THE SANGERYES

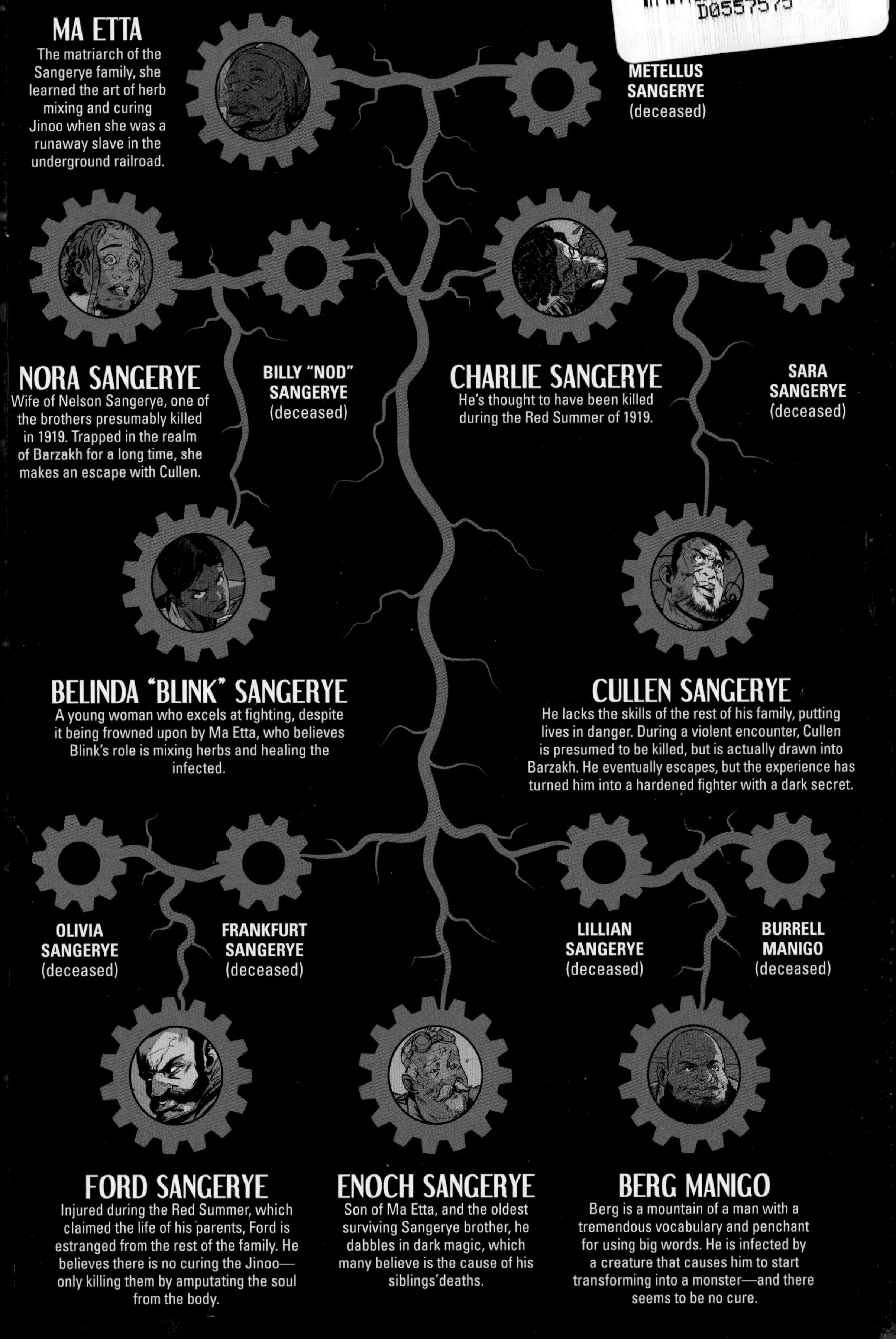
MA ETTA
The matriarch of the Sangerye family, she learned the art of herb mixing and curing Jinoo when she was a runaway slave in the underground railroad.
METELLUS SANGERYE
(deceased)
NORA SANGERYE
Wife of Nelson Sangerye, one of the brothers presumably killed in 1919. Trapped in the realm of Barzakh for a long time, she makes an escape with Cullen.
BILLY "NOD" SANGERYE
(deceased)
CHARLIE SANGERYE
He's thought to have been killed during the Red Summer of 1919.
SARA SANGERYE
(deceased)
BELINDA "BLINK" SANGERYE
A young woman who excels at fighting, despite it being frowned upon by Ma Etta, who believes Blink's role is mixing herbs and healing the infected.
CULLEN SANGERYE
He lacks the skills of the rest of his family, putting lives in danger. During a violent encounter, Cullen is presumed to be killed, but is actually drawn into Barzakh. He eventually escapes, but the experience has turned him into a hardened fighter with a dark secret.
OLIVIA SANGERYE
(deceased)
FRANKFURT SANGERYE
(deceased)
LILLIAN SANGERYE
(deceased)
BURRELL MANIGO
(deceased)
FORD SANGERYE
Injured during the Red Summer, which claimed the life of his parents, Ford is estranged from the rest of the family. He believes there is no curing the Jinoo—only killing them by amputating the soul from the body.
ENOCH SANGERYE
Son of Ma Etta, and the oldest surviving Sangerye brother, he dabbles in dark magic, which many believe is the cause of his siblings'deaths.
BERG MANIGO
Berg is a mountain of a man with a tremendous vocabulary and penchant for using big words. He is infected by a creature that causes him to start transforming into a monster—and there seems to be no cure.

BITER

VOLUME TWO:
RAGE & REDEMPTION

**CHUCK BROWN,
DAVID F. WALKER &
SANFORD GREENE**
creators

**SOFIE DODGSON &
SANFORD GREENE**
color artists

CLAYTON COWLES
letterer

JOHN JENNINGS
backmatter

SHELLY BOND
editor

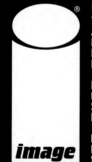

ROOT

RED SUMMER SPECIAL

CHUCK BROWN & DAVID F. WALKER
writers

ETTA
SANFORD GREENE artist
DANIELA MIWA color artist

THE ARSENAL
LISA K. WEBER artist
KELLY FITZPATRICK color artist

RED SUMMER
DANIEL LISH artist

TULSA
CHRIS BRUNNER artist
RICO RENZI color artist

LADIES NIGHT
KHARY RANDOLPH artist
MATT HERMS color artist

BARZAKH
DIETRICH SMITH artist
ANTHONY GEORGE color artist

CLAYTON COWLES letterer
JOHN JENNINGS backmatter
JOE HUGHES editor

BITTER ROOT RED SUMMER SPECIAL

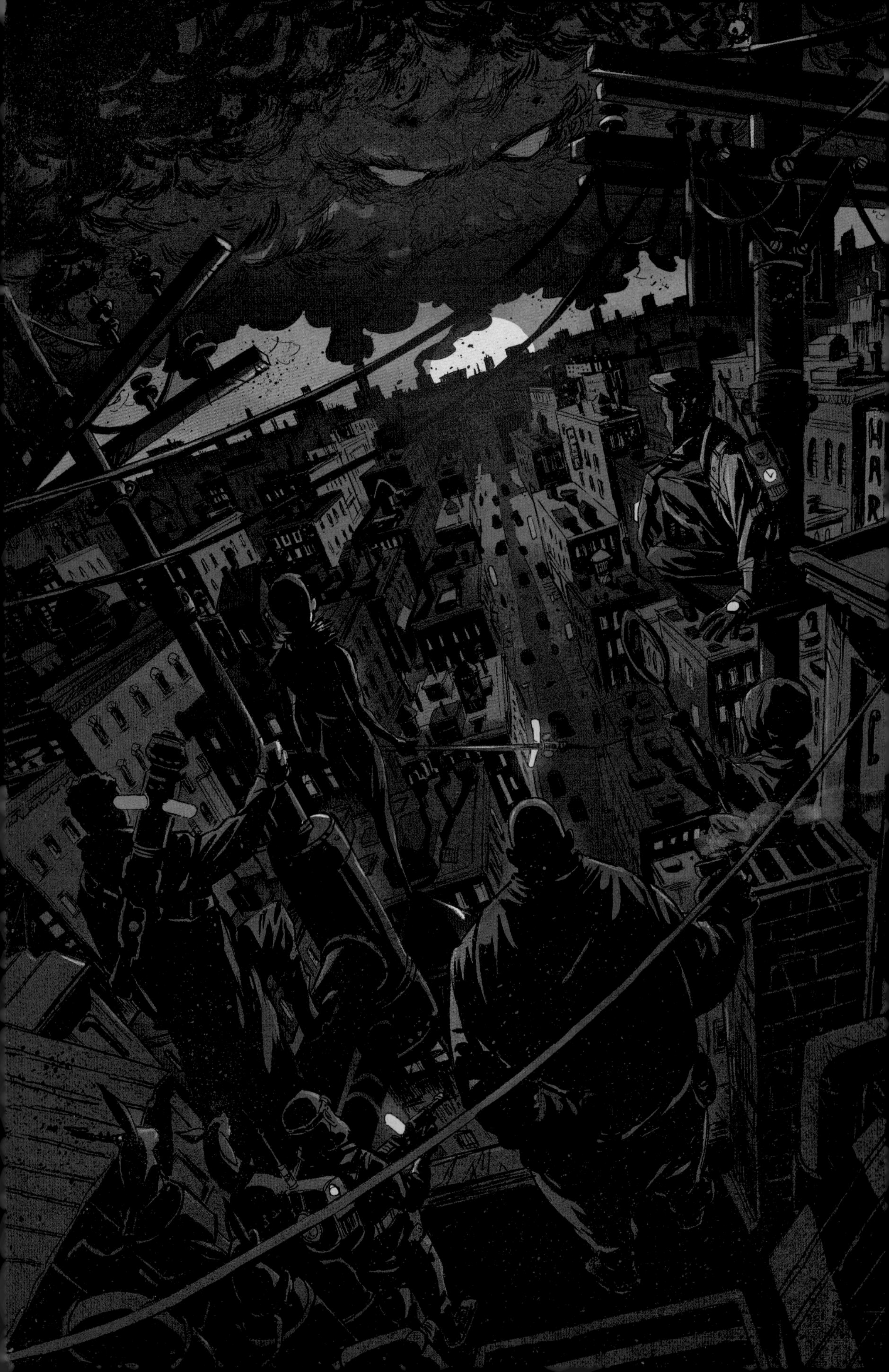

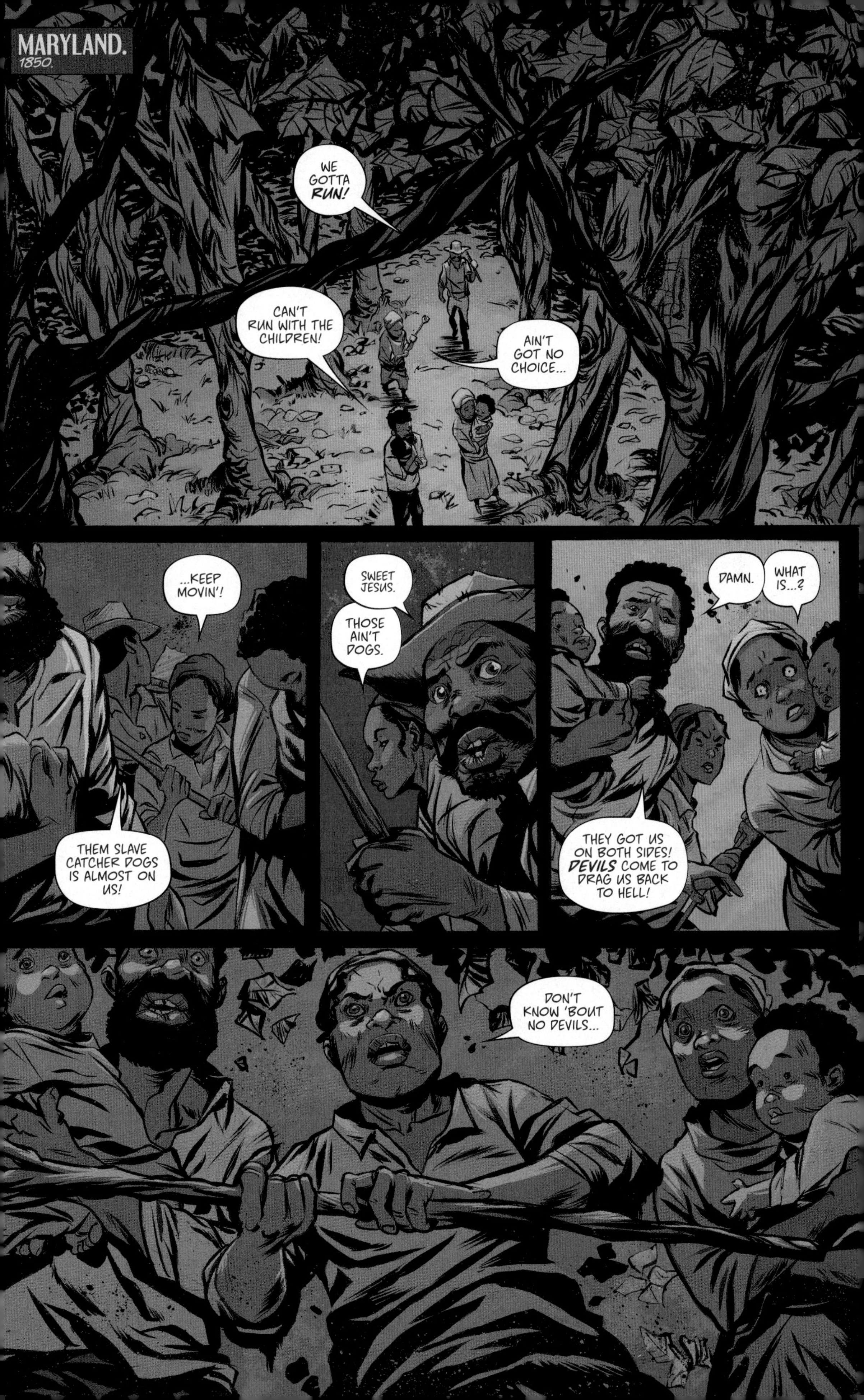
MARYLAND.
1850.
WE GOTTA RUN!
CAN'T RUN WITH THE CHILDREN!
AIN'T GOT NO CHOICE...
...KEEP MOVIN'!
THEM SLAVE CATCHER DOGS IS ALMOST ON US!
SWEET JESUS.
THOSE AIN'T DOGS.
DAMN.
WHAT IS...?
THEY GOT US ON BOTH SIDES! DEVILS COME TO DRAG US BACK TO HELL!
DON'T KNOW 'BOUT NO DEVILS...

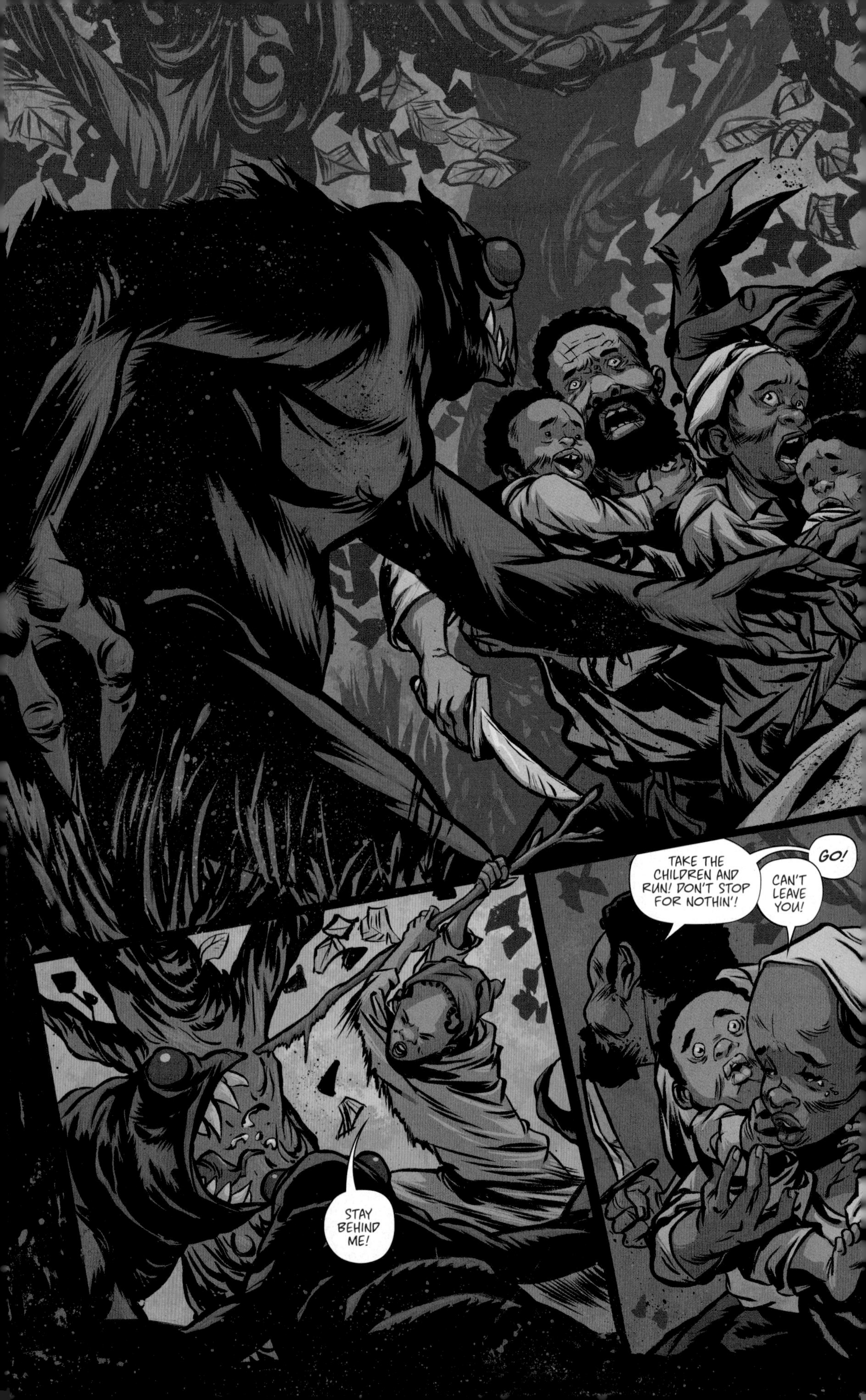
TAKE THE CHILDREN AND RUN! DON'T STOP FOR NOTHIN'!
CAN'T LEAVE YOU!
GO!
STAY BEHIND ME!

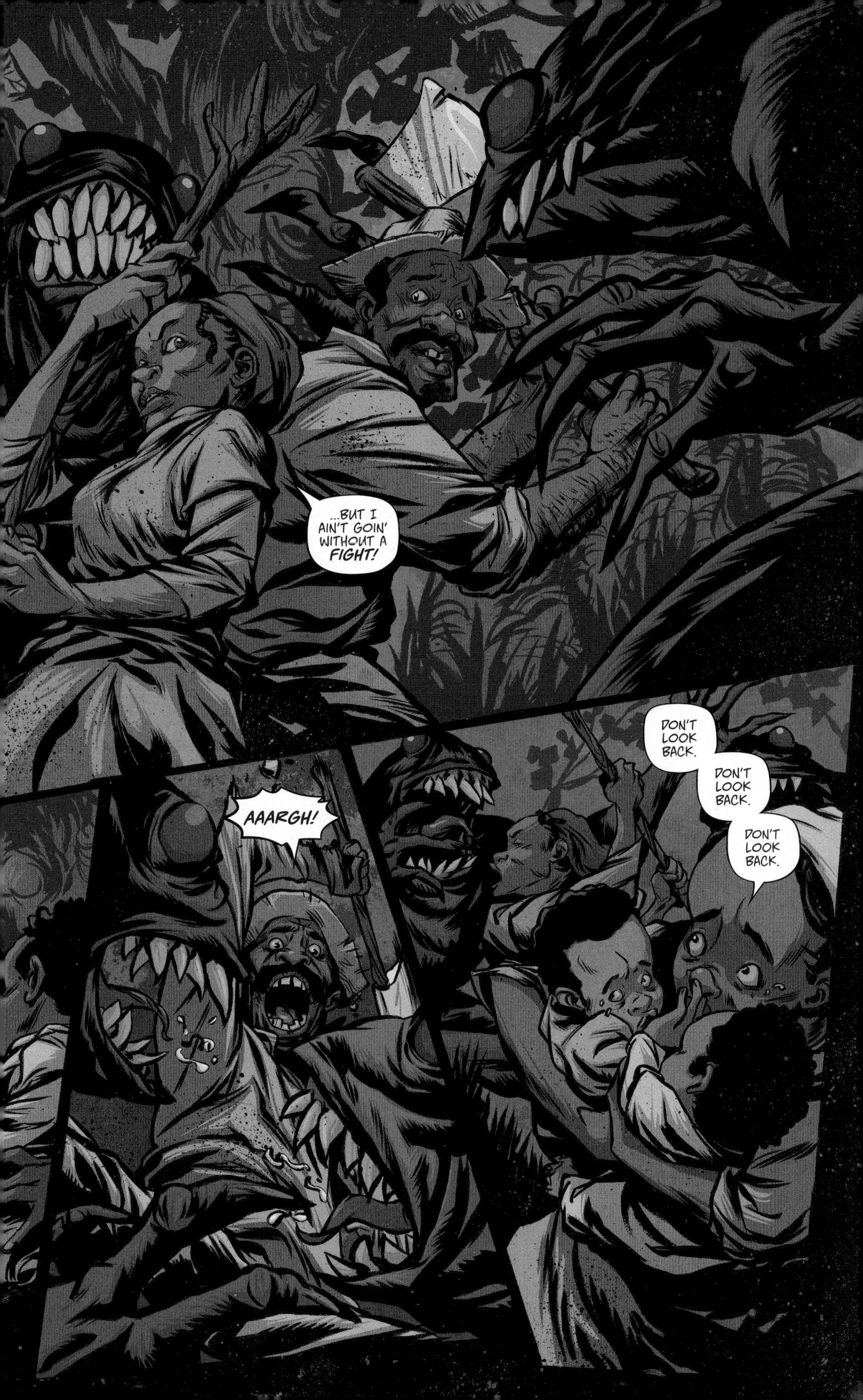
...BUT I AIN'T GOIN' WITHOUT A FIGHT!
AAARGH!
DON'T LOOK BACK.
DON'T LOOK BACK.
DON'T LOOK BACK.

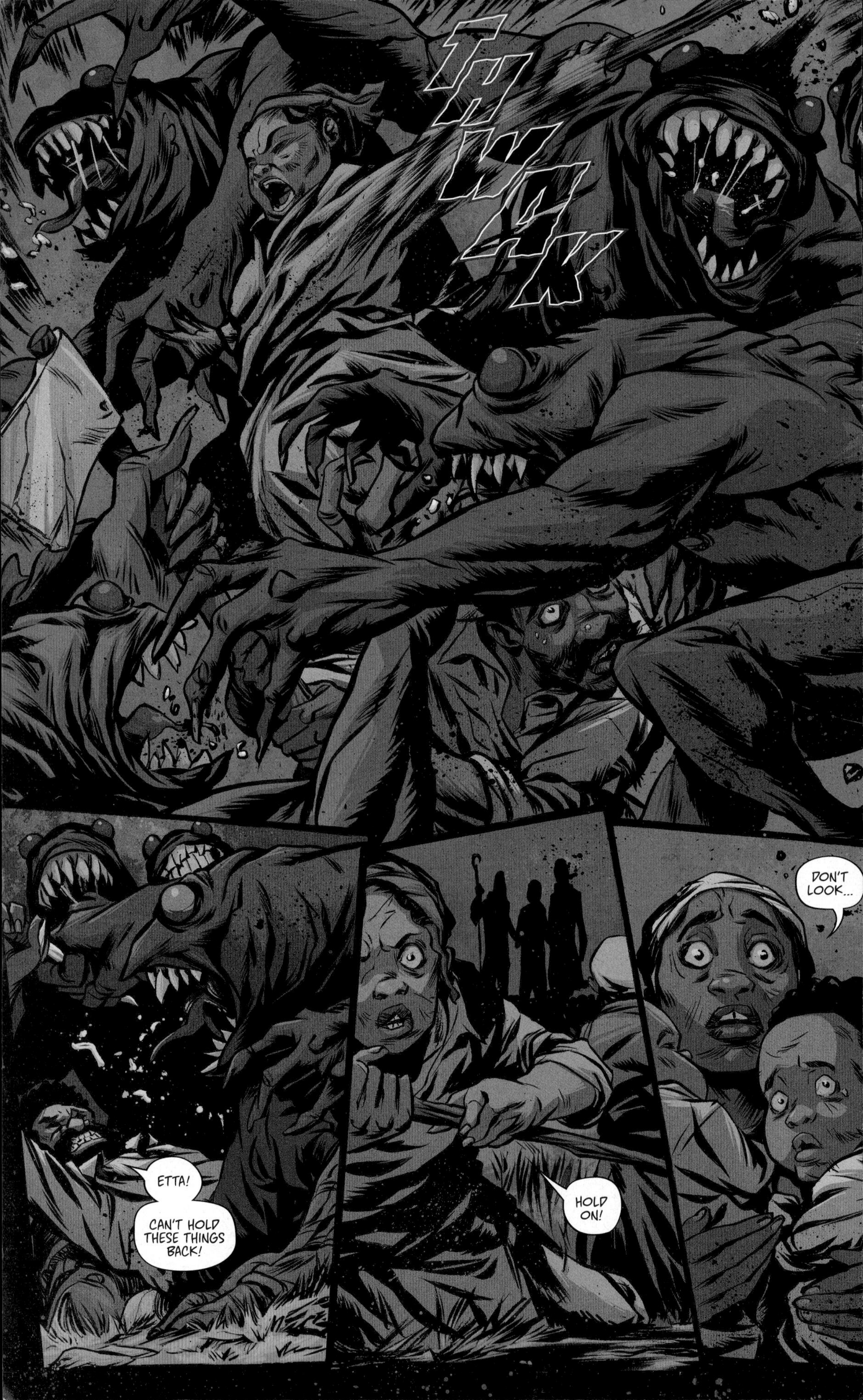
THWAK
ETTA!
CAN'T HOLD THESE THINGS BACK!
HOLD ON!
DON'T LOOK...

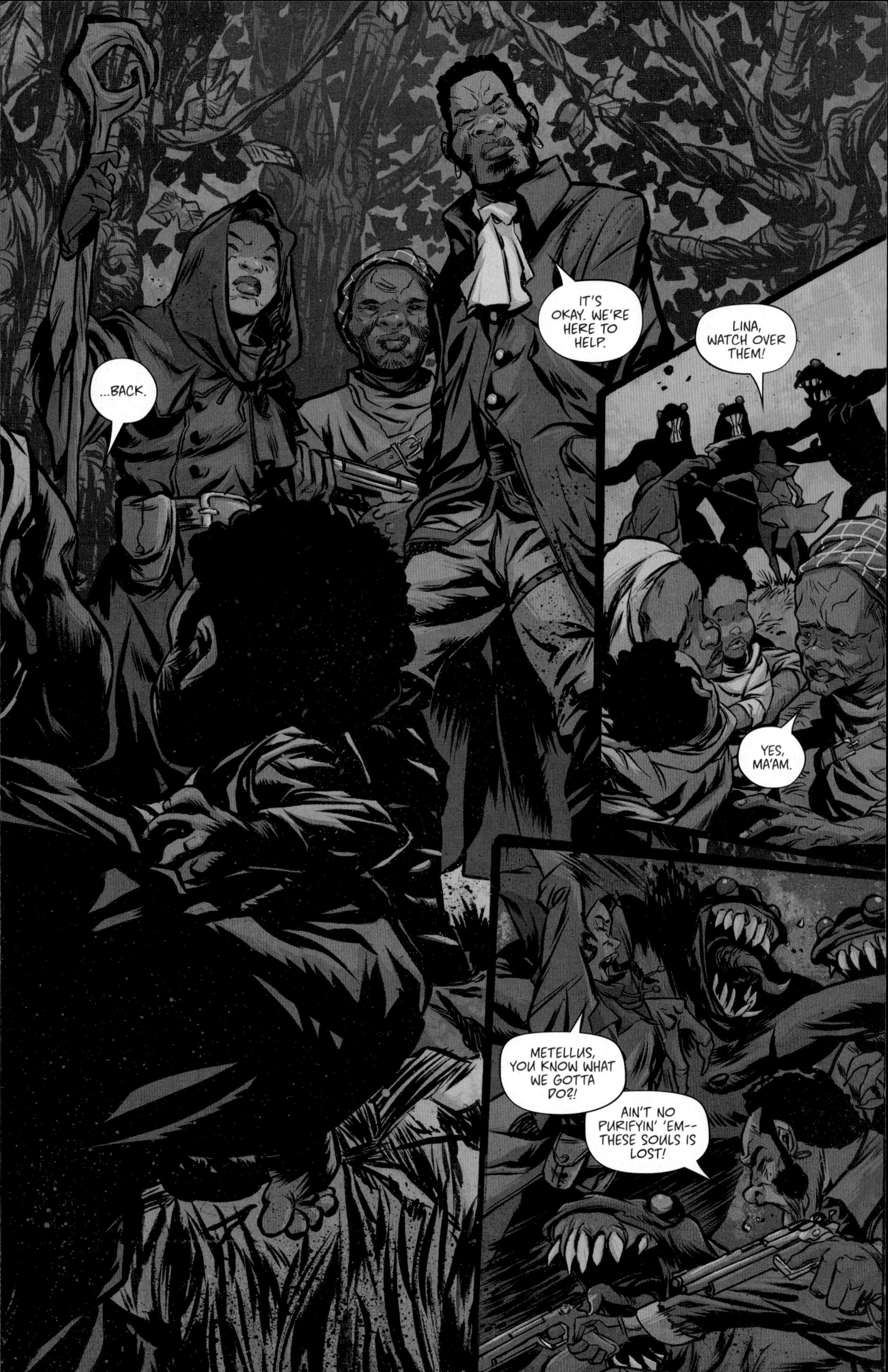

IT'S OKAY. WE'RE HERE TO HELP.
...BACK.
LINA, WATCH OVER THEM!
YES, MA'AM.
METELLUS, YOU KNOW WHAT WE GOTTA DO?!
AIN'T NO PURIFYIN' 'EM-- THESE SOULS IS LOST!

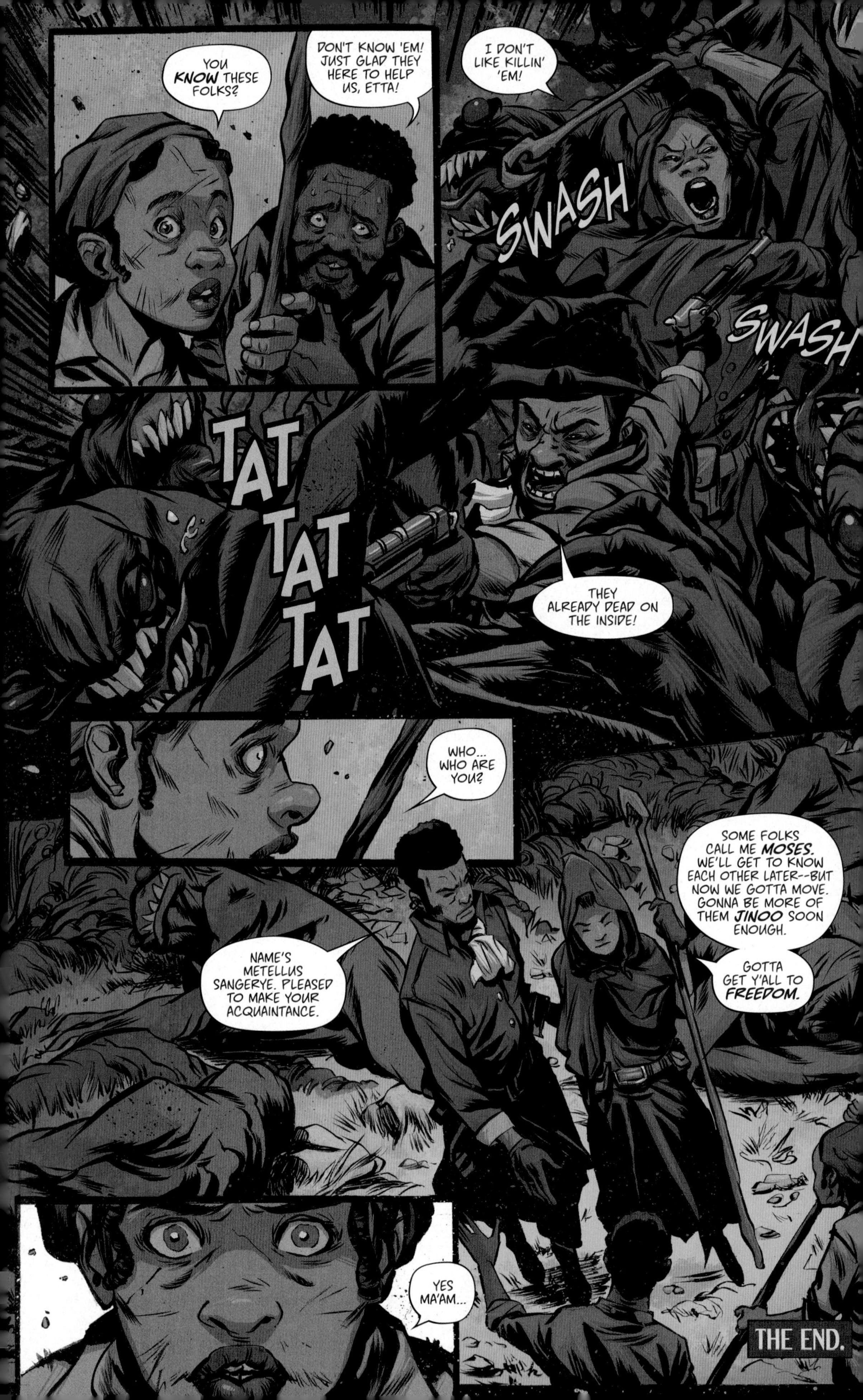

YOU KNOW THESE FOLKS?
DON'T KNOW 'EM! JUST GLAD THEY HERE TO HELP US, ETTA!
I DON'T LIKE KILLIN' 'EM!
SWASH
SWASH
TAT TAT TAT
THEY ALREADY DEAD ON THE INSIDE!
WHO... WHO ARE YOU?
SOME FOLKS CALL ME MOSES. WE'LL GET TO KNOW EACH OTHER LATER--BUT NOW WE GOTTA MOVE. GONNA BE MORE OF THEM JINOO SOON ENOUGH.
NAME'S METELLUS SANGERYE. PLEASED TO MAKE YOUR ACQUAINTANCE.
GOTTA GET Y'ALL TO FREEDOM.
YES MA'AM...
THE END.

BERG IS STRONG, BUT HE HASN'T BEEN FOCUSING ON HIS **STUDIES** SINCE--

I KNOW. I'LL SPEAK TO HIM.

HARLEM. *1904.*

COME ALONG, BERG, YOUR DADDY WANTS TO TALK TO YOU.

DON'T SCURRY ABOUT LIKE A FRIGHTENED **MOUSE**, SON.

COME IN.

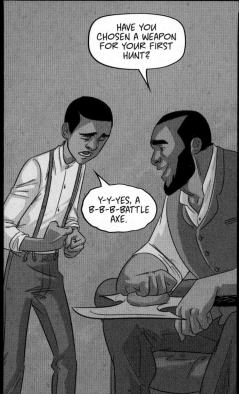

HAVE YOU CHOSEN A WEAPON FOR YOUR FIRST HUNT?

Y-Y-YES, A B-B-B-BATTLE AXE.

CALM DOWN, BURGESS.

I-I-I'M T-T-T-TRYING, B-B-B-BUT AF-AFTER WHAT THE J-J-JINOO DID TO M-M-M-MAMA...

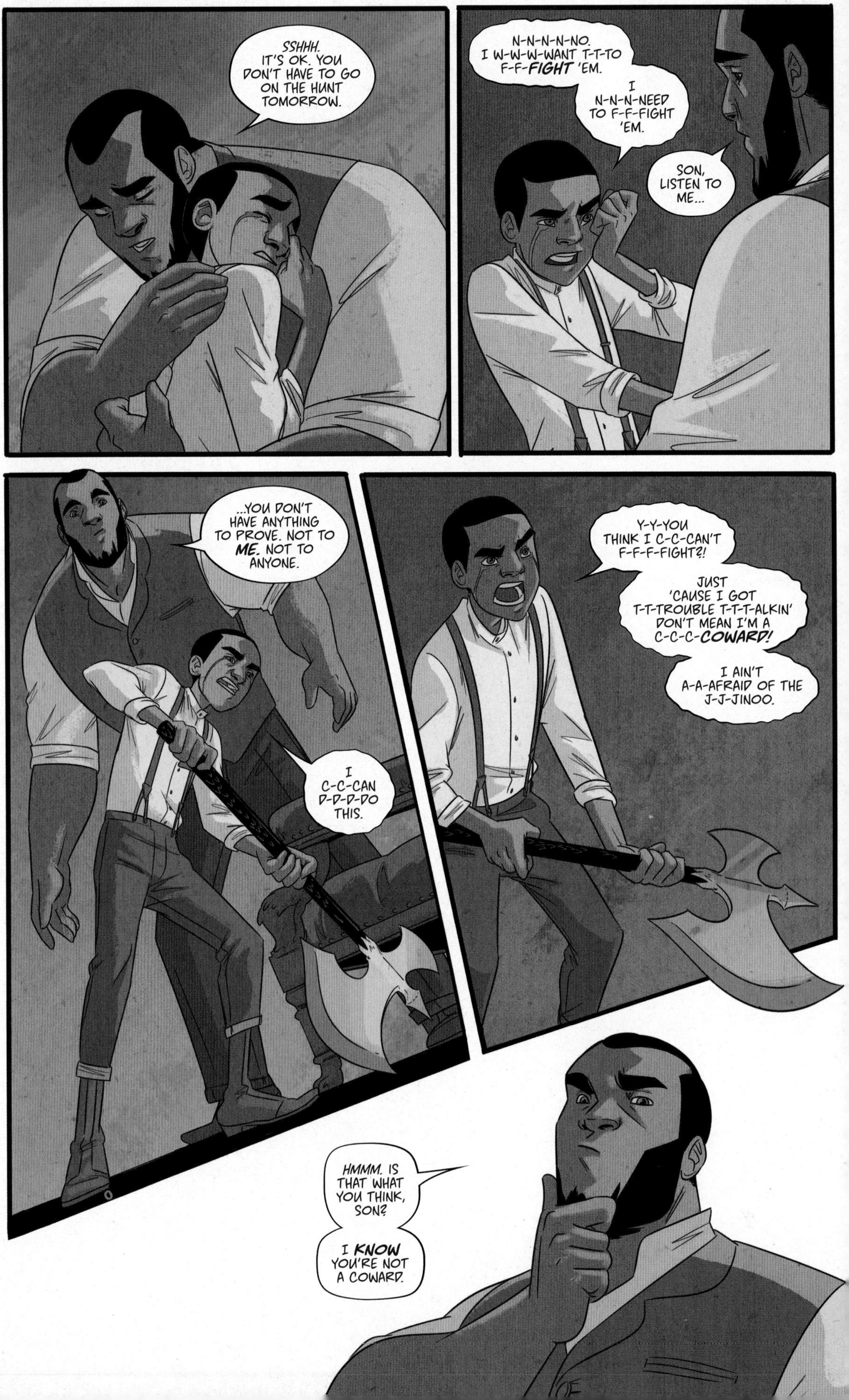
SSHHH. IT'S OK. YOU DON'T HAVE TO GO ON THE HUNT TOMORROW.
N-N-N-N-NO. I W-W-W-WANT T-T-TO F-F-FIGHT 'EM.
I N-N-N-NEED TO F-F-FIGHT 'EM.
SON, LISTEN TO ME...
...YOU DON'T HAVE ANYTHING TO PROVE. NOT TO ME. NOT TO ANYONE.
I C-C-CAN D-D-D-DO THIS.
Y-Y-YOU THINK I C-C-CAN'T F-F-F-FIGHT?!
JUST 'CAUSE I GOT T-T-TROUBLE T-T-T-ALKIN' DON'T MEAN I'M A C-C-C-COWARD!
I AIN'T A-A-AFRAID OF THE J-J-JINOO.
HMMM. IS THAT WHAT YOU THINK, SON?
I KNOW YOU'RE NOT A COWARD.

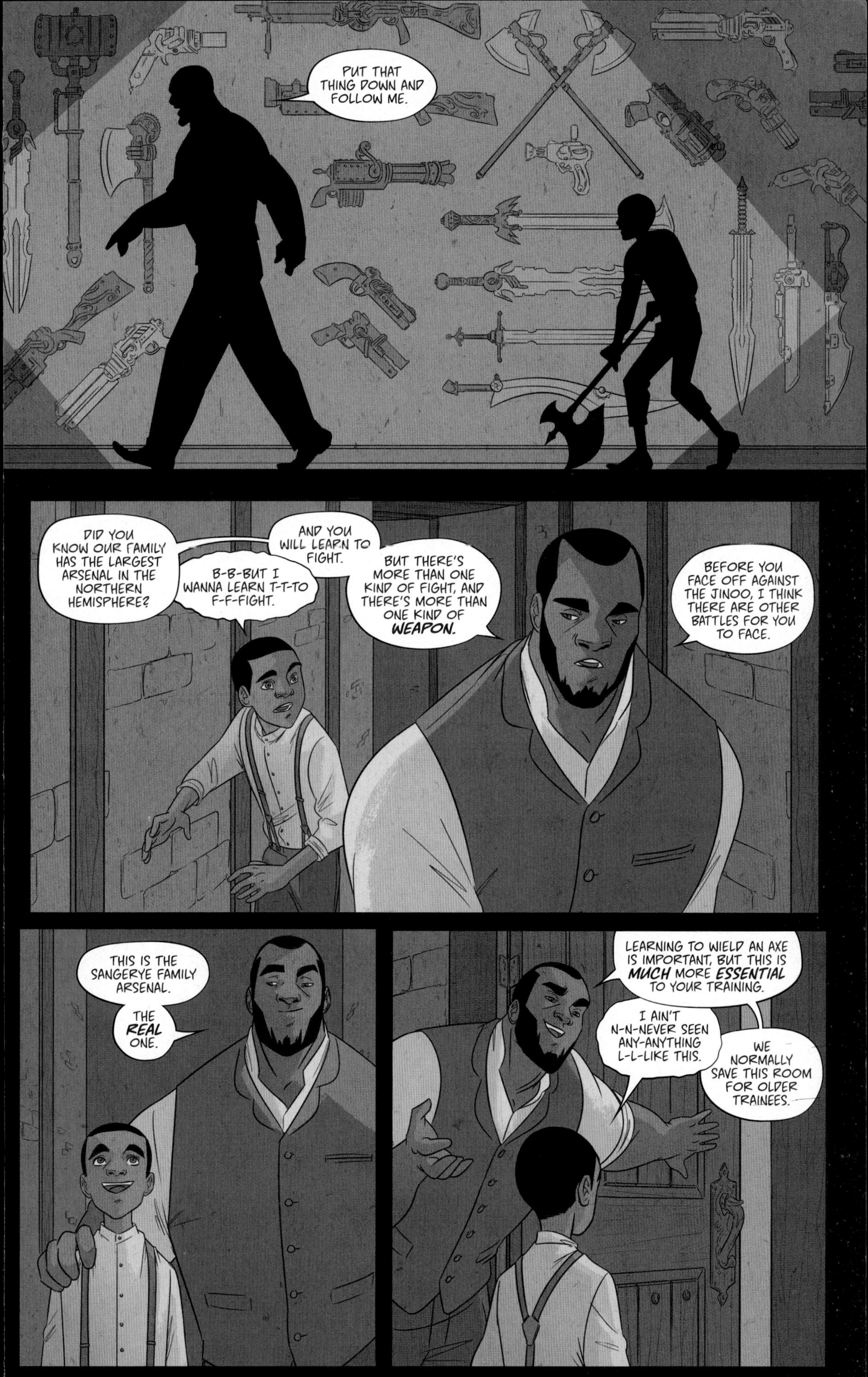
PUT THAT THING DOWN AND FOLLOW ME.
DID YOU KNOW OUR FAMILY HAS THE LARGEST ARSENAL IN THE NORTHERN HEMISPHERE?
B-B-BUT I WANNA LEARN T-T-TO F-F-FIGHT.
AND YOU WILL LEARN TO FIGHT.
BUT THERE'S MORE THAN ONE KIND OF FIGHT, AND THERE'S MORE THAN ONE KIND OF WEAPON.
BEFORE YOU FACE OFF AGAINST THE JINOO, I THINK THERE ARE OTHER BATTLES FOR YOU TO FACE.
THIS IS THE SANGERYE FAMILY ARSENAL.
THE REAL ONE.
LEARNING TO WIELD AN AXE IS IMPORTANT, BUT THIS IS MUCH MORE ESSENTIAL TO YOUR TRAINING.
I AIN'T N-N-NEVER SEEN ANY-ANYTHING L-L-LIKE THIS.
WE NORMALLY SAVE THIS ROOM FOR OLDER TRAINEES.

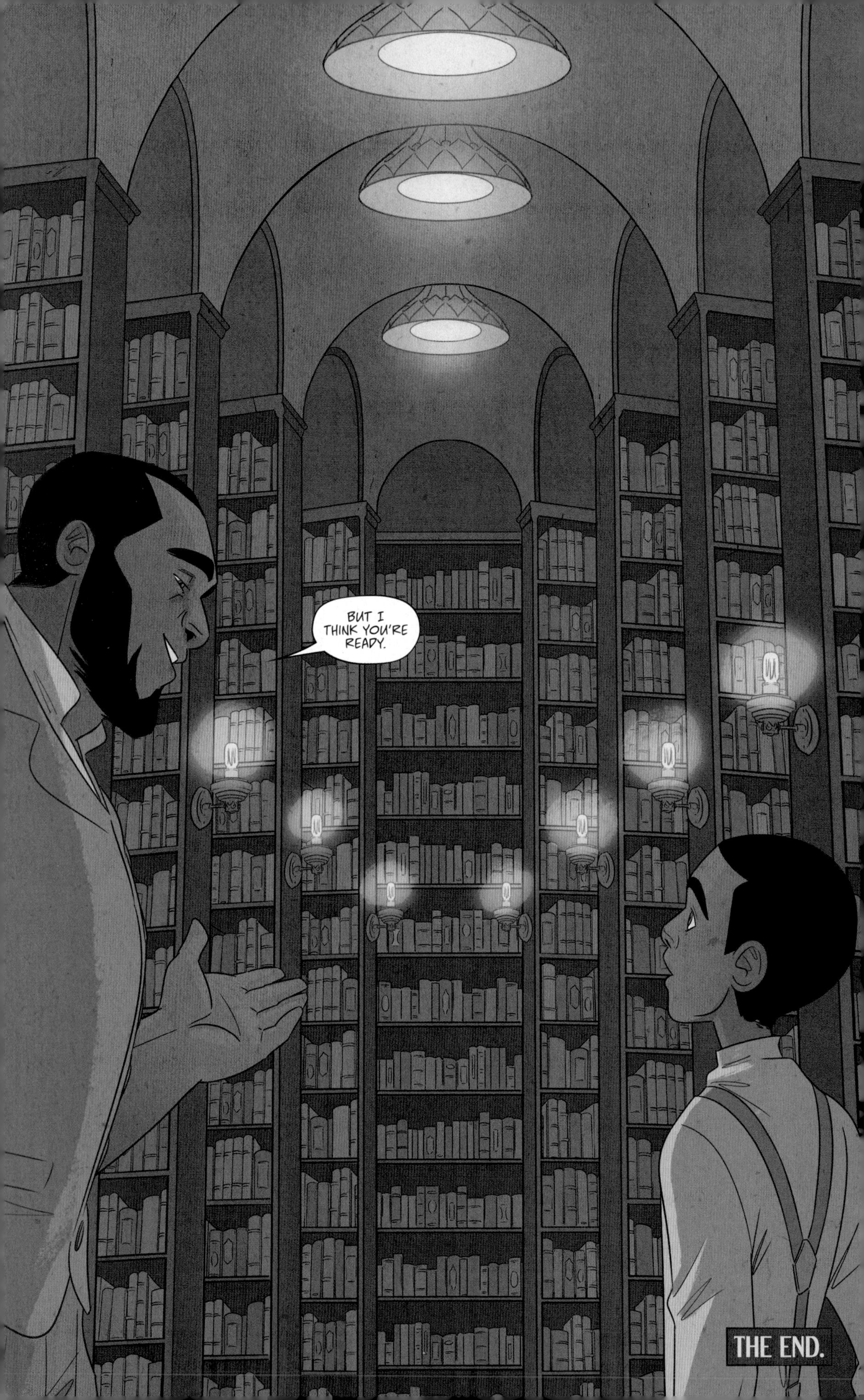
BUT I THINK YOU'RE READY.
THE END.

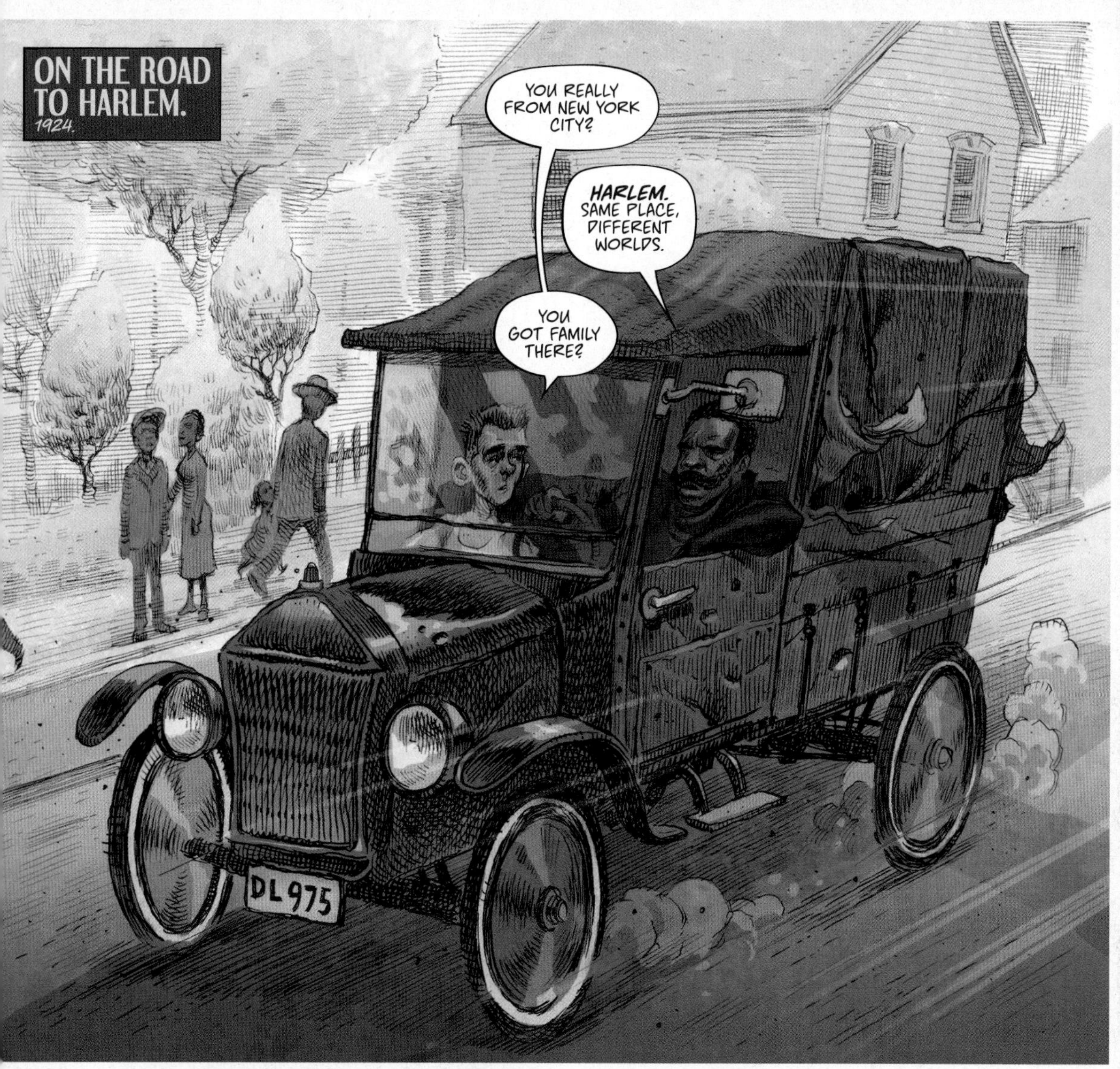
ON THE ROAD TO HARLEM.
1924.
YOU REALLY FROM NEW YORK CITY?
HARLEM. SAME PLACE, DIFFERENT WORLDS.
YOU GOT FAMILY THERE?
DL 975

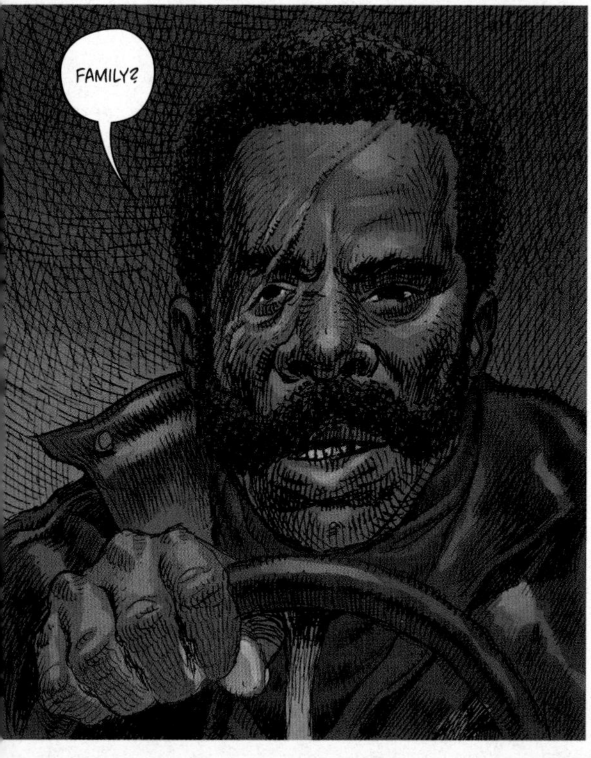
FAMILY?

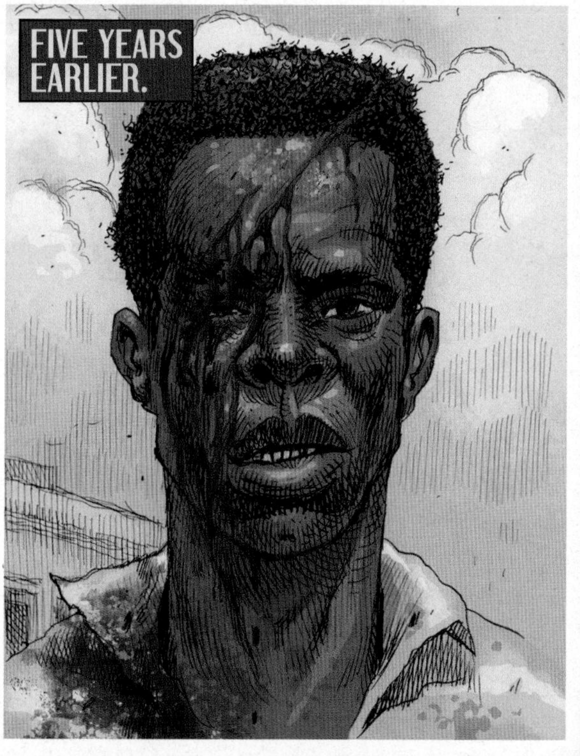
FIVE YEARS EARLIER.

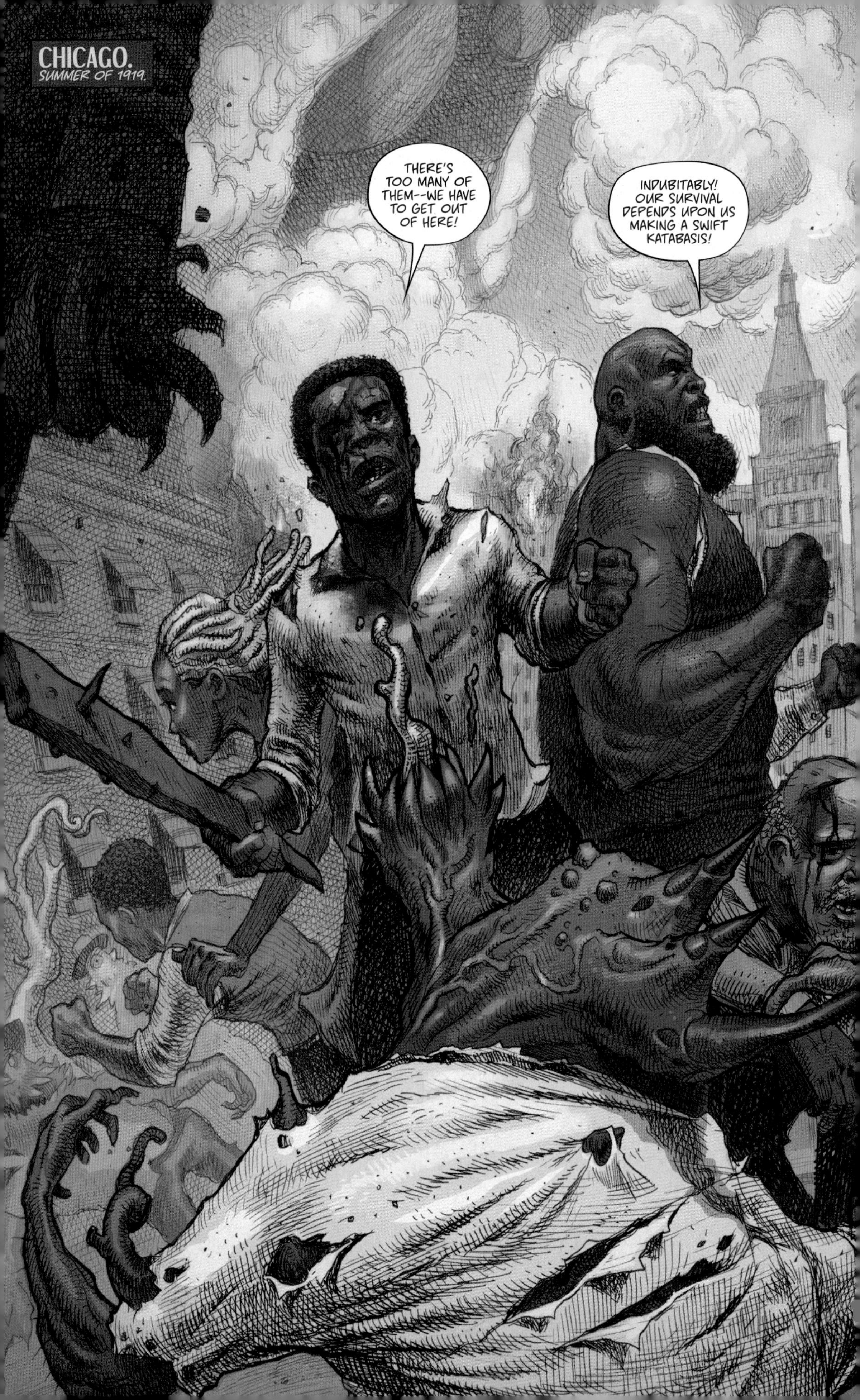
CHICAGO.
SUMMER OF 1919.
THERE'S TOO MANY OF THEM--WE HAVE TO GET OUT OF HERE!
INDUBITABLY! OUR SURVIVAL DEPENDS UPON US MAKING A SWIFT KATABASIS!

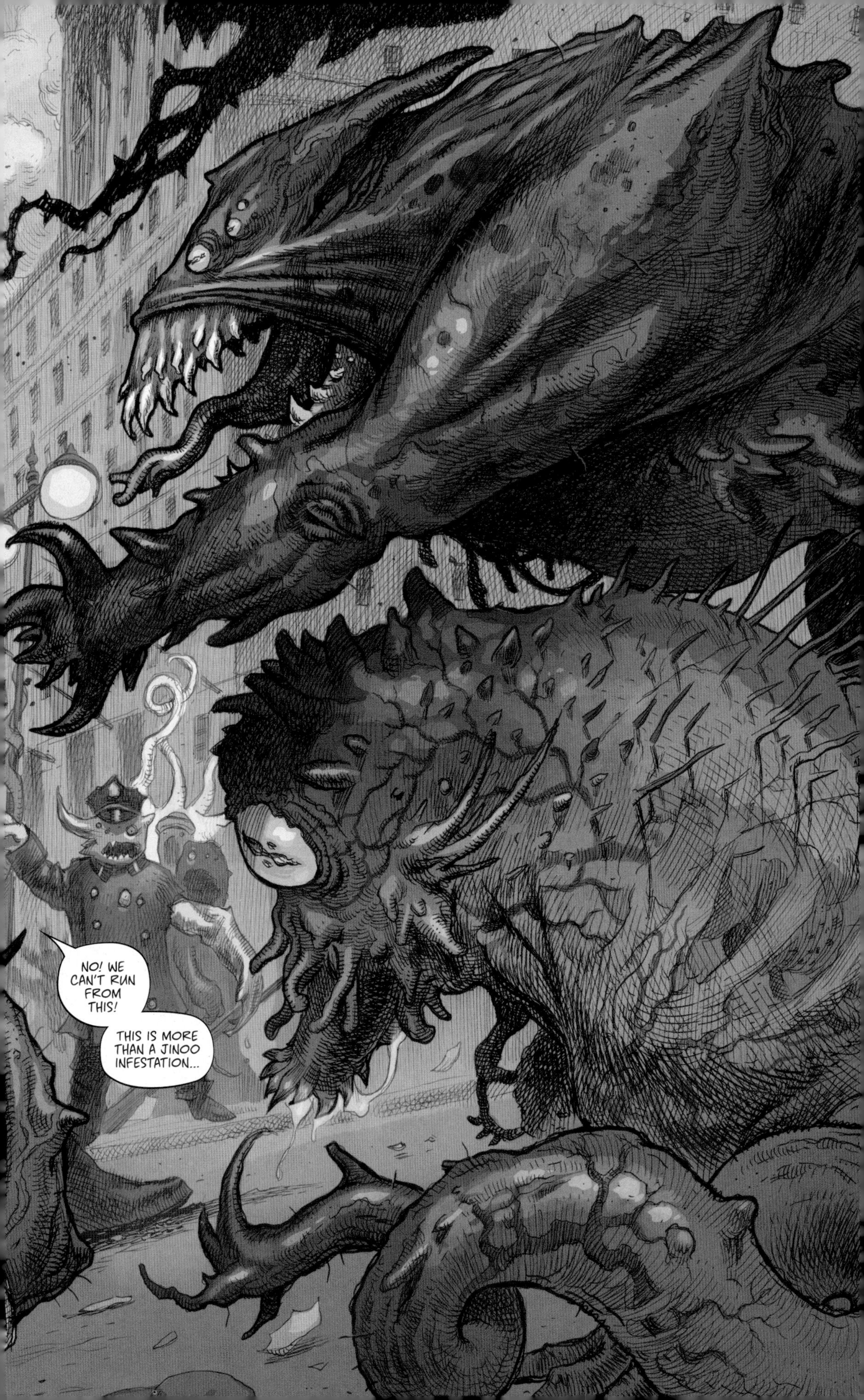
NO! WE CAN'T RUN FROM THIS!
THIS IS MORE THAN A JINOO INFESTATION...

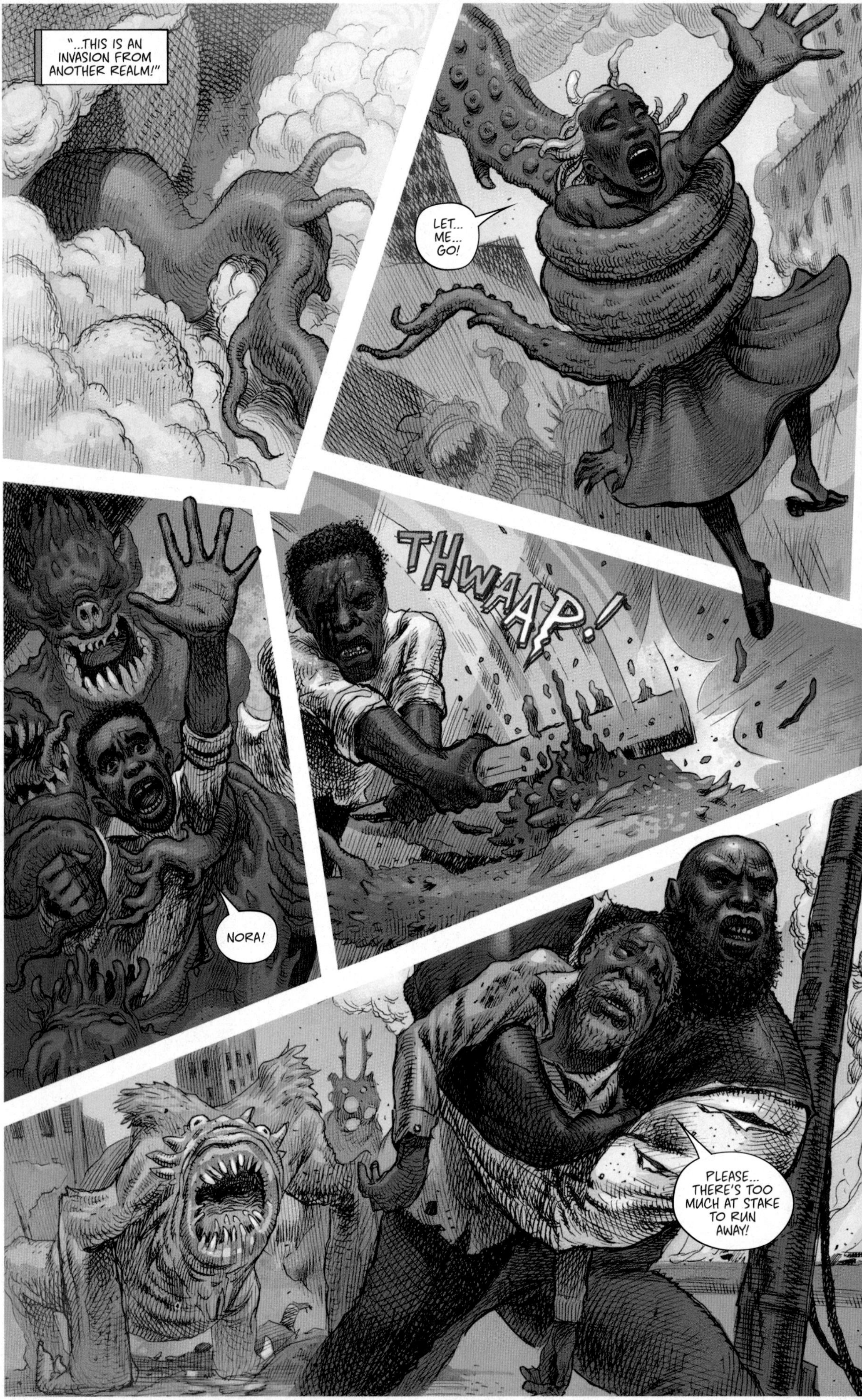
"...THIS IS AN INVASION FROM ANOTHER REALM!"
LET... ME... GO!
THWAAP!
NORA!
PLEASE... THERE'S TOO MUCH AT STAKE TO RUN AWAY!

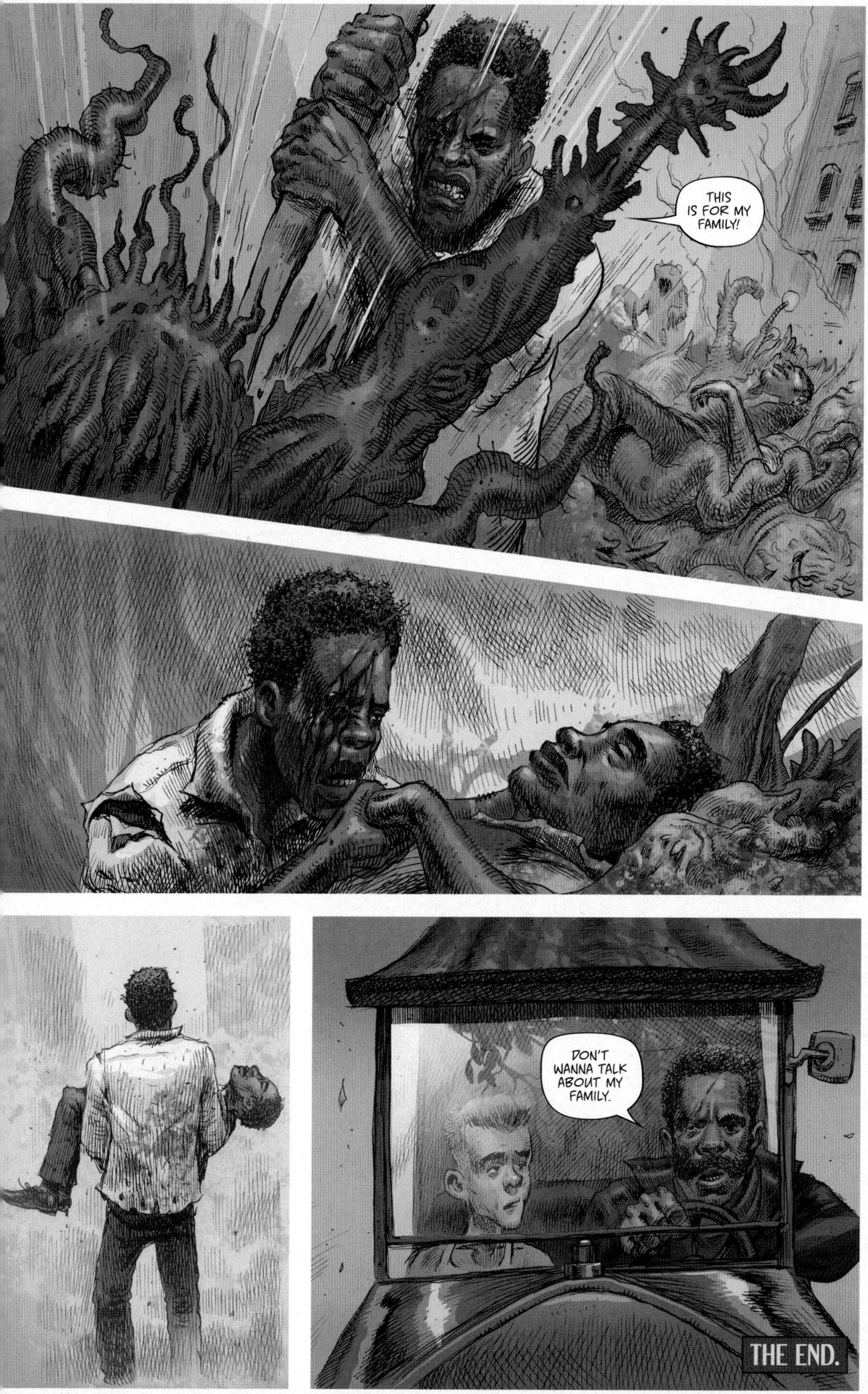
THIS IS FOR MY FAMILY!
DON'T WANNA TALK ABOUT MY FAMILY.
THE END.

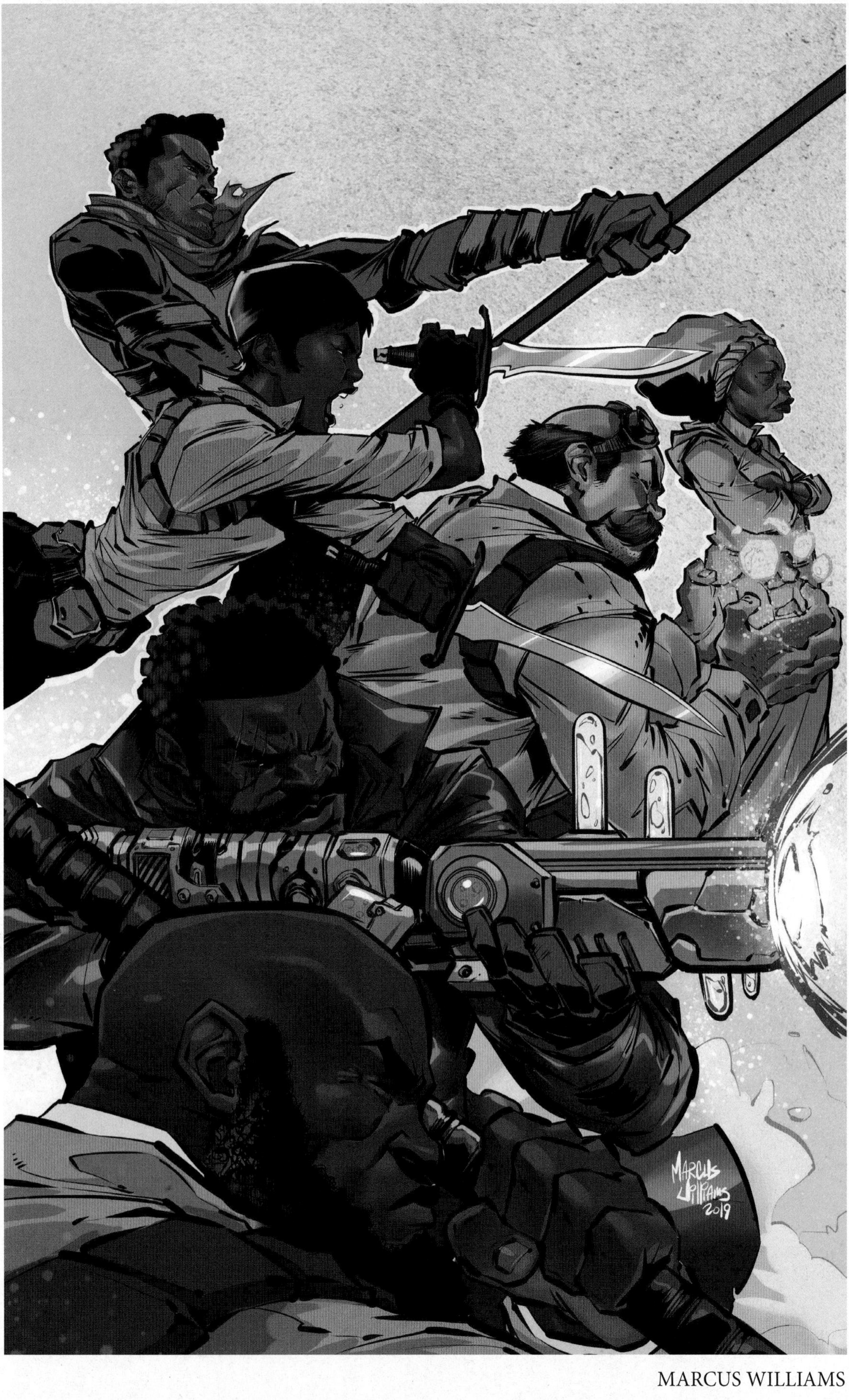
MARCUS
WILLIAMS
2019

MARCUS WILLIAMS

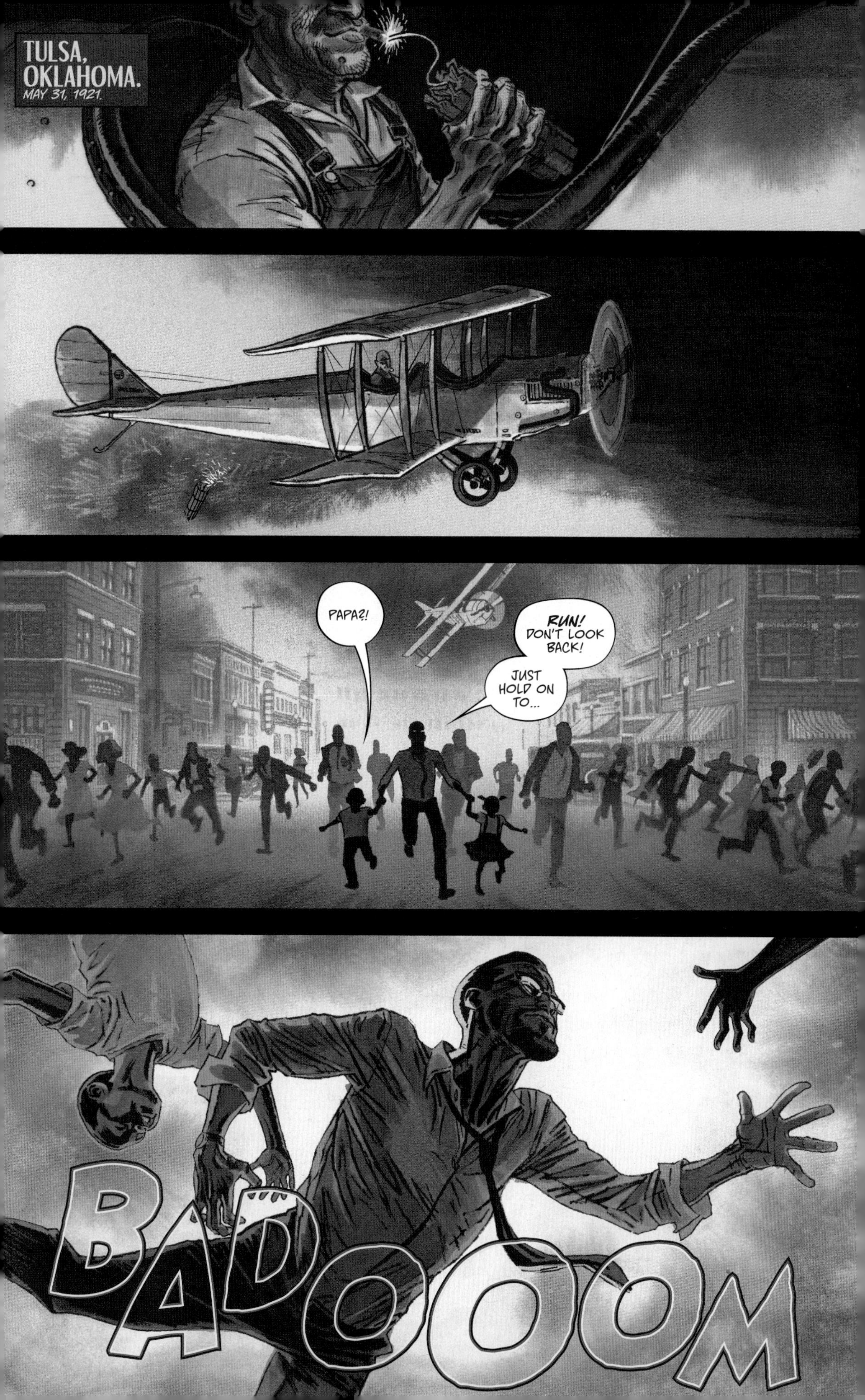
TULSA, OKLAHOMA.
MAY 31, 1921.
PAPA?!
RUN! DON'T LOOK BACK!
JUST HOLD ON TO...
BADOOOM

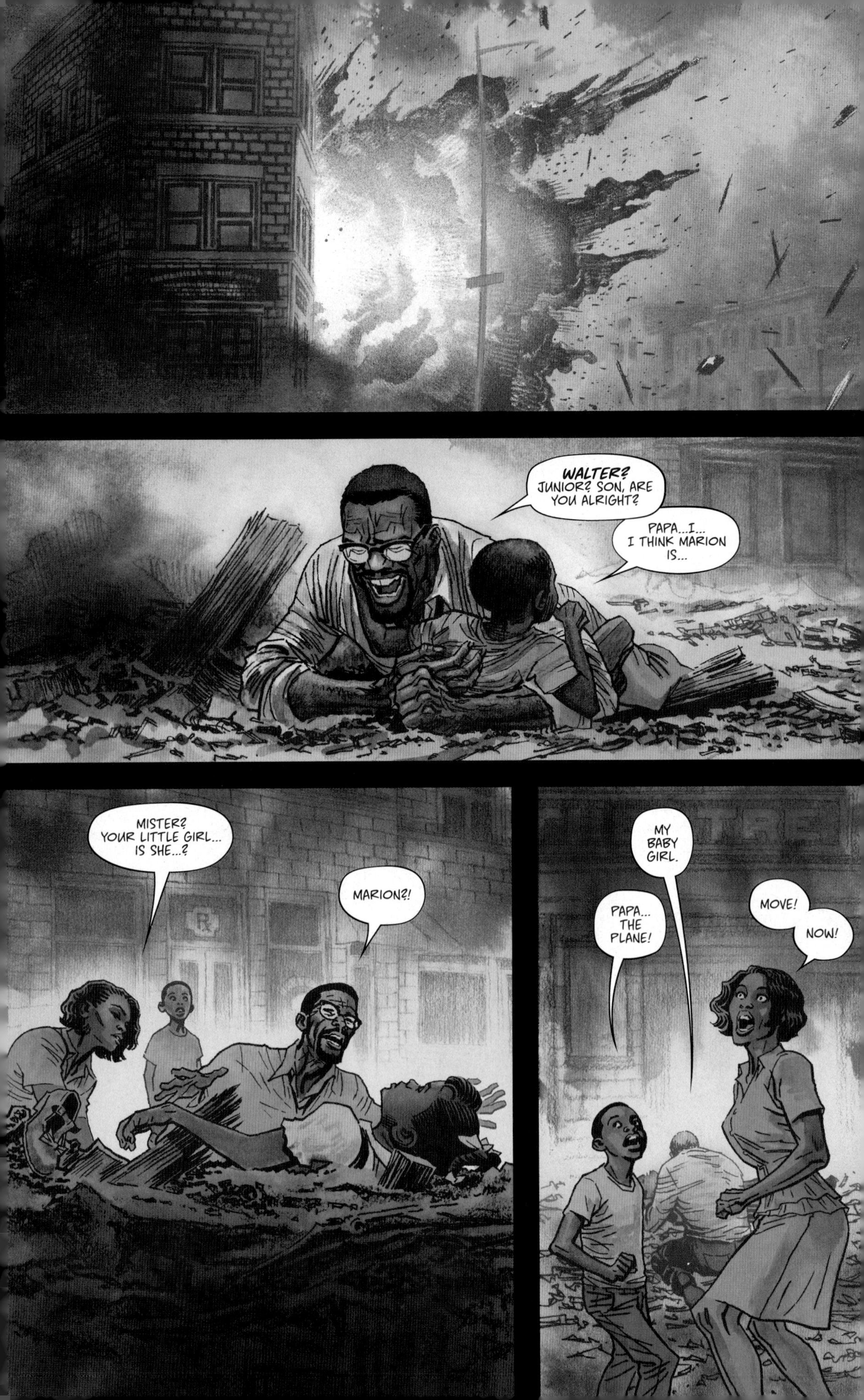
WALTER? JUNIOR? SON, ARE YOU ALRIGHT?
PAPA...I... I THINK MARION IS...
MISTER? YOUR LITTLE GIRL... IS SHE...?
MARION?!
MY BABY GIRL.
PAPA... THE PLANE!
MOVE!
NOW!

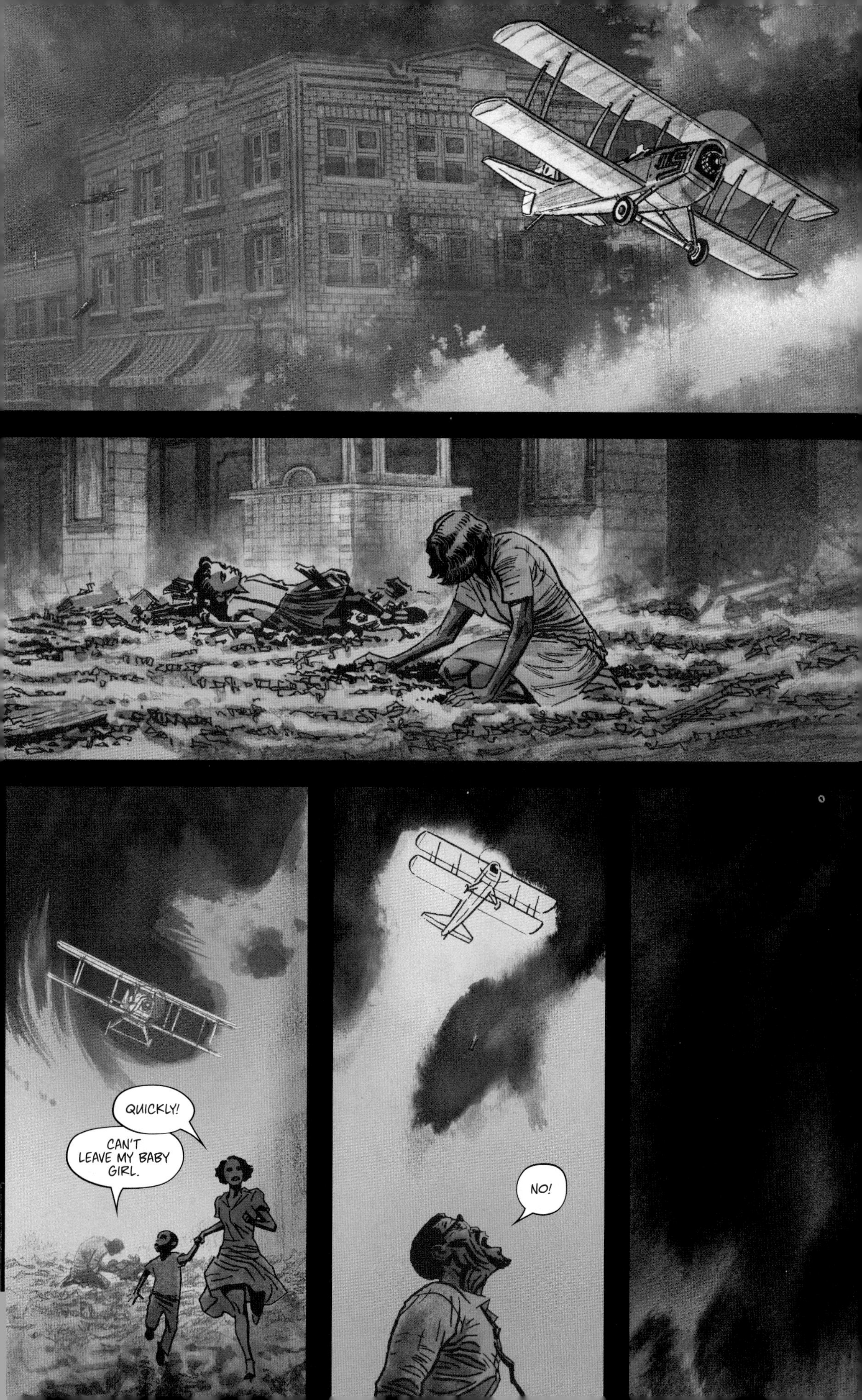
QUICKLY!
CAN'T LEAVE MY BABY GIRL.
NO!

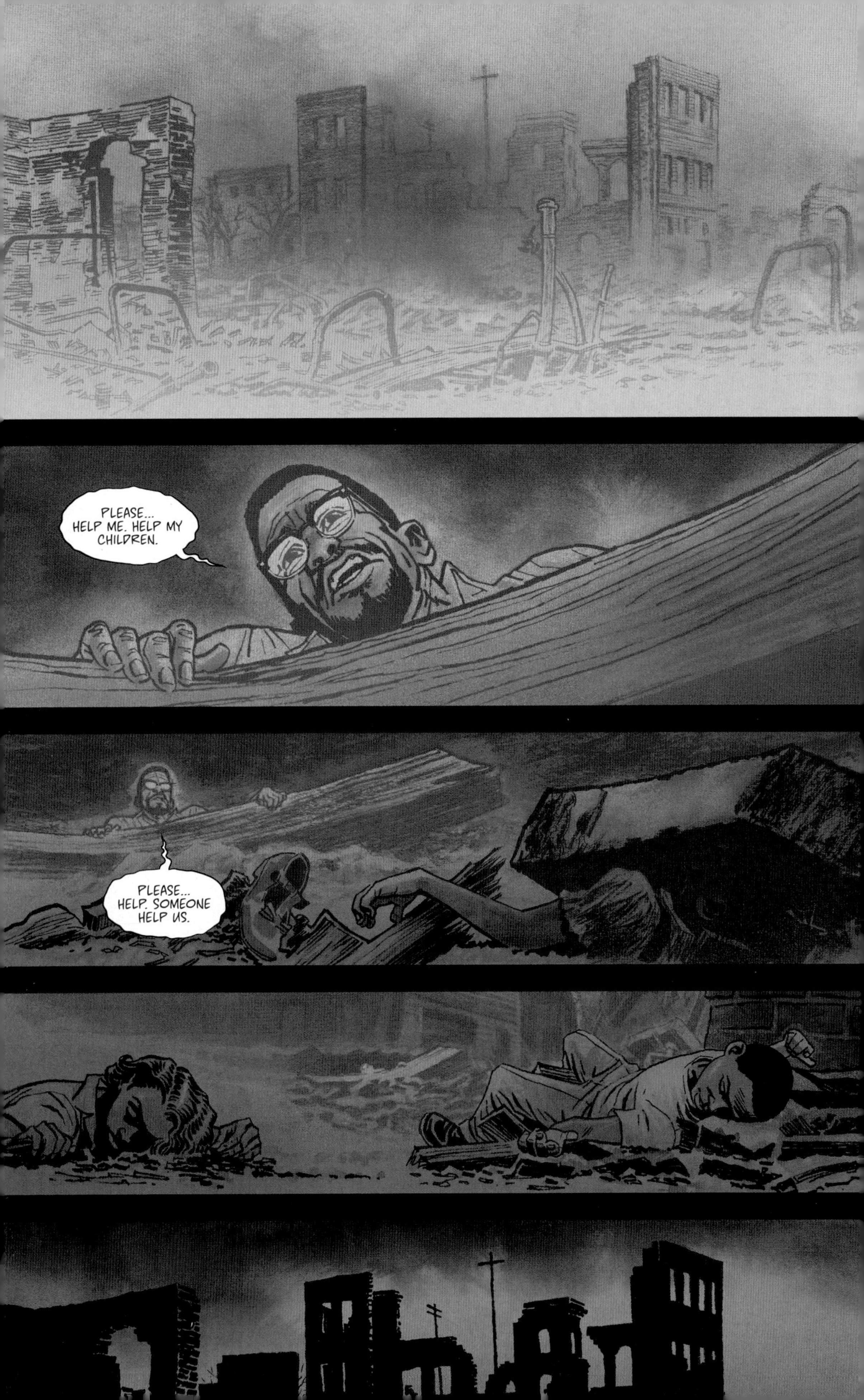
PLEASE... HELP ME. HELP MY CHILDREN.
PLEASE... HELP. SOMEONE HELP US.

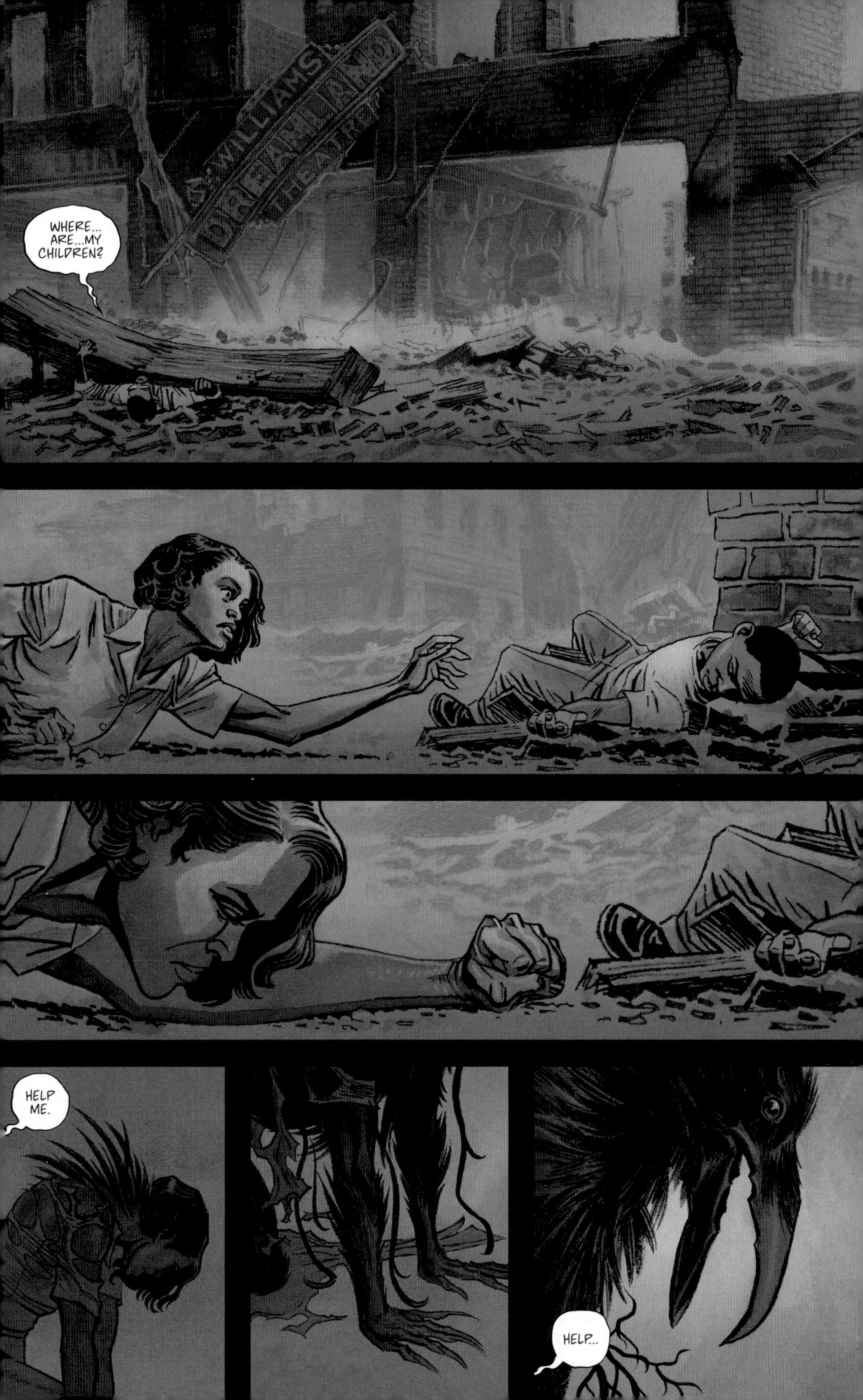
WILLIAMS
DREAMLAND
THEATRE
WHERE... ARE...MY CHILDREN?
HELP ME.
HELP...

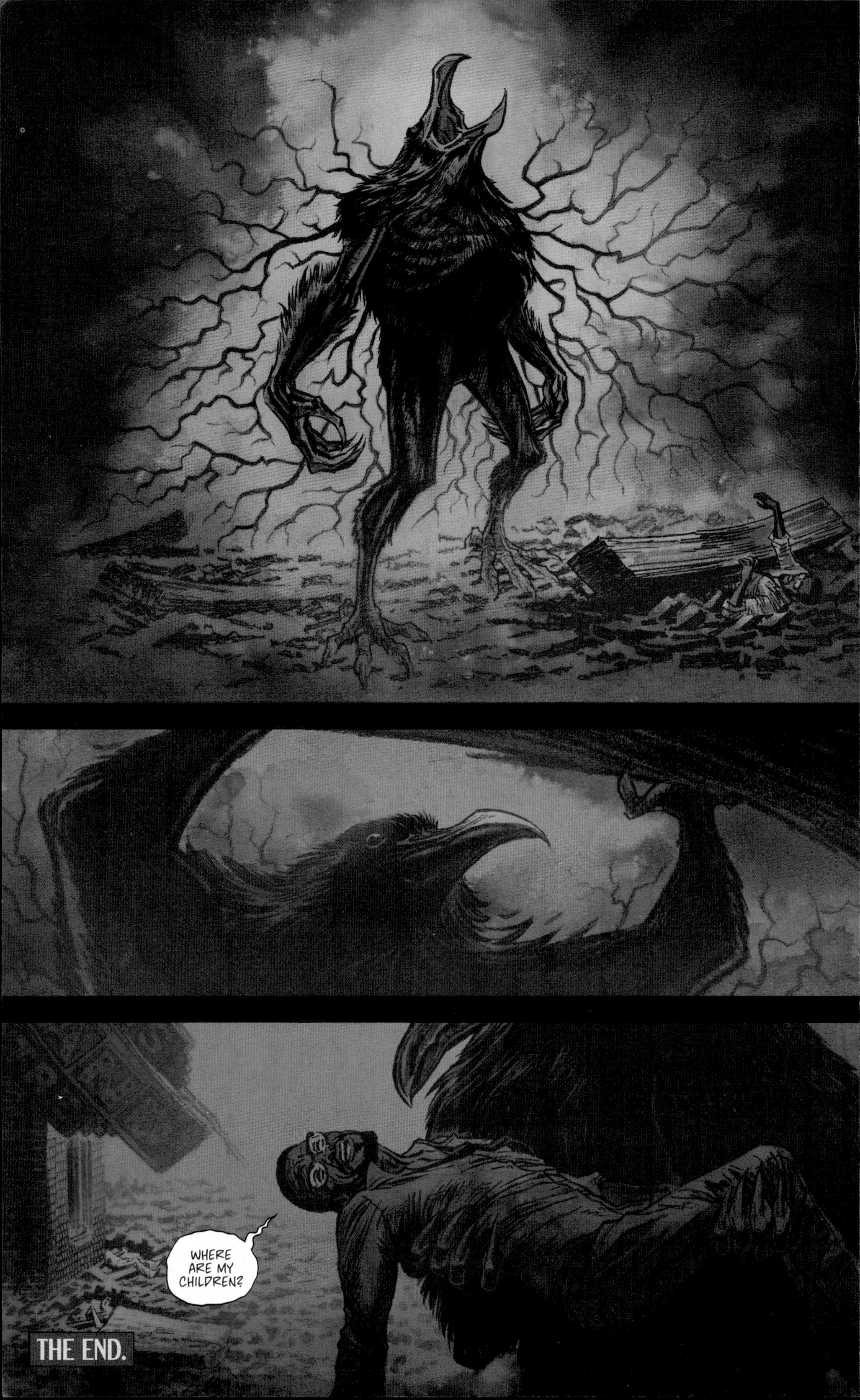
WHERE ARE MY CHILDREN?
THE END.

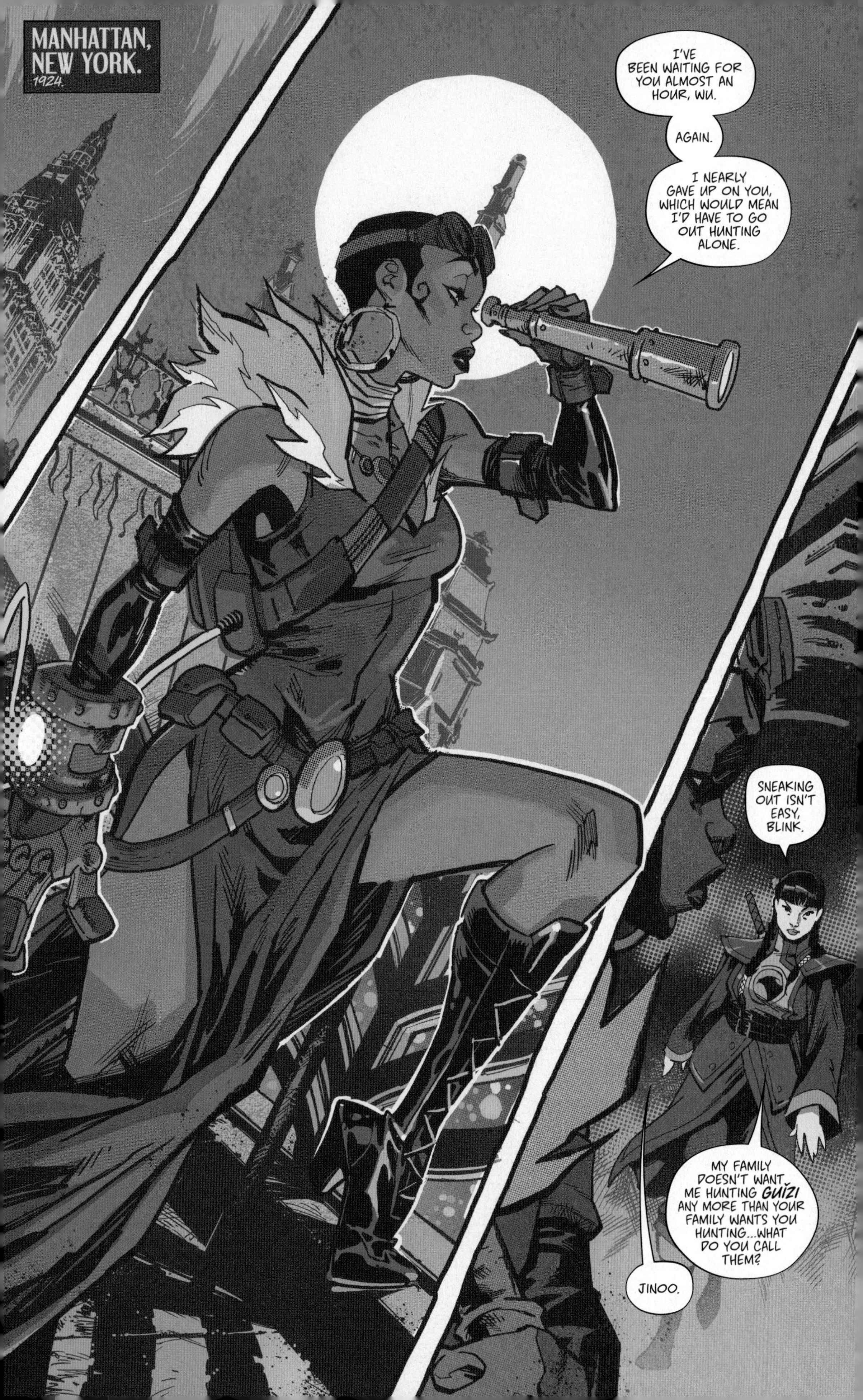
MANHATTAN, NEW YORK.
1924.
I'VE BEEN WAITING FOR YOU ALMOST AN HOUR, WU.
AGAIN.
I NEARLY GAVE UP ON YOU, WHICH WOULD MEAN I'D HAVE TO GO OUT HUNTING ALONE.
SNEAKING OUT ISN'T EASY, BLINK.
MY FAMILY DOESN'T WANT ME HUNTING GUÏZI ANY MORE THAN YOUR FAMILY WANTS YOU HUNTING...WHAT DO YOU CALL THEM?
JINOO.

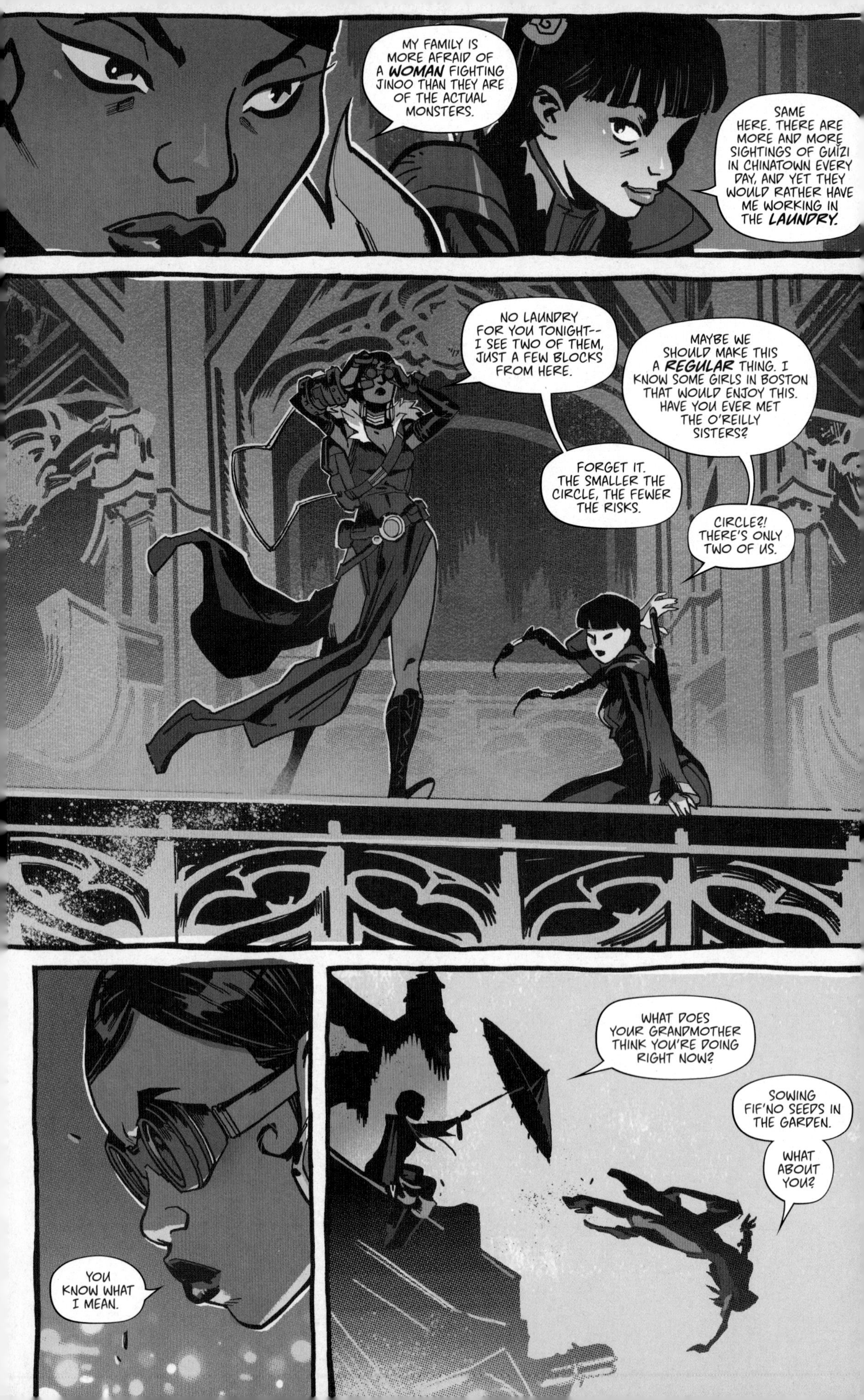

MY FAMILY IS MORE AFRAID OF A WOMAN FIGHTING JINOO THAN THEY ARE OF THE ACTUAL MONSTERS.
SAME HERE. THERE ARE MORE AND MORE SIGHTINGS OF GUÏZI IN CHINATOWN EVERY DAY, AND YET THEY WOULD RATHER HAVE ME WORKING IN THE LAUNDRY.
NO LAUNDRY FOR YOU TONIGHT-- I SEE TWO OF THEM, JUST A FEW BLOCKS FROM HERE.
MAYBE WE SHOULD MAKE THIS A REGULAR THING. I KNOW SOME GIRLS IN BOSTON THAT WOULD ENJOY THIS. HAVE YOU EVER MET THE O'REILLY SISTERS?
FORGET IT. THE SMALLER THE CIRCLE, THE FEWER THE RISKS.
CIRCLE?! THERE'S ONLY TWO OF US.
YOU KNOW WHAT I MEAN.
WHAT DOES YOUR GRANDMOTHER THINK YOU'RE DOING RIGHT NOW?
SOWING FIF'NO SEEDS IN THE GARDEN.
WHAT ABOUT YOU?

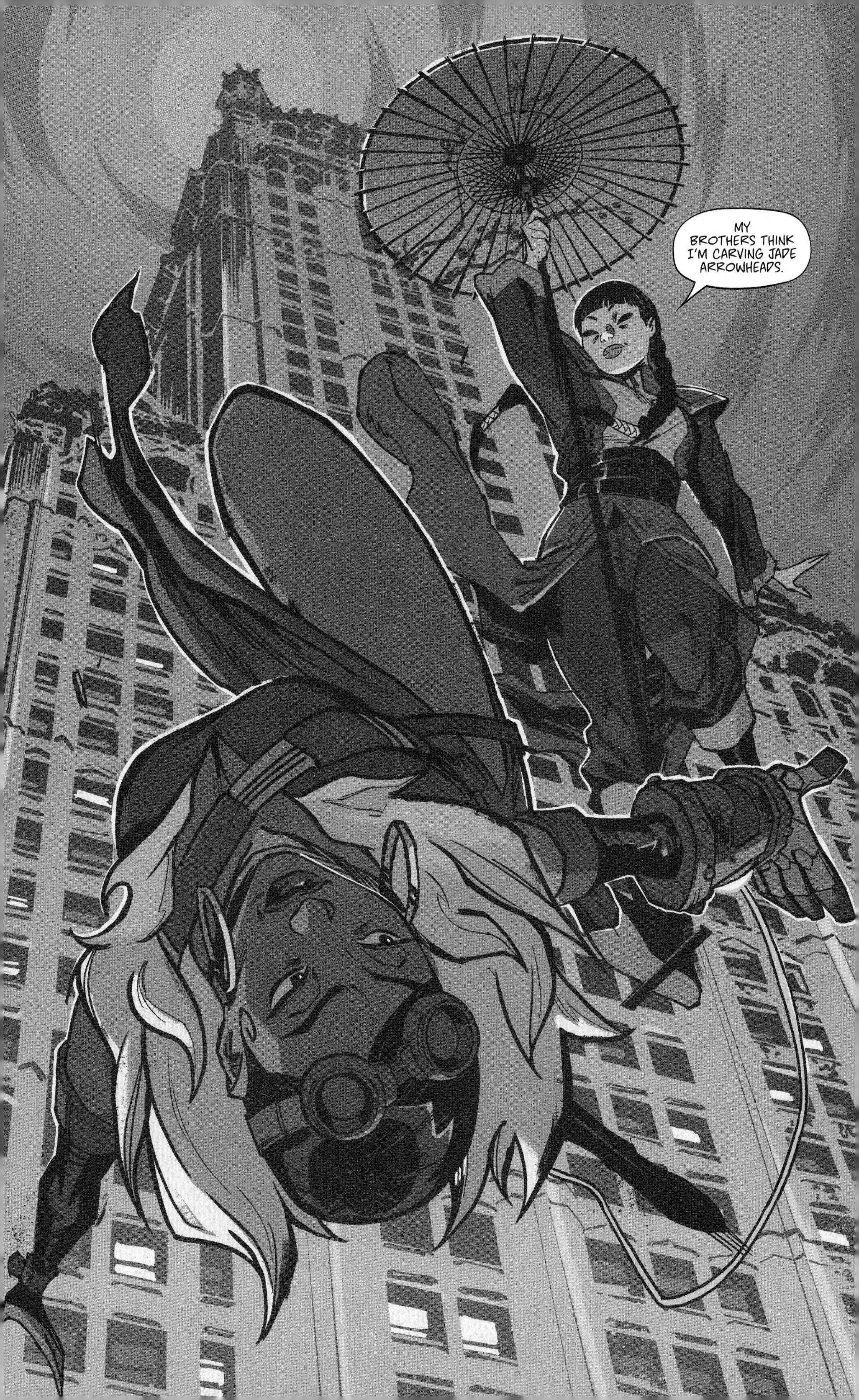
MY BROTHERS THINK I'M CARVING JADE ARROWHEADS.

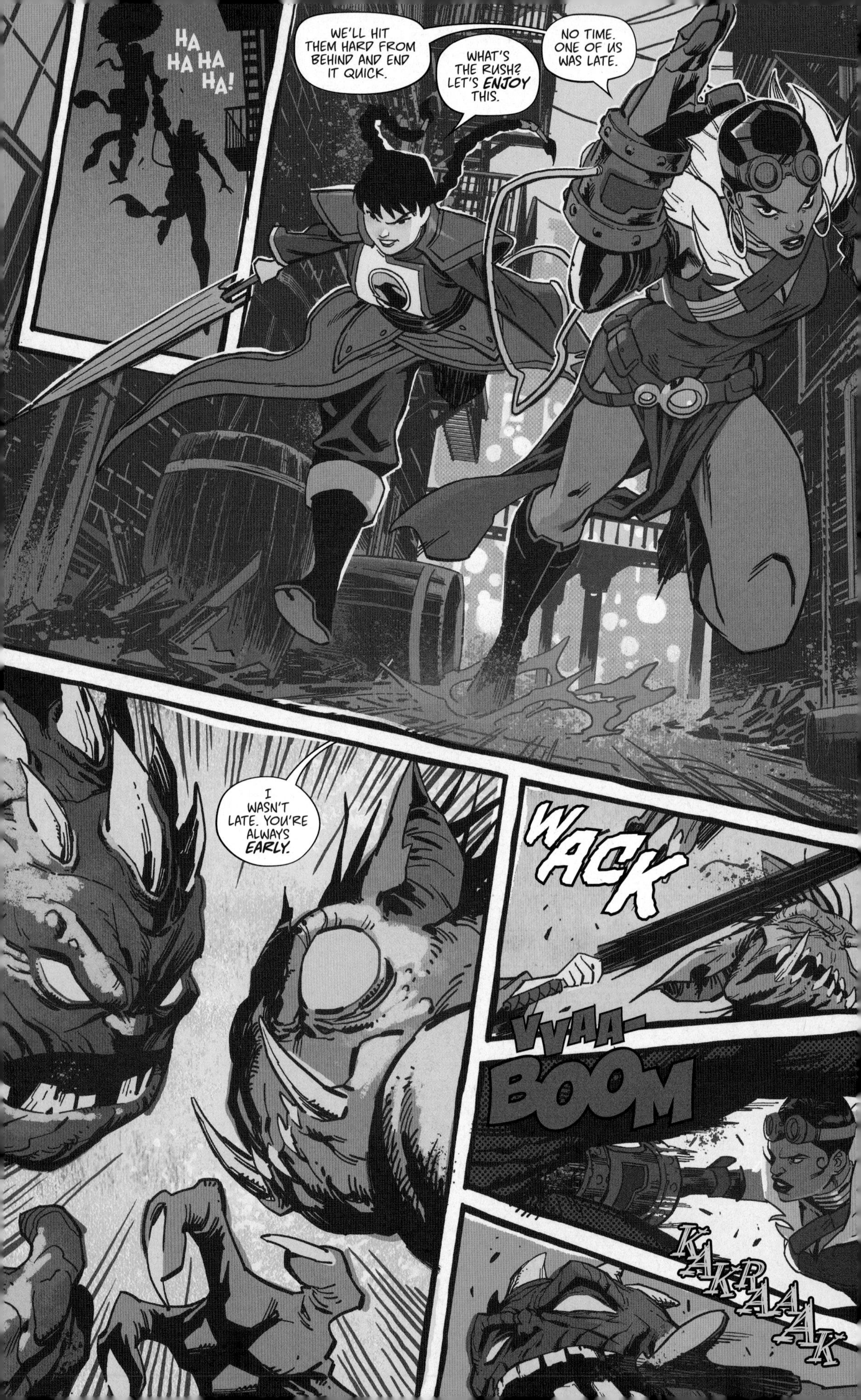
HA
HA HA HA
HA!
WE'LL HIT THEM HARD FROM BEHIND AND END IT QUICK.
WHAT'S THE RUSH? LET'S ENJOY THIS.
NO TIME. ONE OF US WAS LATE.
I WASN'T LATE. YOU'RE ALWAYS EARLY.
WACK
VVAA-BOOM
KAKRAAAK

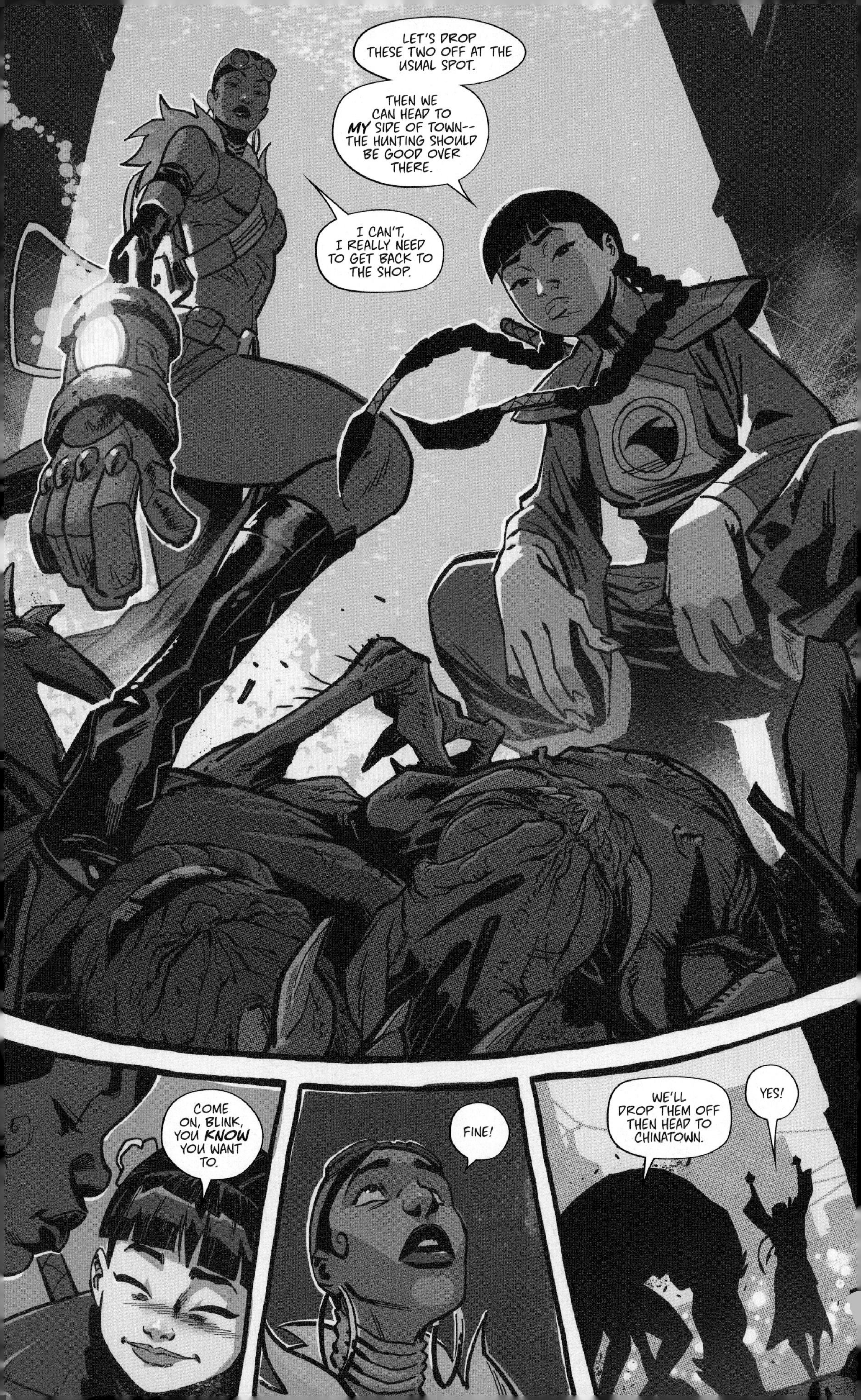
LET'S DROP THESE TWO OFF AT THE USUAL SPOT.
THEN WE CAN HEAD TO MY SIDE OF TOWN-- THE HUNTING SHOULD BE GOOD OVER THERE.
I CAN'T, I REALLY NEED TO GET BACK TO THE SHOP.
COME ON, BLINK, YOU KNOW YOU WANT TO.
FINE!
WE'LL DROP THEM OFF THEN HEAD TO CHINATOWN.
YES!

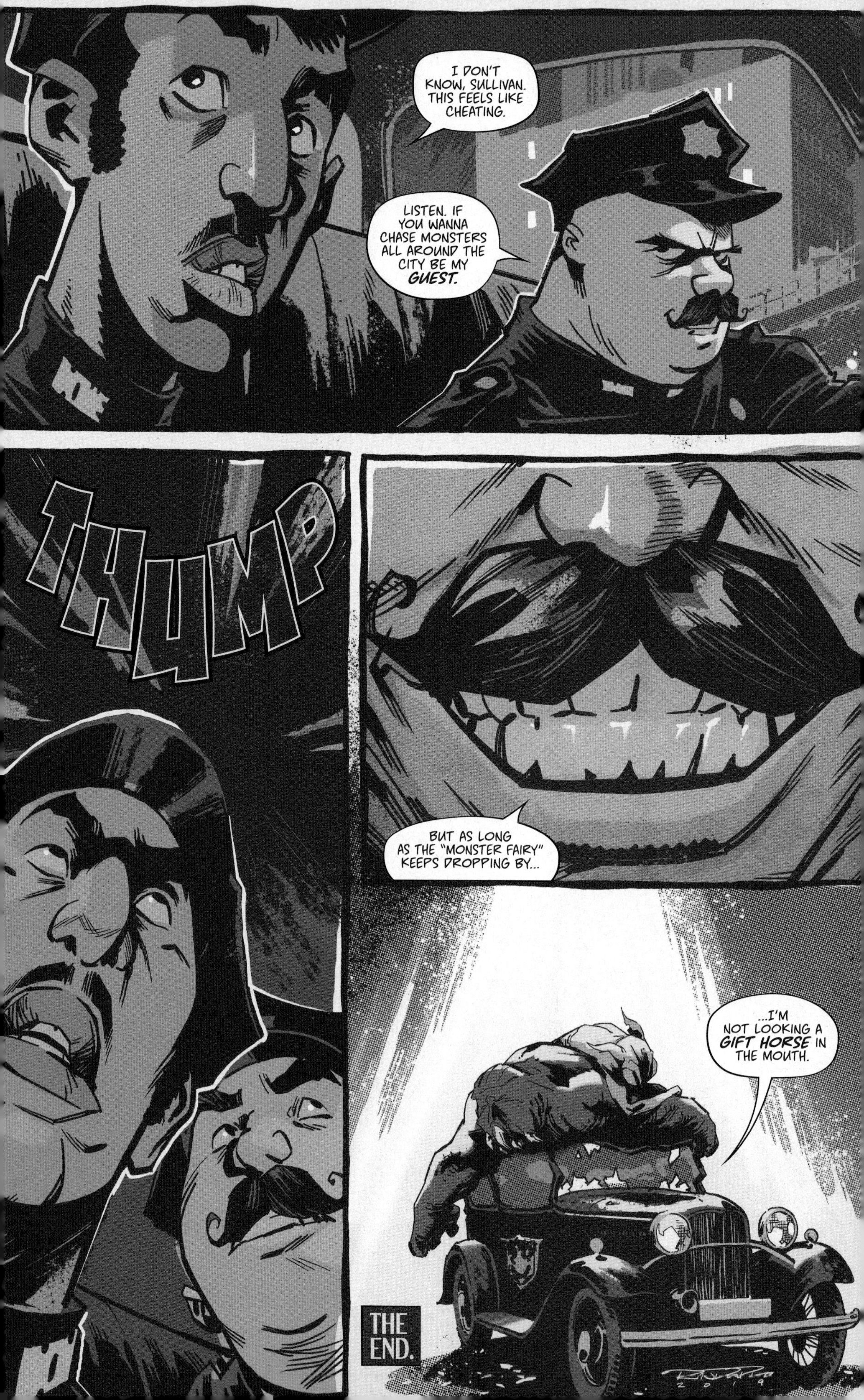
I DON'T KNOW, SULLIVAN. THIS FEELS LIKE CHEATING.
LISTEN. IF YOU WANNA CHASE MONSTERS ALL AROUND THE CITY BE MY GUEST.
THUMP
BUT AS LONG AS THE "MONSTER FAIRY" KEEPS DROPPING BY...
...I'M NOT LOOKING A GIFT HORSE IN THE MOUTH.
THE END.

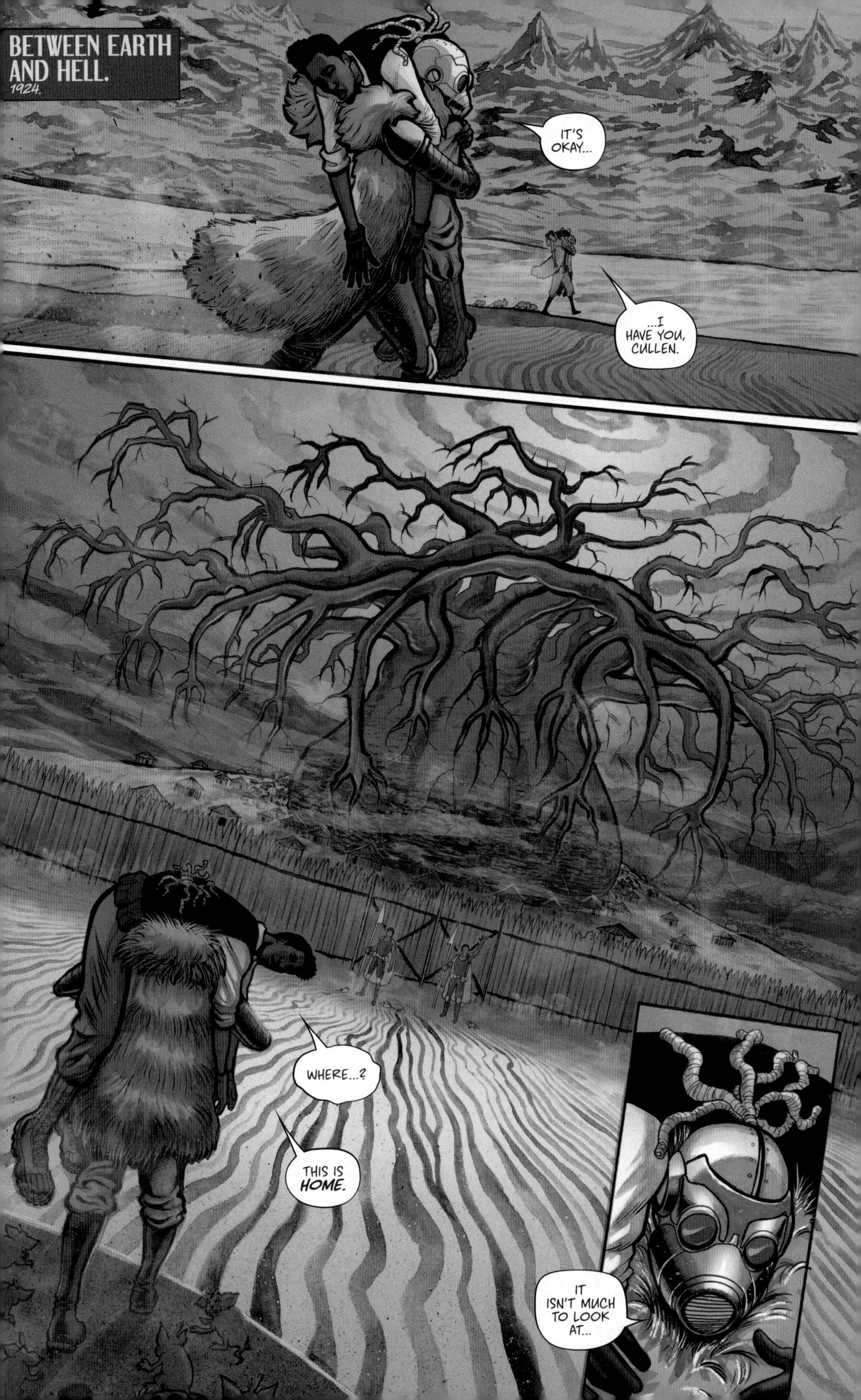
BETWEEN EARTH AND HELL.
1924.
IT'S OKAY...
...I HAVE YOU, CULLEN.
WHERE...?
THIS IS *HOME.*
IT ISN'T MUCH TO LOOK AT...

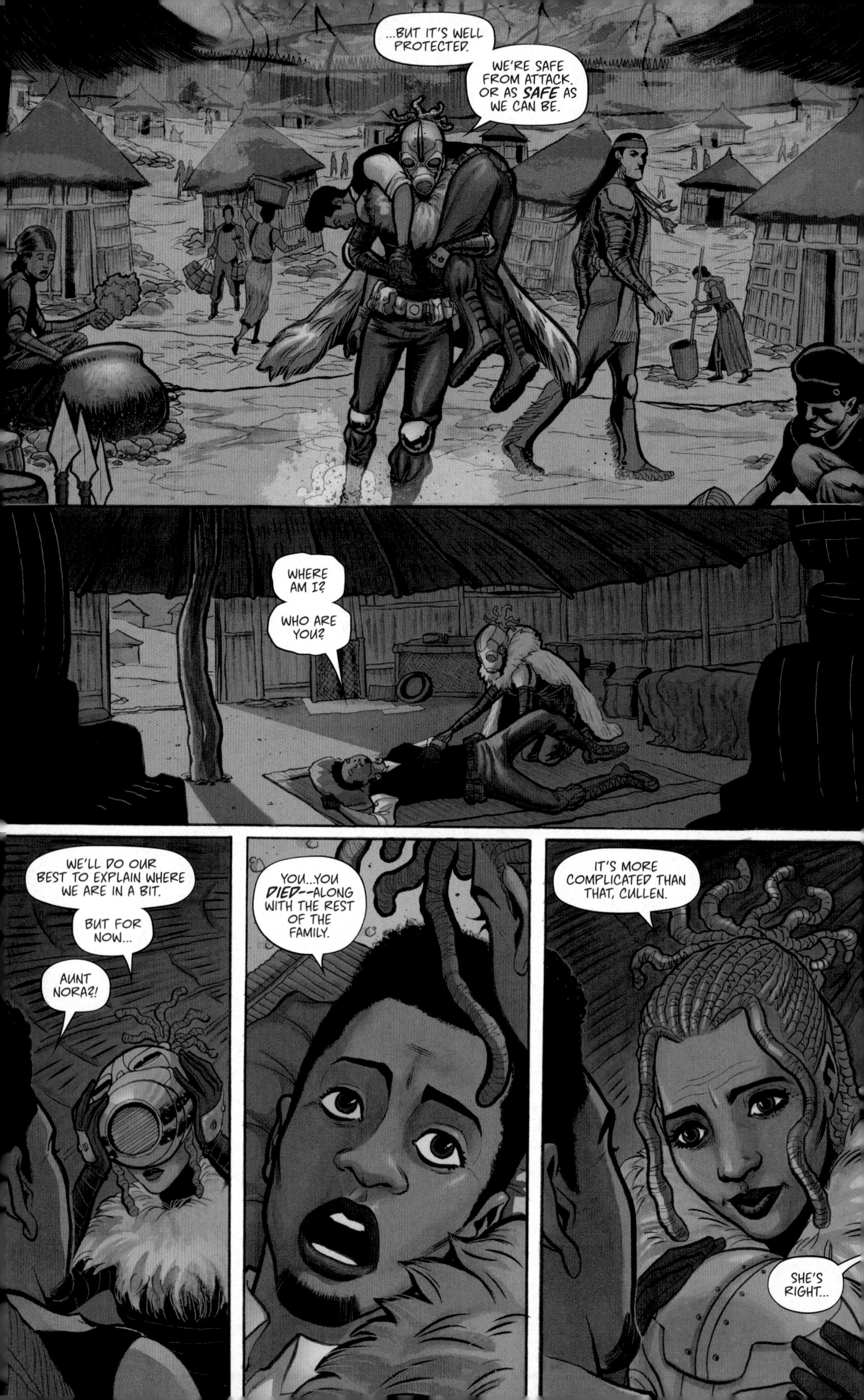

...BUT IT'S WELL PROTECTED.
WE'RE SAFE FROM ATTACK. OR AS SAFE AS WE CAN BE.
WHERE AM I?
WHO ARE YOU?
WE'LL DO OUR BEST TO EXPLAIN WHERE WE ARE IN A BIT.
BUT FOR NOW...
AUNT NORA?!
YOU...YOU DIED--ALONG WITH THE REST OF THE FAMILY.
IT'S MORE COMPLICATED THAN THAT, CULLEN.
SHE'S RIGHT...

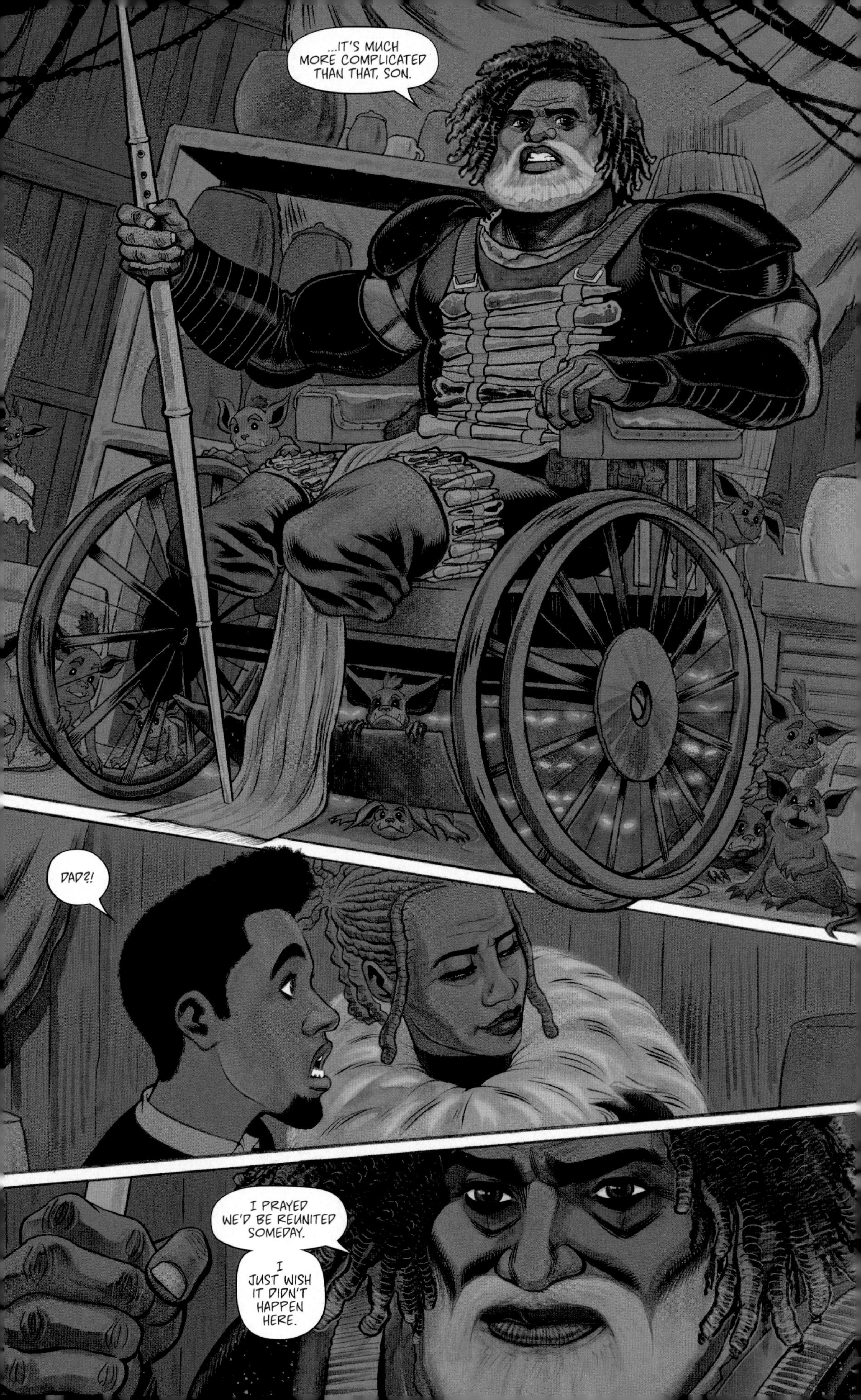
...IT'S MUCH MORE COMPLICATED THAN THAT, SON.
DAD?!
I PRAYED WE'D BE REUNITED SOMEDAY.
I JUST WISH IT DIDN'T HAPPEN HERE.

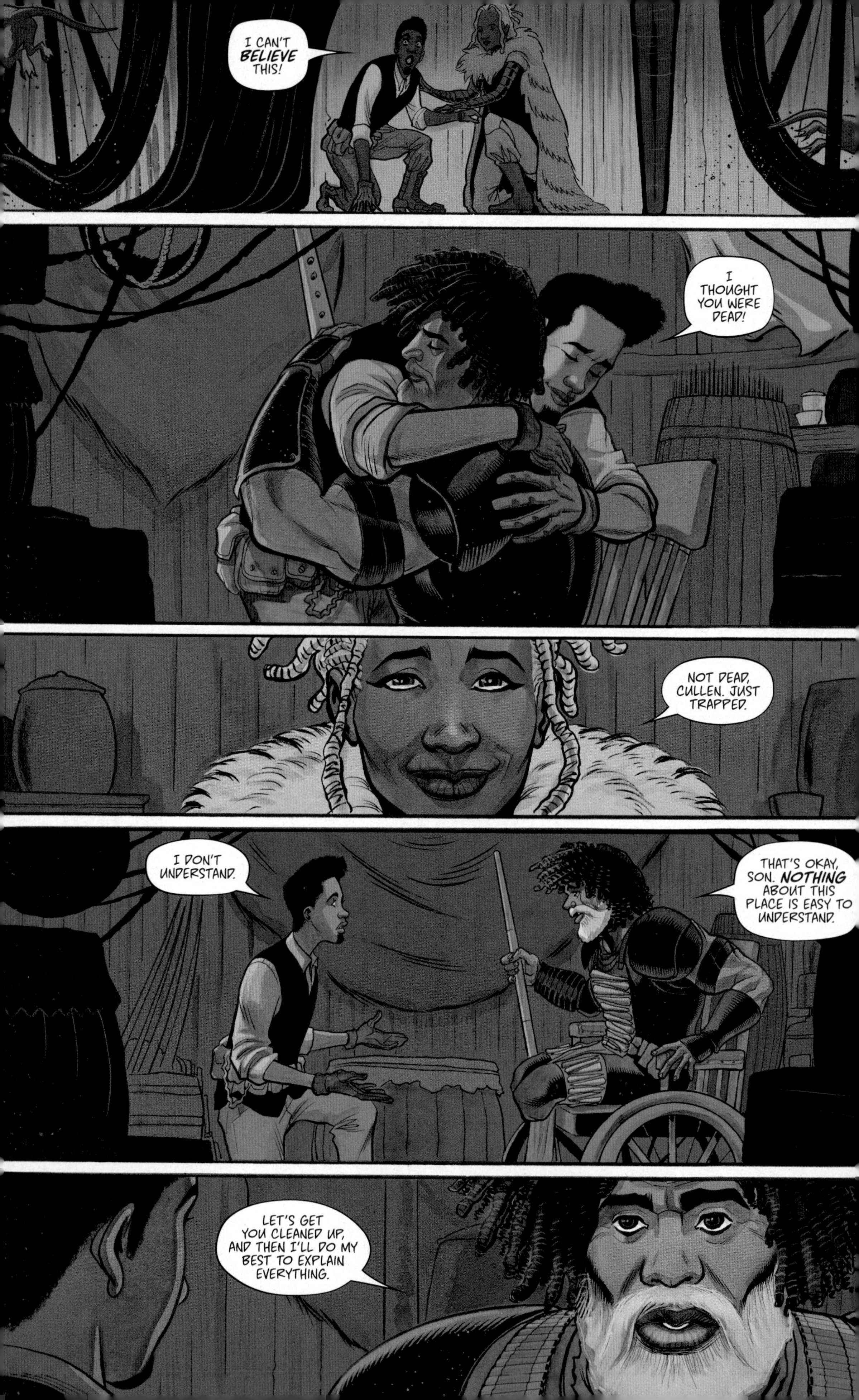
I CAN'T **BELIEVE** THIS!
I THOUGHT YOU WERE DEAD!
NOT DEAD, CULLEN. JUST TRAPPED.
I DON'T UNDERSTAND.
THAT'S OKAY, SON. **NOTHING** ABOUT THIS PLACE IS EASY TO UNDERSTAND.
LET'S GET YOU CLEANED UP, AND THEN I'LL DO MY BEST TO EXPLAIN EVERYTHING.

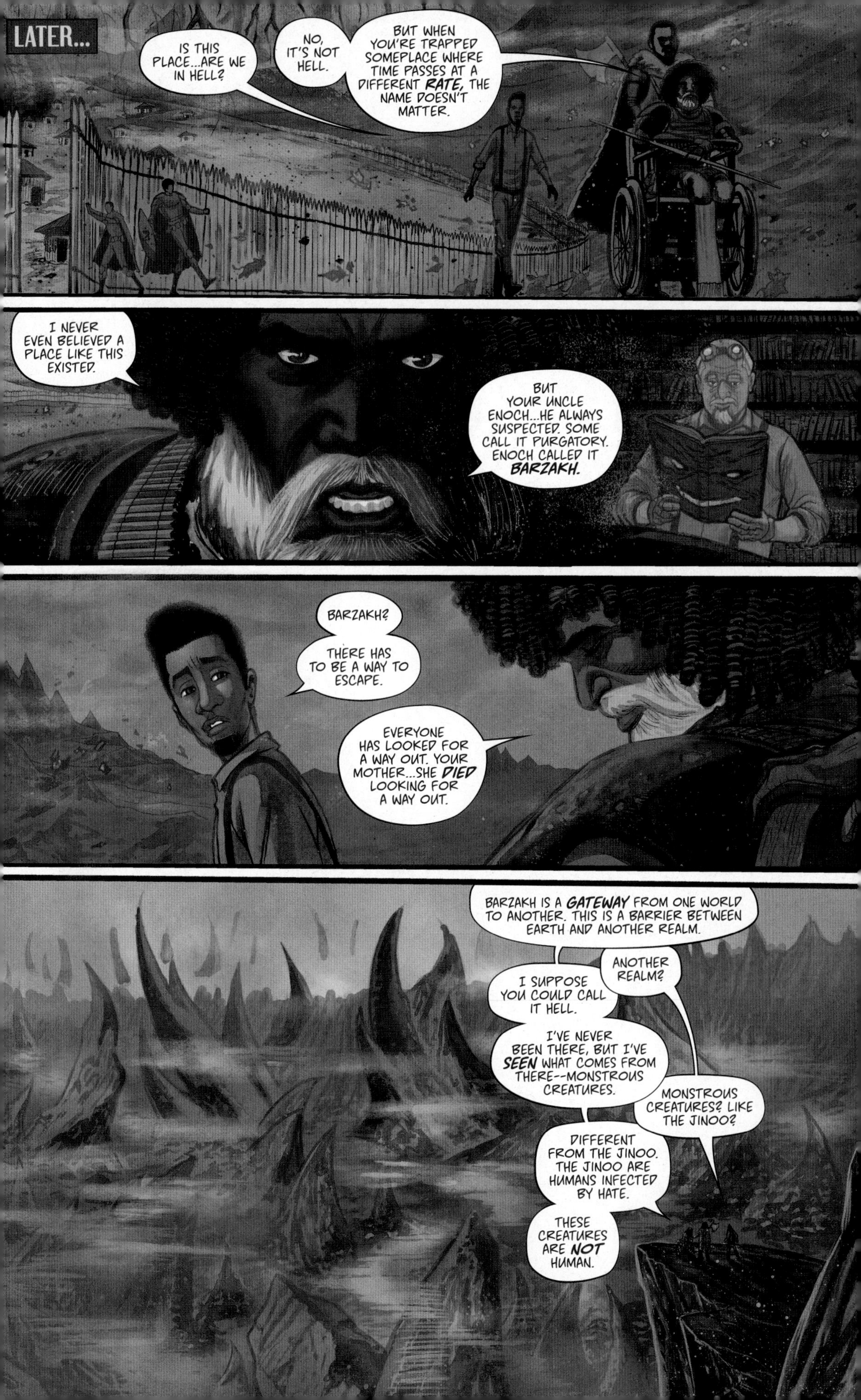
LATER...
IS THIS PLACE...ARE WE IN HELL?
NO, IT'S NOT HELL.
BUT WHEN YOU'RE TRAPPED SOMEPLACE WHERE TIME PASSES AT A DIFFERENT RATE, THE NAME DOESN'T MATTER.
I NEVER EVEN BELIEVED A PLACE LIKE THIS EXISTED.
BUT YOUR UNCLE ENOCH...HE ALWAYS SUSPECTED. SOME CALL IT PURGATORY. ENOCH CALLED IT BARZAKH.
BARZAKH?
THERE HAS TO BE A WAY TO ESCAPE.
EVERYONE HAS LOOKED FOR A WAY OUT. YOUR MOTHER...SHE DIED LOOKING FOR A WAY OUT.
BARZAKH IS A GATEWAY FROM ONE WORLD TO ANOTHER. THIS IS A BARRIER BETWEEN EARTH AND ANOTHER REALM.
ANOTHER REALM?
I SUPPOSE YOU COULD CALL IT HELL.
I'VE NEVER BEEN THERE, BUT I'VE SEEN WHAT COMES FROM THERE--MONSTROUS CREATURES.
MONSTROUS CREATURES? LIKE THE JINOO?
DIFFERENT FROM THE JINOO. THE JINOO ARE HUMANS INFECTED BY HATE.
THESE CREATURES ARE NOT HUMAN.

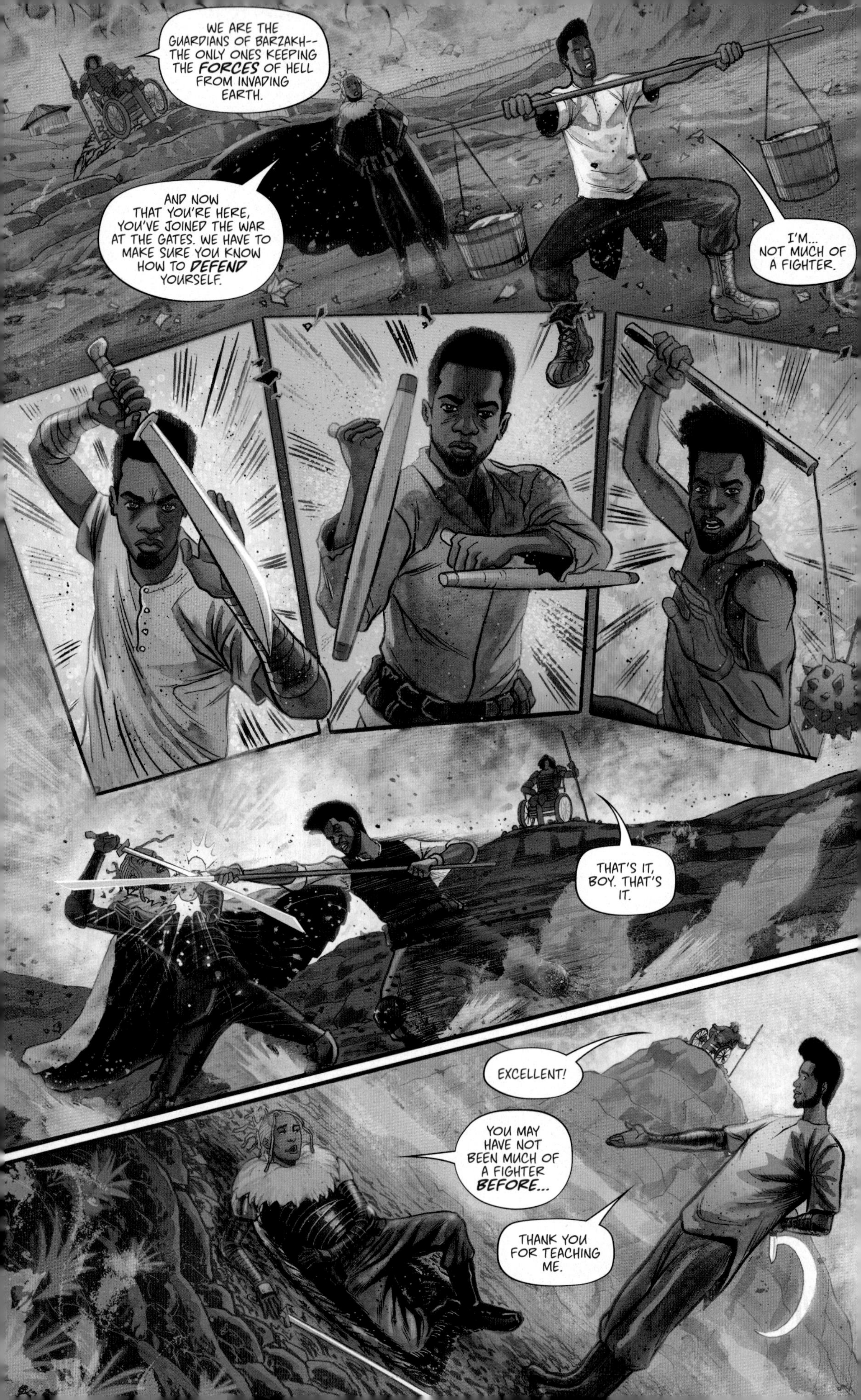
WE ARE THE GUARDIANS OF BARZAKH-- THE ONLY ONES KEEPING THE FORCES OF HELL FROM INVADING EARTH.
AND NOW THAT YOU'RE HERE, YOU'VE JOINED THE WAR AT THE GATES. WE HAVE TO MAKE SURE YOU KNOW HOW TO DEFEND YOURSELF.
I'M... NOT MUCH OF A FIGHTER.
THAT'S IT, BOY. THAT'S IT.
EXCELLENT!
YOU MAY HAVE NOT BEEN MUCH OF A FIGHTER BEFORE...
THANK YOU FOR TEACHING ME.

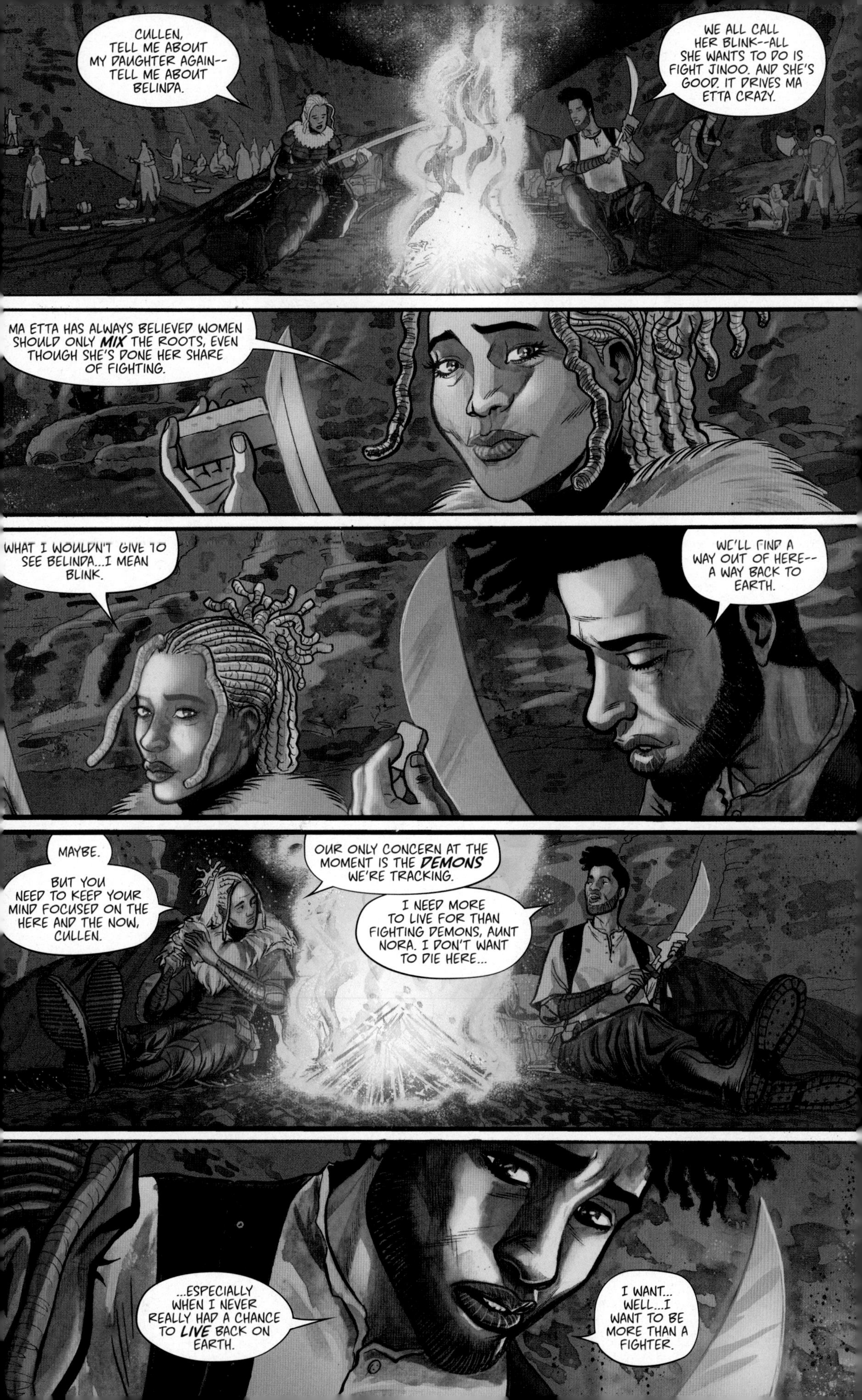

CULLEN, TELL ME ABOUT MY DAUGHTER AGAIN-- TELL ME ABOUT BELINDA.
WE ALL CALL HER BLINK--ALL SHE WANTS TO DO IS FIGHT JINOO. AND SHE'S GOOD. IT DRIVES MA ETTA CRAZY.
MA ETTA HAS ALWAYS BELIEVED WOMEN SHOULD ONLY MIX THE ROOTS, EVEN THOUGH SHE'S DONE HER SHARE OF FIGHTING.
WHAT I WOULDN'T GIVE TO SEE BELINDA...I MEAN BLINK.
WE'LL FIND A WAY OUT OF HERE-- A WAY BACK TO EARTH.
MAYBE.
BUT YOU NEED TO KEEP YOUR MIND FOCUSED ON THE HERE AND THE NOW, CULLEN.
OUR ONLY CONCERN AT THE MOMENT IS THE DEMONS WE'RE TRACKING.
I NEED MORE TO LIVE FOR THAN FIGHTING DEMONS, AUNT NORA. I DON'T WANT TO DIE HERE...
...ESPECIALLY WHEN I NEVER REALLY HAD A CHANCE TO LIVE BACK ON EARTH.
I WANT... WELL...I WANT TO BE MORE THAN A FIGHTER.

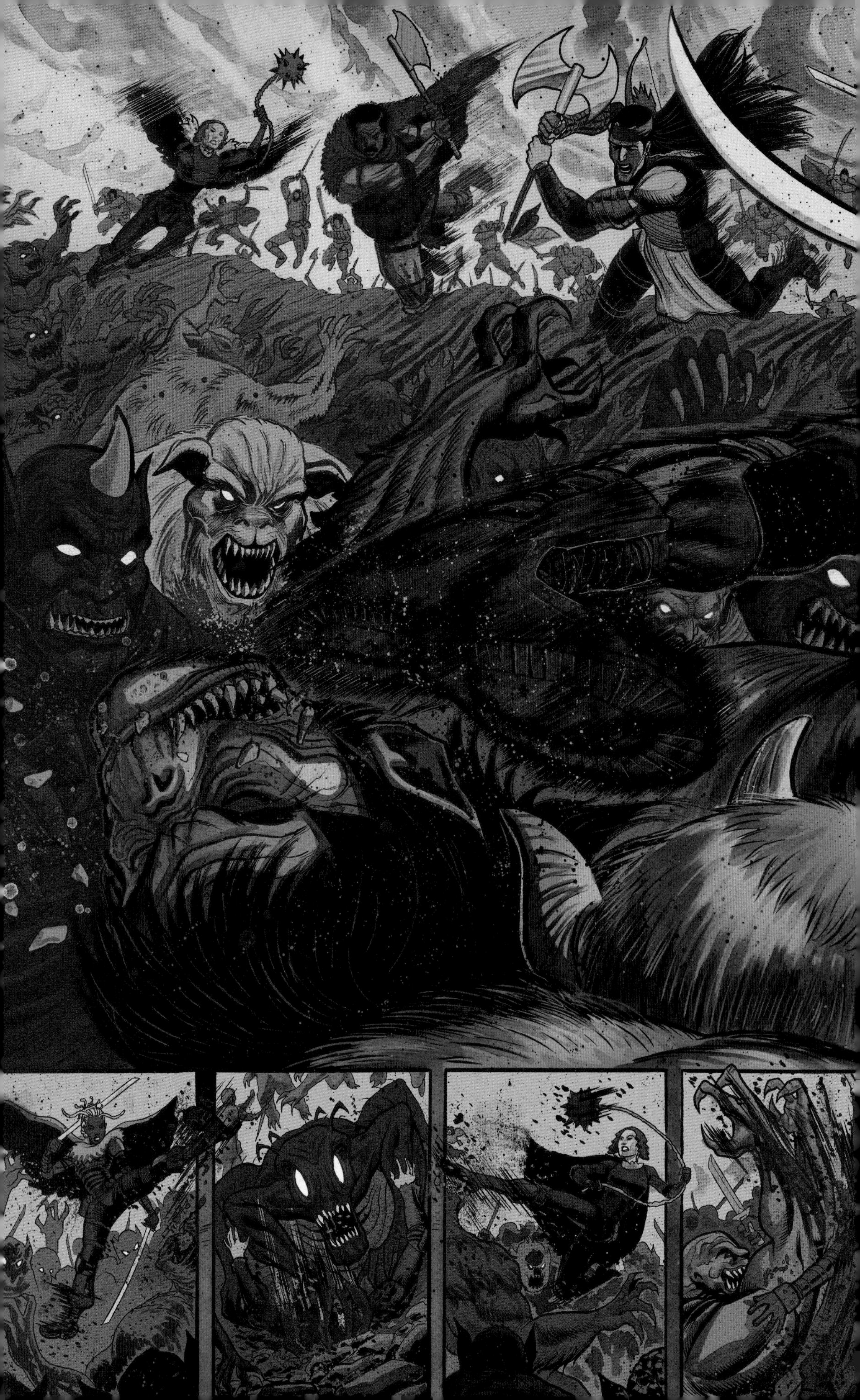

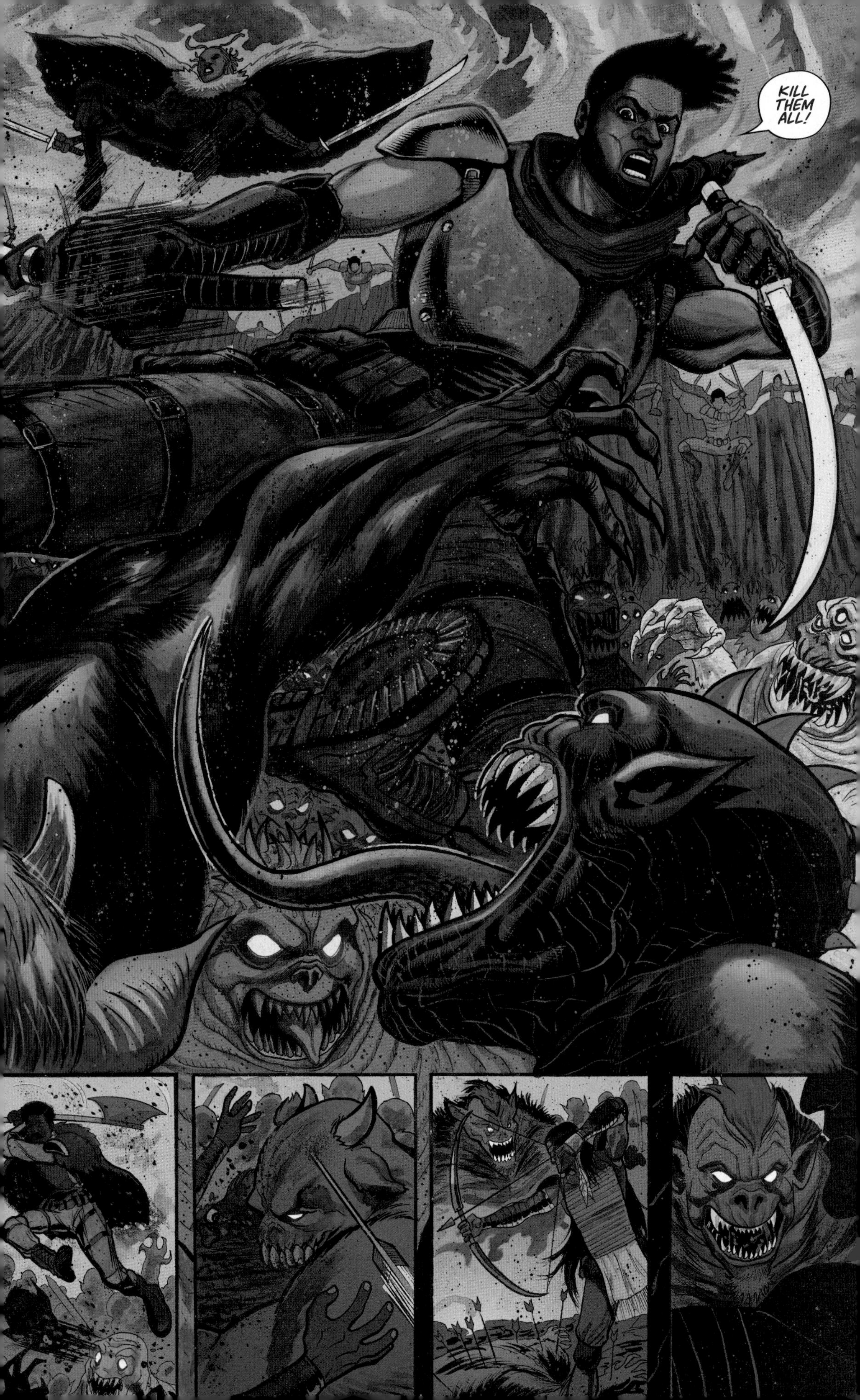
KILL THEM ALL!

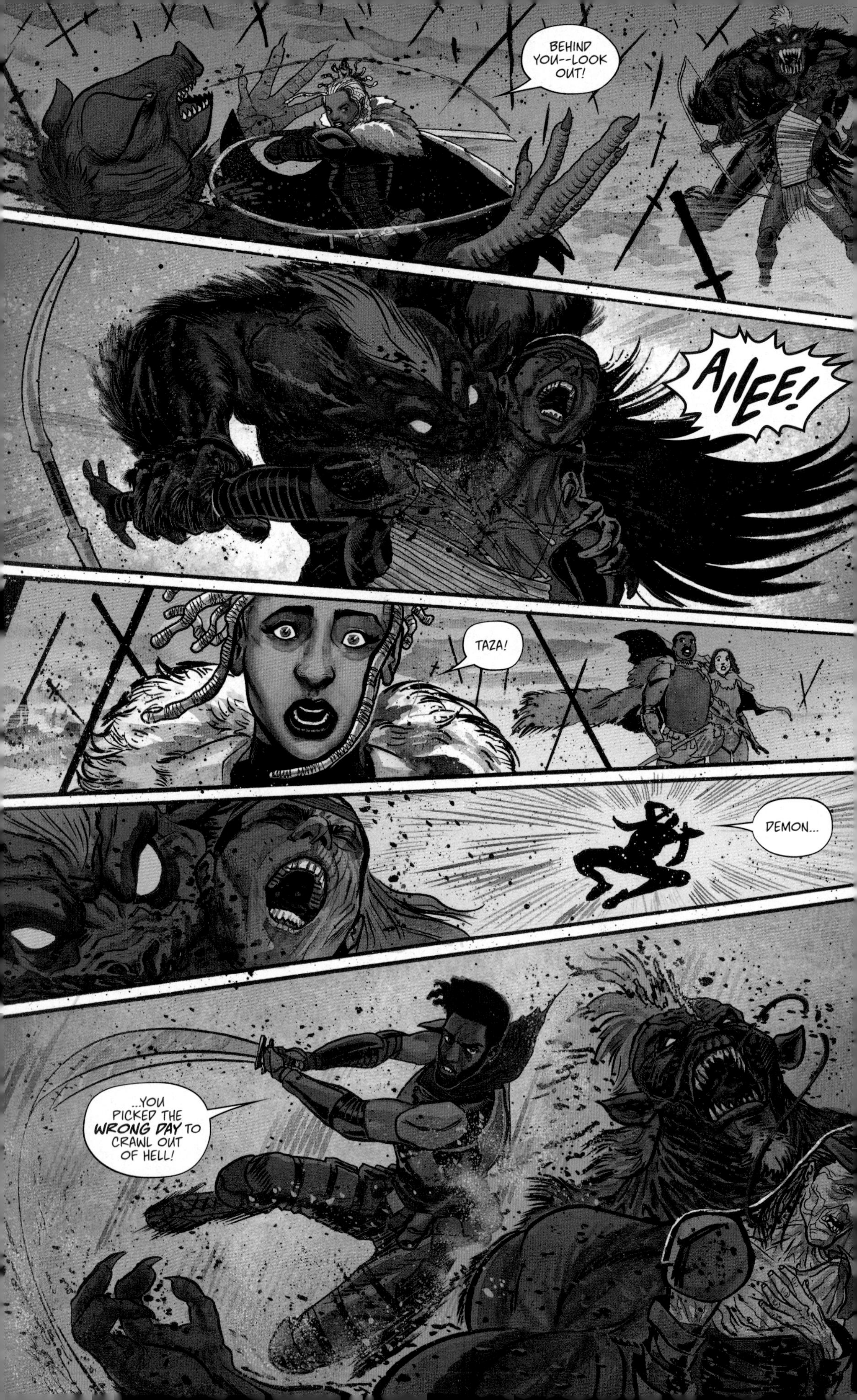
BEHIND YOU--LOOK OUT!
AIEEE!
TAZA!
DEMON...
...YOU PICKED THE **WRONG DAY** TO CRAWL OUT OF HELL!

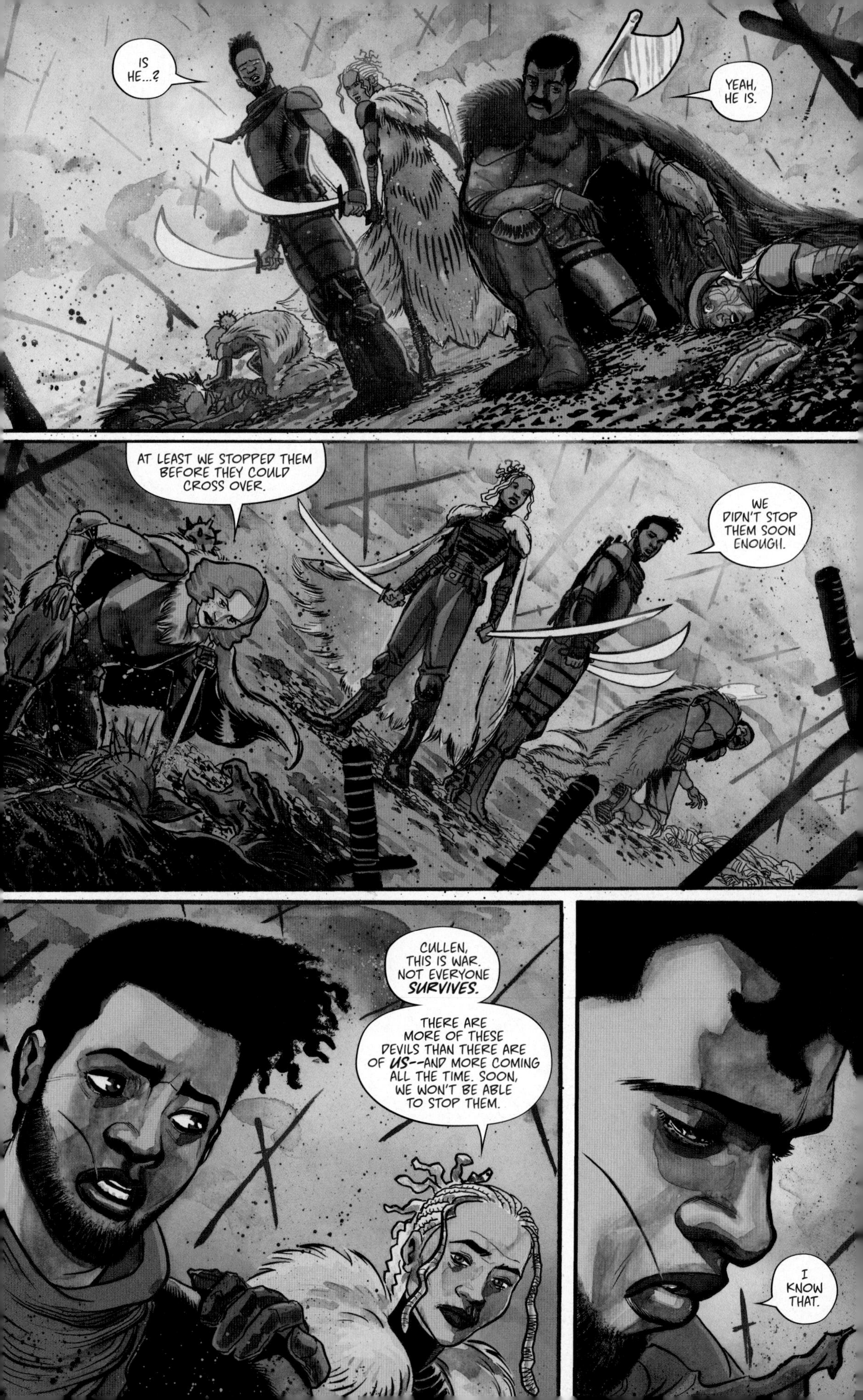
IS HE...?
YEAH, HE IS.
AT LEAST WE STOPPED THEM BEFORE THEY COULD CROSS OVER.
WE DIDN'T STOP THEM SOON ENOUGH.
CULLEN, THIS IS WAR. NOT EVERYONE SURVIVES.
THERE ARE MORE OF THESE DEVILS THAN THERE ARE OF US--AND MORE COMING ALL THE TIME. SOON, WE WON'T BE ABLE TO STOP THEM.
I KNOW THAT.

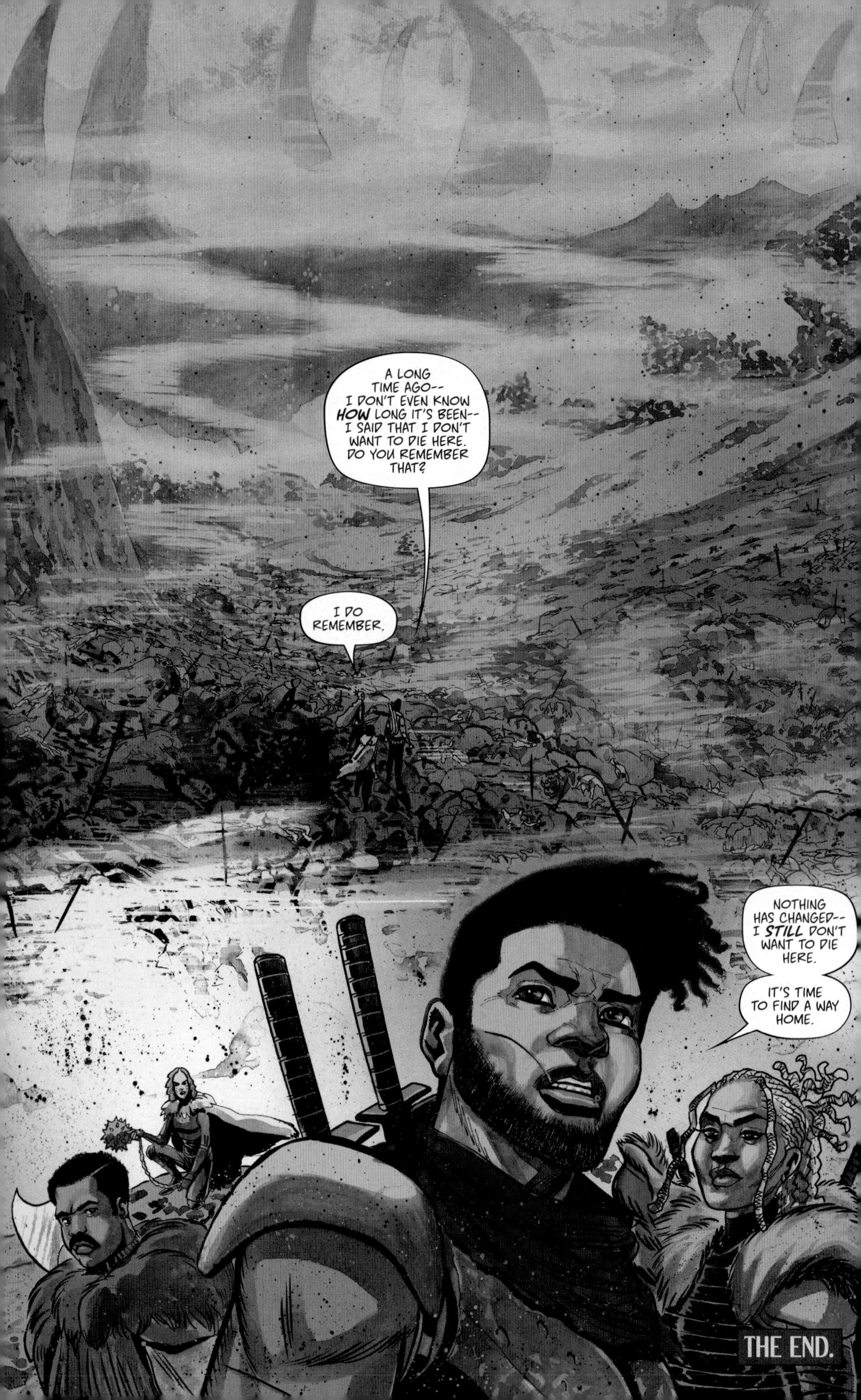
A LONG TIME AGO-- I DON'T EVEN KNOW HOW LONG IT'S BEEN-- I SAID THAT I DON'T WANT TO DIE HERE. DO YOU REMEMBER THAT?
I DO REMEMBER.
NOTHING HAS CHANGED-- I STILL DON'T WANT TO DIE HERE.
IT'S TIME TO FIND A WAY HOME.
THE END.

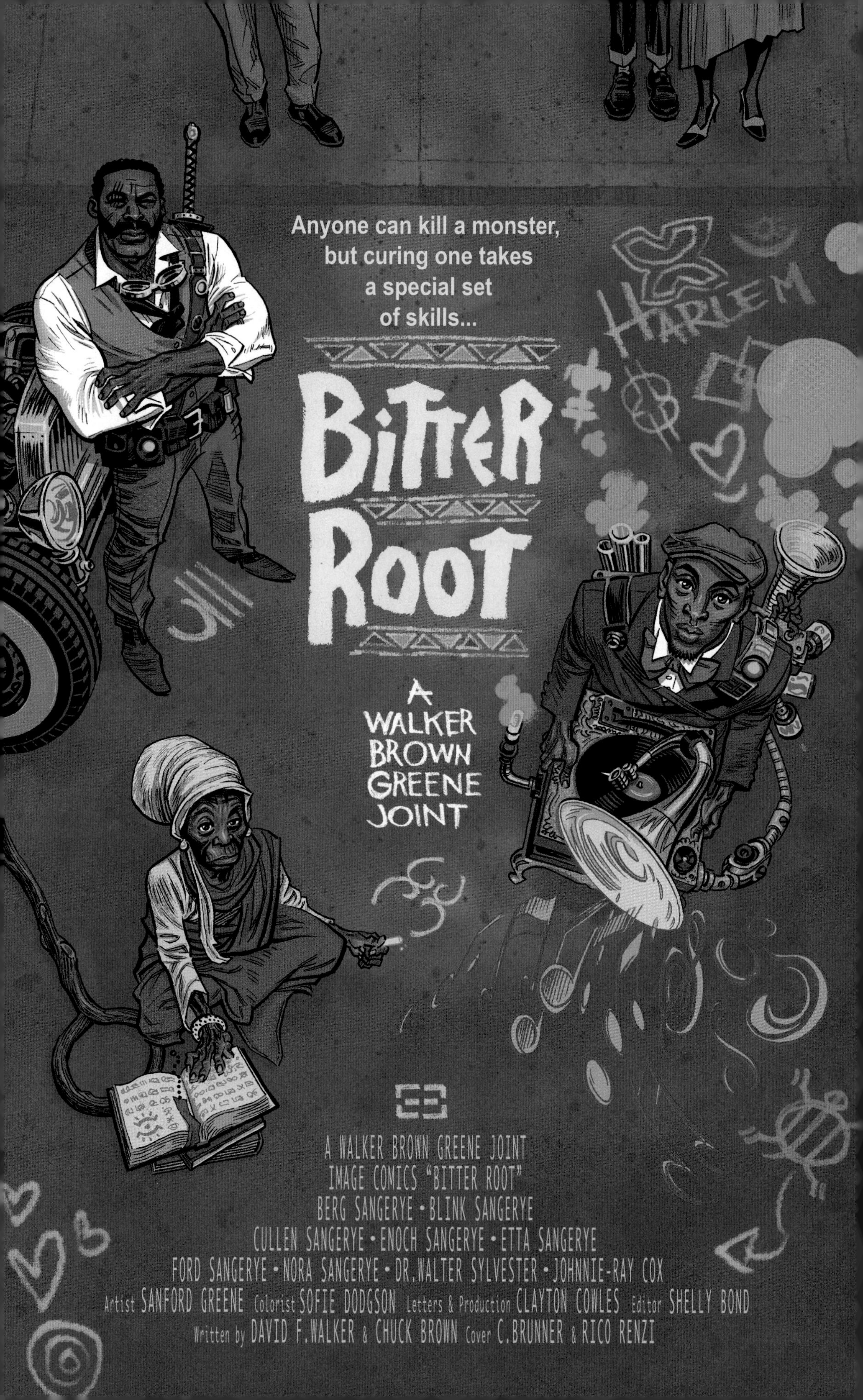
Anyone can kill a monster, but curing one takes a special set of skills...
BITTER ROOT
A WALKER BROWN GREENE JOINT
HARLEM
A WALKER BROWN GREENE JOINT
IMAGE COMICS "BITTER ROOT"
BERG SANGERYE • BLINK SANGERYE
CULLEN SANGERYE • ENOCH SANGERYE • ETTA SANGERYE
FORD SANGERYE • NORA SANGERYE • DR.WALTER SYLVESTER • JOHNNIE-RAY COX
Artist SANFORD GREENE Colorist SOFIE DODGSON Letters & Production CLAYTON COWLES Editor SHELLY BOND
Written by DAVID F.WALKER & CHUCK BROWN Cover C.BRUNNER & RICO RENZI

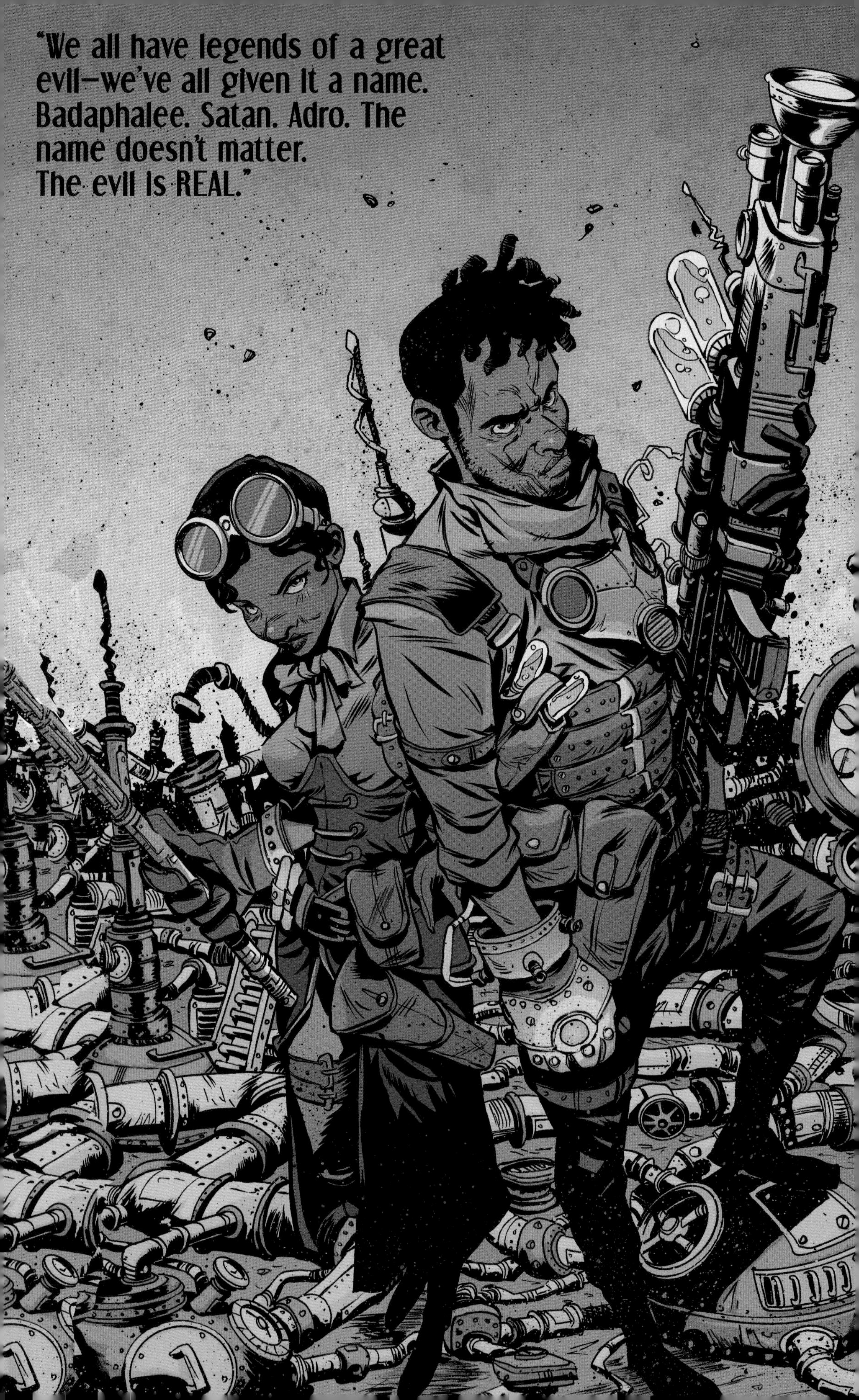
"We all have legends of a great evil—we've all given it a name. Badaphalee. Satan. Adro. The name doesn't matter. The evil is REAL."

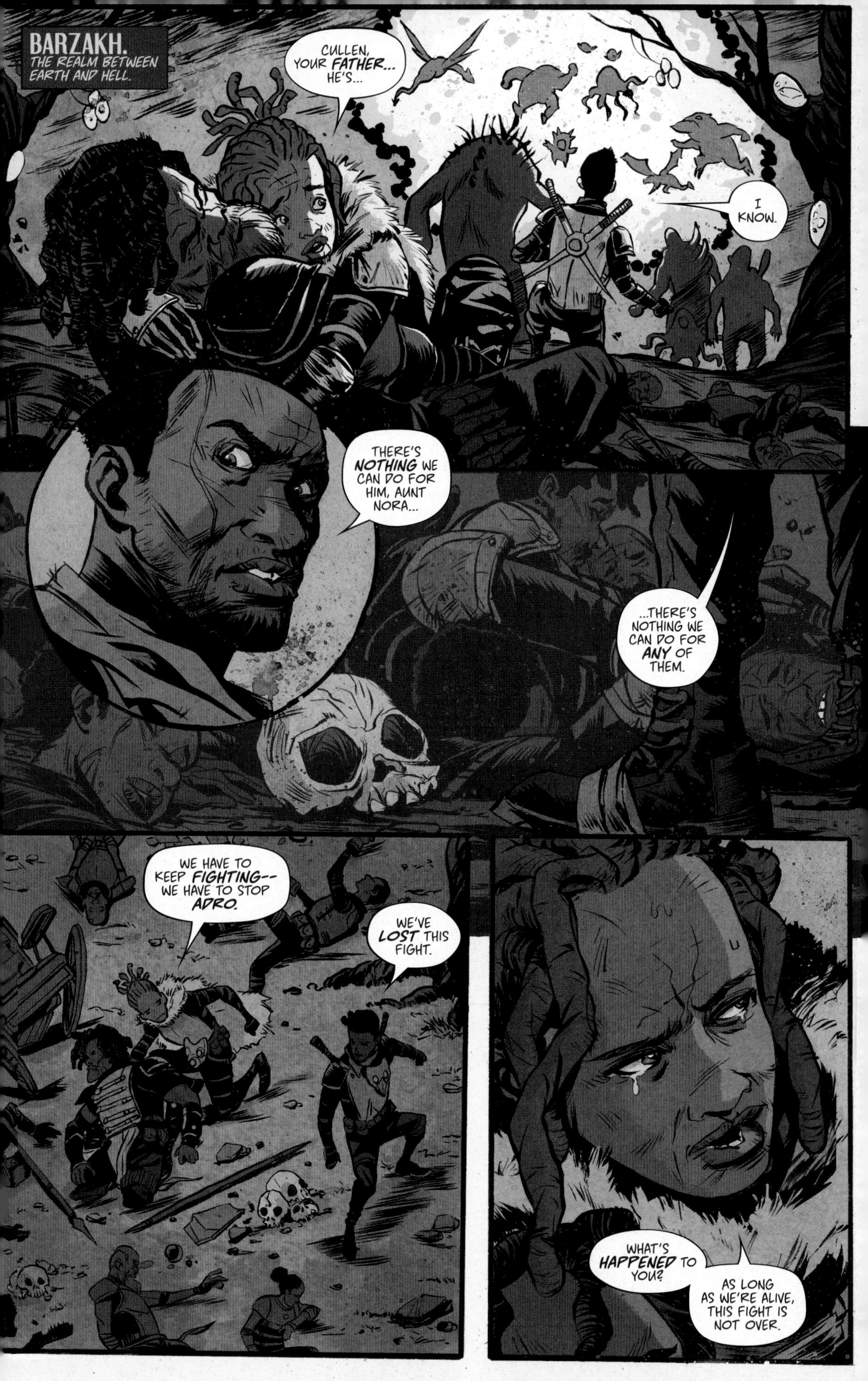
BARZAKH.
THE REALM BETWEEN EARTH AND HELL.
CULLEN, YOUR FATHER... HE'S...
I KNOW.
THERE'S NOTHING WE CAN DO FOR HIM, AUNT NORA...
...THERE'S NOTHING WE CAN DO FOR ANY OF THEM.
WE HAVE TO KEEP FIGHTING-- WE HAVE TO STOP ADRO.
WE'VE LOST THIS FIGHT.
WHAT'S HAPPENED TO YOU?
AS LONG AS WE'RE ALIVE, THIS FIGHT IS NOT OVER.

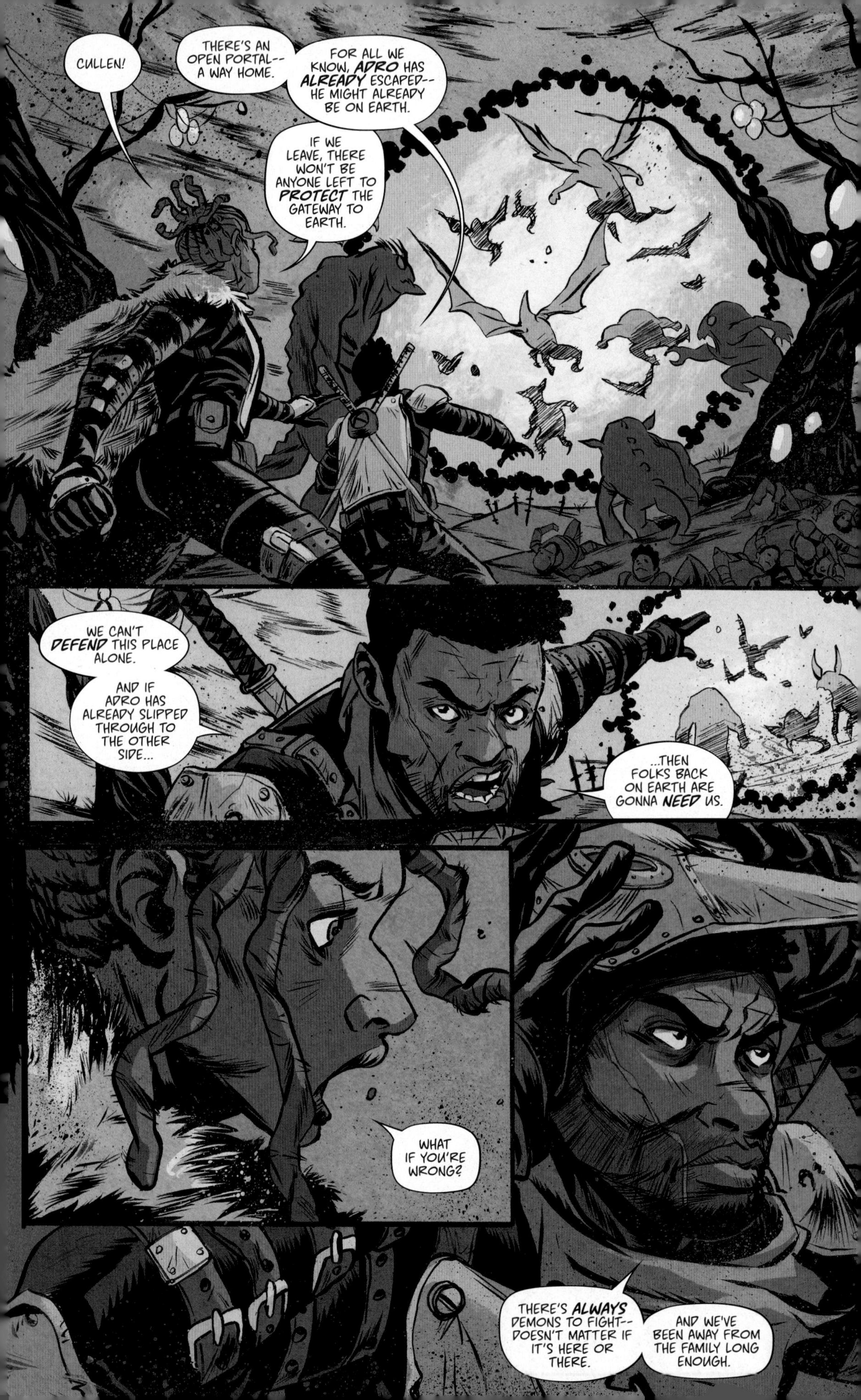
CULLEN!
THERE'S AN OPEN PORTAL-- A WAY HOME.
FOR ALL WE KNOW, ADRO HAS ALREADY ESCAPED-- HE MIGHT ALREADY BE ON EARTH.
IF WE LEAVE, THERE WON'T BE ANYONE LEFT TO PROTECT THE GATEWAY TO EARTH.
WE CAN'T DEFEND THIS PLACE ALONE.
AND IF ADRO HAS ALREADY SLIPPED THROUGH TO THE OTHER SIDE...
...THEN FOLKS BACK ON EARTH ARE GONNA NEED US.
WHAT IF YOU'RE WRONG?
THERE'S ALWAYS DEMONS TO FIGHT-- DOESN'T MATTER IF IT'S HERE OR THERE.
AND WE'VE BEEN AWAY FROM THE FAMILY LONG ENOUGH.

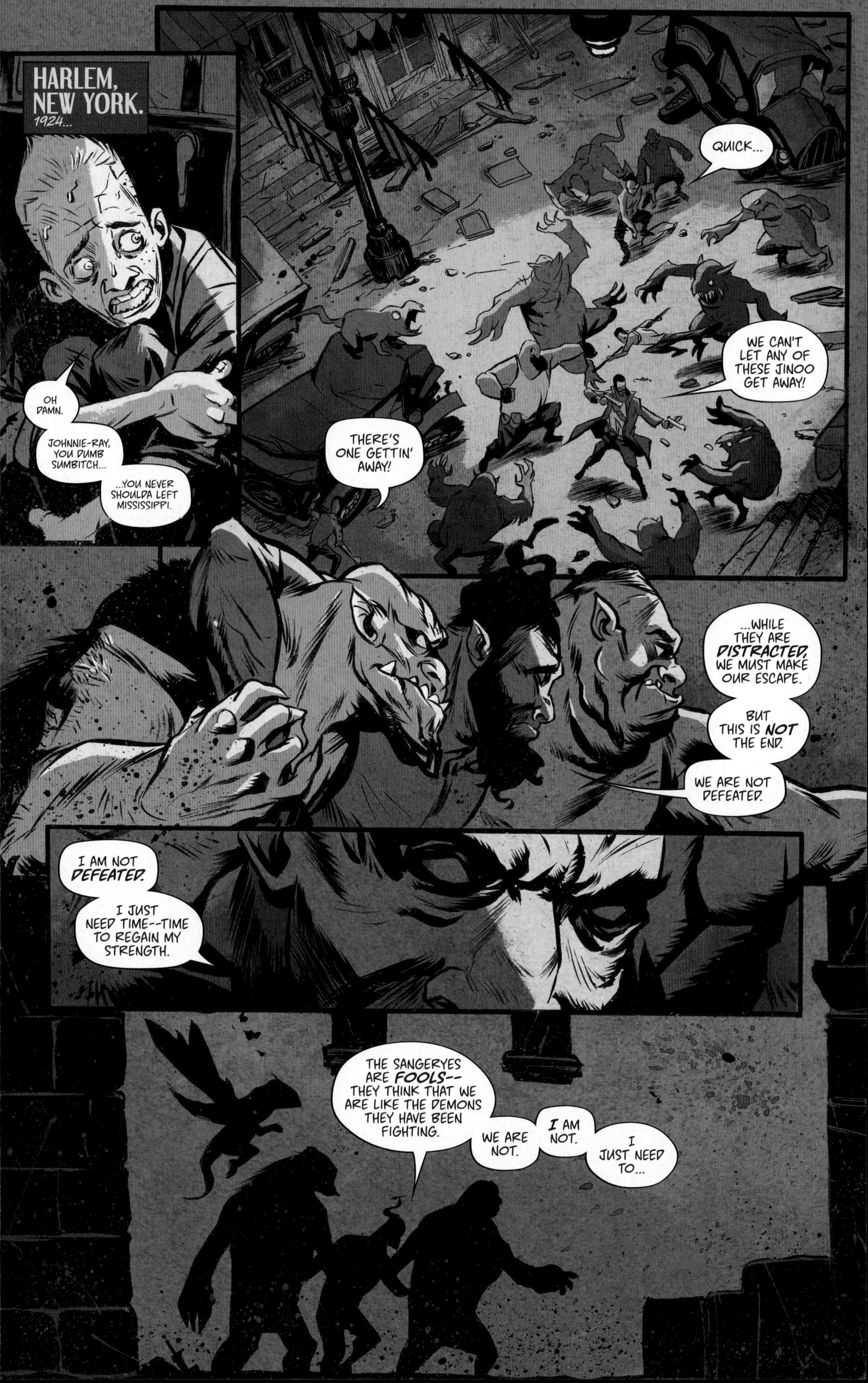
HARLEM, NEW YORK.
1924...
OH DAMN.
JOHNNIE-RAY, YOU DUMB SUMBITCH...
...YOU NEVER SHOULDA LEFT MISSISSIPPI.
QUICK...
WE CAN'T LET ANY OF THESE JINOO GET AWAY!
THERE'S ONE GETTIN' AWAY!
...WHILE THEY ARE DISTRACTED, WE MUST MAKE OUR ESCAPE.
BUT THIS IS NOT THE END.
WE ARE NOT DEFEATED.
I AM NOT DEFEATED.
I JUST NEED TIME--TIME TO REGAIN MY STRENGTH.
THE SANGERYES ARE FOOLS-- THEY THINK THAT WE ARE LIKE THE DEMONS THEY HAVE BEEN FIGHTING.
WE ARE NOT.
I AM NOT.
I JUST NEED TO...

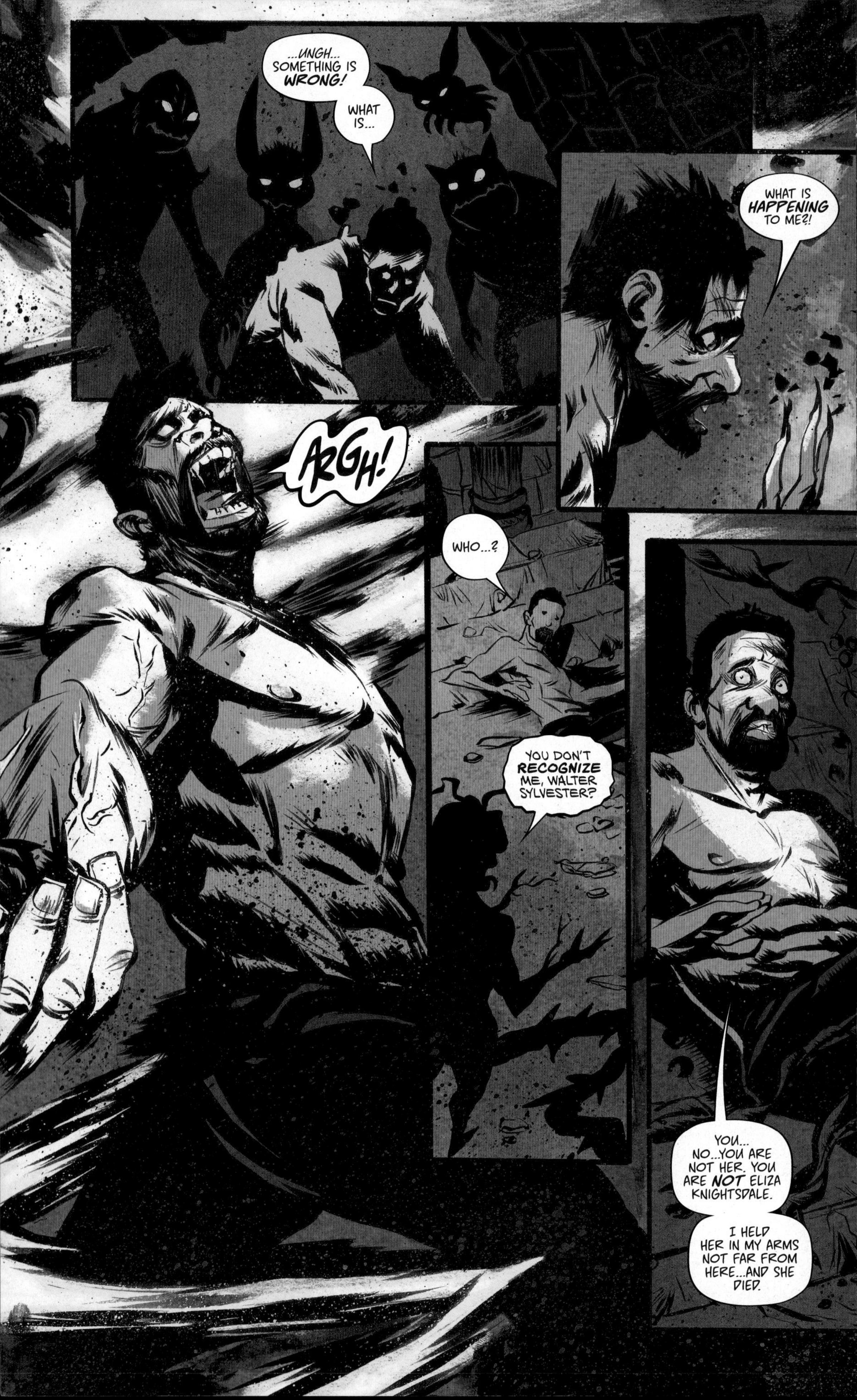
...UNGH... SOMETHING IS **WRONG!**
WHAT IS...
WHAT IS **HAPPENING** TO ME?!
ARGH!
WHO...?
YOU DON'T **RECOGNIZE** ME, WALTER SYLVESTER?
YOU... NO...YOU ARE NOT HER. YOU ARE **NOT** ELIZA KNIGHTSDALE.
I HELD HER IN MY ARMS NOT FAR FROM HERE...AND SHE DIED.

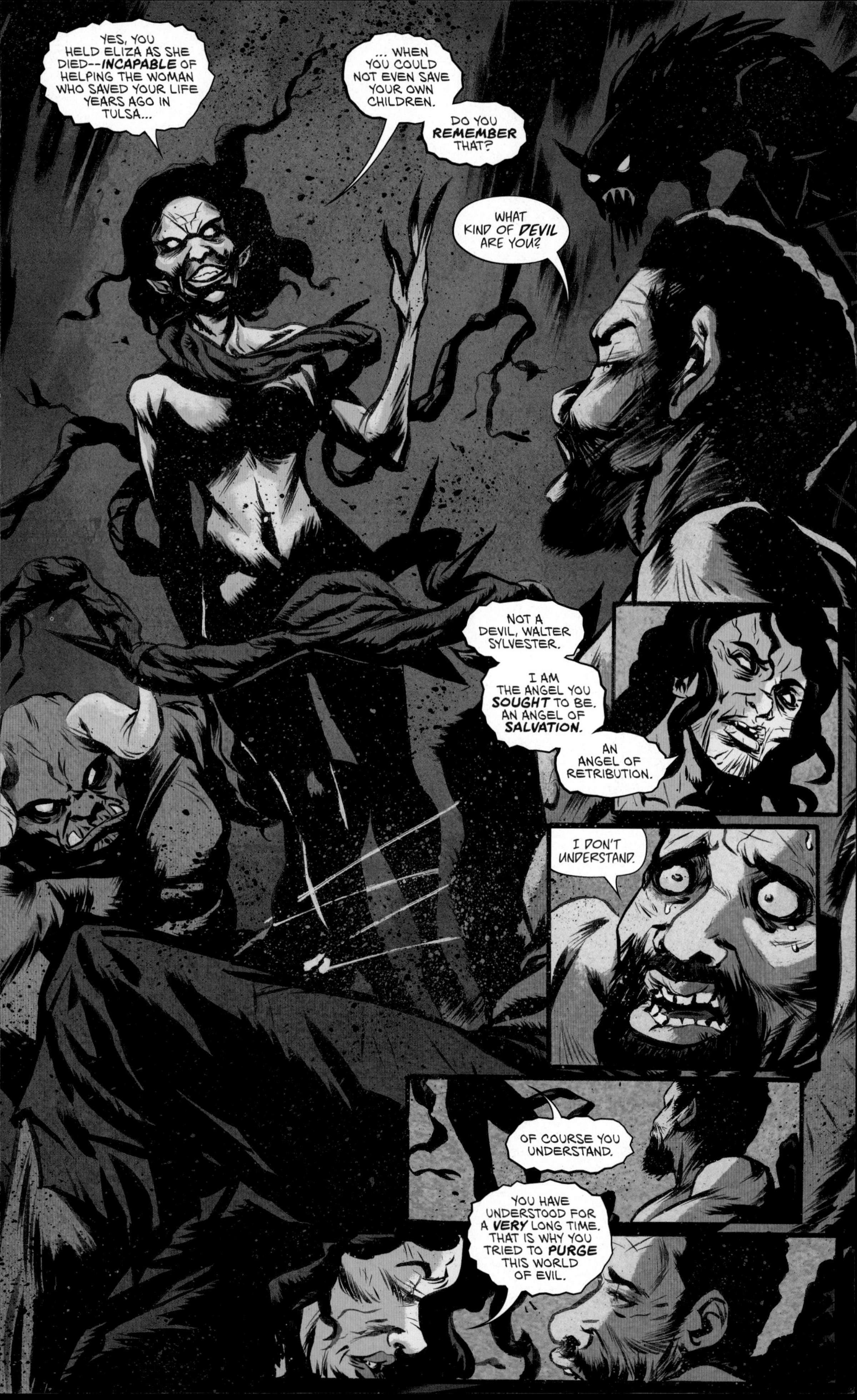
YES, YOU HELD ELIZA AS SHE DIED--INCAPABLE OF HELPING THE WOMAN WHO SAVED YOUR LIFE YEARS AGO IN TULSA...
... WHEN YOU COULD NOT EVEN SAVE YOUR OWN CHILDREN.
DO YOU REMEMBER THAT?
WHAT KIND OF DEVIL ARE YOU?
NOT A DEVIL, WALTER SYLVESTER.
I AM THE ANGEL YOU SOUGHT TO BE. AN ANGEL OF SALVATION.
AN ANGEL OF RETRIBUTION.
I DON'T UNDERSTAND.
OF COURSE YOU UNDERSTAND.
YOU HAVE UNDERSTOOD FOR A VERY LONG TIME. THAT IS WHY YOU TRIED TO PURGE THIS WORLD OF EVIL.

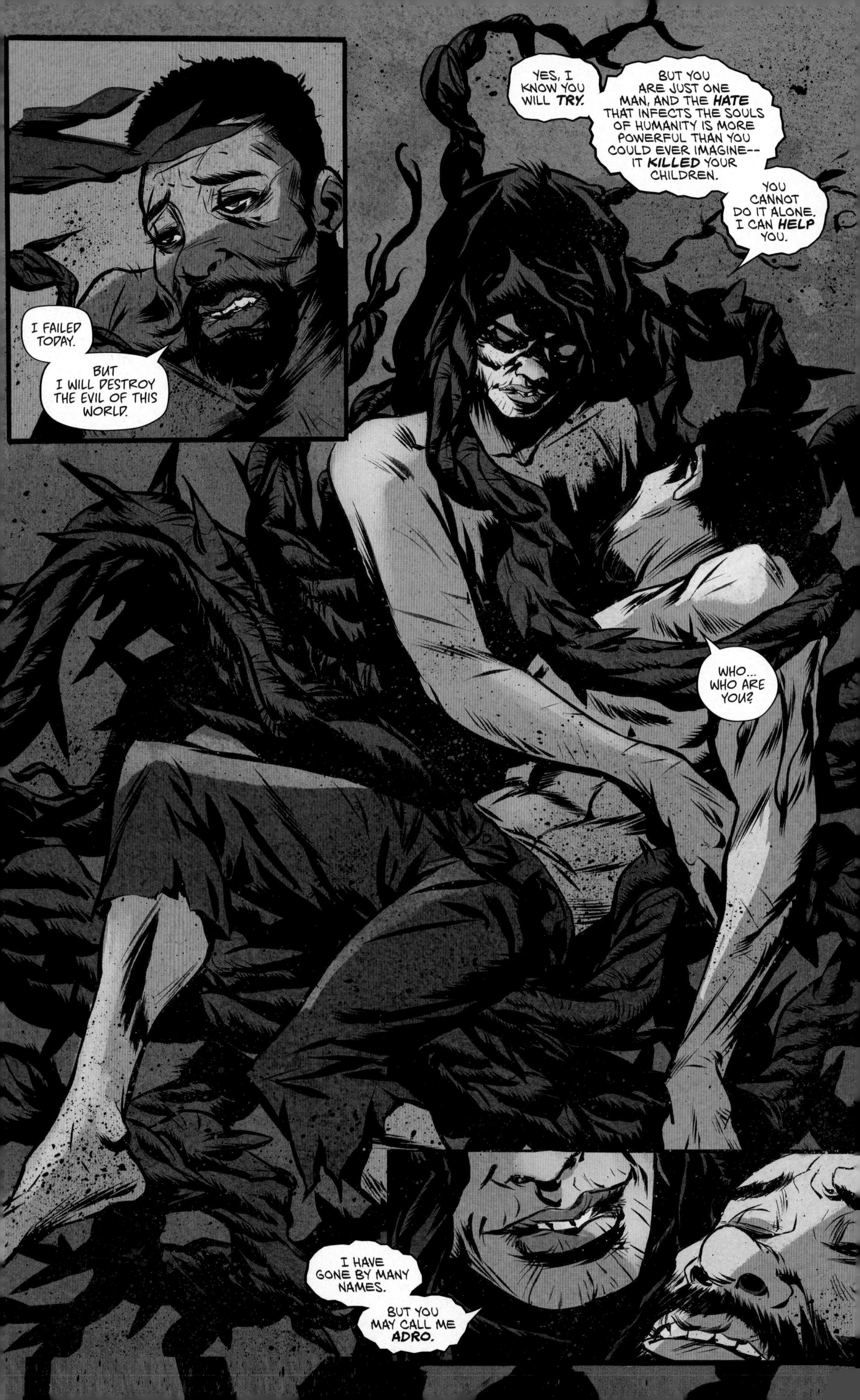
I FAILED TODAY.
BUT I WILL DESTROY THE EVIL OF THIS WORLD.
YES, I KNOW YOU WILL TRY.
BUT YOU ARE JUST ONE MAN, AND THE HATE THAT INFECTS THE SOULS OF HUMANITY IS MORE POWERFUL THAN YOU COULD EVER IMAGINE-- IT KILLED YOUR CHILDREN.
YOU CANNOT DO IT ALONE. I CAN HELP YOU.
WHO... WHO ARE YOU?
I HAVE GONE BY MANY NAMES.
BUT YOU MAY CALL ME ADRO.

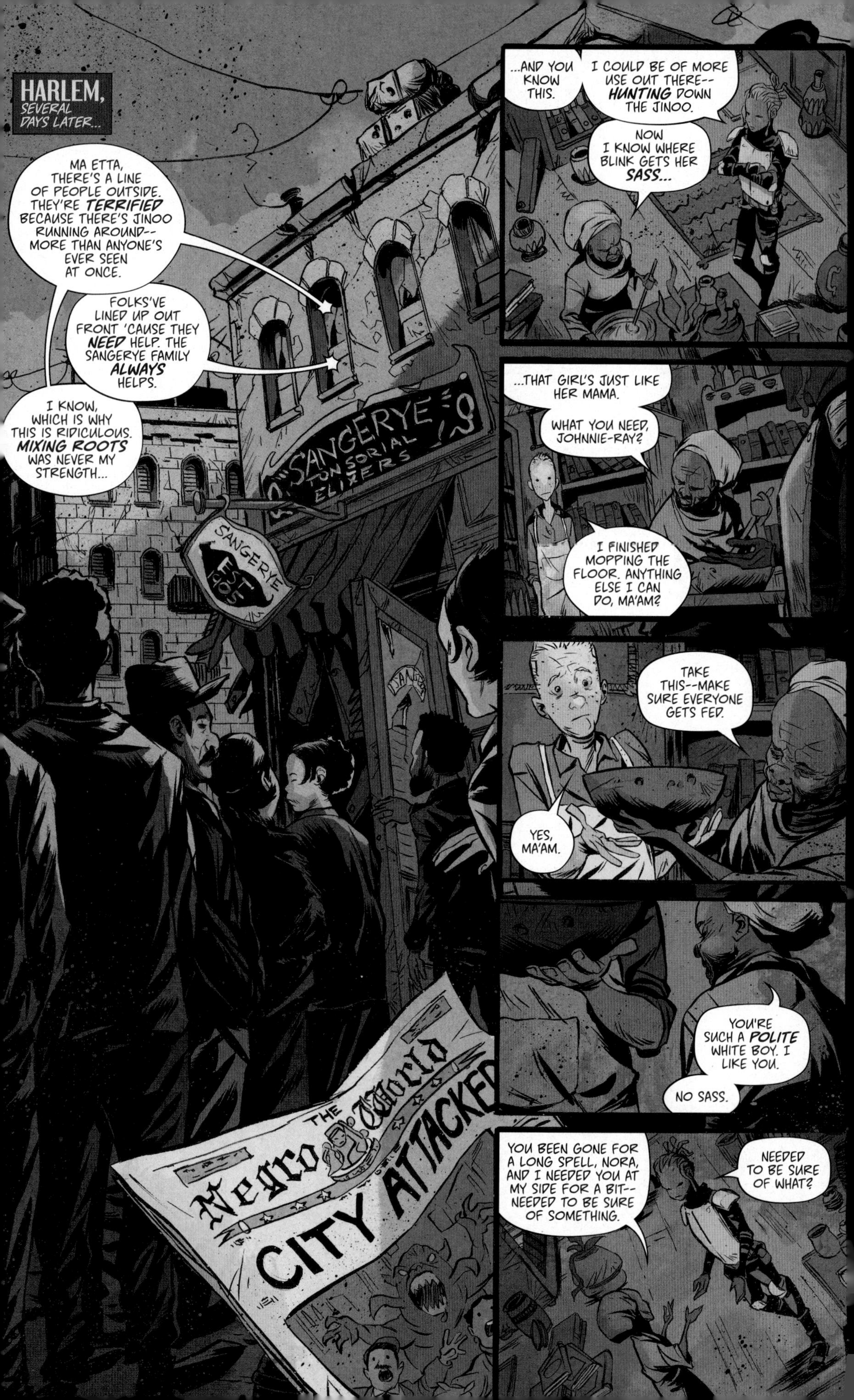
HARLEM, SEVERAL DAYS LATER...
MA ETTA, THERE'S A LINE OF PEOPLE OUTSIDE. THEY'RE TERRIFIED BECAUSE THERE'S JINOO RUNNING AROUND--MORE THAN ANYONE'S EVER SEEN AT ONCE.
FOLKS'VE LINED UP OUT FRONT 'CAUSE THEY NEED HELP. THE SANGERYE FAMILY ALWAYS HELPS.
I KNOW, WHICH IS WHY THIS IS RIDICULOUS. MIXING ROOTS WAS NEVER MY STRENGTH...
SANGERYE TONSORIAL ELIXERS
SANGERYE EST 1905
THE Negro World
CITY ATTACKED
...AND YOU KNOW THIS.
I COULD BE OF MORE USE OUT THERE--HUNTING DOWN THE JINOO.
NOW I KNOW WHERE BLINK GETS HER SASS...
...THAT GIRL'S JUST LIKE HER MAMA.
WHAT YOU NEED, JOHNNIE-RAY?
I FINISHED MOPPING THE FLOOR. ANYTHING ELSE I CAN DO, MA'AM?
TAKE THIS--MAKE SURE EVERYONE GETS FED.
YES, MA'AM.
YOU'RE SUCH A POLITE WHITE BOY. I LIKE YOU.
NO SASS.
YOU BEEN GONE FOR A LONG SPELL, NORA, AND I NEEDED YOU AT MY SIDE FOR A BIT--NEEDED TO BE SURE OF SOMETHING.
NEEDED TO BE SURE OF WHAT?

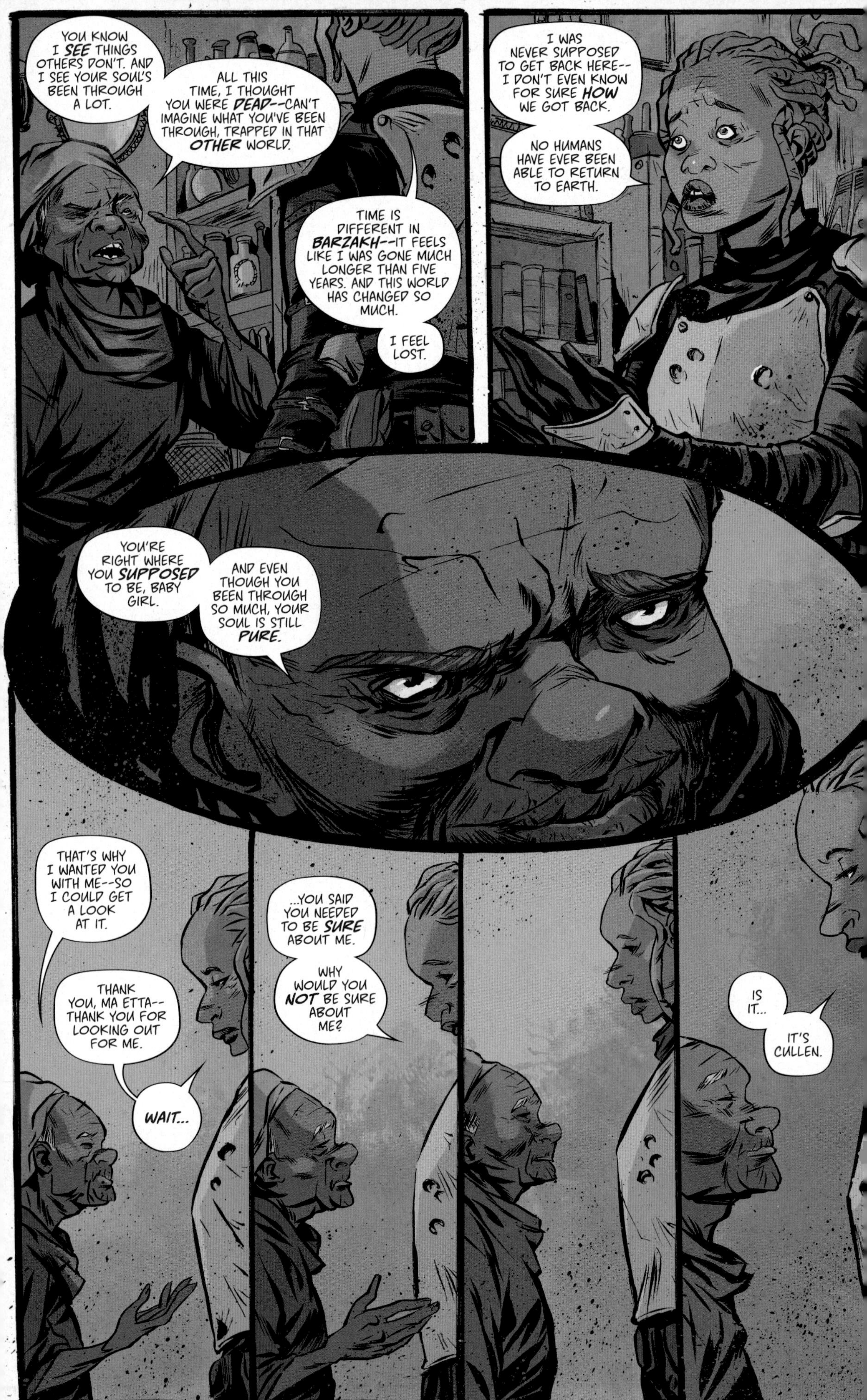
YOU KNOW I SEE THINGS OTHERS DON'T. AND I SEE YOUR SOUL'S BEEN THROUGH A LOT.
ALL THIS TIME, I THOUGHT YOU WERE DEAD--CAN'T IMAGINE WHAT YOU'VE BEEN THROUGH, TRAPPED IN THAT OTHER WORLD.
TIME IS DIFFERENT IN BARZAKH--IT FEELS LIKE I WAS GONE MUCH LONGER THAN FIVE YEARS. AND THIS WORLD HAS CHANGED SO MUCH.
I FEEL LOST.
I WAS NEVER SUPPOSED TO GET BACK HERE--I DON'T EVEN KNOW FOR SURE HOW WE GOT BACK.
NO HUMANS HAVE EVER BEEN ABLE TO RETURN TO EARTH.
YOU'RE RIGHT WHERE YOU SUPPOSED TO BE, BABY GIRL.
AND EVEN THOUGH YOU BEEN THROUGH SO MUCH, YOUR SOUL IS STILL PURE.
THAT'S WHY I WANTED YOU WITH ME--SO I COULD GET A LOOK AT IT.
THANK YOU, MA ETTA--THANK YOU FOR LOOKING OUT FOR ME.
WAIT...
...YOU SAID YOU NEEDED TO BE SURE ABOUT ME.
WHY WOULD YOU NOT BE SURE ABOUT ME?
IS IT...
IT'S CULLEN.

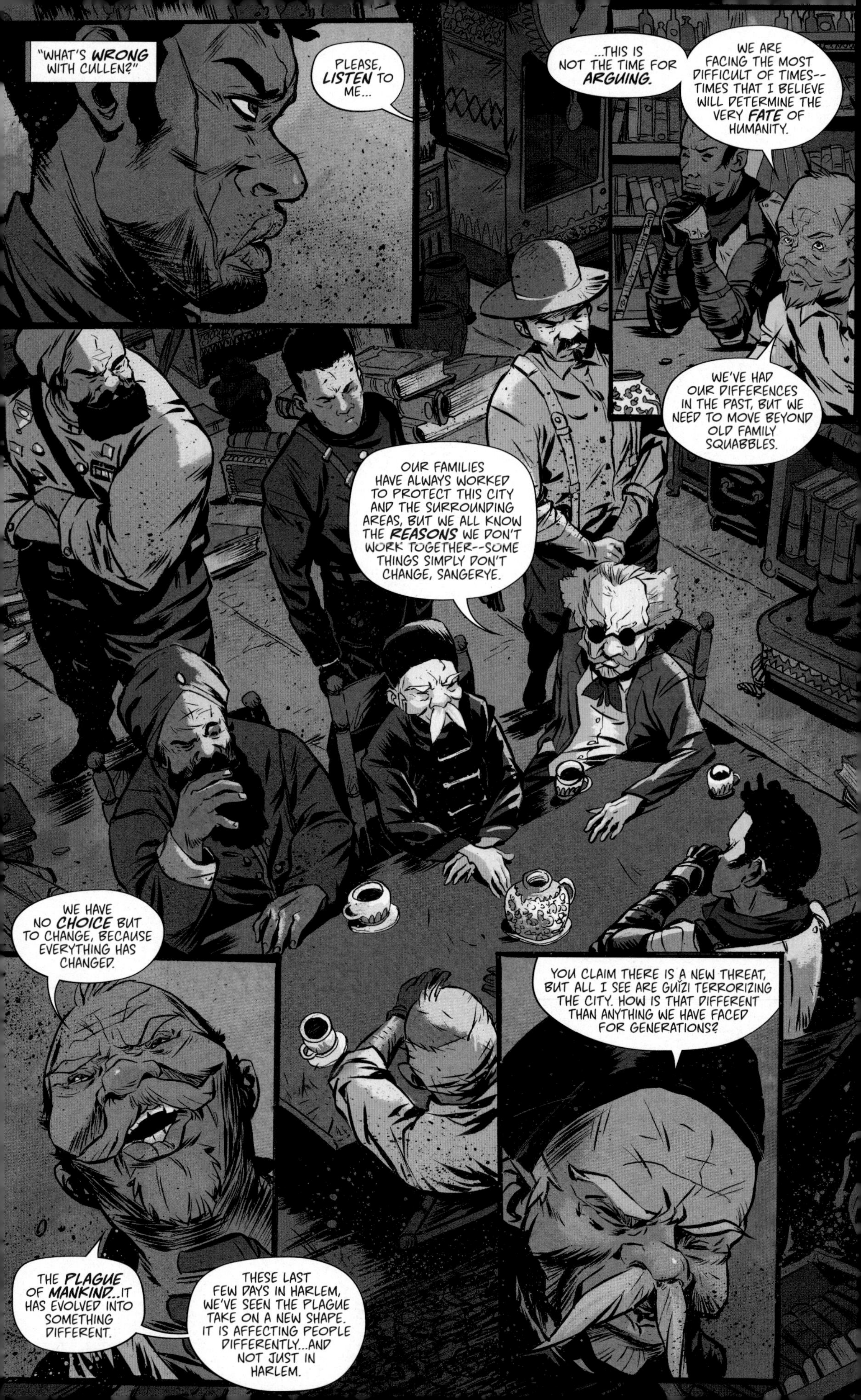
"WHAT'S WRONG WITH CULLEN?"
PLEASE, LISTEN TO ME...
...THIS IS NOT THE TIME FOR ARGUING.
WE ARE FACING THE MOST DIFFICULT OF TIMES--TIMES THAT I BELIEVE WILL DETERMINE THE VERY FATE OF HUMANITY.
WE'VE HAD OUR DIFFERENCES IN THE PAST, BUT WE NEED TO MOVE BEYOND OLD FAMILY SQUABBLES.
OUR FAMILIES HAVE ALWAYS WORKED TO PROTECT THIS CITY AND THE SURROUNDING AREAS, BUT WE ALL KNOW THE REASONS WE DON'T WORK TOGETHER--SOME THINGS SIMPLY DON'T CHANGE, SANGERYE.
WE HAVE NO CHOICE BUT TO CHANGE, BECAUSE EVERYTHING HAS CHANGED.
YOU CLAIM THERE IS A NEW THREAT, BUT ALL I SEE ARE GUÏZI TERRORIZING THE CITY. HOW IS THAT DIFFERENT THAN ANYTHING WE HAVE FACED FOR GENERATIONS?
THE PLAGUE OF MANKIND...IT HAS EVOLVED INTO SOMETHING DIFFERENT.
THESE LAST FEW DAYS IN HARLEM, WE'VE SEEN THE PLAGUE TAKE ON A NEW SHAPE. IT IS AFFECTING PEOPLE DIFFERENTLY...AND NOT JUST IN HARLEM.

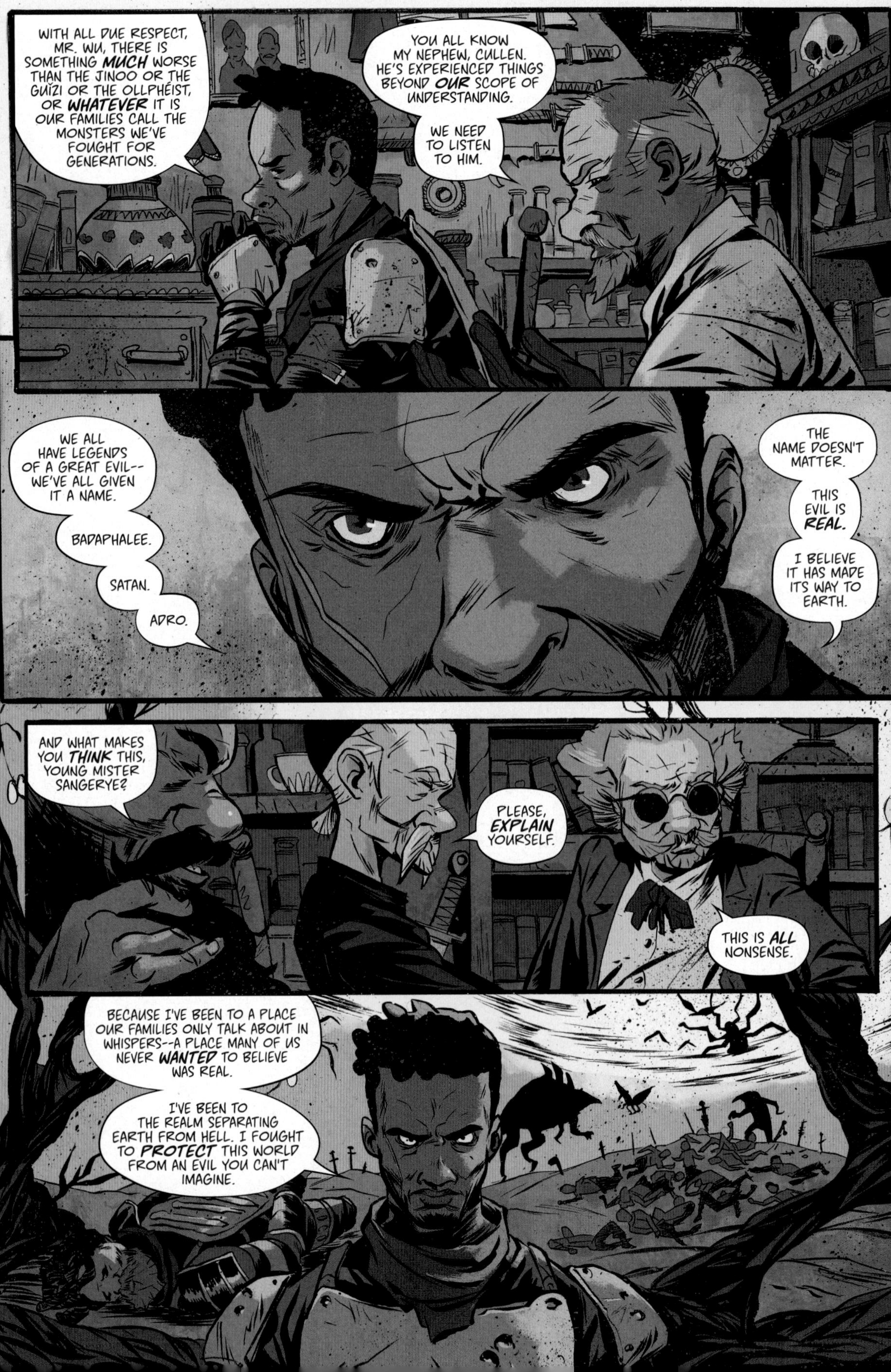
WITH ALL DUE RESPECT, MR. WU, THERE IS SOMETHING MUCH WORSE THAN THE JINOO OR THE GUÏZI OR THE OLLPHÉIST, OR WHATEVER IT IS OUR FAMILIES CALL THE MONSTERS WE'VE FOUGHT FOR GENERATIONS.
YOU ALL KNOW MY NEPHEW, CULLEN. HE'S EXPERIENCED THINGS BEYOND OUR SCOPE OF UNDERSTANDING.
WE NEED TO LISTEN TO HIM.
WE ALL HAVE LEGENDS OF A GREAT EVIL--WE'VE ALL GIVEN IT A NAME.
BADAPHALEE.
SATAN.
ADRO.
THE NAME DOESN'T MATTER.
THIS EVIL IS REAL.
I BELIEVE IT HAS MADE ITS WAY TO EARTH.
AND WHAT MAKES YOU THINK THIS, YOUNG MISTER SANGERYE?
PLEASE, EXPLAIN YOURSELF.
THIS IS ALL NONSENSE.
BECAUSE I'VE BEEN TO A PLACE OUR FAMILIES ONLY TALK ABOUT IN WHISPERS--A PLACE MANY OF US NEVER WANTED TO BELIEVE WAS REAL.
I'VE BEEN TO THE REALM SEPARATING EARTH FROM HELL. I FOUGHT TO PROTECT THIS WORLD FROM AN EVIL YOU CAN'T IMAGINE.

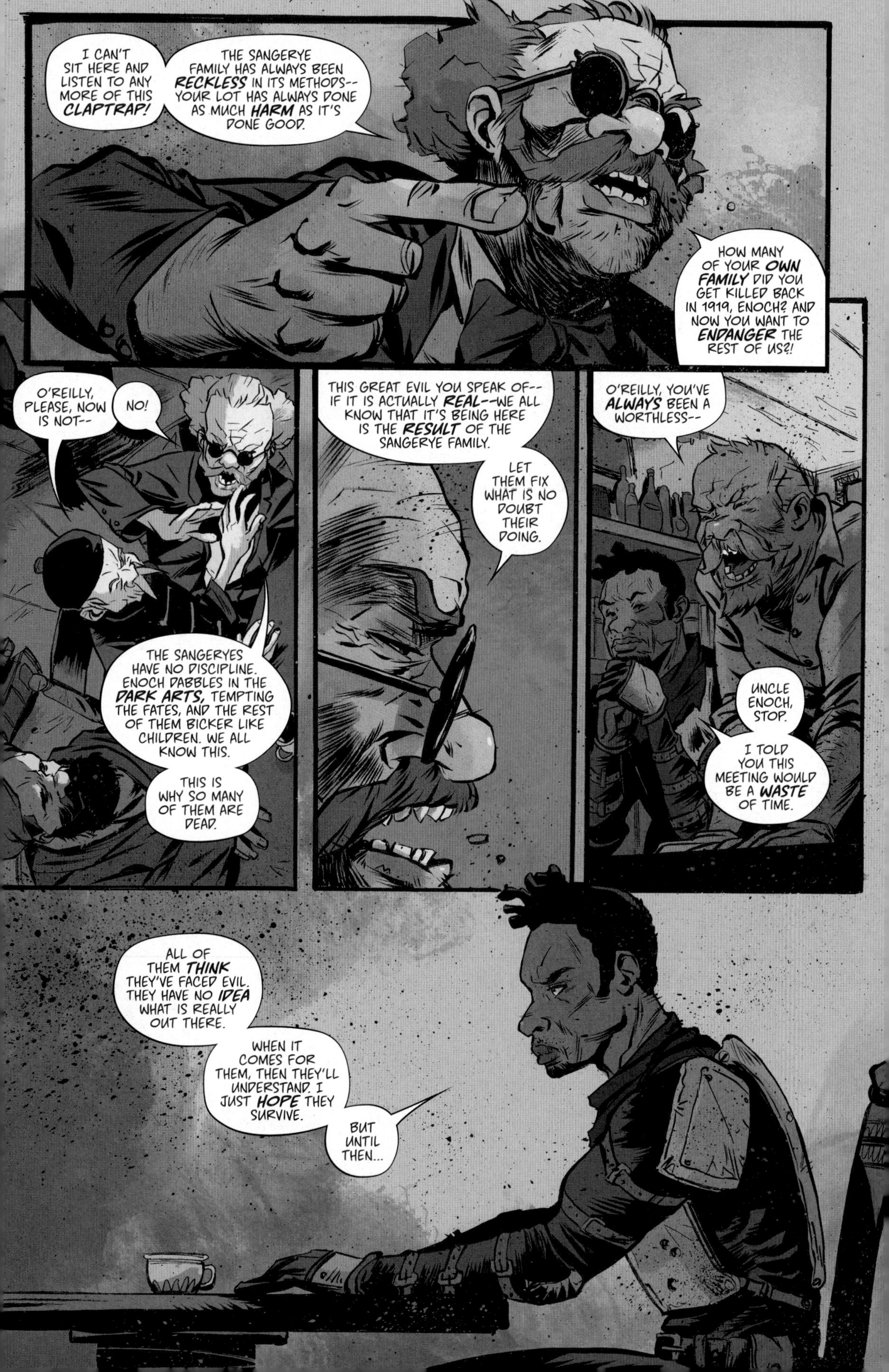
I CAN'T SIT HERE AND LISTEN TO ANY MORE OF THIS CLAPTRAP!
THE SANGERYE FAMILY HAS ALWAYS BEEN RECKLESS IN ITS METHODS--YOUR LOT HAS ALWAYS DONE AS MUCH HARM AS IT'S DONE GOOD.
HOW MANY OF YOUR OWN FAMILY DID YOU GET KILLED BACK IN 1919, ENOCH? AND NOW YOU WANT TO ENDANGER THE REST OF US?!
O'REILLY, PLEASE, NOW IS NOT--
NO!
THE SANGERYES HAVE NO DISCIPLINE. ENOCH DABBLES IN THE DARK ARTS, TEMPTING THE FATES, AND THE REST OF THEM BICKER LIKE CHILDREN. WE ALL KNOW THIS.
THIS IS WHY SO MANY OF THEM ARE DEAD.
THIS GREAT EVIL YOU SPEAK OF--IF IT IS ACTUALLY REAL--WE ALL KNOW THAT IT'S BEING HERE IS THE RESULT OF THE SANGERYE FAMILY.
LET THEM FIX WHAT IS NO DOUBT THEIR DOING.
O'REILLY, YOU'VE ALWAYS BEEN A WORTHLESS--
UNCLE ENOCH, STOP.
I TOLD YOU THIS MEETING WOULD BE A WASTE OF TIME.
ALL OF THEM THINK THEY'VE FACED EVIL. THEY HAVE NO IDEA WHAT IS REALLY OUT THERE.
WHEN IT COMES FOR THEM, THEN THEY'LL UNDERSTAND. I JUST HOPE THEY SURVIVE.
BUT UNTIL THEN...

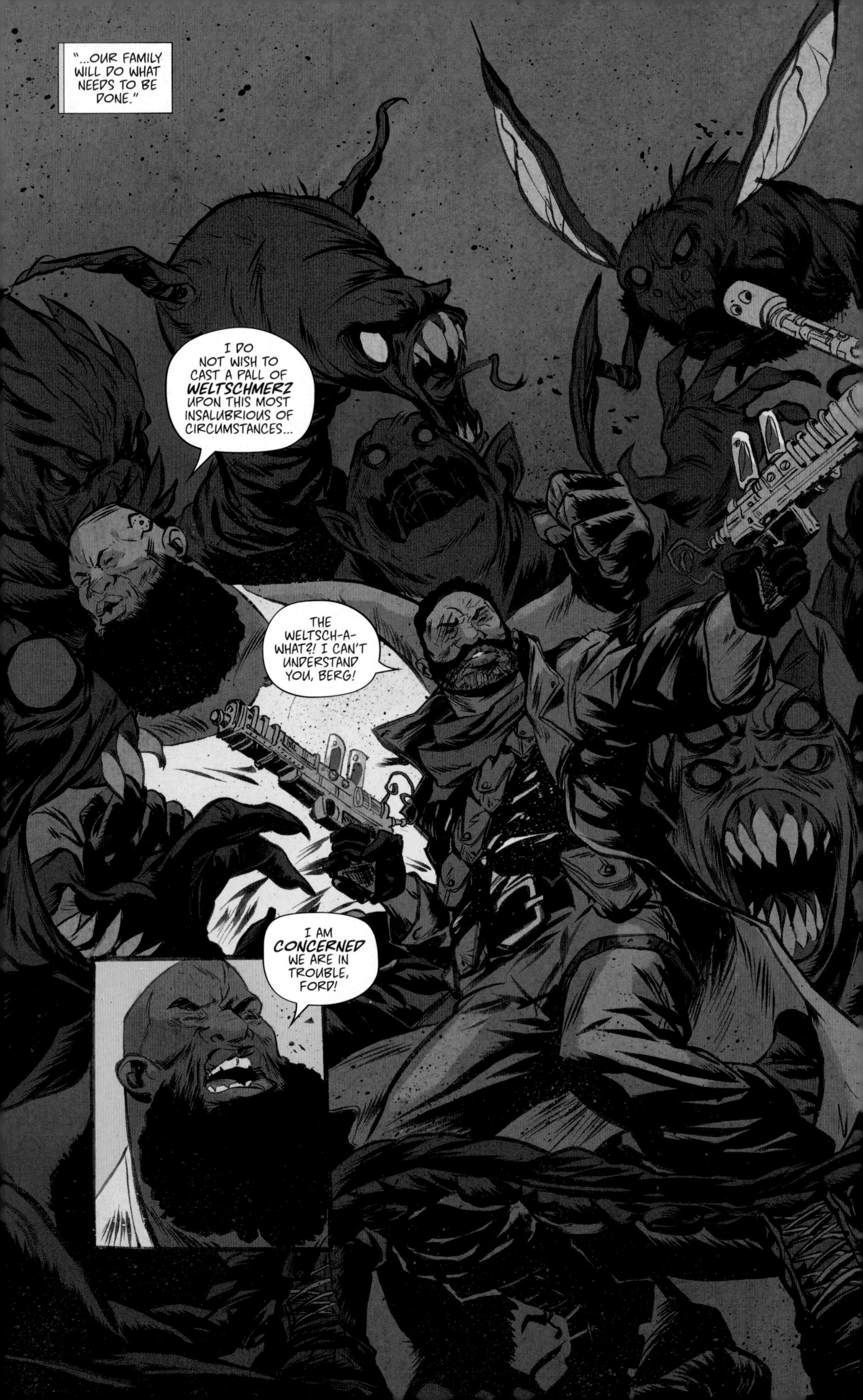
"...OUR FAMILY WILL DO WHAT NEEDS TO BE DONE."
I DO NOT WISH TO CAST A PALL OF WELTSCHMERZ UPON THIS MOST INSALUBRIOUS OF CIRCUMSTANCES...
THE WELTSCH-A-WHAT?! I CAN'T UNDERSTAND YOU, BERG!
I AM CONCERNED WE ARE IN TROUBLE, FORD!

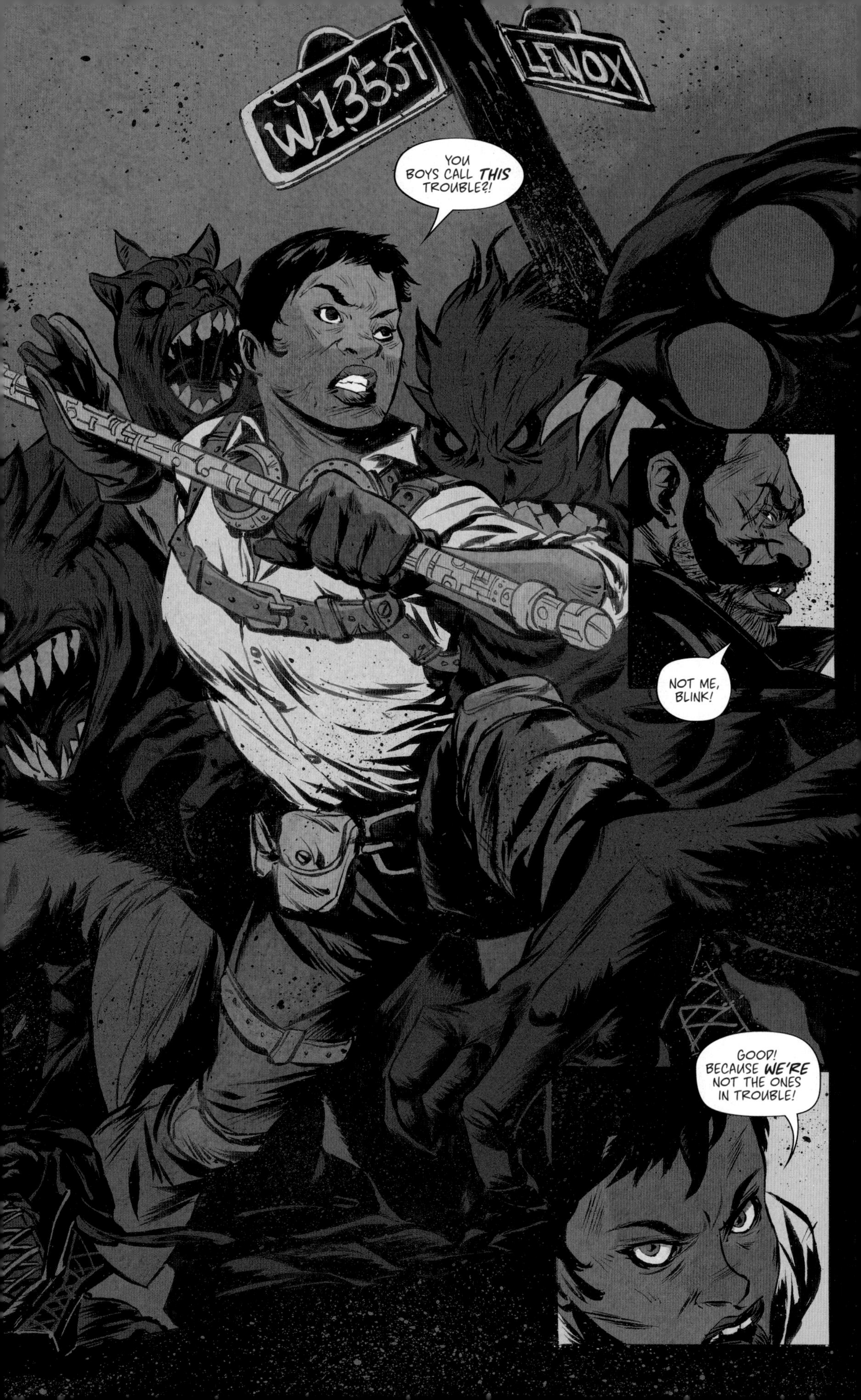
W. 135 ST
LENOX
YOU BOYS CALL THIS TROUBLE?!
NOT ME, BLINK!
GOOD! BECAUSE WE'RE NOT THE ONES IN TROUBLE!

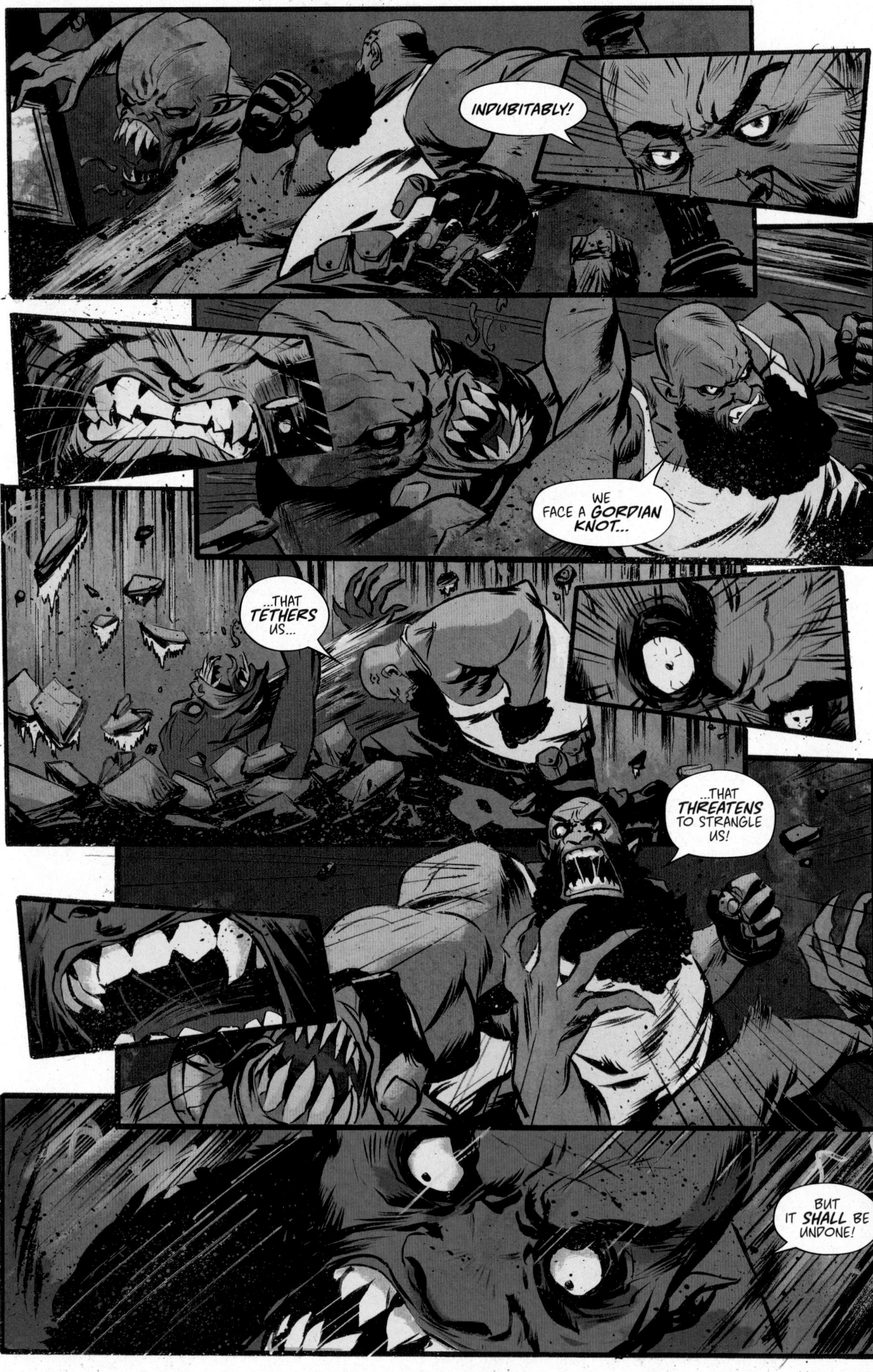
INDUBITABLY!
WE FACE A GORDIAN KNOT...
...THAT TETHERS US...
...THAT THREATENS TO STRANGLE US!
BUT IT SHALL BE UNDONE!

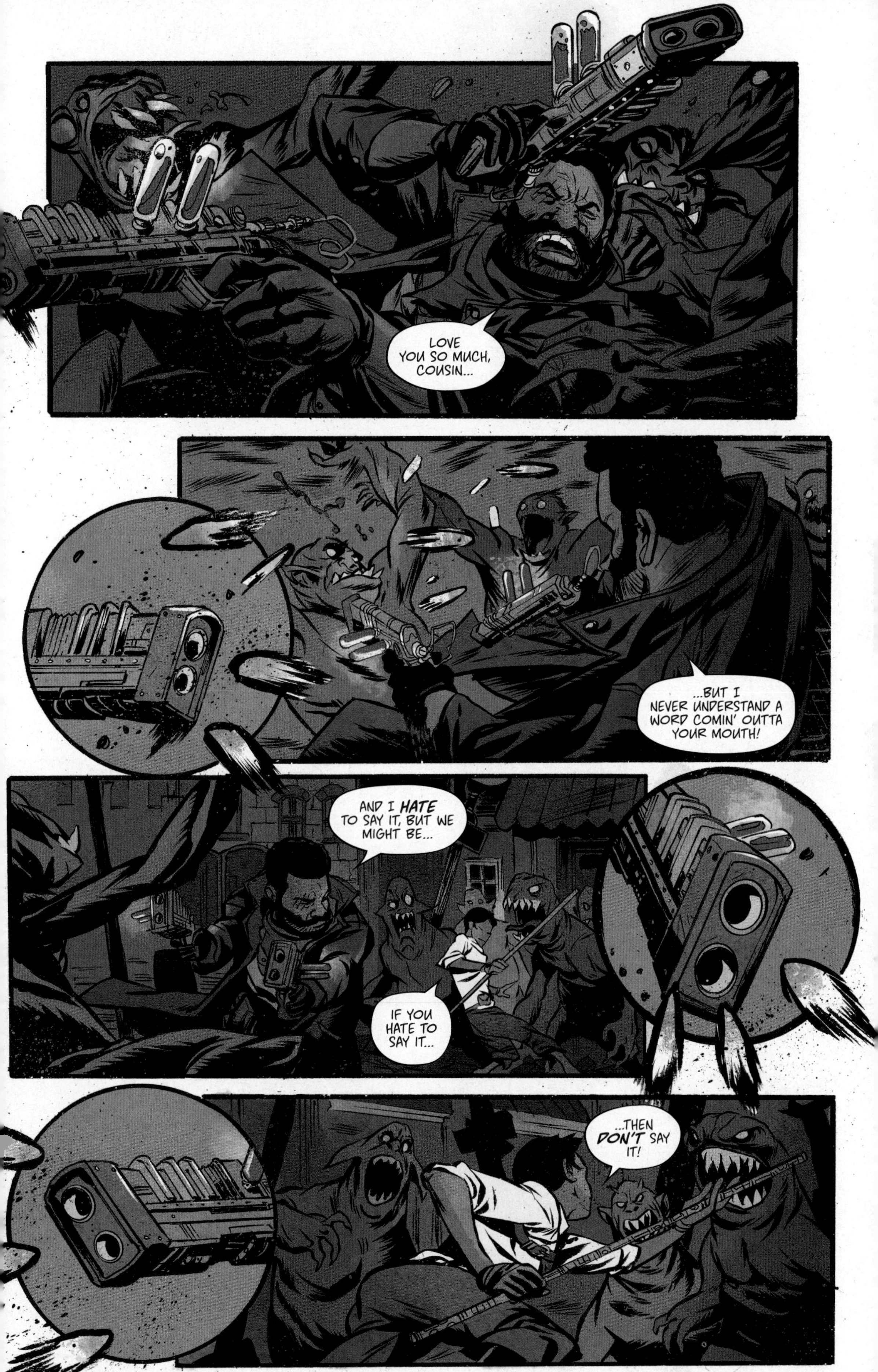
LOVE YOU SO MUCH, COUSIN...
...BUT I NEVER UNDERSTAND A WORD COMIN' OUTTA YOUR MOUTH!
AND I HATE TO SAY IT, BUT WE MIGHT BE...
IF YOU HATE TO SAY IT...
...THEN DON'T SAY IT!

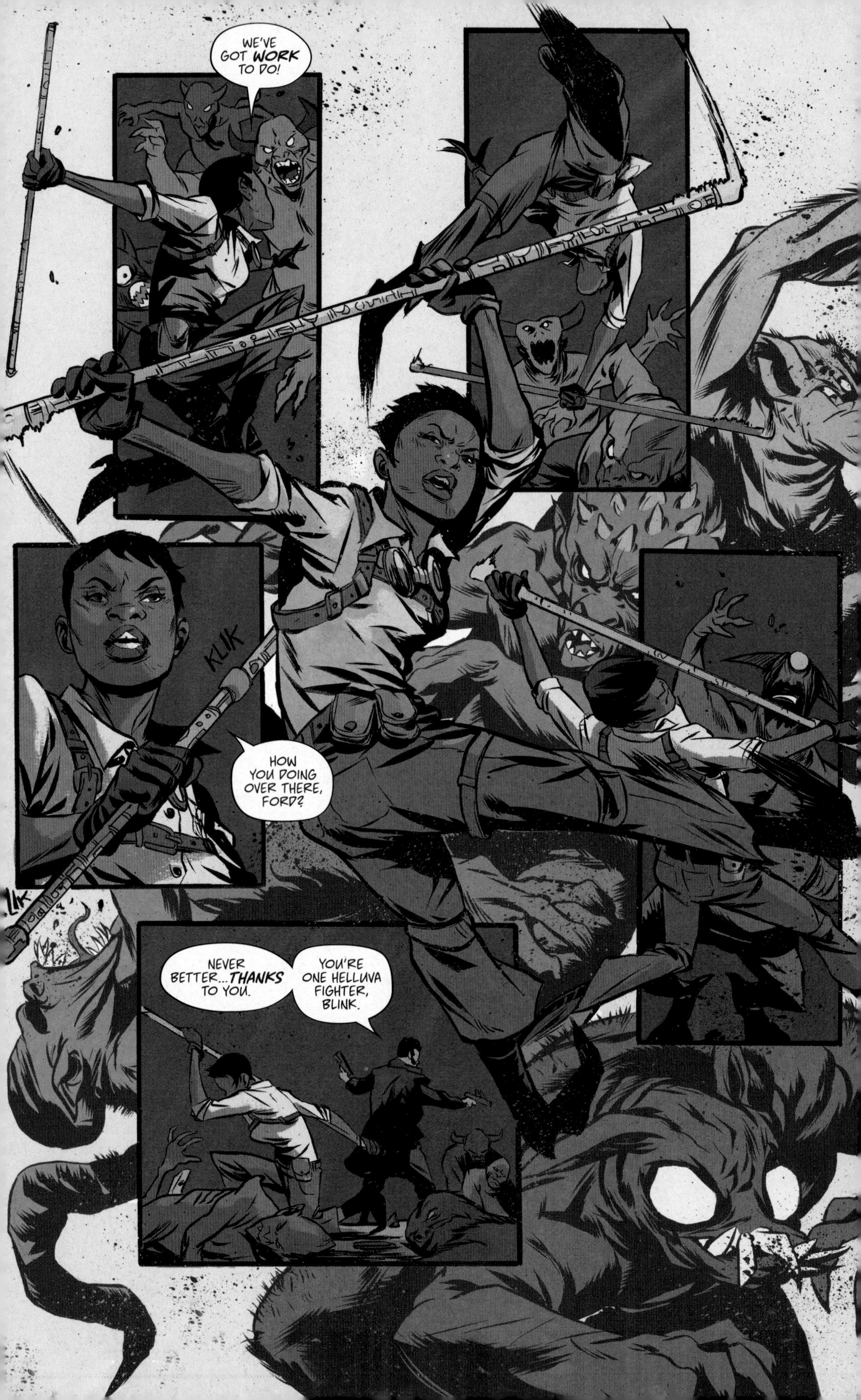

WE'VE GOT **WORK** TO DO!
KLIK
HOW YOU DOING OVER THERE, FORD?
KLIK
NEVER BETTER... **THANKS** TO YOU.
YOU'RE ONE HELLUVA FIGHTER, BLINK.

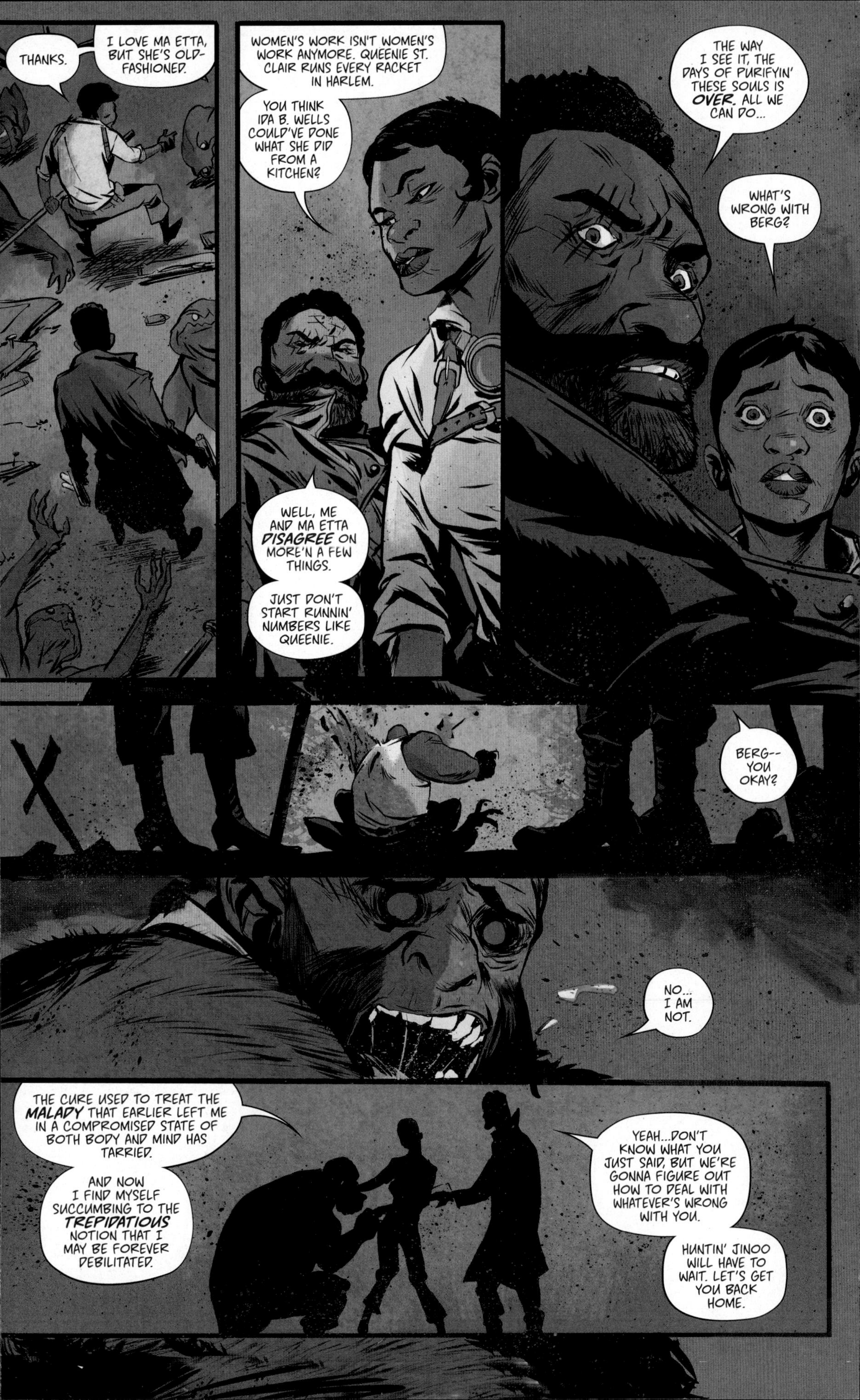
THANKS.
I LOVE MA ETTA, BUT SHE'S OLD-FASHIONED.
WOMEN'S WORK ISN'T WOMEN'S WORK ANYMORE. QUEENIE ST. CLAIR RUNS EVERY RACKET IN HARLEM.
YOU THINK IDA B. WELLS COULD'VE DONE WHAT SHE DID FROM A KITCHEN?
WELL, ME AND MA ETTA DISAGREE ON MORE'N A FEW THINGS.
JUST DON'T START RUNNIN' NUMBERS LIKE QUEENIE.
THE WAY I SEE IT, THE DAYS OF PURIFYIN' THESE SOULS IS OVER. ALL WE CAN DO...
WHAT'S WRONG WITH BERG?
BERG-- YOU OKAY?
NO... I AM NOT.
THE CURE USED TO TREAT THE MALADY THAT EARLIER LEFT ME IN A COMPROMISED STATE OF BOTH BODY AND MIND HAS TARRIED.
AND NOW I FIND MYSELF SUCCUMBING TO THE TREPIDATIOUS NOTION THAT I MAY BE FOREVER DEBILITATED.
YEAH...DON'T KNOW WHAT YOU JUST SAID, BUT WE'RE GONNA FIGURE OUT HOW TO DEAL WITH WHATEVER'S WRONG WITH YOU.
HUNTIN' JINOO WILL HAVE TO WAIT. LET'S GET YOU BACK HOME.

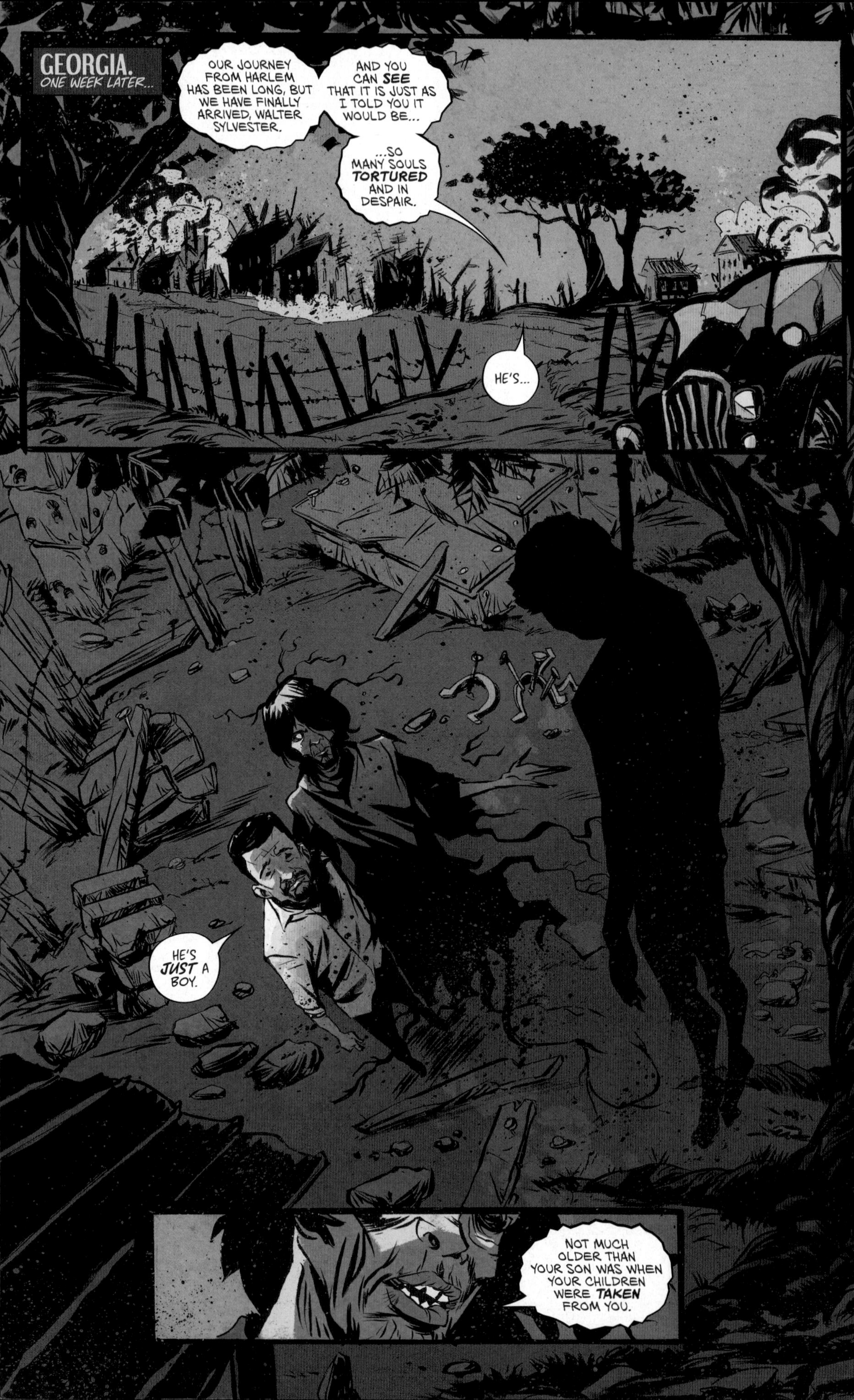
GEORGIA.
ONE WEEK LATER...
OUR JOURNEY FROM HARLEM HAS BEEN LONG, BUT WE HAVE FINALLY ARRIVED, WALTER SYLVESTER.
AND YOU CAN SEE THAT IT IS JUST AS I TOLD YOU IT WOULD BE...
...SO MANY SOULS TORTURED AND IN DESPAIR.
HE'S...
HE'S JUST A BOY.
NOT MUCH OLDER THAN YOUR SON WAS WHEN YOUR CHILDREN WERE TAKEN FROM YOU.

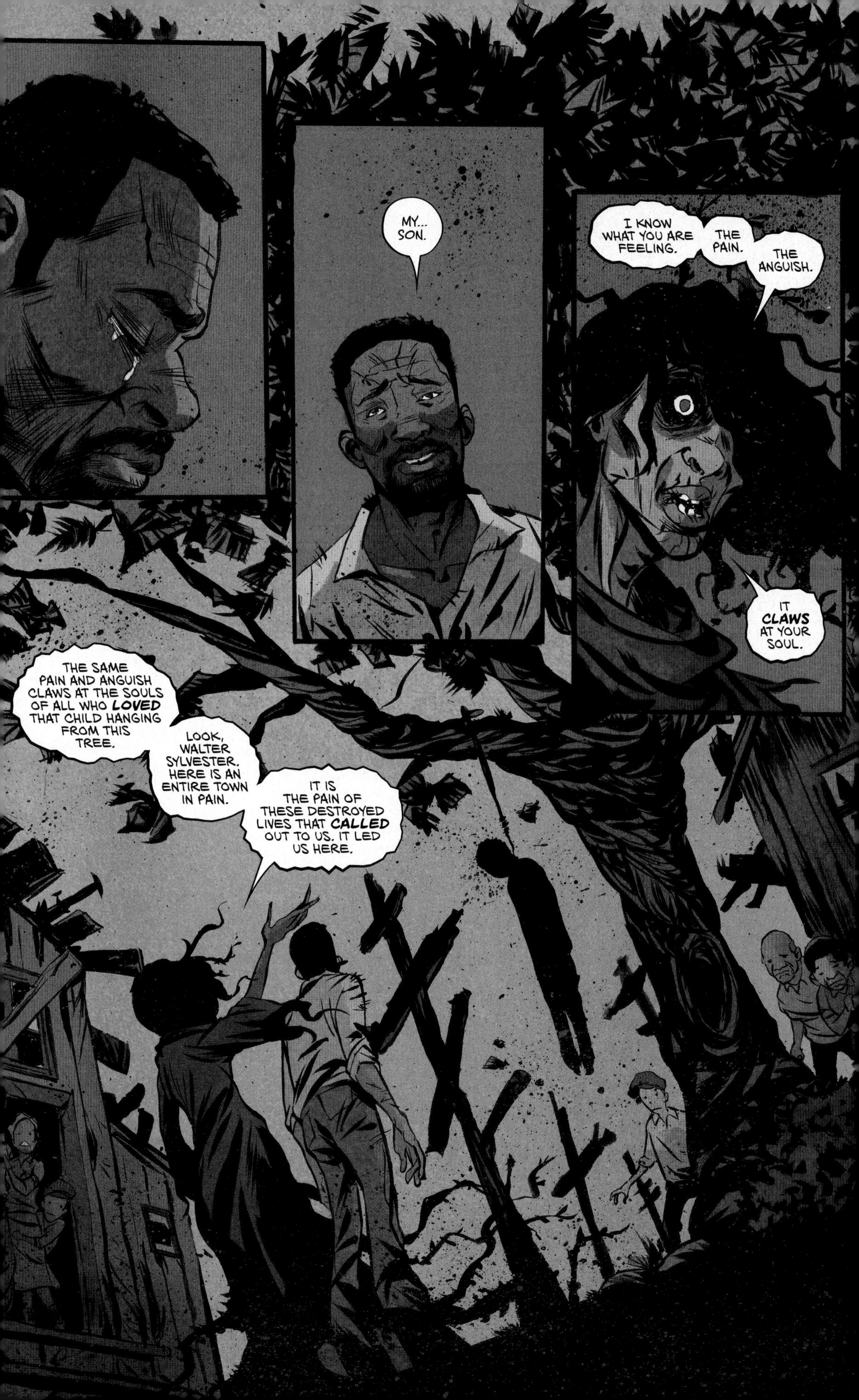
MY... SON.
I KNOW WHAT YOU ARE FEELING.
THE PAIN.
THE ANGUISH.
IT CLAWS AT YOUR SOUL.
THE SAME PAIN AND ANGUISH CLAWS AT THE SOULS OF ALL WHO LOVED THAT CHILD HANGING FROM THIS TREE.
LOOK, WALTER SYLVESTER. HERE IS AN ENTIRE TOWN IN PAIN.
IT IS THE PAIN OF THESE DESTROYED LIVES THAT CALLED OUT TO US. IT LED US HERE.

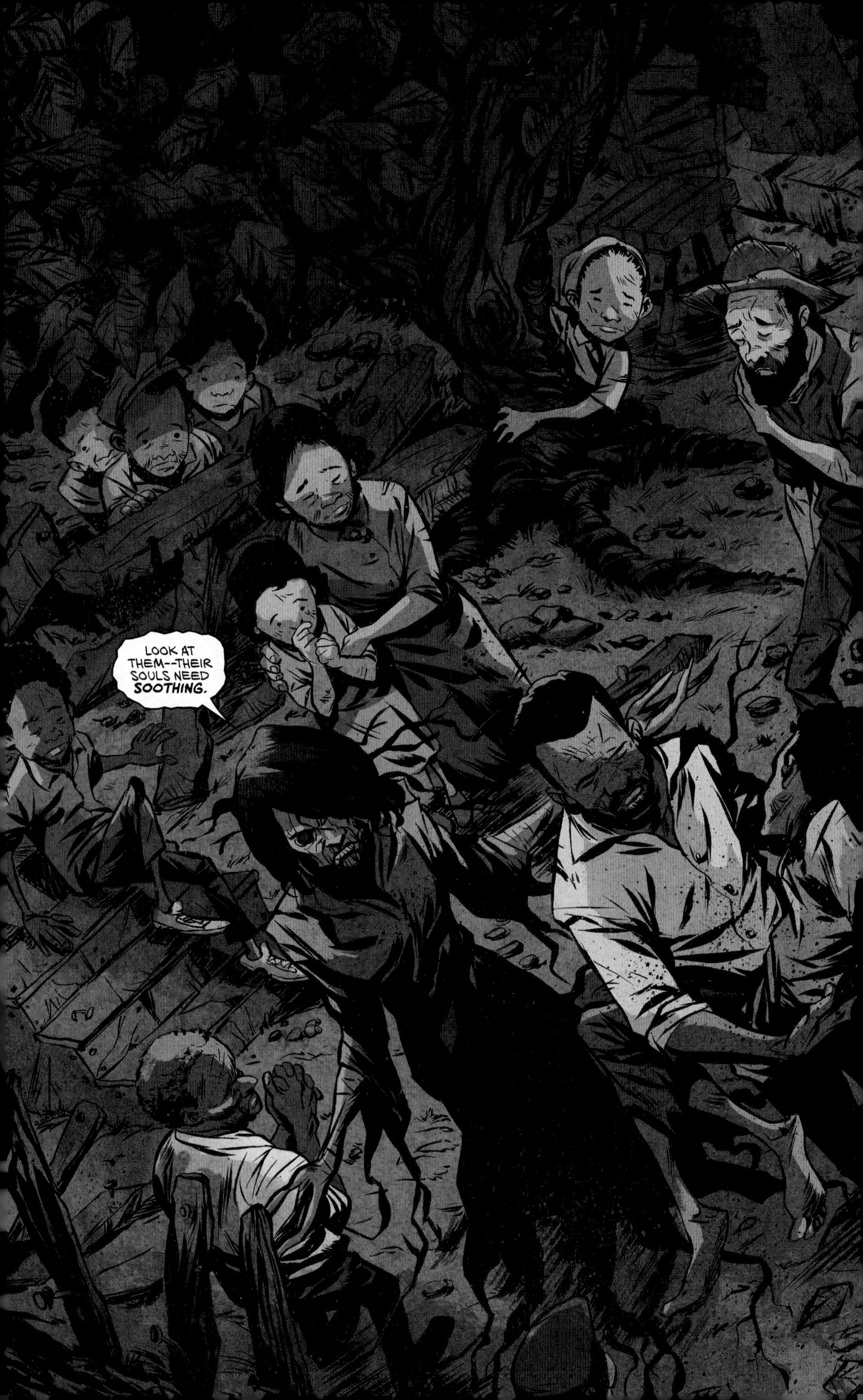
LOOK AT THEM--THEIR SOULS NEED SOOTHING.

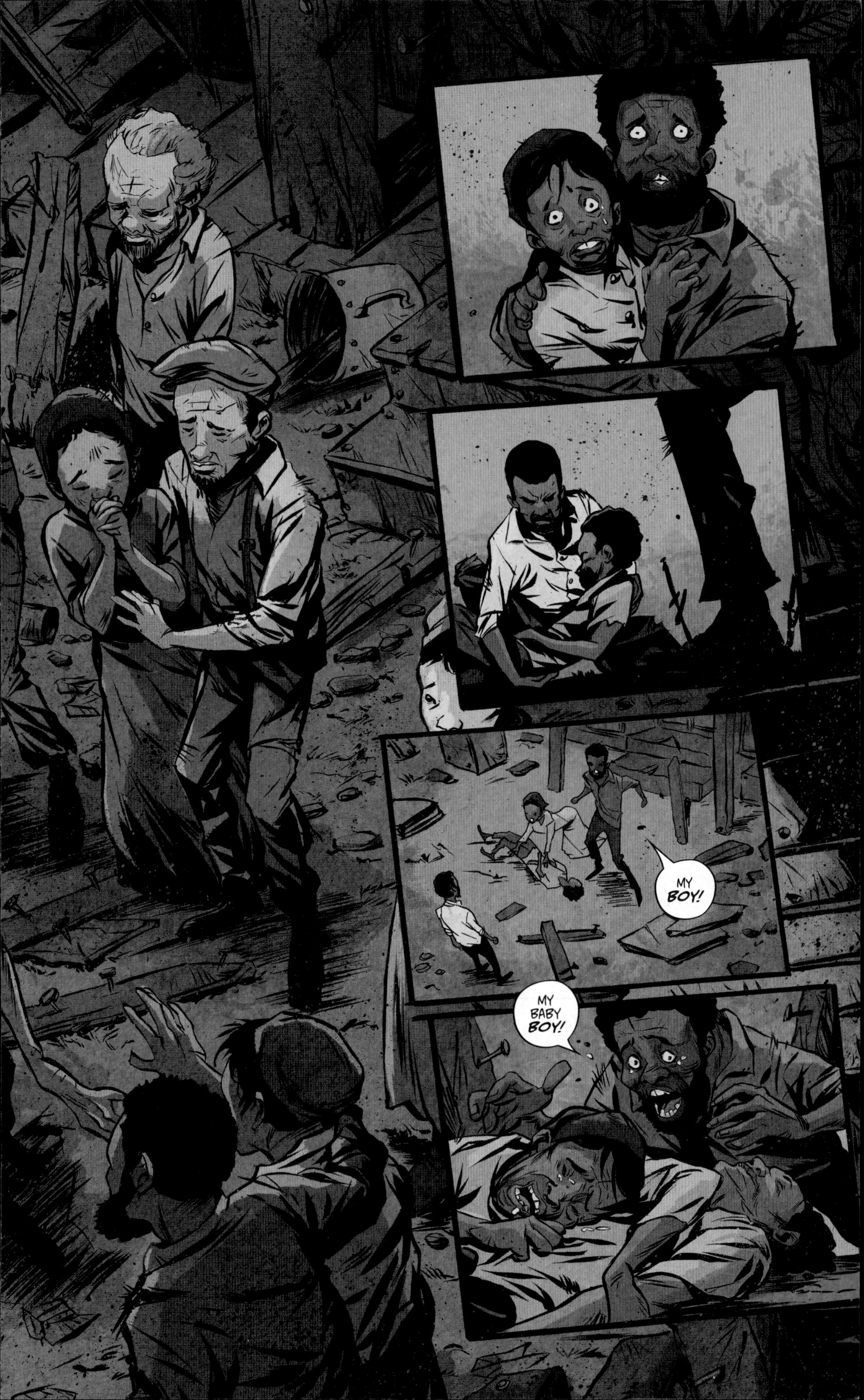
MY BOY!
MY BABY BOY!

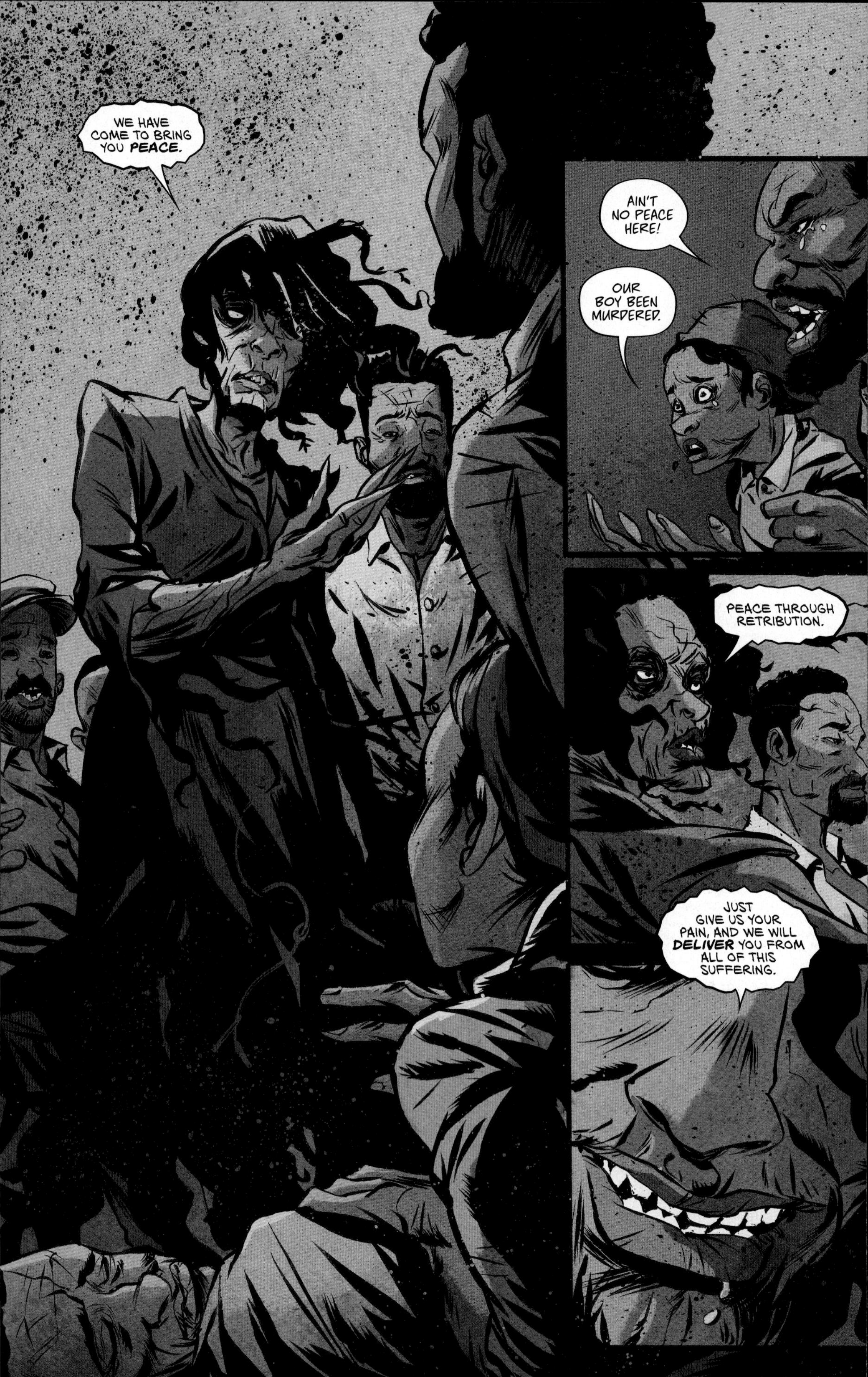
WE HAVE COME TO BRING YOU **PEACE.**
AIN'T NO PEACE HERE!
OUR BOY BEEN MURDERED.
PEACE THROUGH RETRIBUTION.
JUST GIVE US YOUR PAIN, AND WE WILL **DELIVER** YOU FROM ALL OF THIS SUFFERING.

Once upon a time
in Harlem, N.Y.

Bitter
Root

Do not let a bitter root
grow to defile many

DAVID F. WALKER • CHUCK BROWN • SANFORD GREENE

IMAGE COMICS "BITTER ROOT"

CULLEN SANGERYE • BERG SANGERYE • BLINK SANGERYE • ENOCH SANGERYE • ETTA SANGERYE
FORD SANGERYE • NORA SANGERYE • DR. WALTER SYLVESTER • JOHNNIE-RAY COX
Artist SANFORD GREENE Colorist SOFIE DODGSON Letters & Production CLAYTON COWLES Editor SHELLY BOND
Written by DAVID F. WALKER & CHUCK BROWN Cover ELIZA IVANOVA

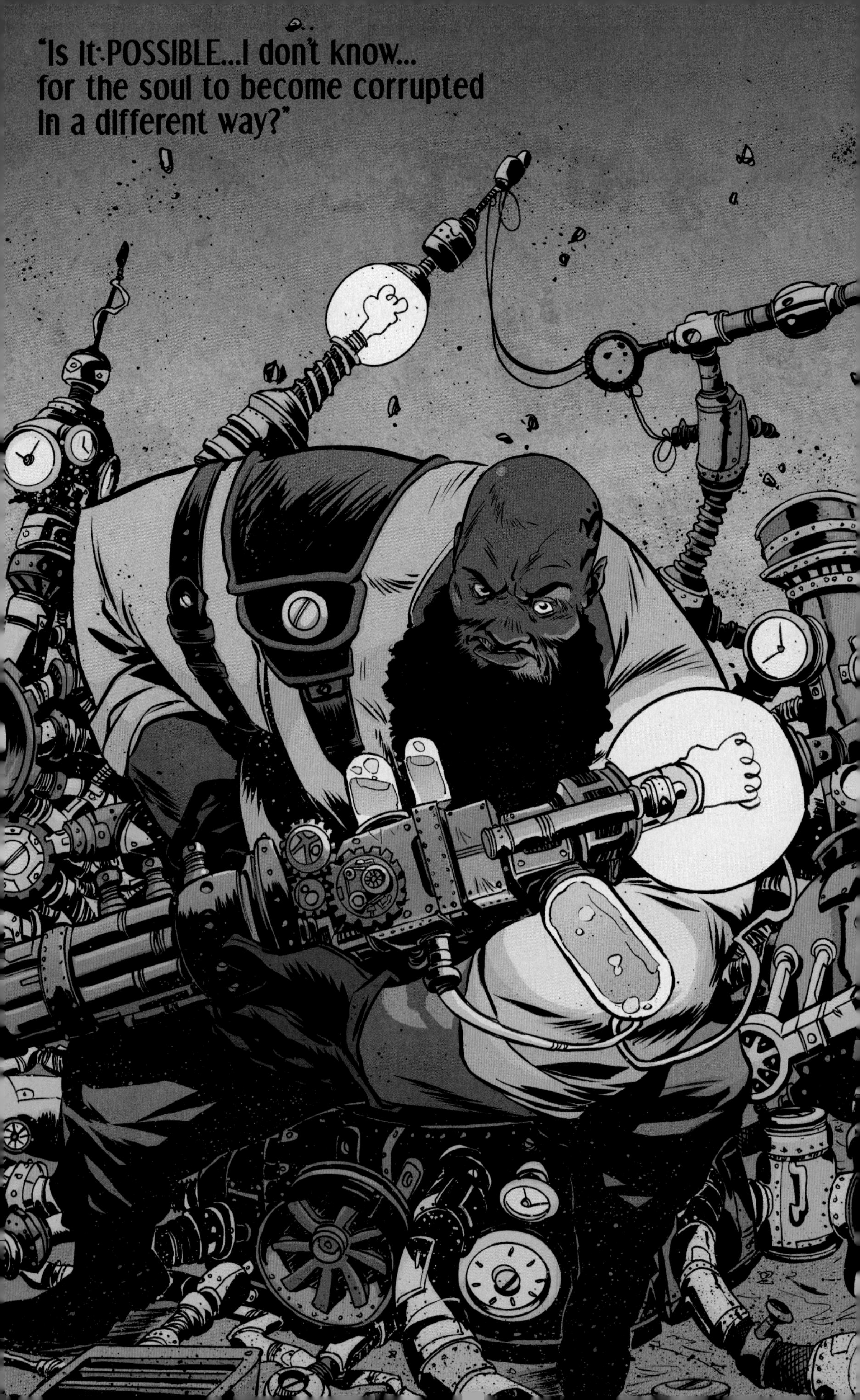
"Is it:POSSIBLE...I don't know...
for the soul to become corrupted
in a different way?"

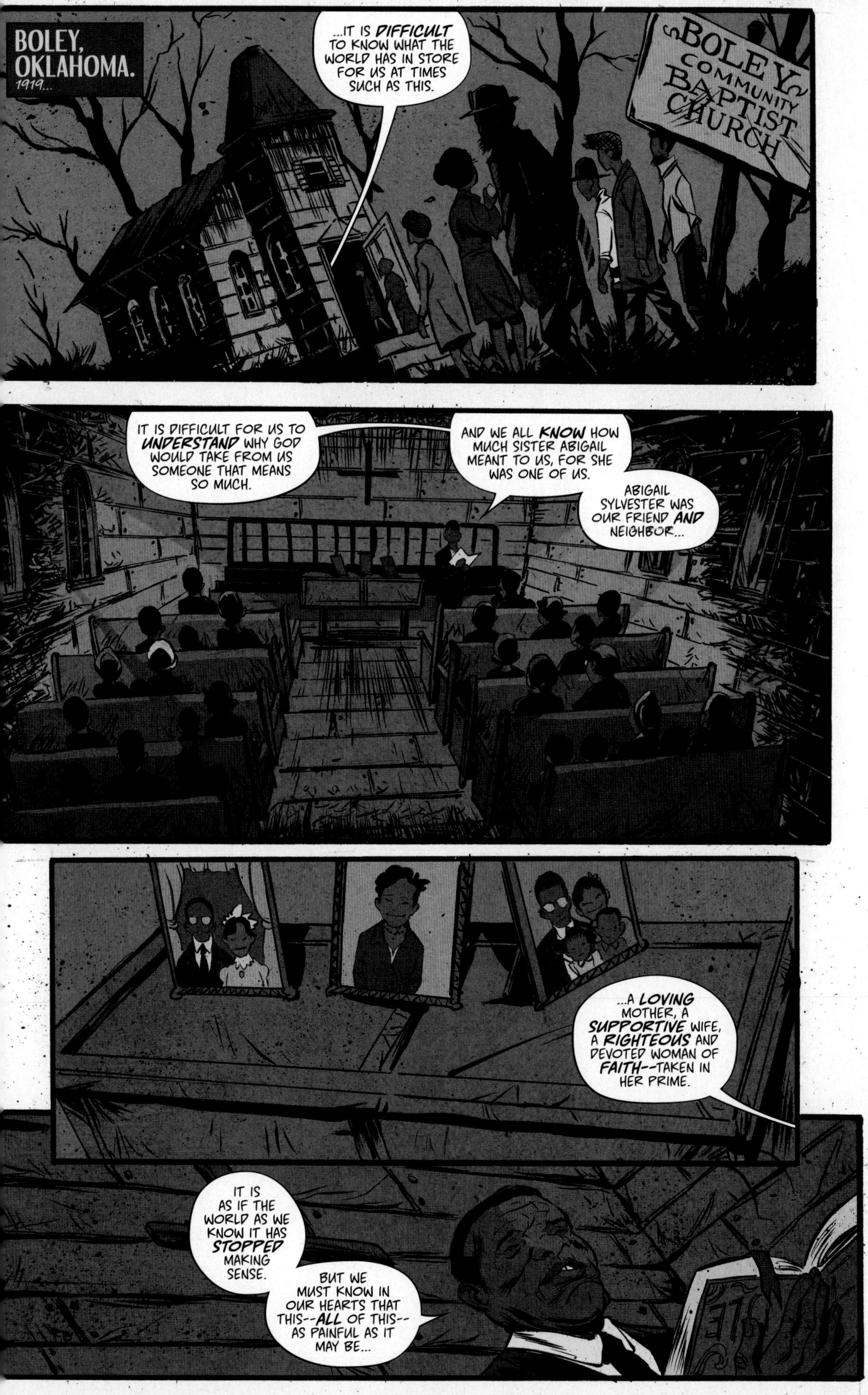
BOLEY, OKLAHOMA. 1919...
...IT IS DIFFICULT TO KNOW WHAT THE WORLD HAS IN STORE FOR US AT TIMES SUCH AS THIS.
BOLEY COMMUNITY BAPTIST CHURCH
IT IS DIFFICULT FOR US TO UNDERSTAND WHY GOD WOULD TAKE FROM US SOMEONE THAT MEANS SO MUCH.
AND WE ALL KNOW HOW MUCH SISTER ABIGAIL MEANT TO US, FOR SHE WAS ONE OF US.
ABIGAIL SYLVESTER WAS OUR FRIEND AND NEIGHBOR...
...A LOVING MOTHER, A SUPPORTIVE WIFE, A RIGHTEOUS AND DEVOTED WOMAN OF FAITH--TAKEN IN HER PRIME.
IT IS AS IF THE WORLD AS WE KNOW IT HAS STOPPED MAKING SENSE.
BUT WE MUST KNOW IN OUR HEARTS THAT THIS--ALL OF THIS--AS PAINFUL AS IT MAY BE...

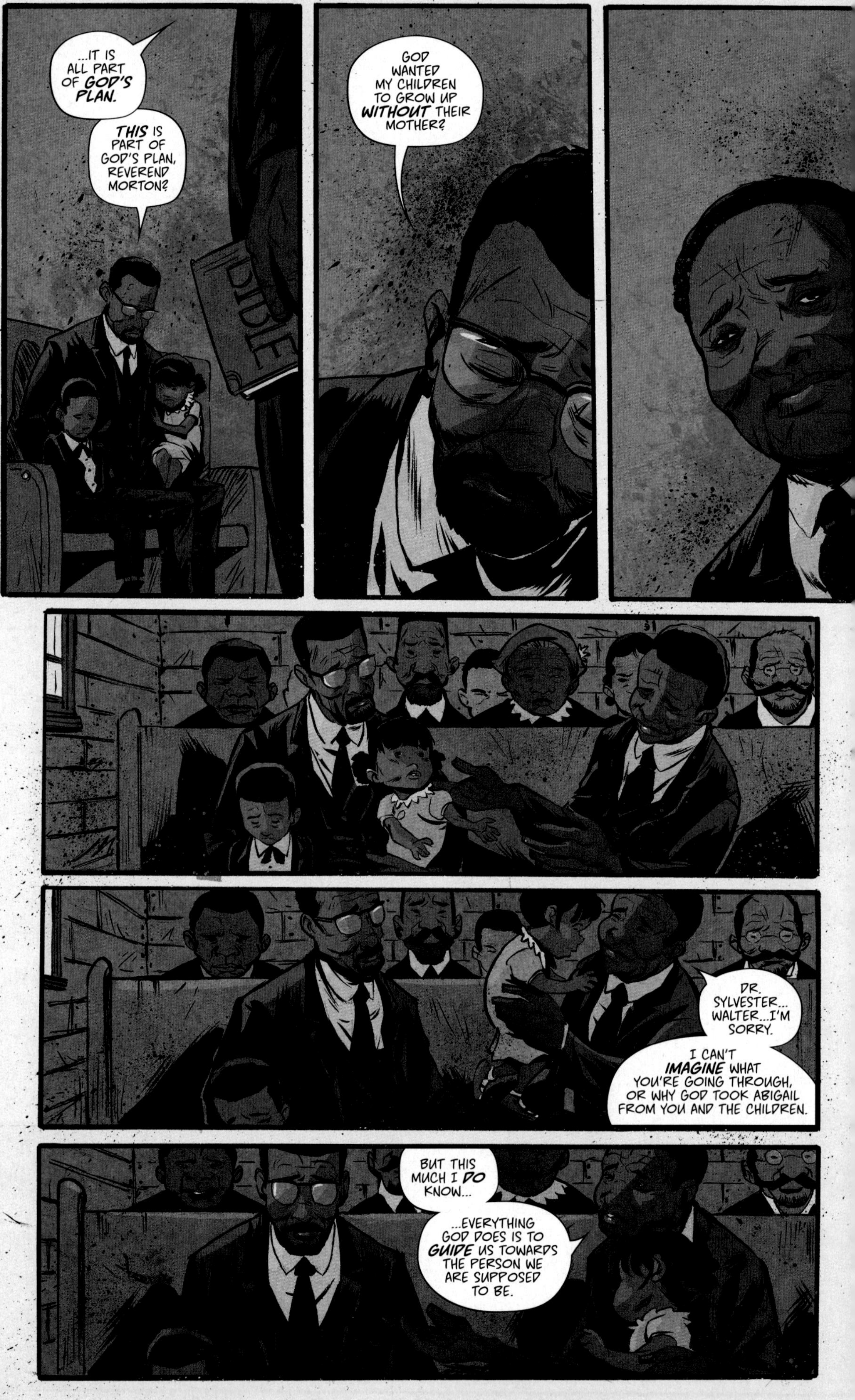

...IT IS ALL PART OF GOD'S PLAN.
THIS IS PART OF GOD'S PLAN, REVEREND MORTON?
BIBLE
GOD WANTED MY CHILDREN TO GROW UP WITHOUT THEIR MOTHER?
DR. SYLVESTER... WALTER...I'M SORRY.
I CAN'T IMAGINE WHAT YOU'RE GOING THROUGH, OR WHY GOD TOOK ABIGAIL FROM YOU AND THE CHILDREN.
BUT THIS MUCH I DO KNOW...
...EVERYTHING GOD DOES IS TO GUIDE US TOWARDS THE PERSON WE ARE SUPPOSED TO BE.

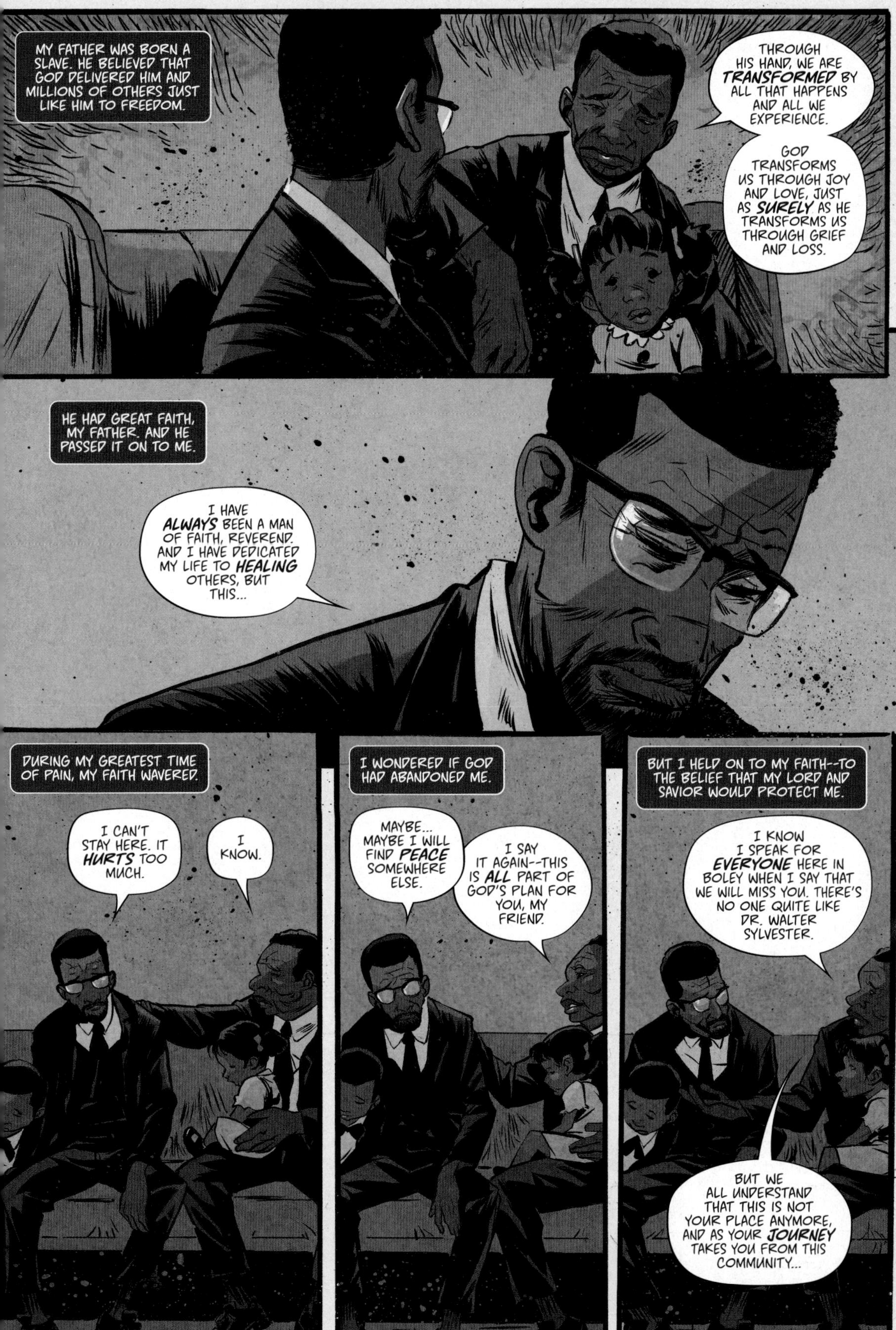
MY FATHER WAS BORN A SLAVE. HE BELIEVED THAT GOD DELIVERED HIM AND MILLIONS OF OTHERS JUST LIKE HIM TO FREEDOM.
THROUGH HIS HAND, WE ARE TRANSFORMED BY ALL THAT HAPPENS AND ALL WE EXPERIENCE.
GOD TRANSFORMS US THROUGH JOY AND LOVE, JUST AS SURELY AS HE TRANSFORMS US THROUGH GRIEF AND LOSS.
HE HAD GREAT FAITH, MY FATHER. AND HE PASSED IT ON TO ME.
I HAVE ALWAYS BEEN A MAN OF FAITH, REVEREND. AND I HAVE DEDICATED MY LIFE TO HEALING OTHERS, BUT THIS...
DURING MY GREATEST TIME OF PAIN, MY FAITH WAVERED.
I CAN'T STAY HERE. IT HURTS TOO MUCH.
I KNOW.
I WONDERED IF GOD HAD ABANDONED ME.
MAYBE... MAYBE I WILL FIND PEACE SOMEWHERE ELSE.
I SAY IT AGAIN--THIS IS ALL PART OF GOD'S PLAN FOR YOU, MY FRIEND.
BUT I HELD ON TO MY FAITH--TO THE BELIEF THAT MY LORD AND SAVIOR WOULD PROTECT ME.
I KNOW I SPEAK FOR EVERYONE HERE IN BOLEY WHEN I SAY THAT WE WILL MISS YOU. THERE'S NO ONE QUITE LIKE DR. WALTER SYLVESTER.
BUT WE ALL UNDERSTAND THAT THIS IS NOT YOUR PLACE ANYMORE, AND AS YOUR JOURNEY TAKES YOU FROM THIS COMMUNITY...

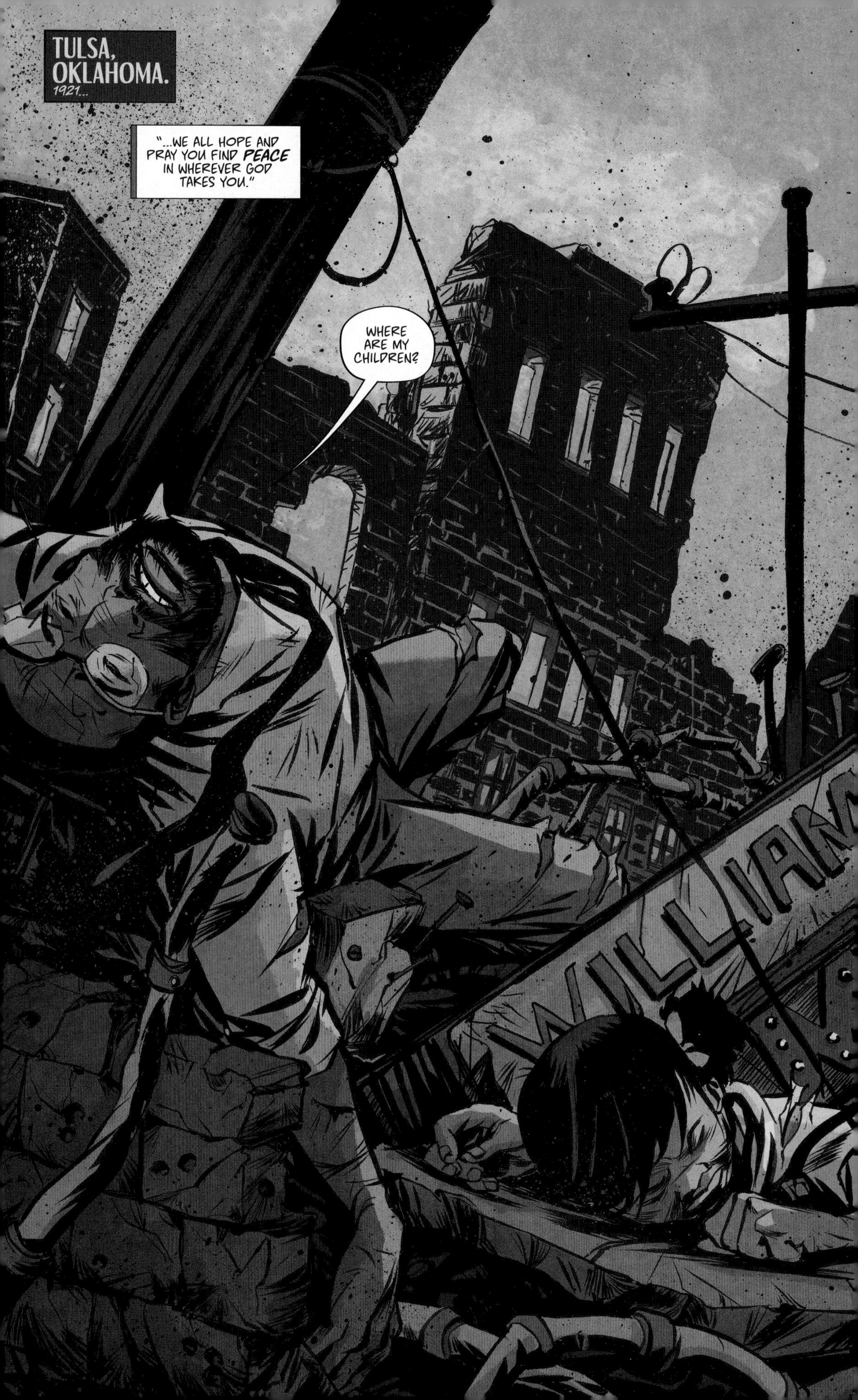
TULSA, OKLAHOMA.
1921...
"...WE ALL HOPE AND PRAY YOU FIND PEACE IN WHEREVER GOD TAKES YOU."
WHERE ARE MY CHILDREN?
WILLIAM

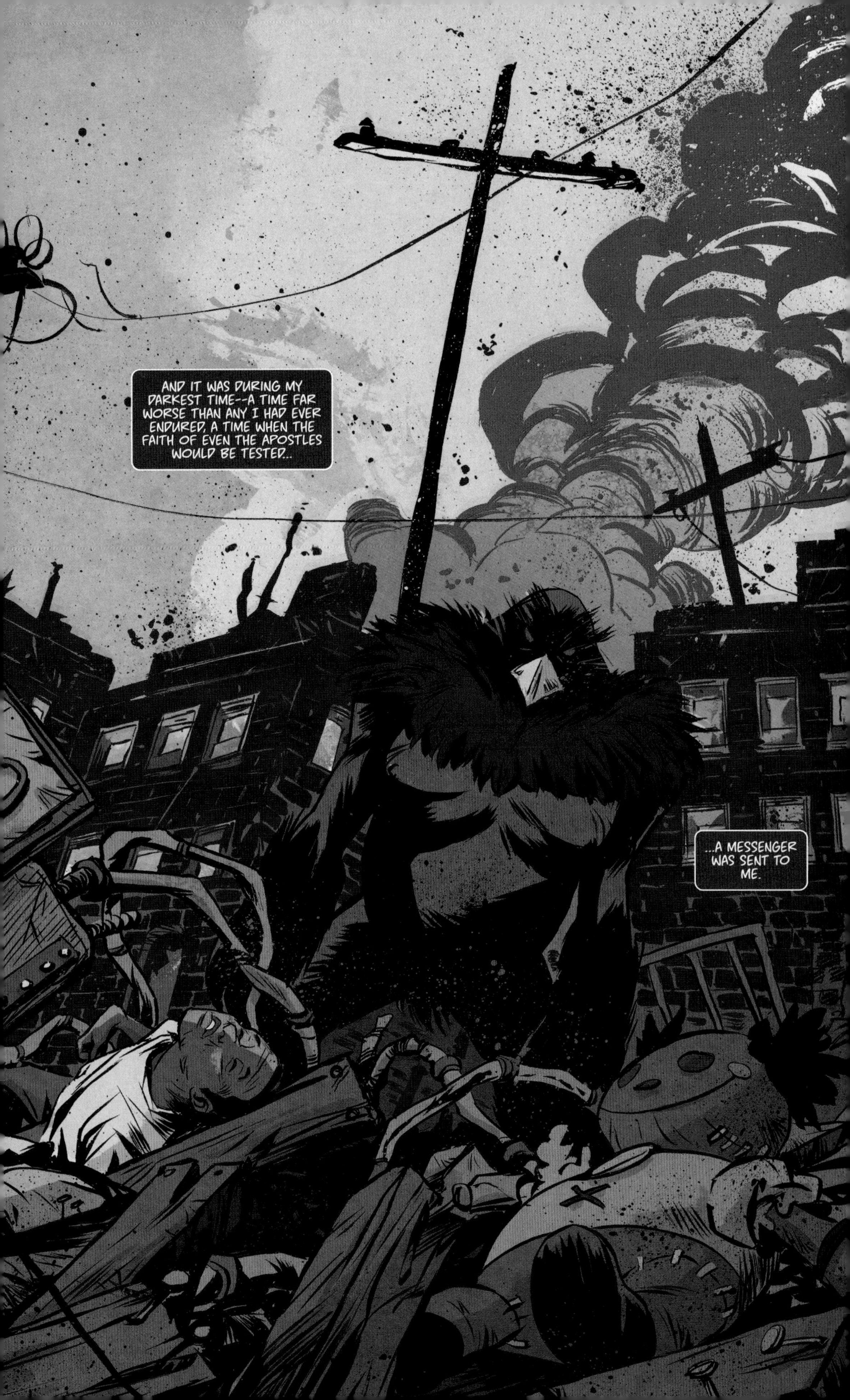
AND IT WAS DURING MY DARKEST TIME--A TIME FAR WORSE THAN ANY I HAD EVER ENDURED, A TIME WHEN THE FAITH OF EVEN THE APOSTLES WOULD BE TESTED...
...A MESSENGER WAS SENT TO ME.

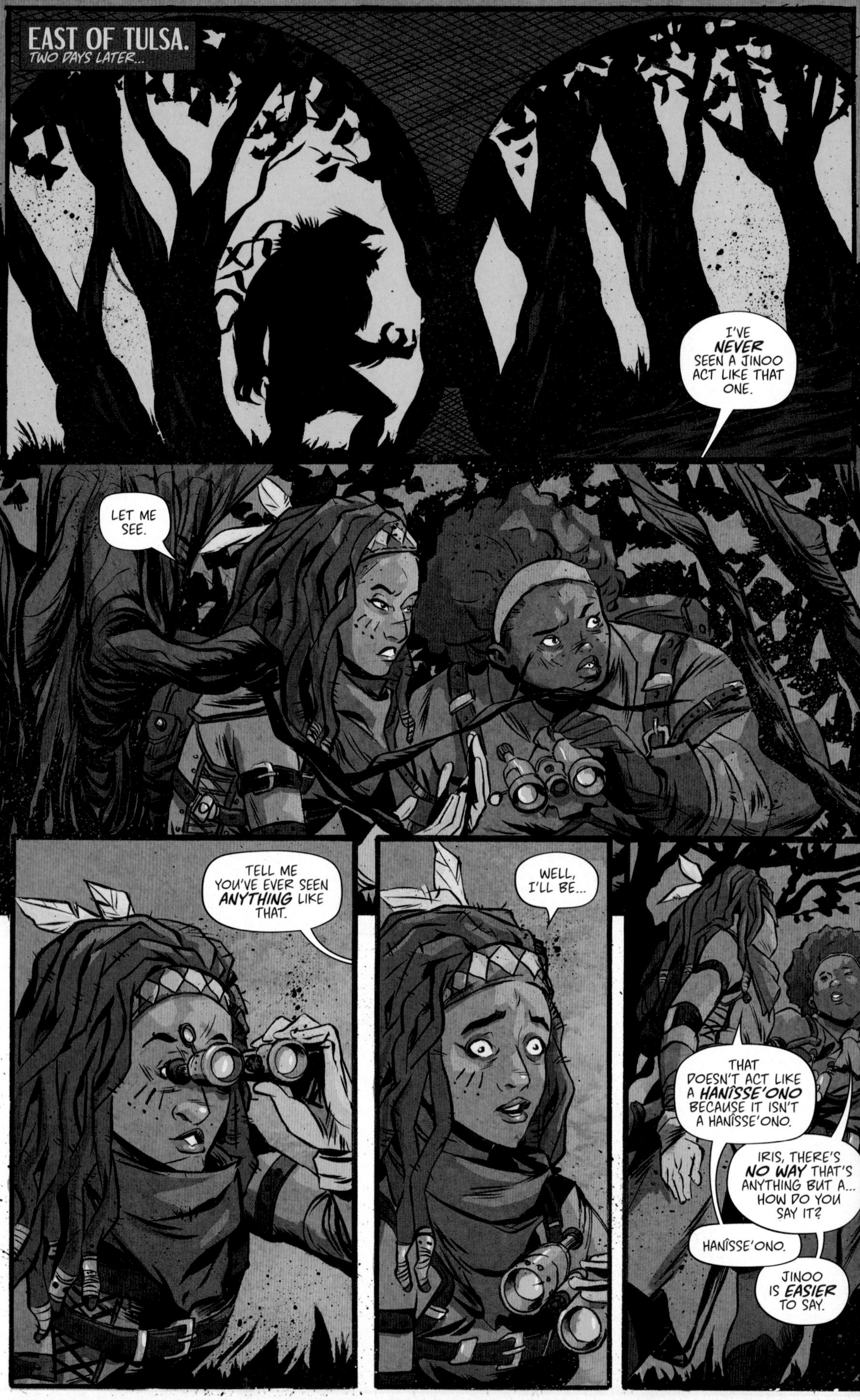
EAST OF TULSA.
TWO DAYS LATER...
I'VE NEVER SEEN A JINOO ACT LIKE THAT ONE.
LET ME SEE.
TELL ME YOU'VE EVER SEEN ANYTHING LIKE THAT.
WELL, I'LL BE...
THAT DOESN'T ACT LIKE A HANÎSSE'ONO BECAUSE IT ISN'T A HANÎSSE'ONO.
IRIS, THERE'S NO WAY THAT'S ANYTHING BUT A... HOW DO YOU SAY IT?
HANÎSSE'ONO.
JINOO IS EASIER TO SAY.

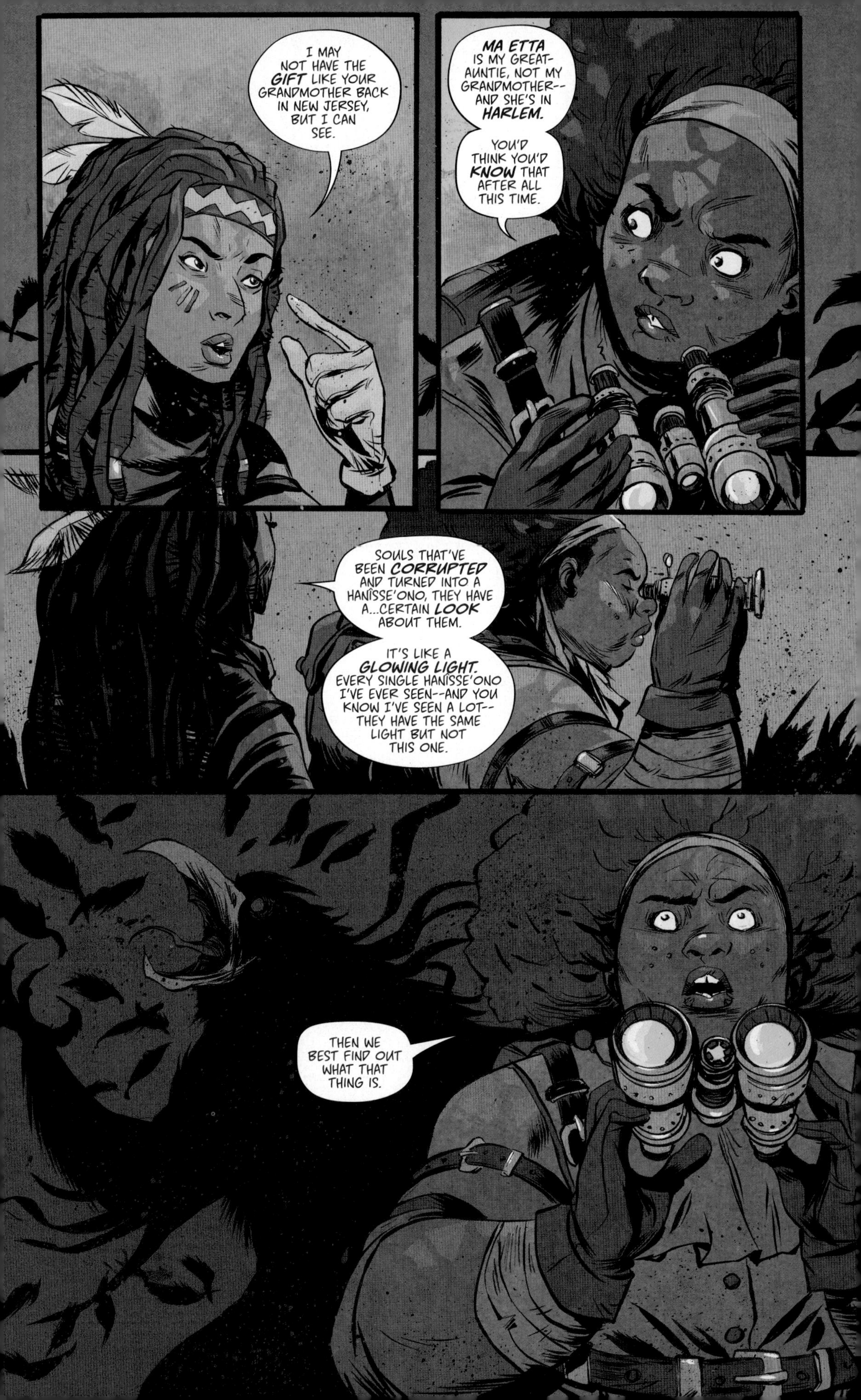
I MAY NOT HAVE THE GIFT LIKE YOUR GRANDMOTHER BACK IN NEW JERSEY, BUT I CAN SEE.
MA ETTA IS MY GREAT-AUNTIE, NOT MY GRANDMOTHER-- AND SHE'S IN HARLEM.
YOU'D THINK YOU'D KNOW THAT AFTER ALL THIS TIME.
SOULS THAT'VE BEEN CORRUPTED AND TURNED INTO A HANÍSSE'ONO, THEY HAVE A...CERTAIN LOOK ABOUT THEM.
IT'S LIKE A GLOWING LIGHT. EVERY SINGLE HANÍSSE'ONO I'VE EVER SEEN--AND YOU KNOW I'VE SEEN A LOT-- THEY HAVE THE SAME LIGHT BUT NOT THIS ONE.
THEN WE BEST FIND OUT WHAT THAT THING IS.

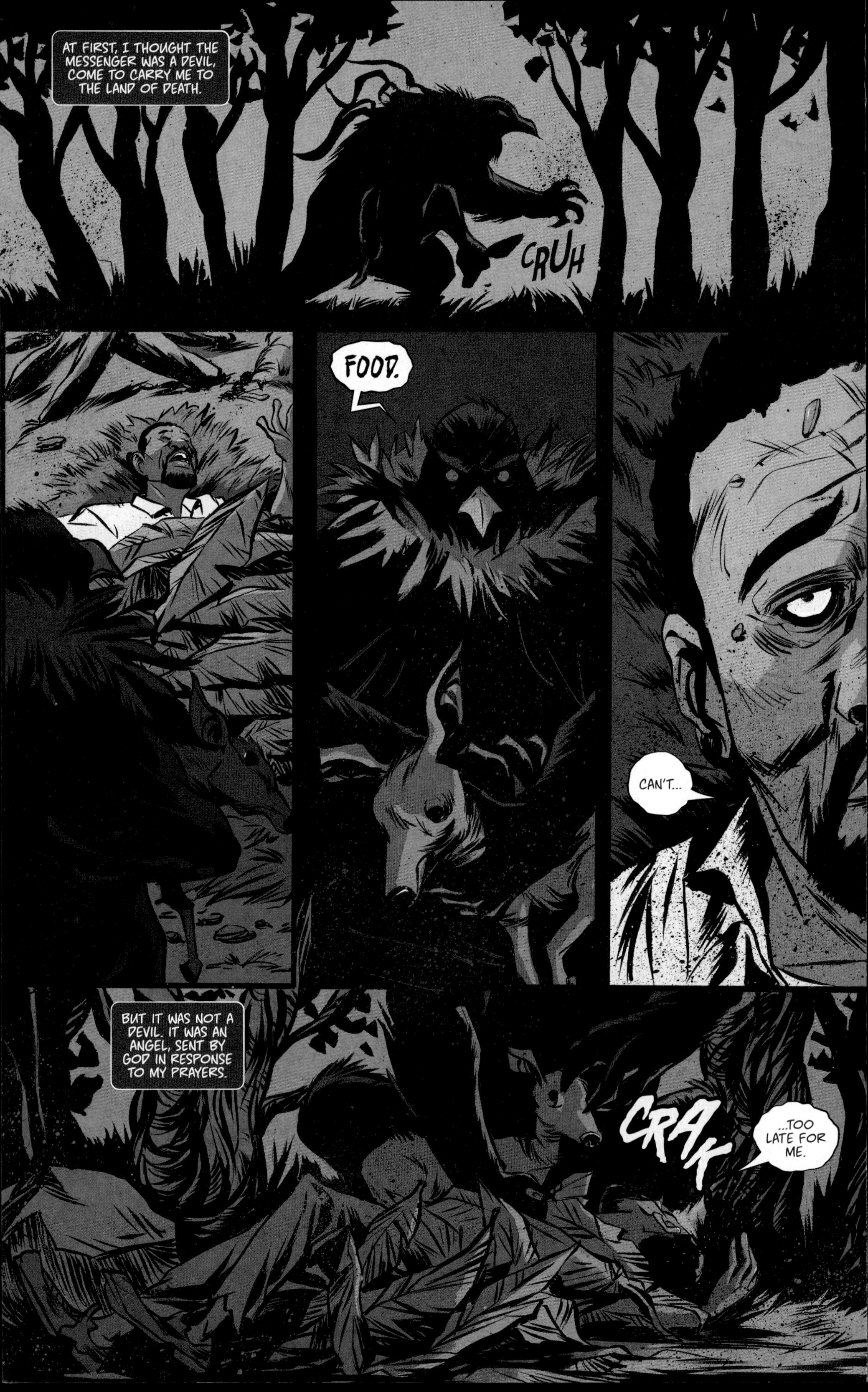
AT FIRST, I THOUGHT THE MESSENGER WAS A DEVIL, COME TO CARRY ME TO THE LAND OF DEATH.
CRUH
FOOD.
CAN'T...
BUT IT WAS NOT A DEVIL. IT WAS AN ANGEL, SENT BY GOD IN RESPONSE TO MY PRAYERS.
CRAK
...TOO LATE FOR ME.

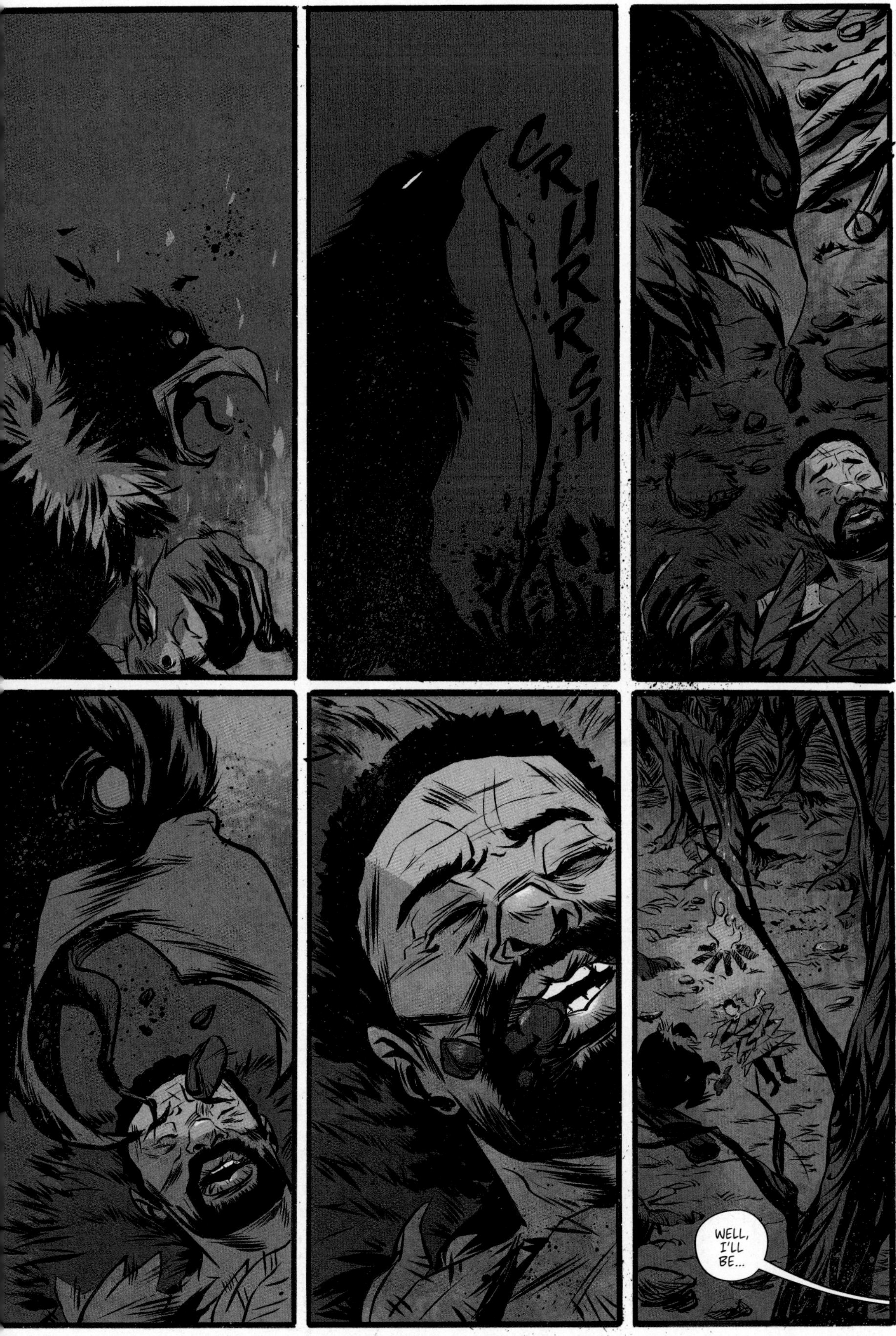
CRURRSH
WELL, I'LL BE...

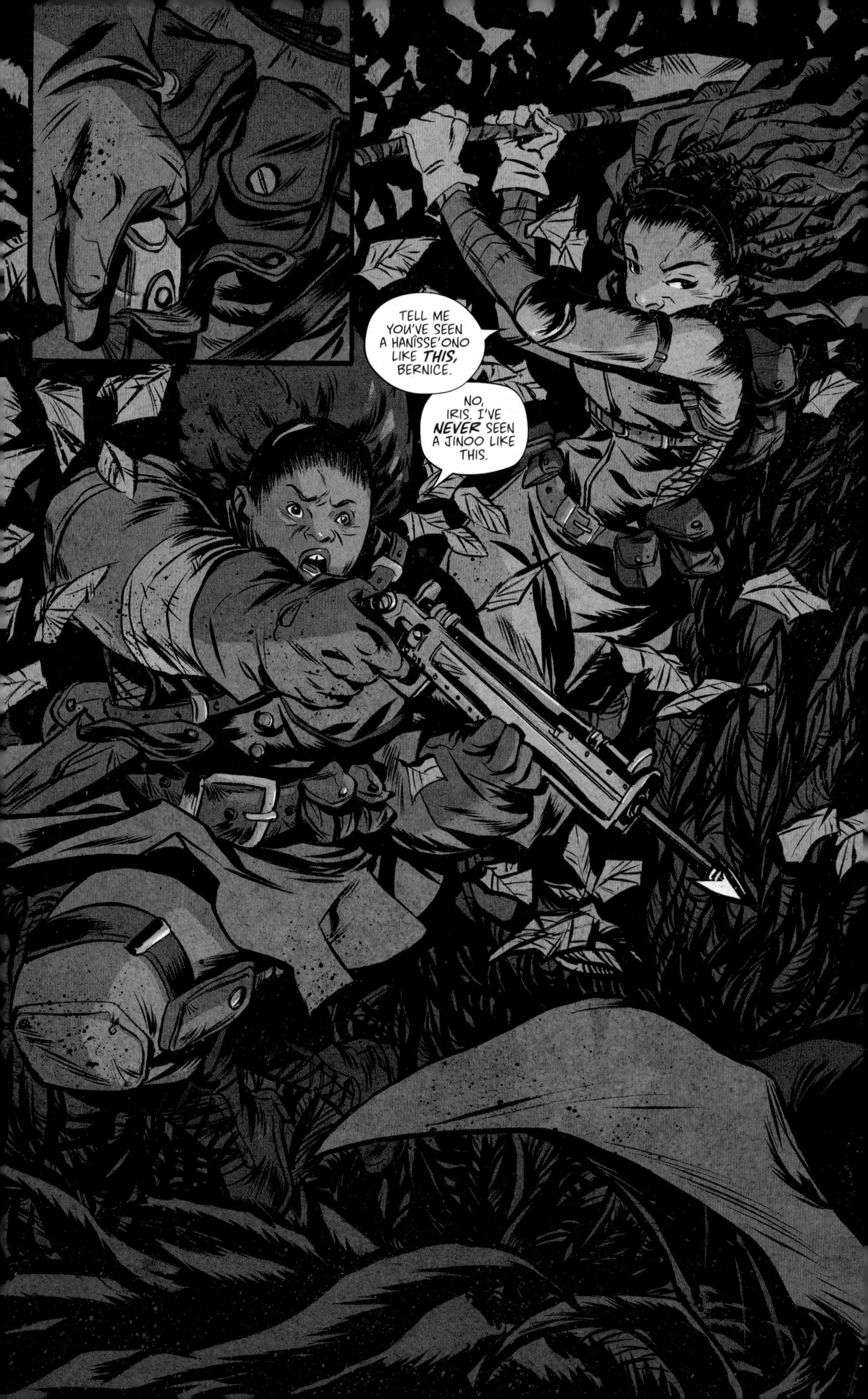
TELL ME YOU'VE SEEN A HANÎSSE'ONO LIKE **THIS,** BERNICE.
NO, IRIS. I'VE **NEVER** SEEN A JINOO LIKE THIS.

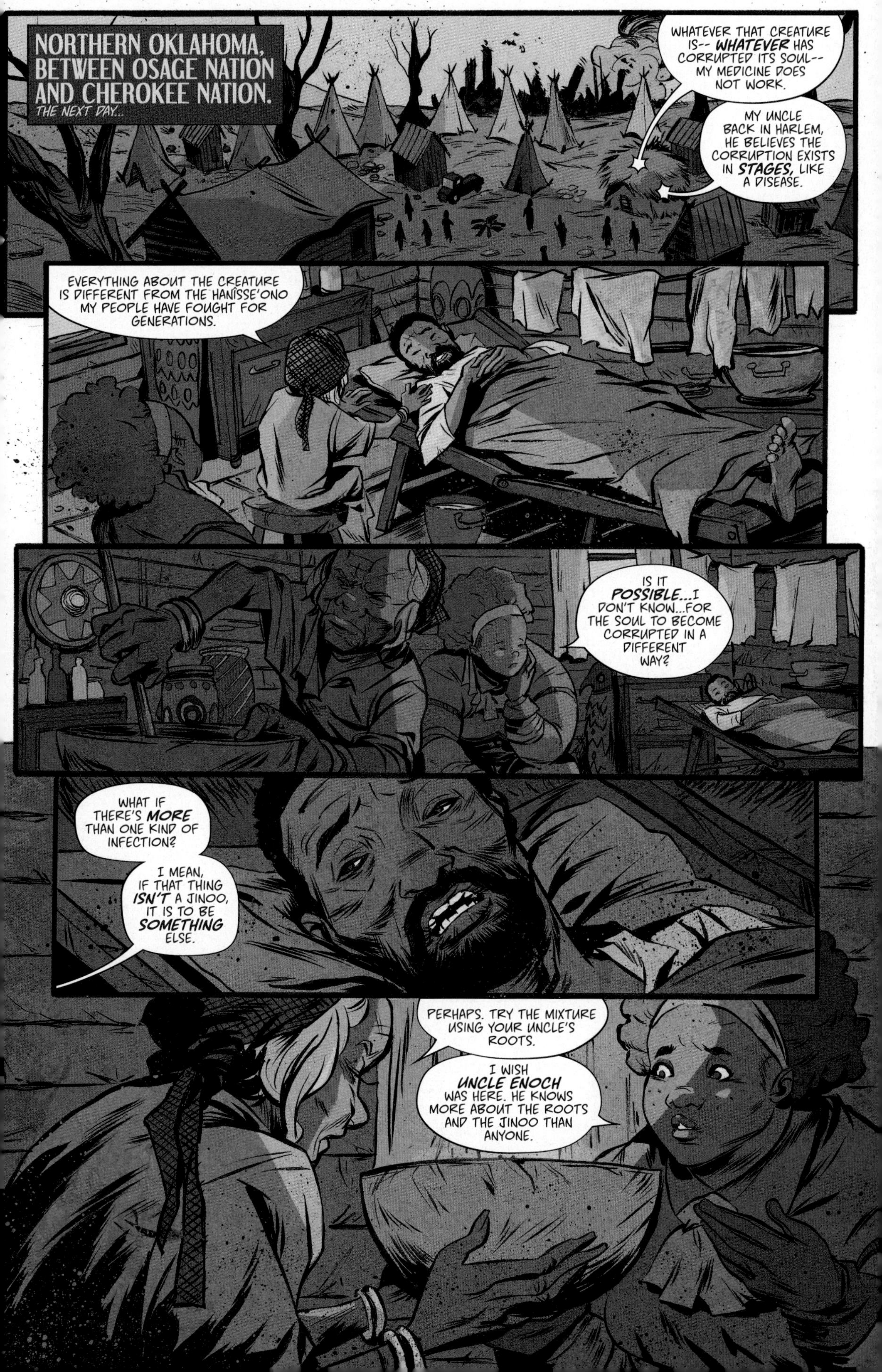
NORTHERN OKLAHOMA, BETWEEN OSAGE NATION AND CHEROKEE NATION.
THE NEXT DAY...
WHATEVER THAT CREATURE IS-- WHATEVER HAS CORRUPTED ITS SOUL-- MY MEDICINE DOES NOT WORK.
MY UNCLE BACK IN HARLEM, HE BELIEVES THE CORRUPTION EXISTS IN STAGES, LIKE A DISEASE.
EVERYTHING ABOUT THE CREATURE IS DIFFERENT FROM THE HANISSE'ONO MY PEOPLE HAVE FOUGHT FOR GENERATIONS.
IS IT POSSIBLE...I DON'T KNOW...FOR THE SOUL TO BECOME CORRUPTED IN A DIFFERENT WAY?
WHAT IF THERE'S MORE THAN ONE KIND OF INFECTION?
I MEAN, IF THAT THING ISN'T A JINOO, IT IS TO BE SOMETHING ELSE.
PERHAPS. TRY THE MIXTURE USING YOUR UNCLE'S ROOTS.
I WISH UNCLE ENOCH WAS HERE. HE KNOWS MORE ABOUT THE ROOTS AND THE JINOO THAN ANYONE.

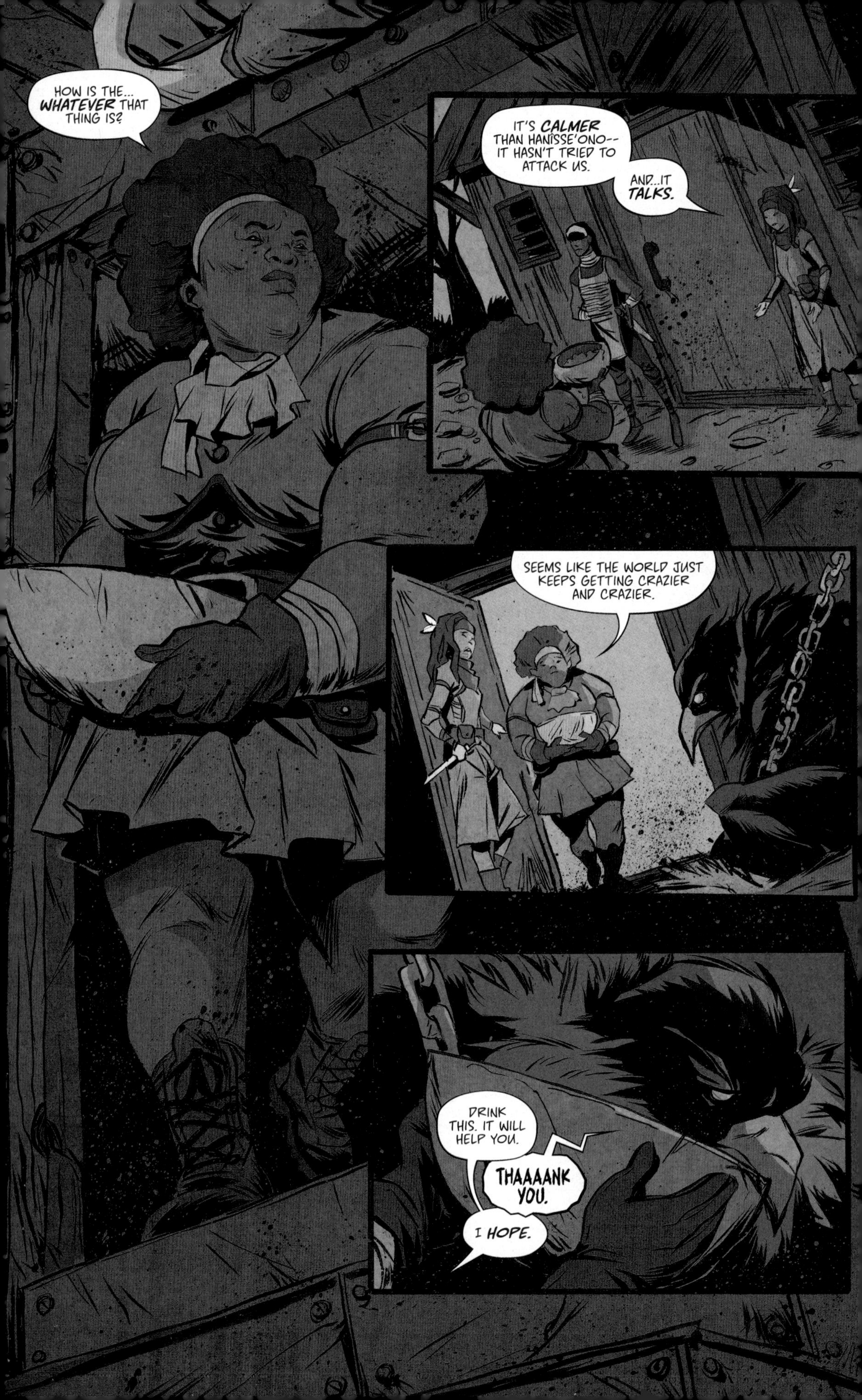
HOW IS THE... WHATEVER THAT THING IS?
IT'S CALMER THAN HANISSE'ONO-- IT HASN'T TRIED TO ATTACK US.
AND...IT TALKS.
SEEMS LIKE THE WORLD JUST KEEPS GETTING CRAZIER AND CRAZIER.
DRINK THIS. IT WILL HELP YOU.
THAAAANK YOU.
I HOPE.

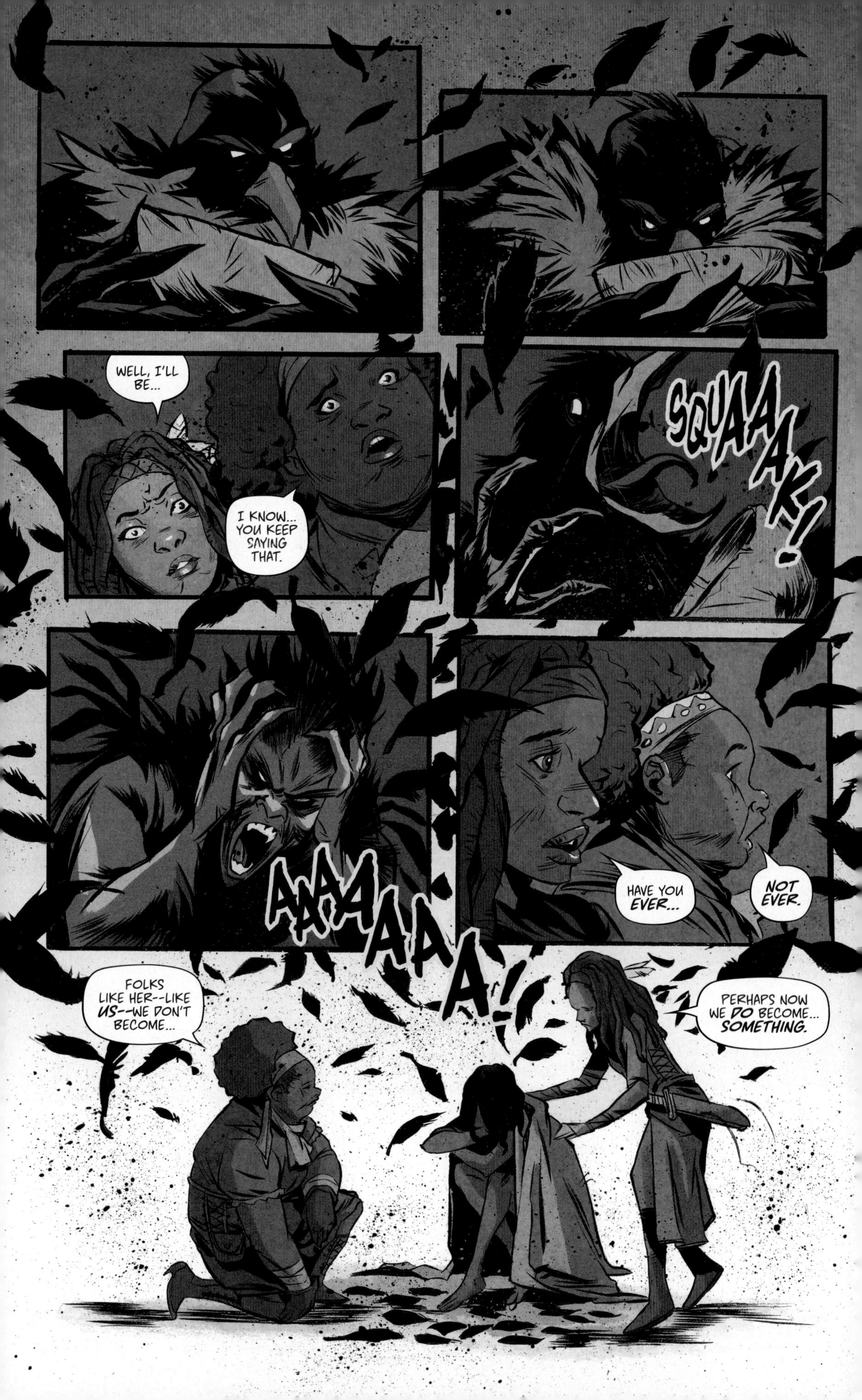
WELL, I'LL BE...
I KNOW... YOU KEEP SAYING THAT.
SQUAAAK!
AAAAAAAA!
HAVE YOU EVER...
NOT EVER.
FOLKS LIKE HER--LIKE US--WE DON'T BECOME...
PERHAPS NOW WE DO BECOME... SOMETHING.

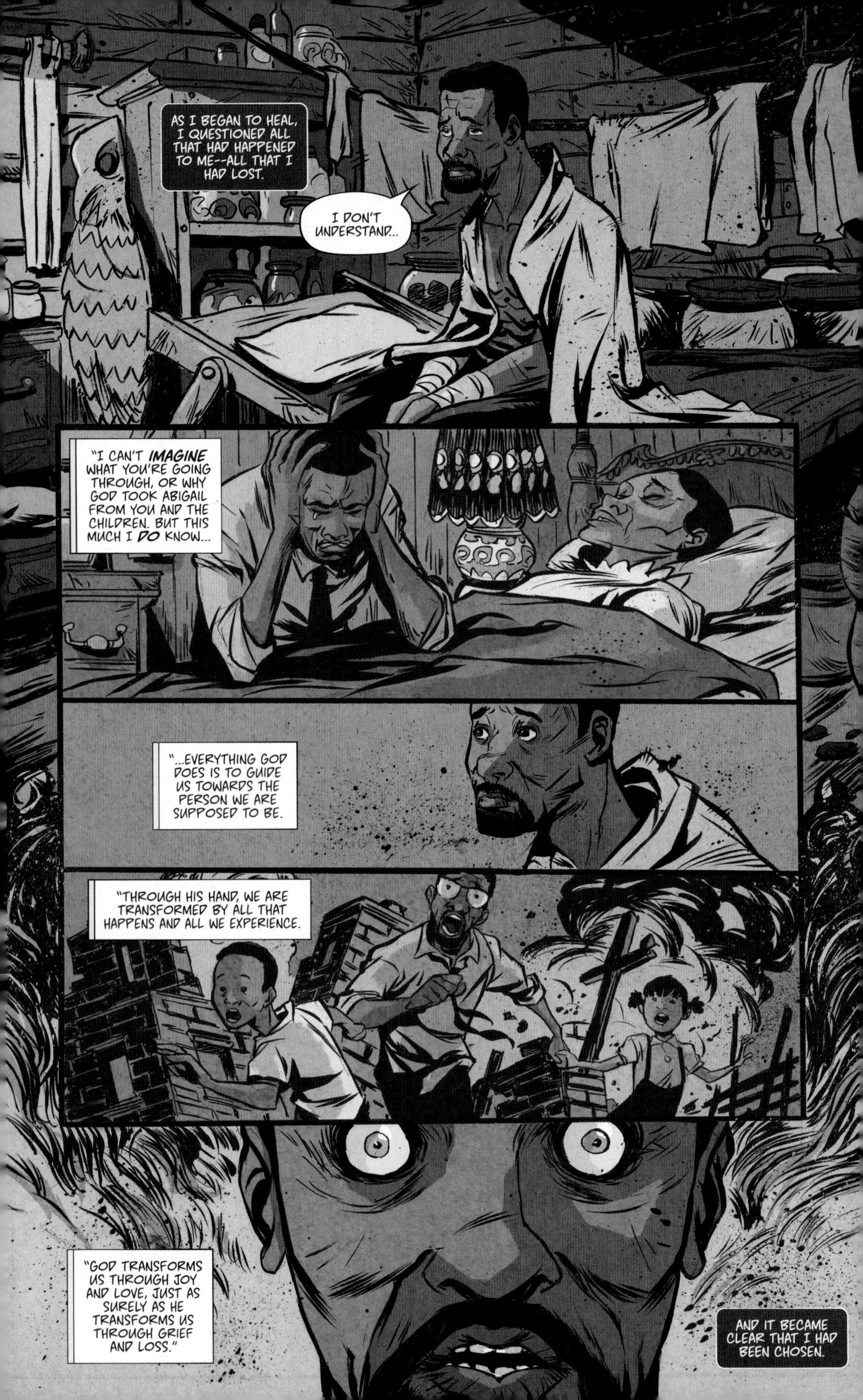
AS I BEGAN TO HEAL, I QUESTIONED ALL THAT HAD HAPPENED TO ME--ALL THAT I HAD LOST.
I DON'T UNDERSTAND...
"I CAN'T IMAGINE WHAT YOU'RE GOING THROUGH, OR WHY GOD TOOK ABIGAIL FROM YOU AND THE CHILDREN. BUT THIS MUCH I DO KNOW...
"...EVERYTHING GOD DOES IS TO GUIDE US TOWARDS THE PERSON WE ARE SUPPOSED TO BE.
"THROUGH HIS HAND, WE ARE TRANSFORMED BY ALL THAT HAPPENS AND ALL WE EXPERIENCE.
"GOD TRANSFORMS US THROUGH JOY AND LOVE, JUST AS SURELY AS HE TRANSFORMS US THROUGH GRIEF AND LOSS."
AND IT BECAME CLEAR THAT I HAD BEEN CHOSEN.

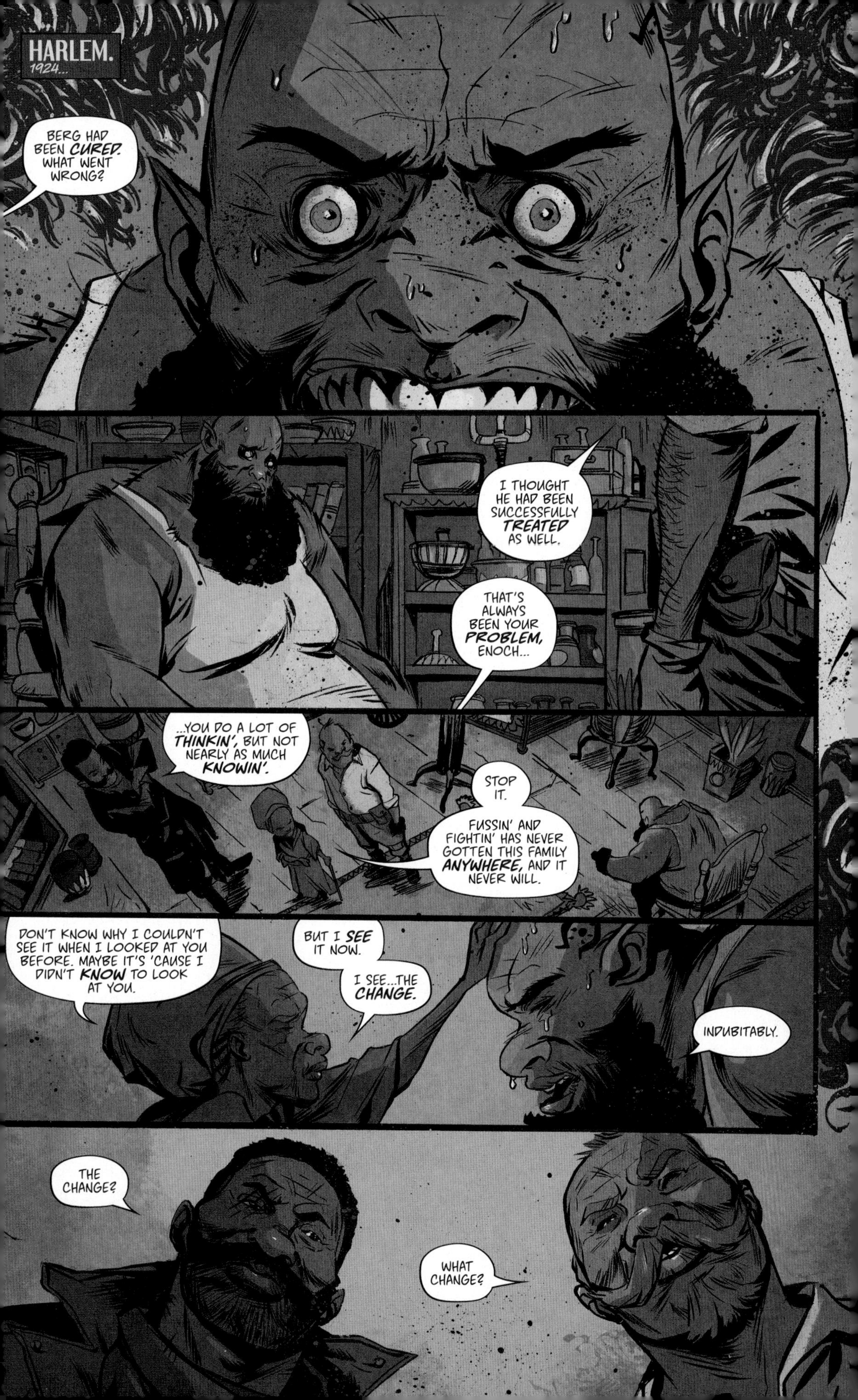
HARLEM.
1924...
BERG HAD BEEN CURED. WHAT WENT WRONG?
I THOUGHT HE HAD BEEN SUCCESSFULLY TREATED AS WELL.
THAT'S ALWAYS BEEN YOUR PROBLEM, ENOCH...
...YOU DO A LOT OF THINKIN', BUT NOT NEARLY AS MUCH KNOWIN'.
STOP IT.
FUSSIN' AND FIGHTIN' HAS NEVER GOTTEN THIS FAMILY ANYWHERE, AND IT NEVER WILL.
DON'T KNOW WHY I COULDN'T SEE IT WHEN I LOOKED AT YOU BEFORE. MAYBE IT'S 'CAUSE I DIDN'T KNOW TO LOOK AT YOU.
BUT I SEE IT NOW.
I SEE...THE CHANGE.
INDUBITABLY.
THE CHANGE?
WHAT CHANGE?

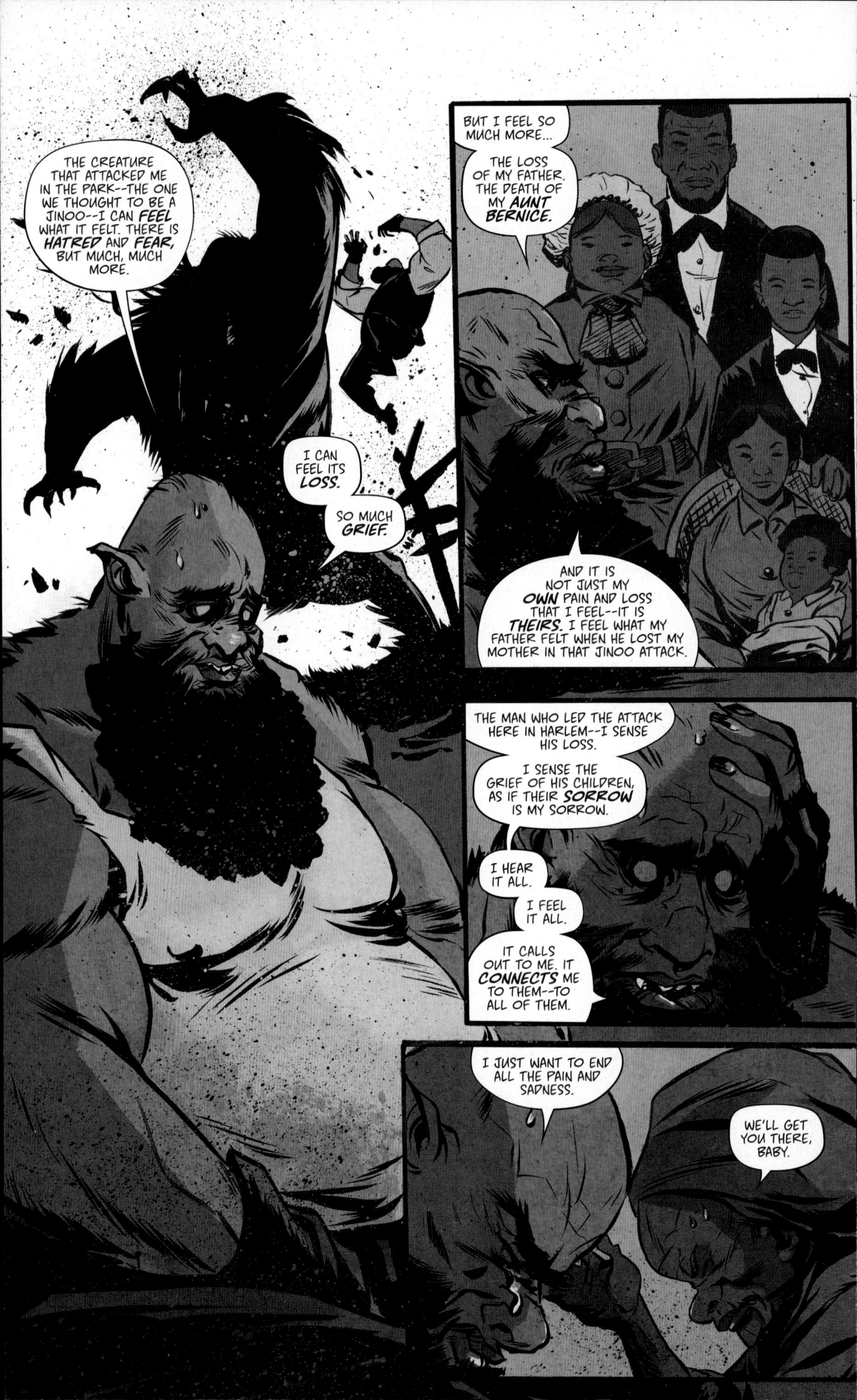
THE CREATURE THAT ATTACKED ME IN THE PARK--THE ONE WE THOUGHT TO BE A JINOO--I CAN FEEL WHAT IT FELT. THERE IS HATRED AND FEAR, BUT MUCH, MUCH MORE.
I CAN FEEL ITS LOSS.
SO MUCH GRIEF.
BUT I FEEL SO MUCH MORE...
THE LOSS OF MY FATHER. THE DEATH OF MY AUNT BERNICE.
AND IT IS NOT JUST MY OWN PAIN AND LOSS THAT I FEEL--IT IS THEIRS. I FEEL WHAT MY FATHER FELT WHEN HE LOST MY MOTHER IN THAT JINOO ATTACK.
THE MAN WHO LED THE ATTACK HERE IN HARLEM--I SENSE HIS LOSS.
I SENSE THE GRIEF OF HIS CHILDREN, AS IF THEIR SORROW IS MY SORROW.
I HEAR IT ALL.
I FEEL IT ALL.
IT CALLS OUT TO ME. IT CONNECTS ME TO THEM--TO ALL OF THEM.
I JUST WANT TO END ALL THE PAIN AND SADNESS.
WE'LL GET YOU THERE, BABY.

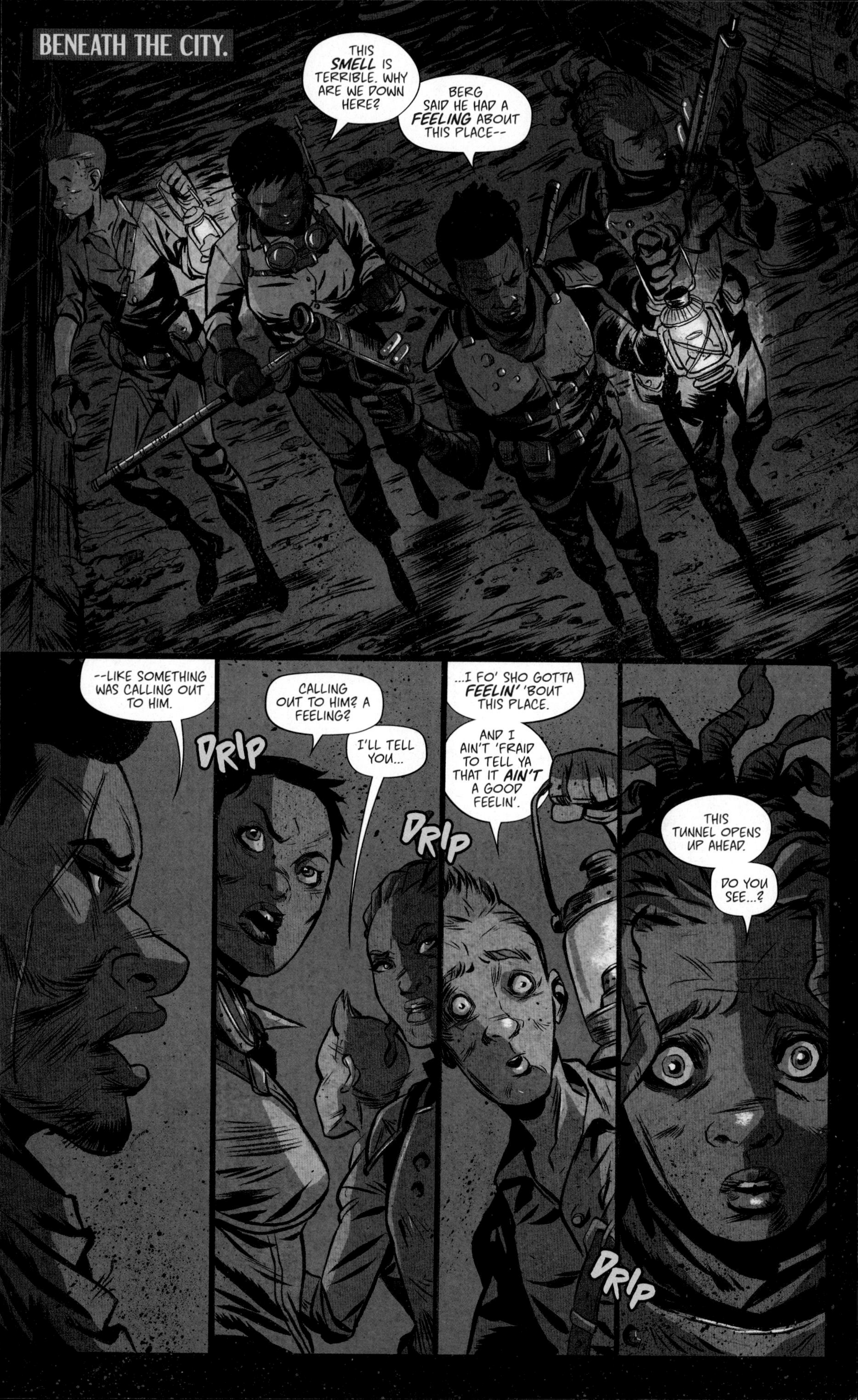
BENEATH THE CITY.
THIS SMELL IS TERRIBLE. WHY ARE WE DOWN HERE?
BERG SAID HE HAD A FEELING ABOUT THIS PLACE--
--LIKE SOMETHING WAS CALLING OUT TO HIM.
DRIP
CALLING OUT TO HIM? A FEELING?
I'LL TELL YOU...
DRIP
...I FO' SHO GOTTA FEELIN' 'BOUT THIS PLACE.
AND I AIN'T 'FRAID TO TELL YA THAT IT AIN'T A GOOD FEELIN'.
THIS TUNNEL OPENS UP AHEAD.
DO YOU SEE...?
DRIP

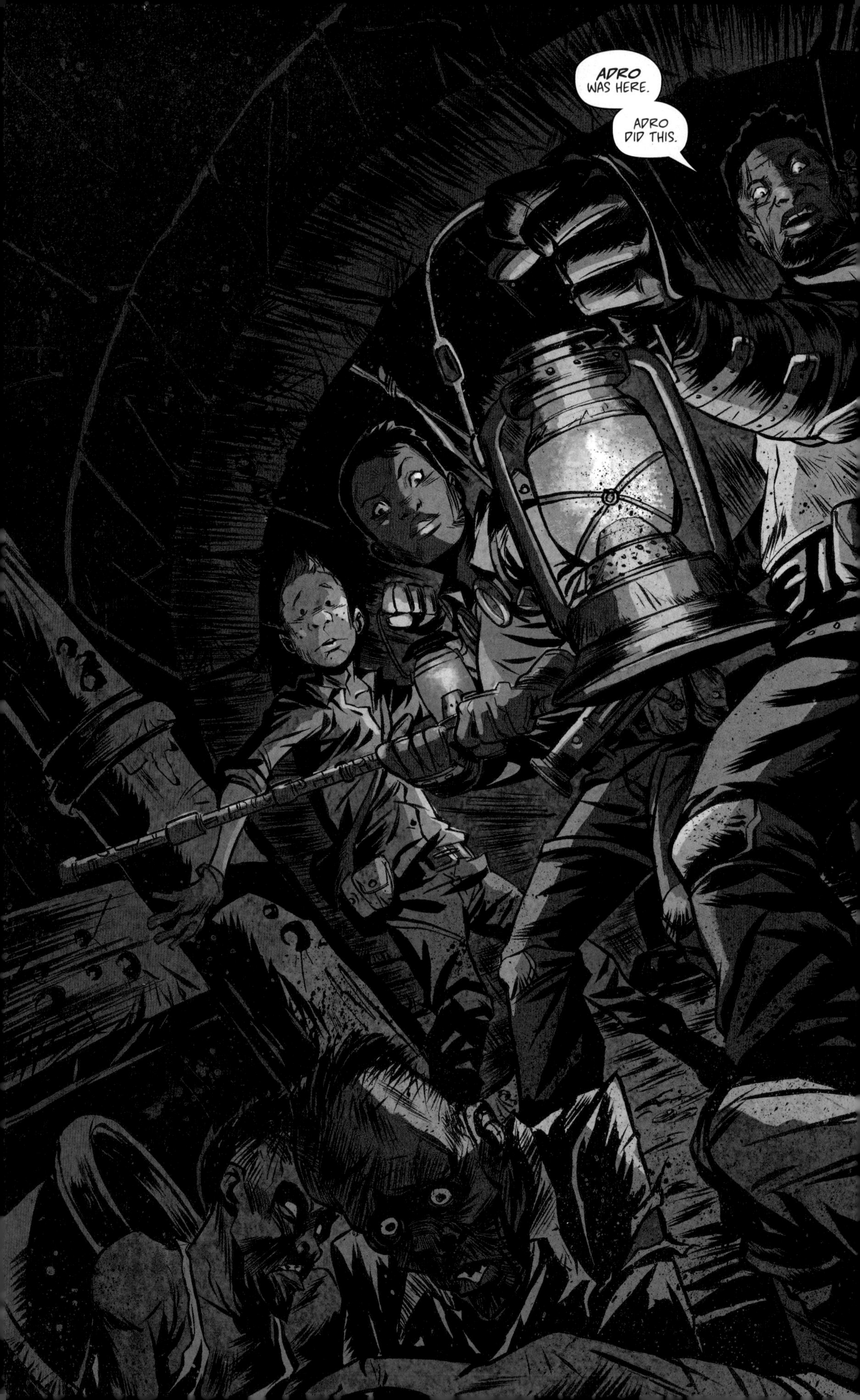
ADRO WAS HERE.
ADRO DID THIS.

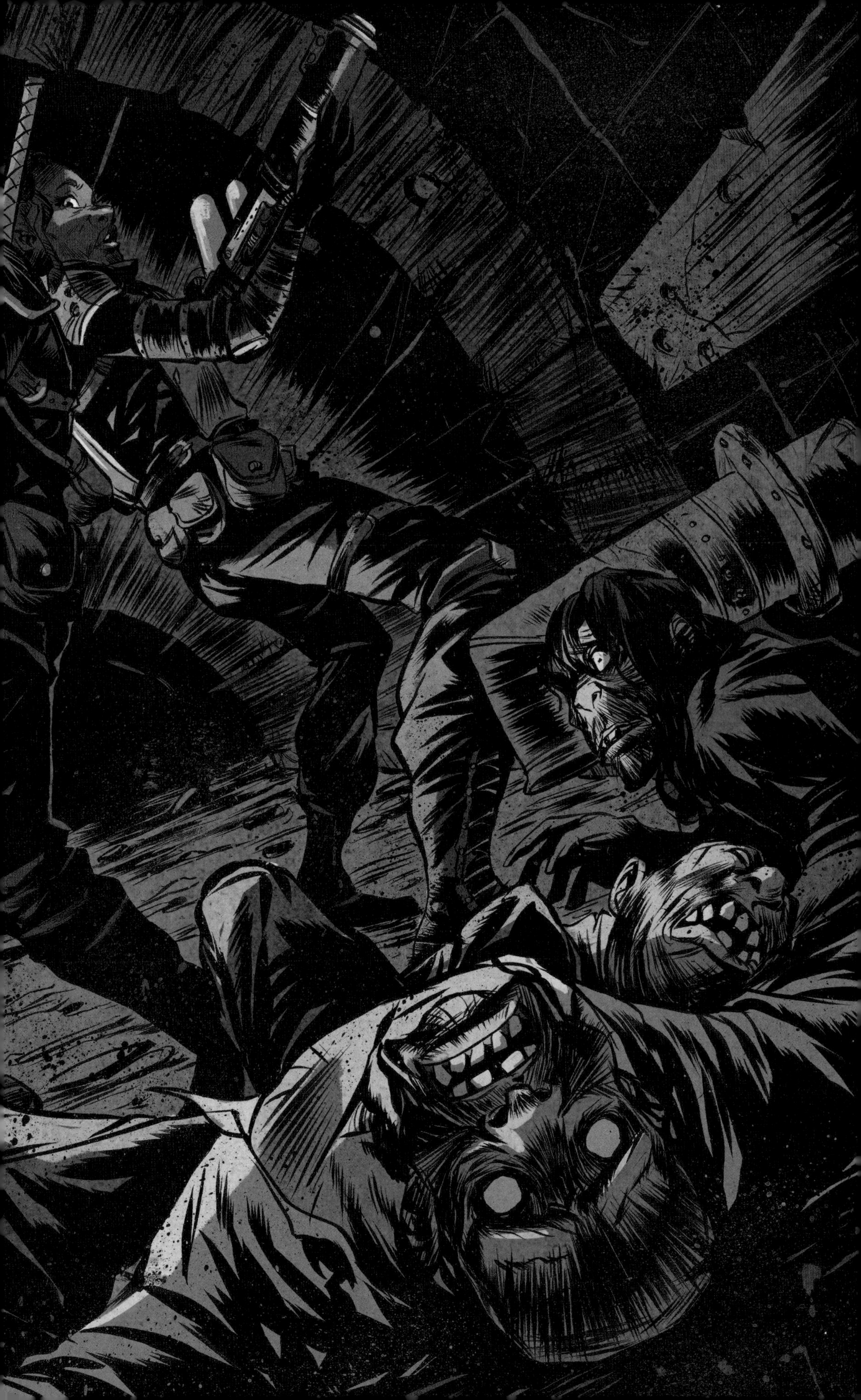

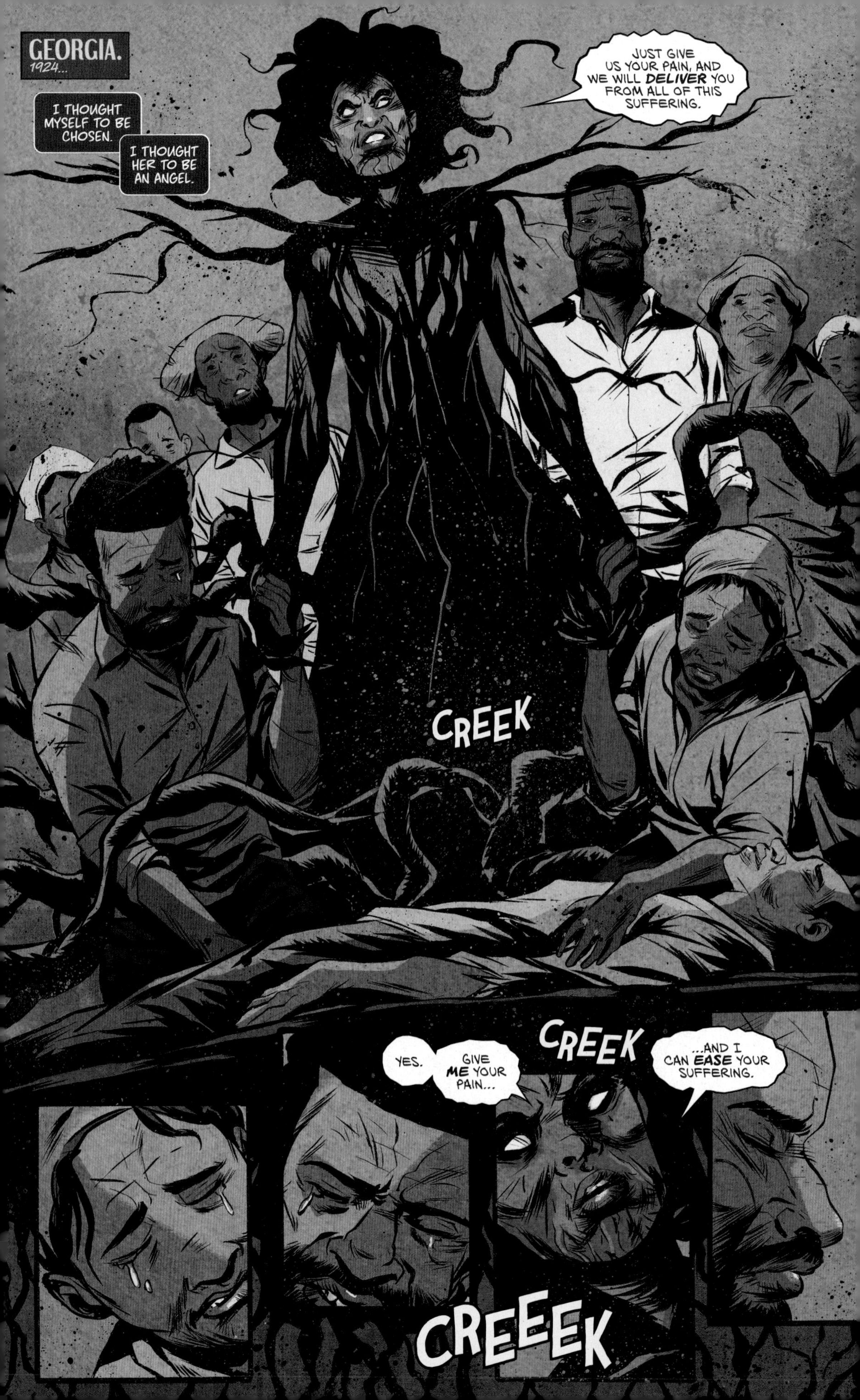
GEORGIA. 1924...
I THOUGHT MYSELF TO BE CHOSEN.
I THOUGHT HER TO BE AN ANGEL.
JUST GIVE US YOUR PAIN, AND WE WILL DELIVER YOU FROM ALL OF THIS SUFFERING.
CREEK
YES.
GIVE ME YOUR PAIN...
CREEK
...AND I CAN EASE YOUR SUFFERING.
CREEEK

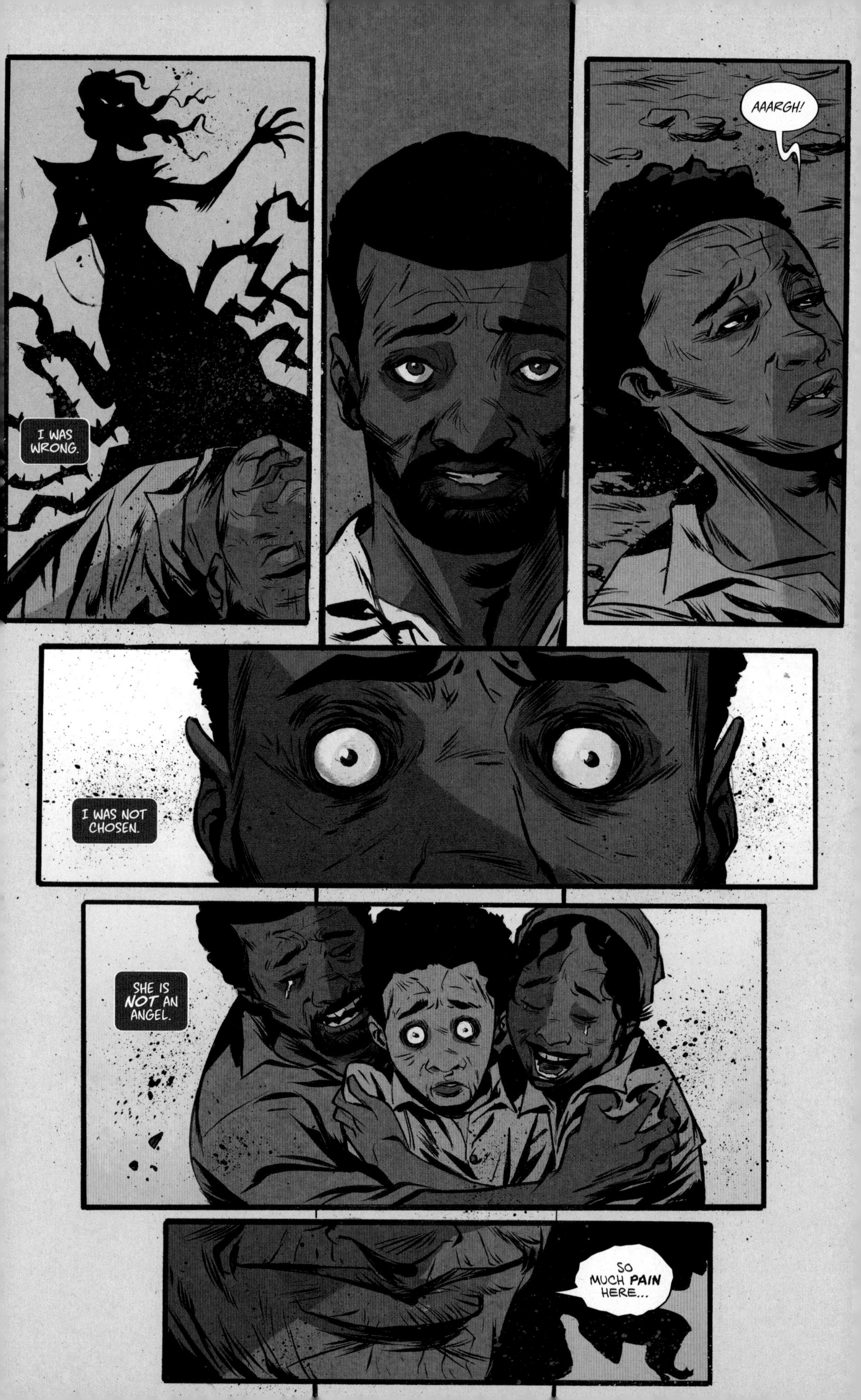
I WAS WRONG.
AAARGH!
I WAS NOT CHOSEN.
SHE IS NOT AN ANGEL.
SO MUCH PAIN HERE...

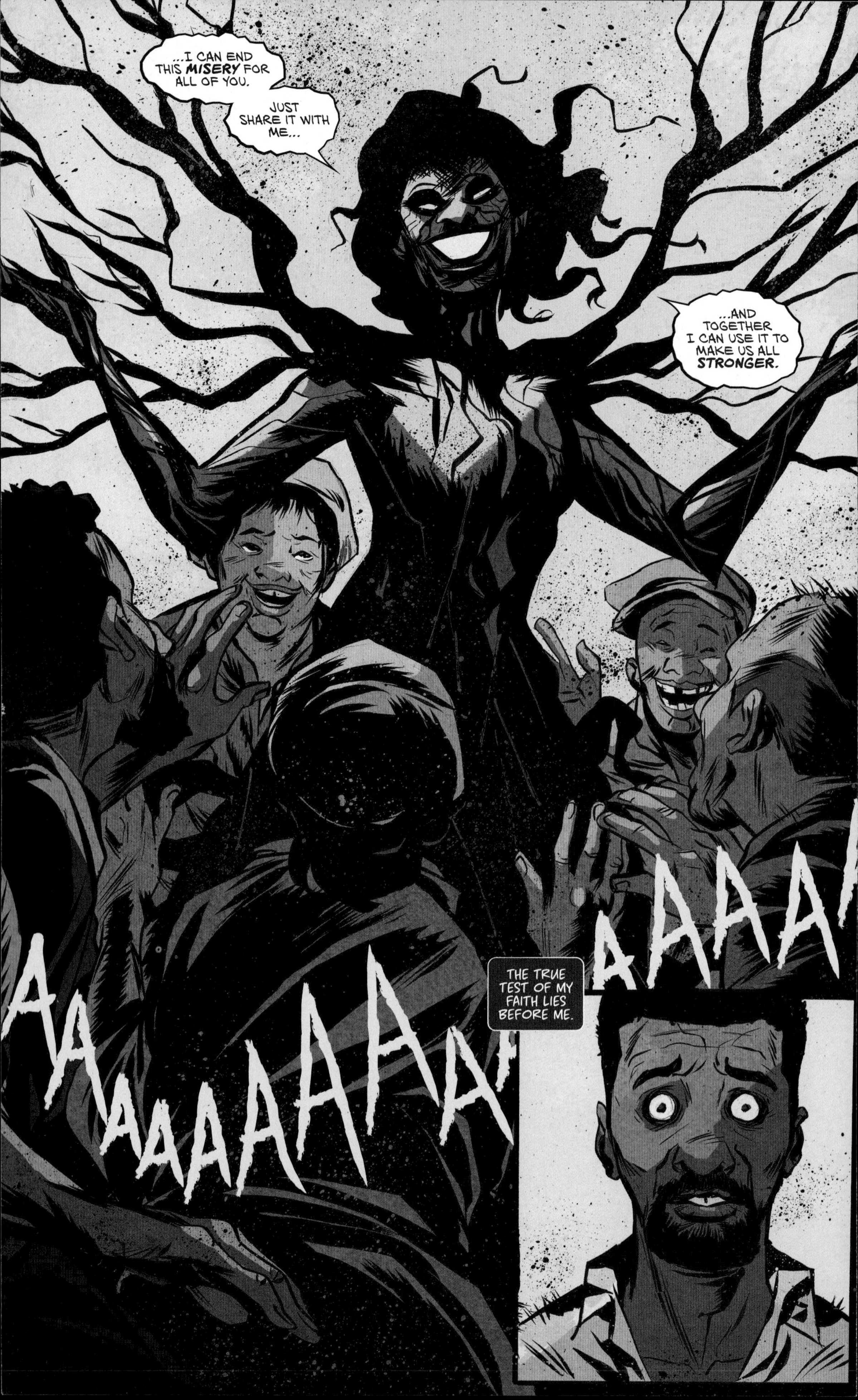
...I CAN END THIS MISERY FOR ALL OF YOU.
JUST SHARE IT WITH ME...
...AND TOGETHER I CAN USE IT TO MAKE US ALL STRONGER.
AAAAAAAAAAAAA
THE TRUE TEST OF MY FAITH LIES BEFORE ME.

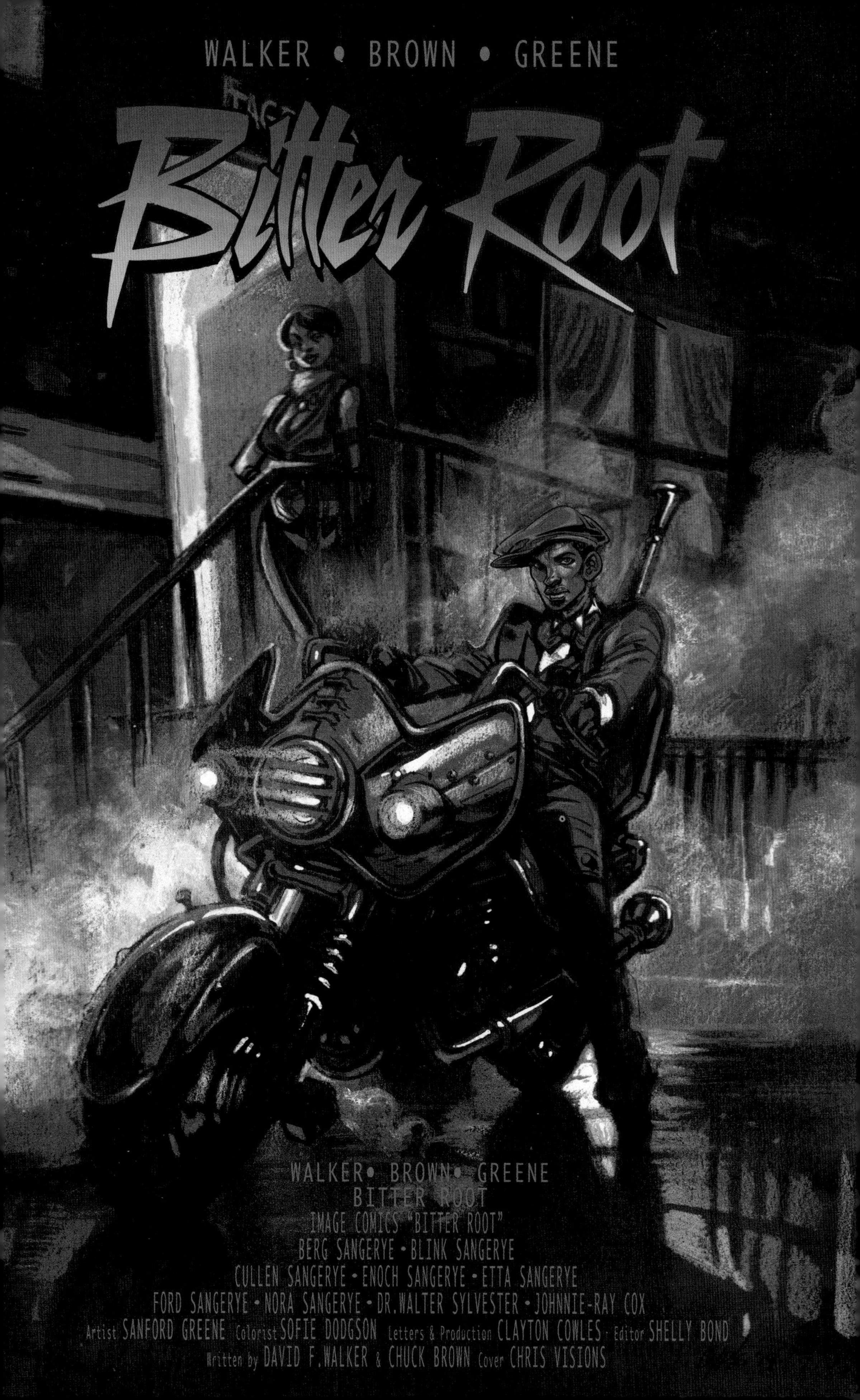
WALKER • BROWN • GREENE
Bitter Root
WALKER • BROWN • GREENE
BITTER ROOT
IMAGE COMICS "BITTER ROOT"
BERG SANGERYE • BLINK SANGERYE
CULLEN SANGERYE • ENOCH SANGERYE • ETTA SANGERYE
FORD SANGERYE • NORA SANGERYE • DR.WALTER SYLVESTER • JOHNNIE-RAY COX
Artist SANFORD GREENE Colorist SOFIE DODGSON Letters & Production CLAYTON COWLES · Editor SHELLY BOND
Written by DAVID F.WALKER & CHUCK BROWN Cover CHRIS VISIONS

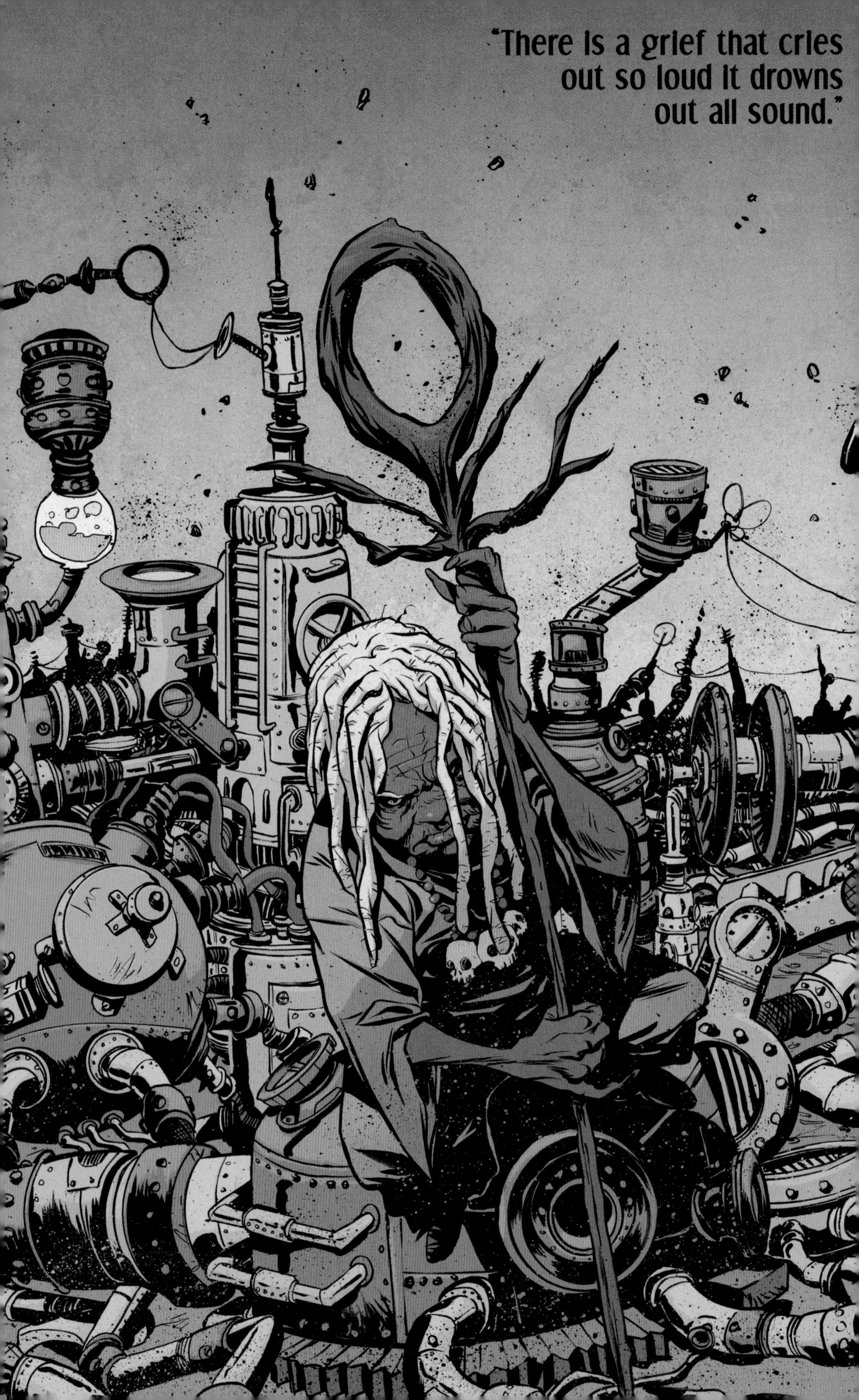
"There is a grief that cries out so loud it drowns out all sound."

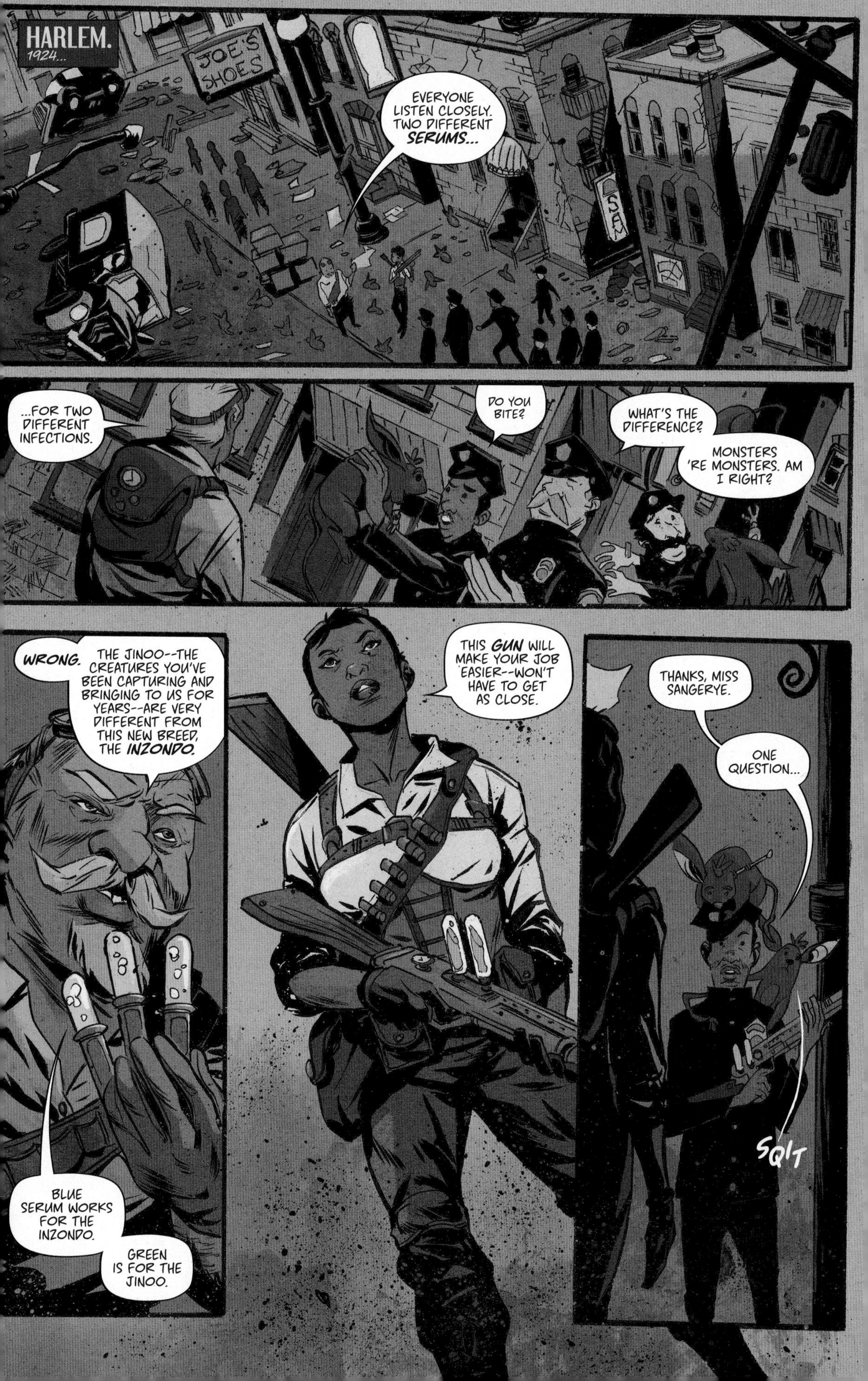
HARLEM. 1924...
JOE'S SHOES
EVERYONE LISTEN CLOSELY. TWO DIFFERENT SERUMS...
SAM
...FOR TWO DIFFERENT INFECTIONS.
DO YOU BITE?
WHAT'S THE DIFFERENCE?
MONSTERS 'RE MONSTERS. AM I RIGHT?
WRONG.
THE JINOO--THE CREATURES YOU'VE BEEN CAPTURING AND BRINGING TO US FOR YEARS--ARE VERY DIFFERENT FROM THIS NEW BREED, THE INZONDO.
BLUE SERUM WORKS FOR THE INZONDO.
GREEN IS FOR THE JINOO.
THIS GUN WILL MAKE YOUR JOB EASIER--WON'T HAVE TO GET AS CLOSE.
THANKS, MISS SANGERYE.
ONE QUESTION...
SQIT

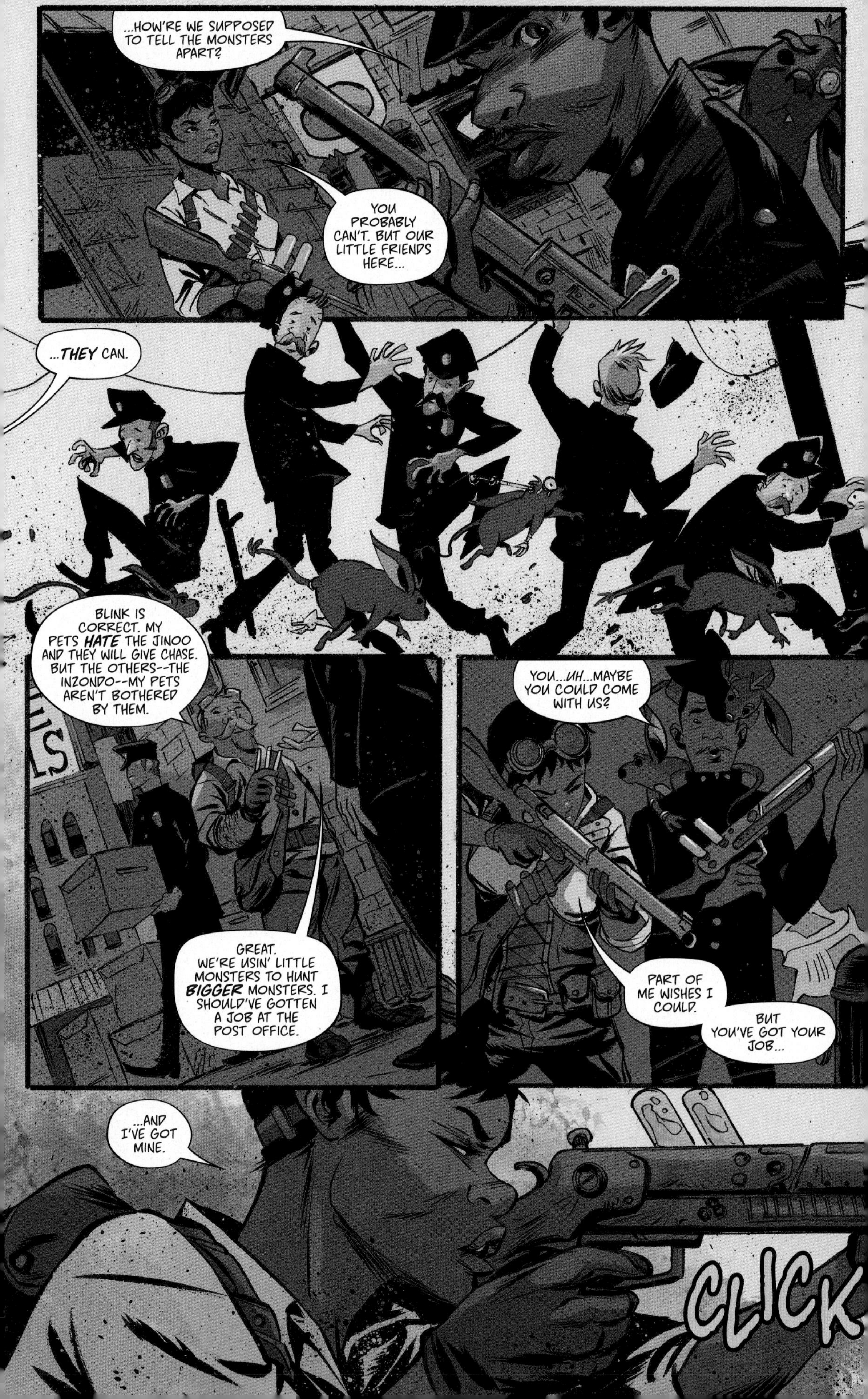
...HOW'RE WE SUPPOSED TO TELL THE MONSTERS APART?
YOU PROBABLY CAN'T. BUT OUR LITTLE FRIENDS HERE...
...THEY CAN.
BLINK IS CORRECT. MY PETS HATE THE JINOO AND THEY WILL GIVE CHASE. BUT THE OTHERS--THE INZONDO--MY PETS AREN'T BOTHERED BY THEM.
GREAT. WE'RE USIN' LITTLE MONSTERS TO HUNT BIGGER MONSTERS. I SHOULD'VE GOTTEN A JOB AT THE POST OFFICE.
YOU...UH...MAYBE YOU COULD COME WITH US?
PART OF ME WISHES I COULD.
BUT YOU'VE GOT YOUR JOB...
...AND I'VE GOT MINE.
CLICK

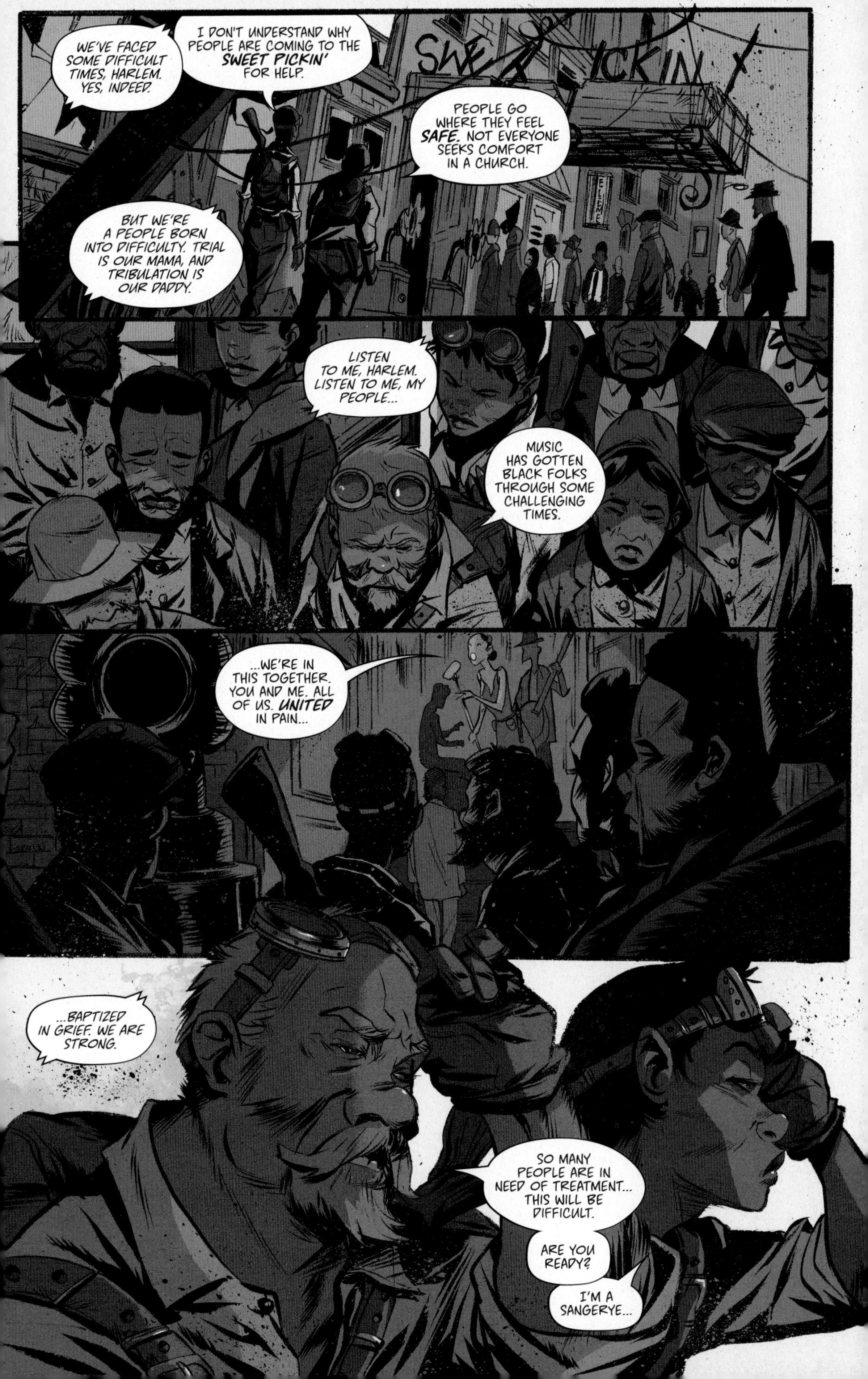
WE'VE FACED SOME DIFFICULT TIMES, HARLEM. YES, INDEED.
I DON'T UNDERSTAND WHY PEOPLE ARE COMING TO THE SWEET PICKIN' FOR HELP.
PEOPLE GO WHERE THEY FEEL SAFE. NOT EVERYONE SEEKS COMFORT IN A CHURCH.
BUT WE'RE A PEOPLE BORN INTO DIFFICULTY. TRIAL IS OUR MAMA, AND TRIBULATION IS OUR DADDY.
LISTEN TO ME, HARLEM. LISTEN TO ME, MY PEOPLE...
MUSIC HAS GOTTEN BLACK FOLKS THROUGH SOME CHALLENGING TIMES.
...WE'RE IN THIS TOGETHER. YOU AND ME. ALL OF US. UNITED IN PAIN...
...BAPTIZED IN GRIEF. WE ARE STRONG.
SO MANY PEOPLE ARE IN NEED OF TREATMENT... THIS WILL BE DIFFICULT.
ARE YOU READY?
I'M A SANGERYE...

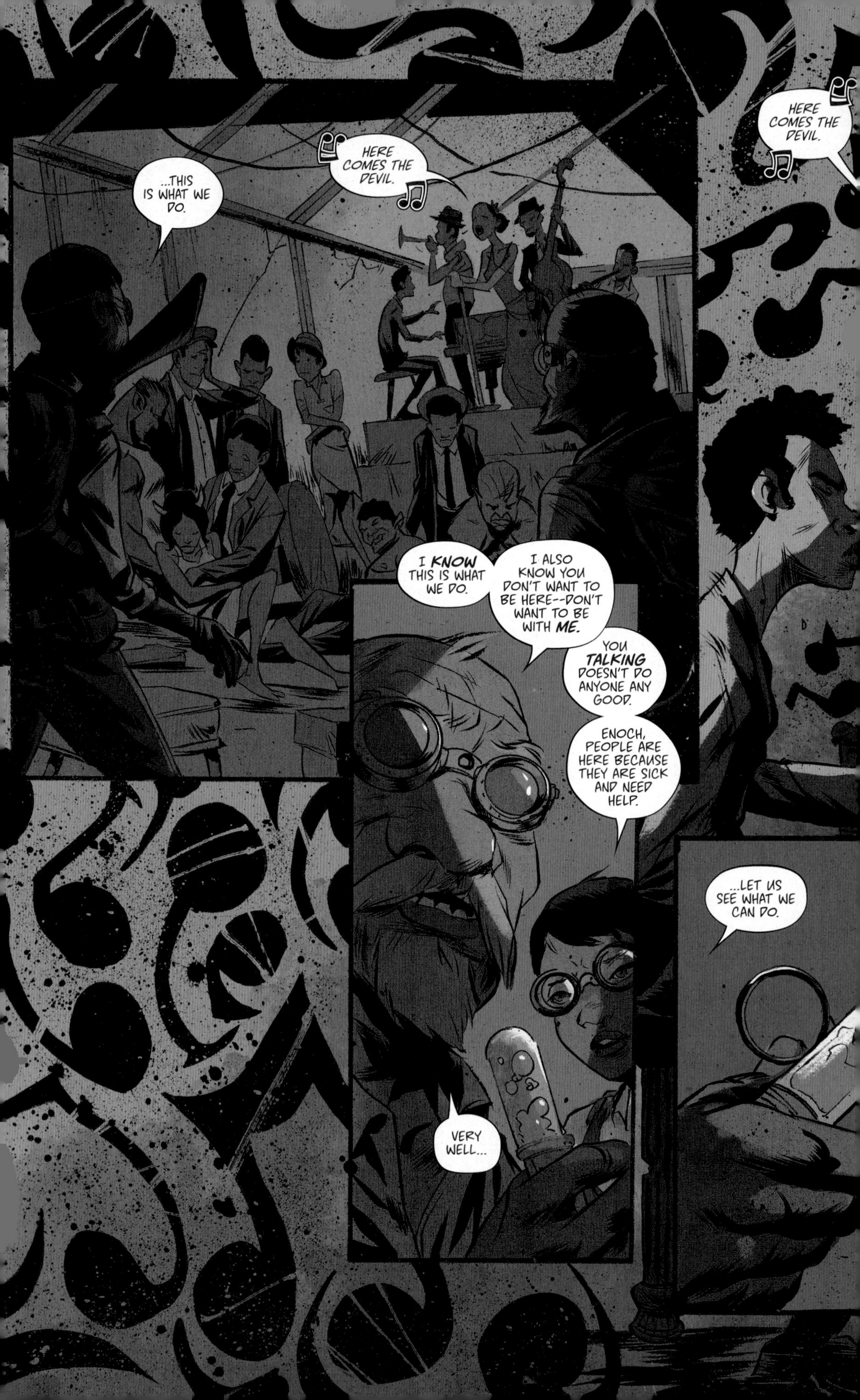

...THIS IS WHAT WE DO.
HERE COMES THE DEVIL.
HERE COMES THE DEVIL.
I KNOW THIS IS WHAT WE DO.
I ALSO KNOW YOU DON'T WANT TO BE HERE--DON'T WANT TO BE WITH ME.
YOU TALKING DOESN'T DO ANYONE ANY GOOD.
ENOCH, PEOPLE ARE HERE BECAUSE THEY ARE SICK AND NEED HELP.
VERY WELL...
...LET US SEE WHAT WE CAN DO.

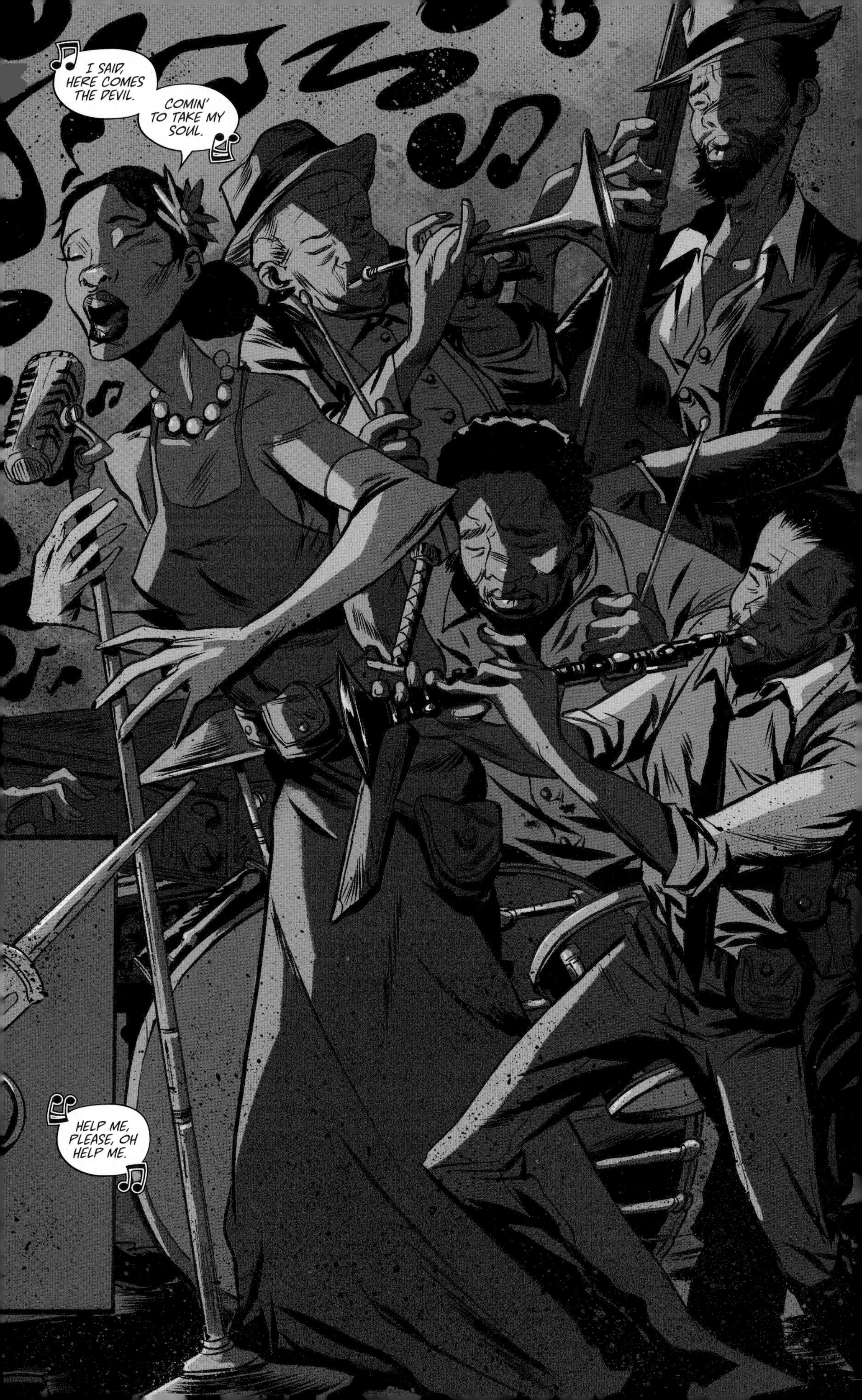
I SAID, HERE COMES THE DEVIL.
COMIN' TO TAKE MY SOUL.
HELP ME, PLEASE, OH HELP ME.

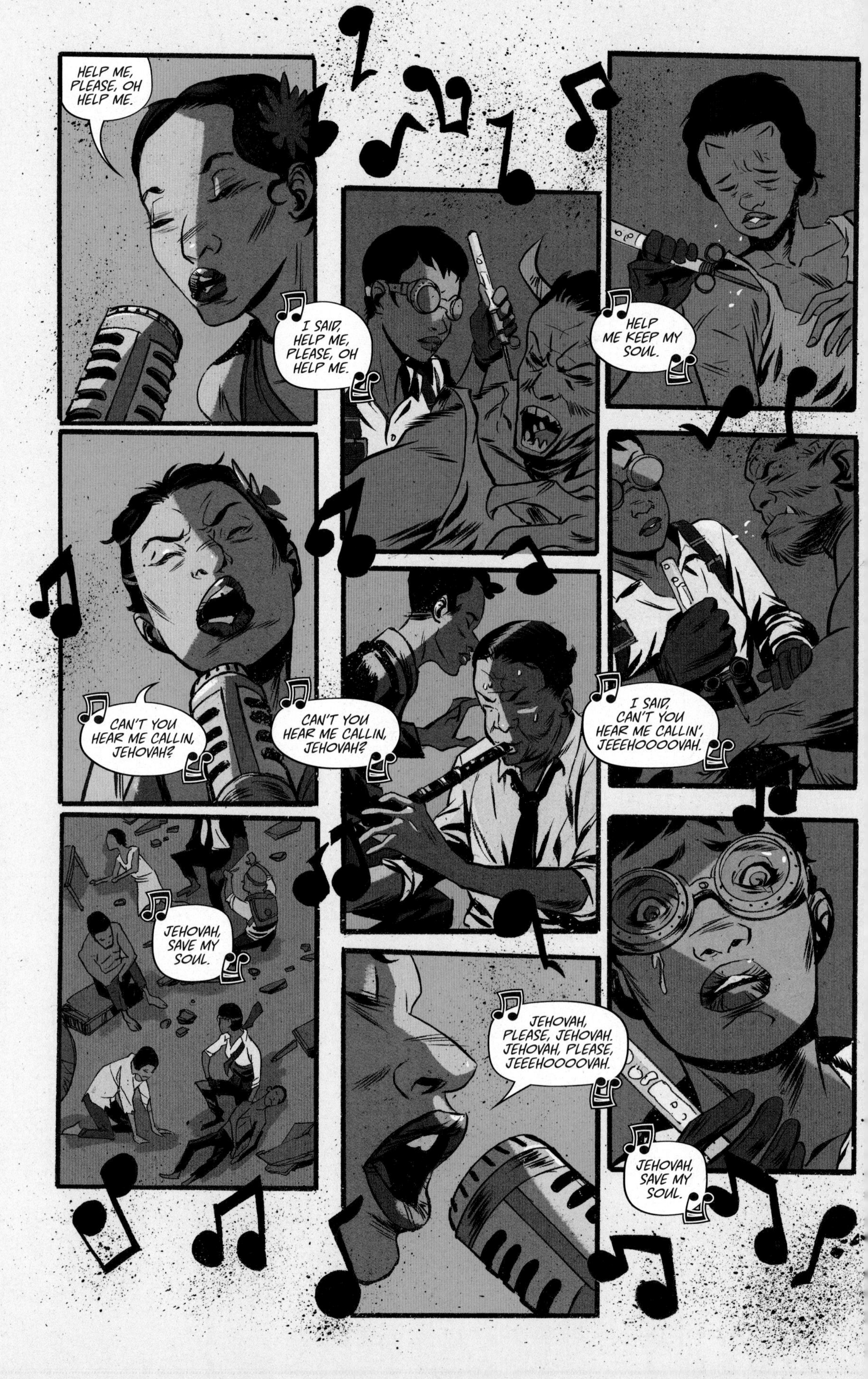
HELP ME, PLEASE, OH HELP ME.
I SAID, HELP ME, PLEASE, OH HELP ME.
HELP ME KEEP MY SOUL.
CAN'T YOU HEAR ME CALLIN, JEHOVAH?
CAN'T YOU HEAR ME CALLIN, JEHOVAH?
I SAID, CAN'T YOU HEAR ME CALLIN', JEEEHOOOOVAH.
JEHOVAH, SAVE MY SOUL.
JEHOVAH, PLEASE, JEHOVAH. JEHOVAH, PLEASE, JEEEHOOOOVAH.
JEHOVAH, SAVE MY SOUL.

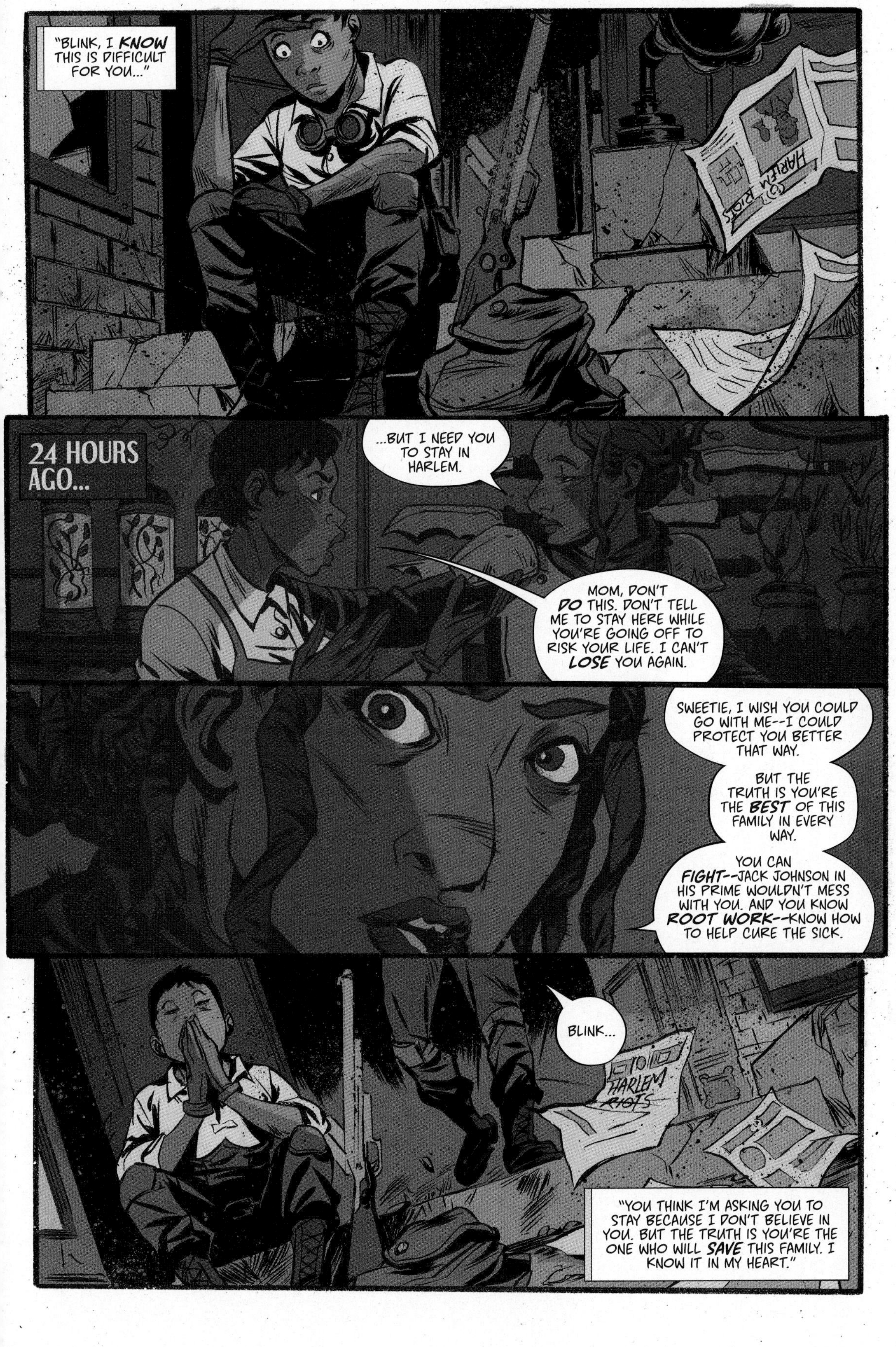
"BLINK, I KNOW THIS IS DIFFICULT FOR YOU..."
HARLEM RIOTS
24 HOURS AGO...
...BUT I NEED YOU TO STAY IN HARLEM.
MOM, DON'T DO THIS. DON'T TELL ME TO STAY HERE WHILE YOU'RE GOING OFF TO RISK YOUR LIFE. I CAN'T LOSE YOU AGAIN.
SWEETIE, I WISH YOU COULD GO WITH ME--I COULD PROTECT YOU BETTER THAT WAY.
BUT THE TRUTH IS YOU'RE THE BEST OF THIS FAMILY IN EVERY WAY.
YOU CAN FIGHT--JACK JOHNSON IN HIS PRIME WOULDN'T MESS WITH YOU. AND YOU KNOW ROOT WORK--KNOW HOW TO HELP CURE THE SICK.
BLINK...
HARLEM RIOTS
"YOU THINK I'M ASKING YOU TO STAY BECAUSE I DON'T BELIEVE IN YOU. BUT THE TRUTH IS YOU'RE THE ONE WHO WILL SAVE THIS FAMILY. I KNOW IT IN MY HEART."

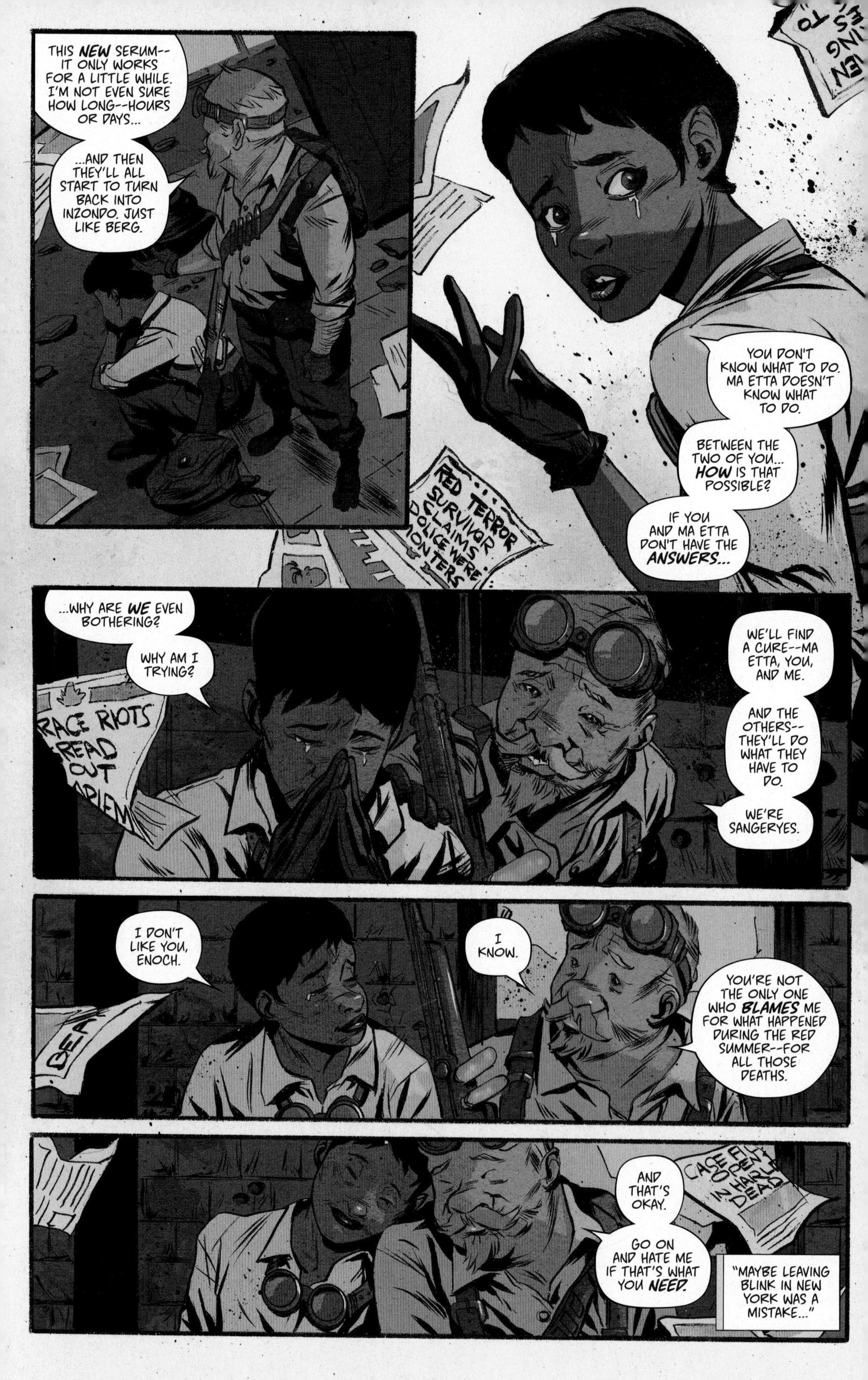

THIS NEW SERUM--IT ONLY WORKS FOR A LITTLE WHILE. I'M NOT EVEN SURE HOW LONG--HOURS OR DAYS...
...AND THEN THEY'LL ALL START TO TURN BACK INTO INZONDO. JUST LIKE BERG.
YOU DON'T KNOW WHAT TO DO. MA ETTA DOESN'T KNOW WHAT TO DO.
BETWEEN THE TWO OF YOU... HOW IS THAT POSSIBLE?
IF YOU AND MA ETTA DON'T HAVE THE ANSWERS...
RED TERROR SURVIVOR CLAIMS POLICE WERE
...WHY ARE WE EVEN BOTHERING?
WHY AM I TRYING?
WE'LL FIND A CURE--MA ETTA, YOU, AND ME.
AND THE OTHERS--THEY'LL DO WHAT THEY HAVE TO DO.
WE'RE SANGERYES.
I DON'T LIKE YOU, ENOCH.
I KNOW.
YOU'RE NOT THE ONLY ONE WHO BLAMES ME FOR WHAT HAPPENED DURING THE RED SUMMER--FOR ALL THOSE DEATHS.
AND THAT'S OKAY.
GO ON AND HATE ME IF THAT'S WHAT YOU NEED.
"MAYBE LEAVING BLINK IN NEW YORK WAS A MISTAKE..."

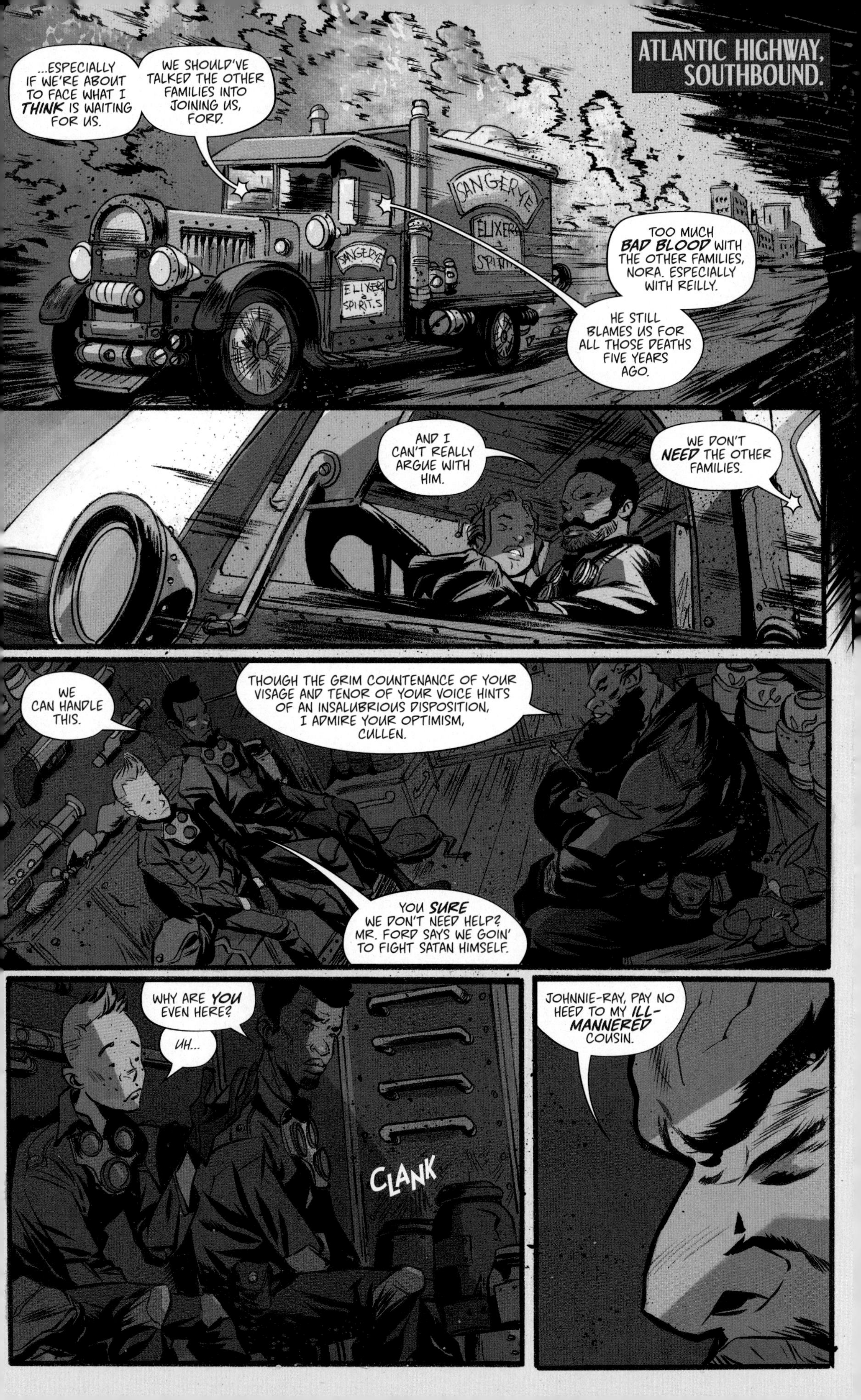
ATLANTIC HIGHWAY, SOUTHBOUND.
WE SHOULD'VE TALKED THE OTHER FAMILIES INTO JOINING US, FORD.
...ESPECIALLY IF WE'RE ABOUT TO FACE WHAT I THINK IS WAITING FOR US.
SANGERYE
ELIXERS
SPIRITS
SANGERYE
ELIXERS & SPIRITS
TOO MUCH BAD BLOOD WITH THE OTHER FAMILIES, NORA. ESPECIALLY WITH REILLY.
HE STILL BLAMES US FOR ALL THOSE DEATHS FIVE YEARS AGO.
AND I CAN'T REALLY ARGUE WITH HIM.
WE DON'T NEED THE OTHER FAMILIES.
WE CAN HANDLE THIS.
THOUGH THE GRIM COUNTENANCE OF YOUR VISAGE AND TENOR OF YOUR VOICE HINTS OF AN INSALUBRIOUS DISPOSITION, I ADMIRE YOUR OPTIMISM, CULLEN.
YOU SURE WE DON'T NEED HELP? MR. FORD SAYS WE GOIN' TO FIGHT SATAN HIMSELF.
WHY ARE YOU EVEN HERE?
UH...
CLANK
JOHNNIE-RAY, PAY NO HEED TO MY ILL-MANNERED COUSIN.

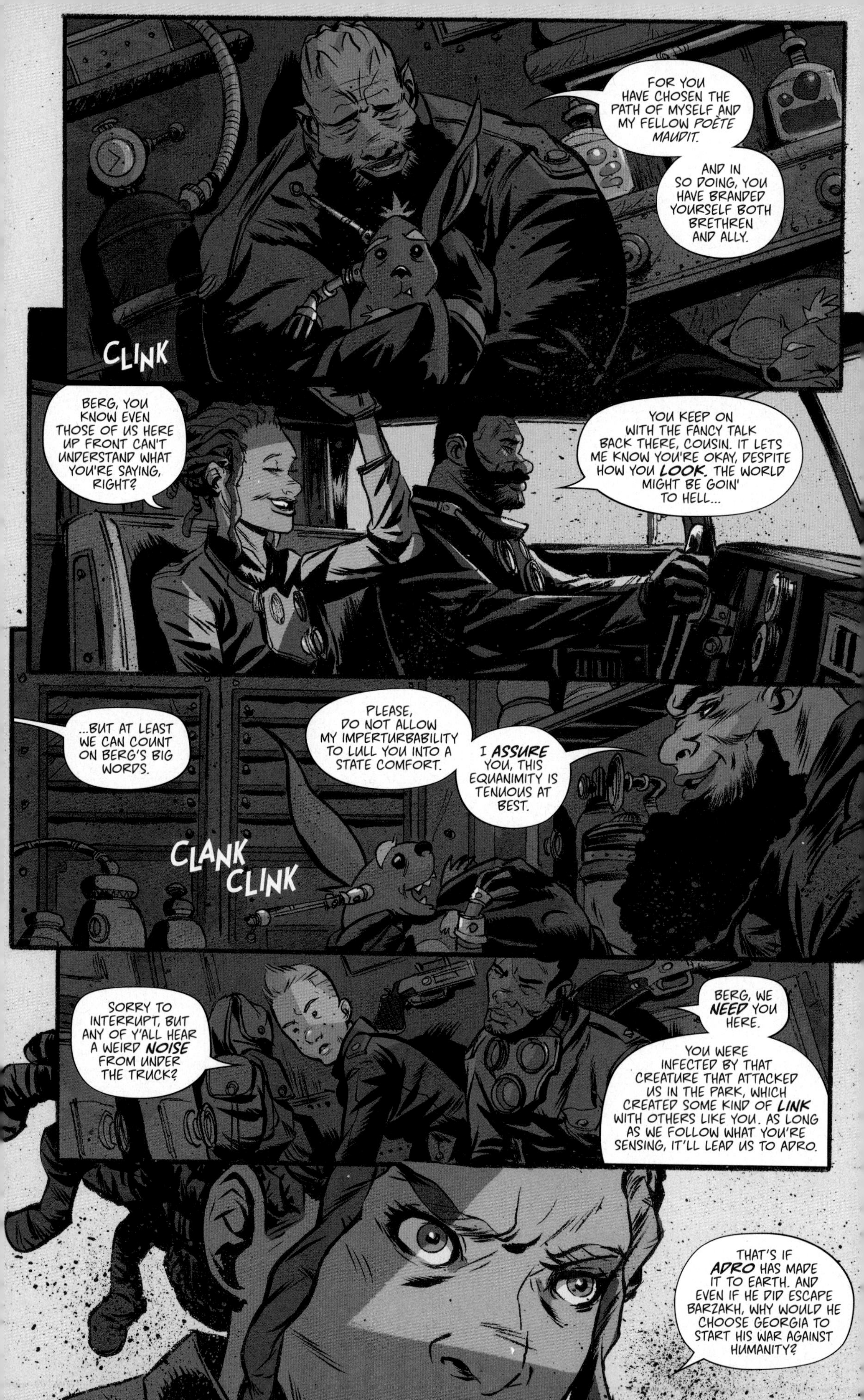
FOR YOU HAVE CHOSEN THE PATH OF MYSELF AND MY FELLOW POÈTE MAUDIT.
AND IN SO DOING, YOU HAVE BRANDED YOURSELF BOTH BRETHREN AND ALLY.
CLINK
BERG, YOU KNOW EVEN THOSE OF US HERE UP FRONT CAN'T UNDERSTAND WHAT YOU'RE SAYING, RIGHT?
YOU KEEP ON WITH THE FANCY TALK BACK THERE, COUSIN. IT LETS ME KNOW YOU'RE OKAY, DESPITE HOW YOU LOOK. THE WORLD MIGHT BE GOIN' TO HELL...
...BUT AT LEAST WE CAN COUNT ON BERG'S BIG WORDS.
PLEASE, DO NOT ALLOW MY IMPERTURBABILITY TO LULL YOU INTO A STATE COMFORT.
I ASSURE YOU, THIS EQUANIMITY IS TENUOUS AT BEST.
CLANK
CLINK
SORRY TO INTERRUPT, BUT ANY OF Y'ALL HEAR A WEIRD NOISE FROM UNDER THE TRUCK?
BERG, WE NEED YOU HERE.
YOU WERE INFECTED BY THAT CREATURE THAT ATTACKED US IN THE PARK, WHICH CREATED SOME KIND OF LINK WITH OTHERS LIKE YOU. AS LONG AS WE FOLLOW WHAT YOU'RE SENSING, IT'LL LEAD US TO ADRO.
THAT'S IF ADRO HAS MADE IT TO EARTH. AND EVEN IF HE DID ESCAPE BARZAKH, WHY WOULD HE CHOOSE GEORGIA TO START HIS WAR AGAINST HUMANITY?

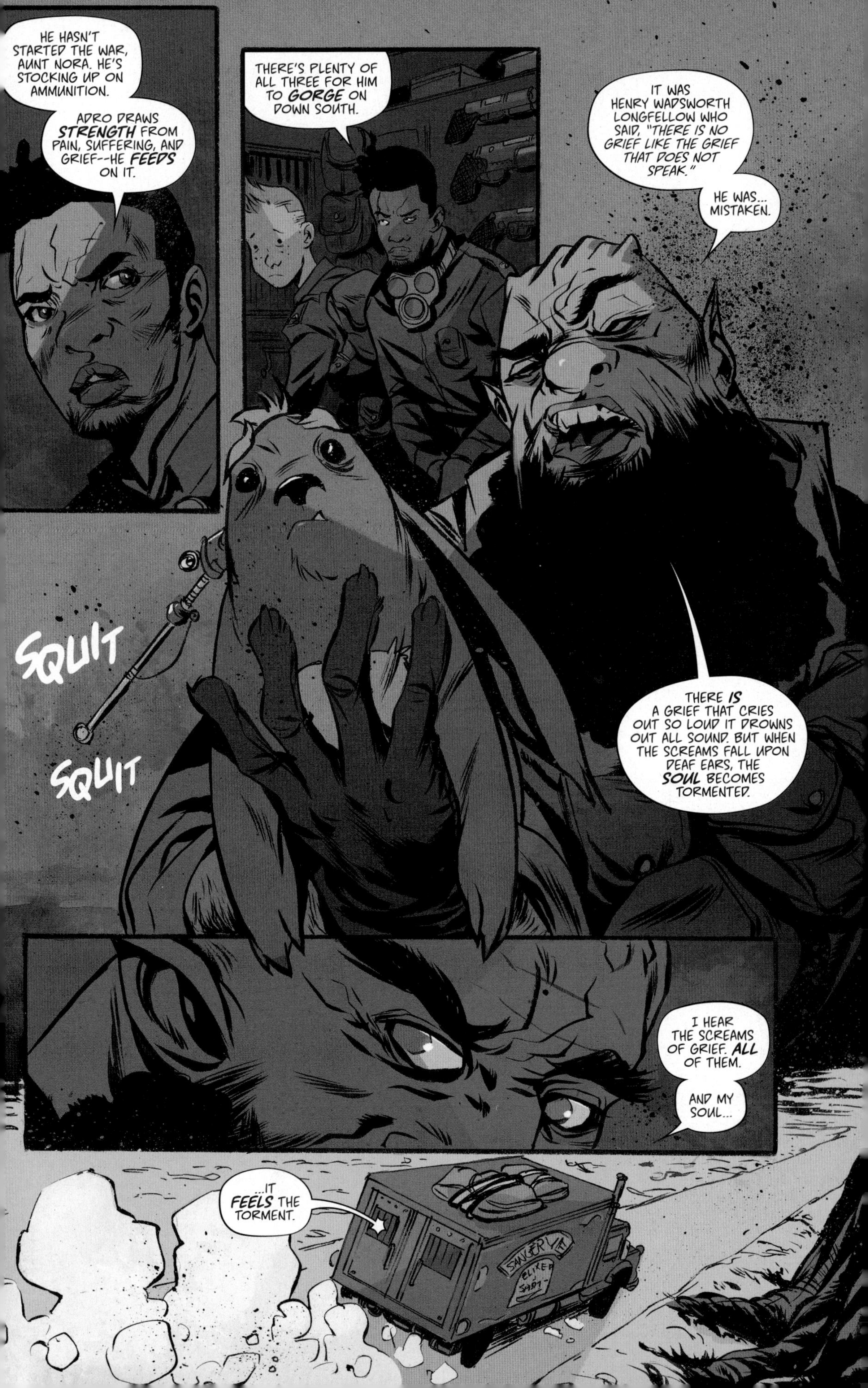
HE HASN'T STARTED THE WAR, AUNT NORA. HE'S STOCKING UP ON AMMUNITION.
ADRO DRAWS STRENGTH FROM PAIN, SUFFERING, AND GRIEF--HE FEEDS ON IT.
THERE'S PLENTY OF ALL THREE FOR HIM TO GORGE ON DOWN SOUTH.
IT WAS HENRY WADSWORTH LONGFELLOW WHO SAID, "THERE IS NO GRIEF LIKE THE GRIEF THAT DOES NOT SPEAK."
HE WAS... MISTAKEN.
SQUIT
SQUIT
THERE IS A GRIEF THAT CRIES OUT SO LOUD IT DROWNS OUT ALL SOUND. BUT WHEN THE SCREAMS FALL UPON DEAF EARS, THE SOUL BECOMES TORMENTED.
I HEAR THE SCREAMS OF GRIEF. ALL OF THEM.
AND MY SOUL...
...IT FEELS THE TORMENT.

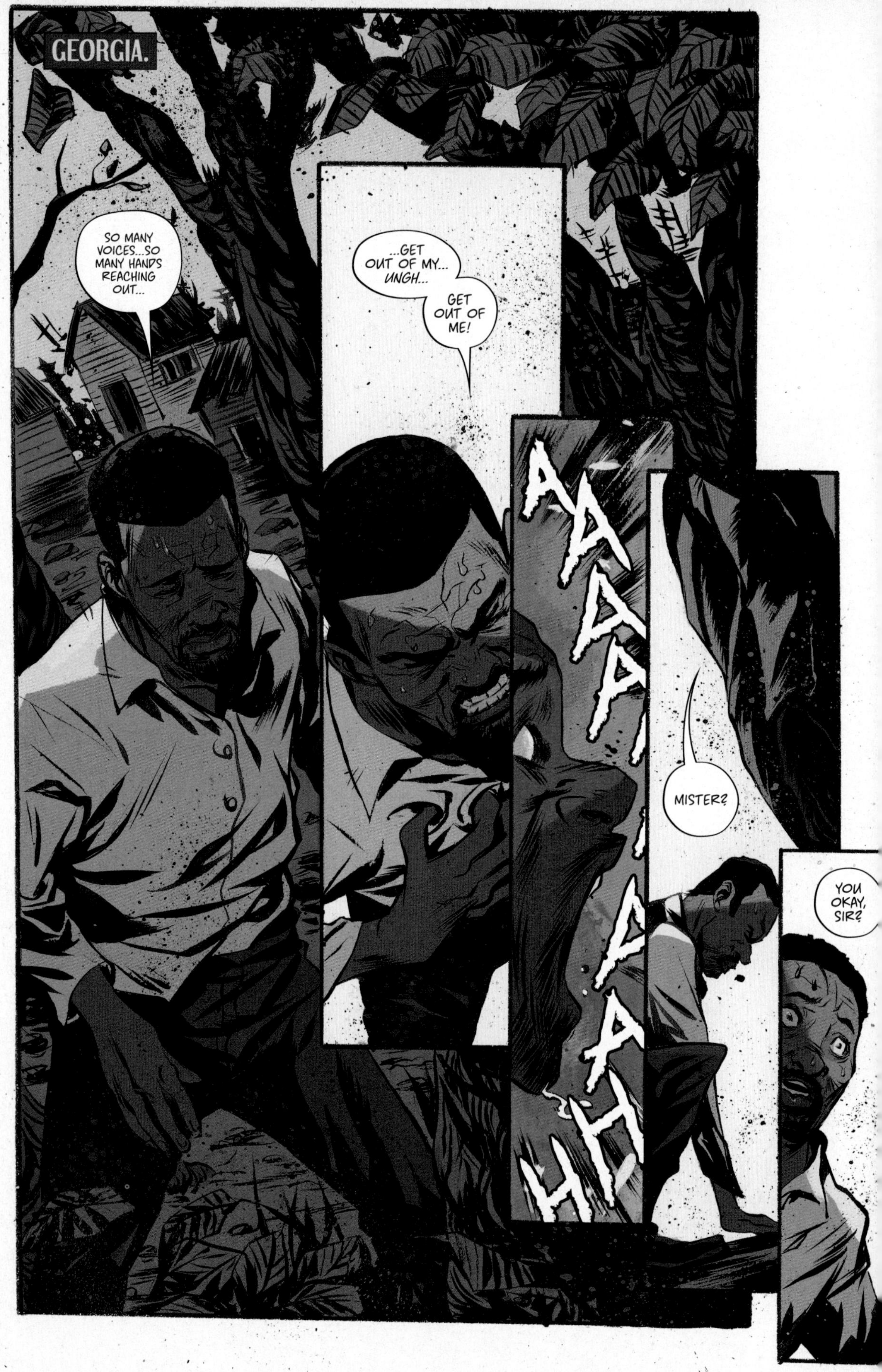
GEORGIA.
SO MANY VOICES...SO MANY HANDS REACHING OUT...
...GET OUT OF MY... UNGH...
GET OUT OF ME!
AAAAAAAHHH
MISTER?
YOU OKAY, SIR?

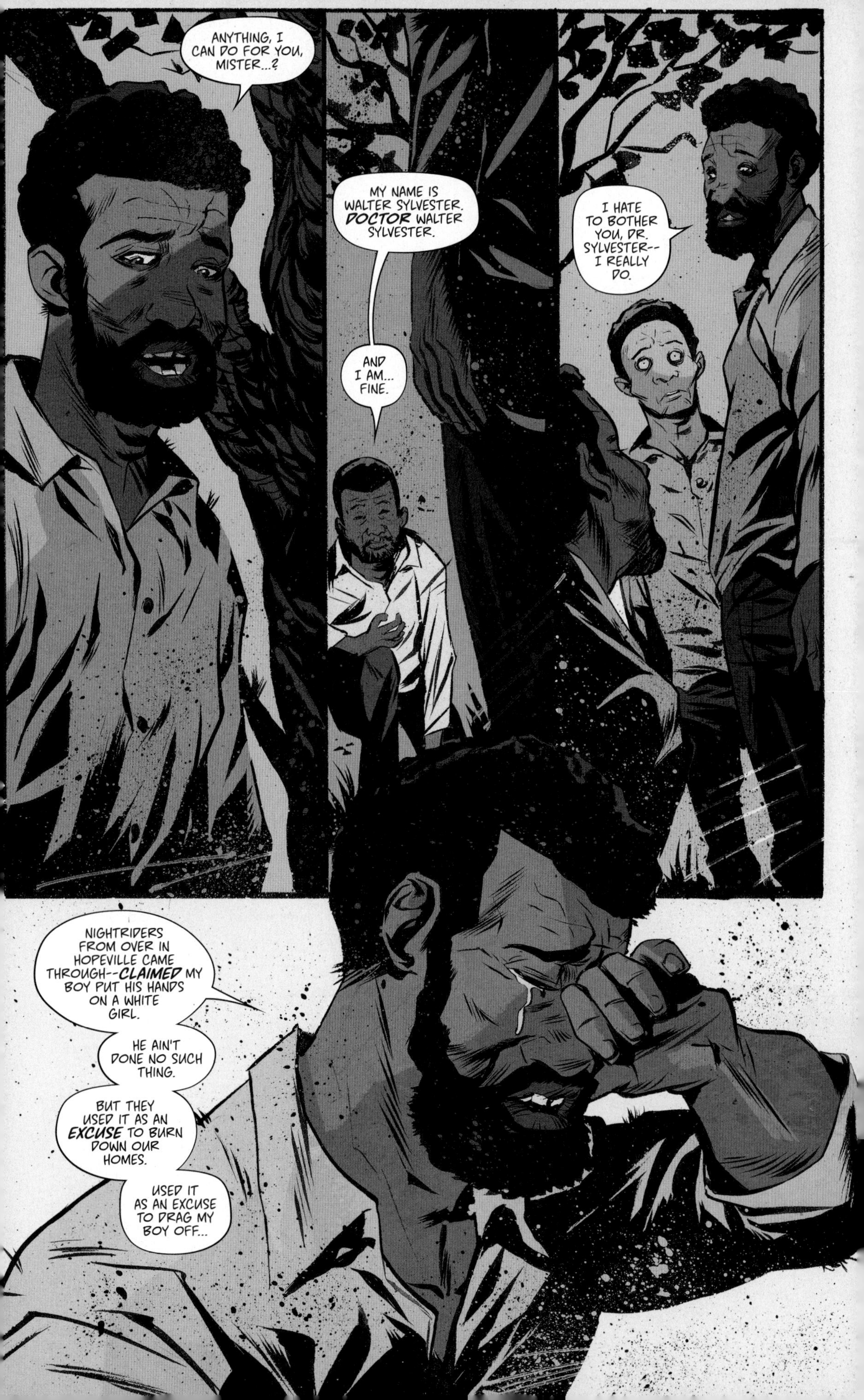
ANYTHING, I CAN DO FOR YOU, MISTER...?
MY NAME IS WALTER SYLVESTER. DOCTOR WALTER SYLVESTER.
AND I AM... FINE.
I HATE TO BOTHER YOU, DR. SYLVESTER-- I REALLY DO.
NIGHTRIDERS FROM OVER IN HOPEVILLE CAME THROUGH--CLAIMED MY BOY PUT HIS HANDS ON A WHITE GIRL.
HE AIN'T DONE NO SUCH THING.
BUT THEY USED IT AS AN EXCUSE TO BURN DOWN OUR HOMES.
USED IT AS AN EXCUSE TO DRAG MY BOY OFF...

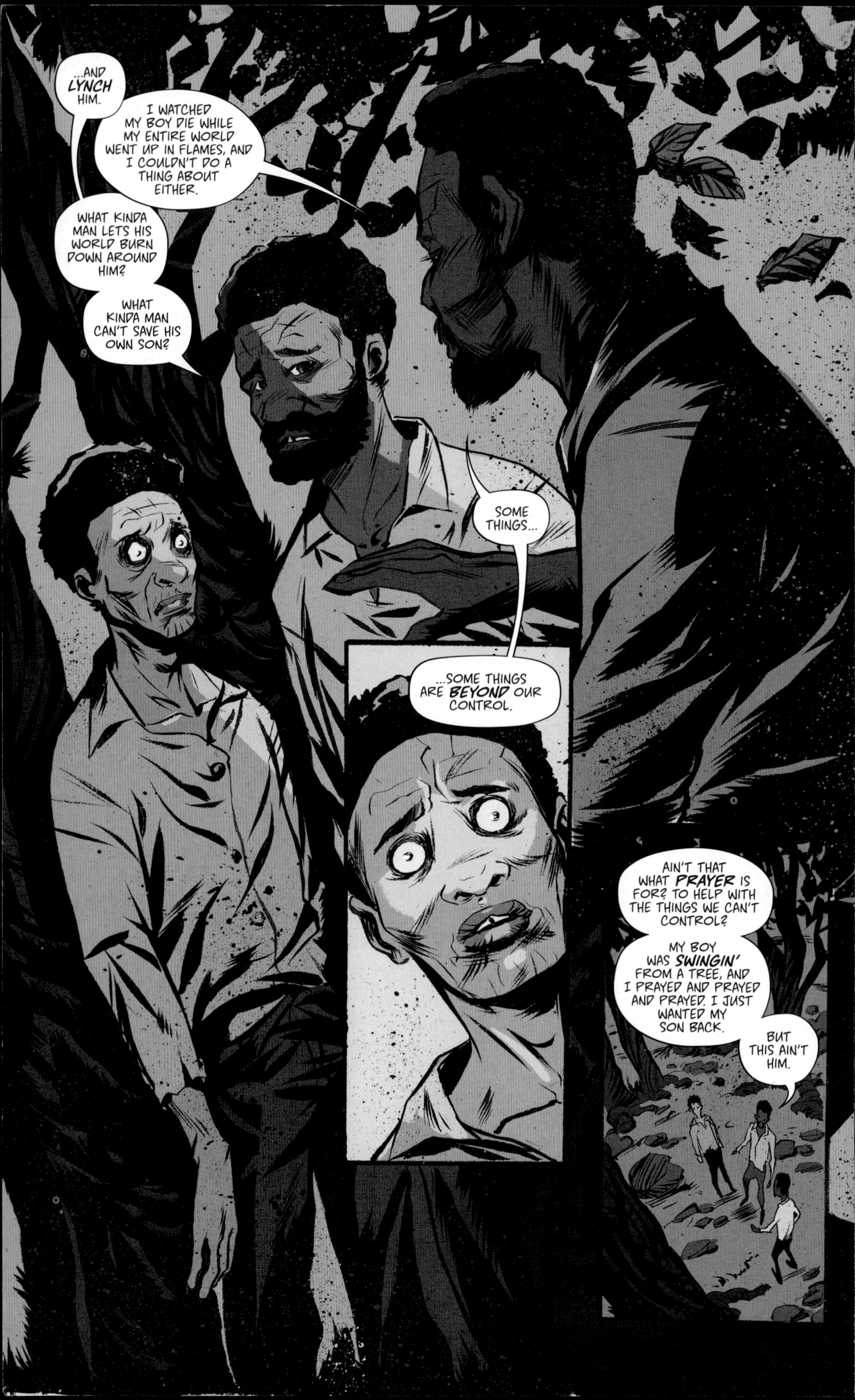
...AND LYNCH HIM.
I WATCHED MY BOY DIE WHILE MY ENTIRE WORLD WENT UP IN FLAMES, AND I COULDN'T DO A THING ABOUT EITHER.
WHAT KINDA MAN LETS HIS WORLD BURN DOWN AROUND HIM?
WHAT KINDA MAN CAN'T SAVE HIS OWN SON?
SOME THINGS...
...SOME THINGS ARE BEYOND OUR CONTROL.
AIN'T THAT WHAT PRAYER IS FOR? TO HELP WITH THE THINGS WE CAN'T CONTROL?
MY BOY WAS SWINGIN' FROM A TREE, AND I PRAYED AND PRAYED AND PRAYED. I JUST WANTED MY SON BACK.
BUT THIS AIN'T HIM.

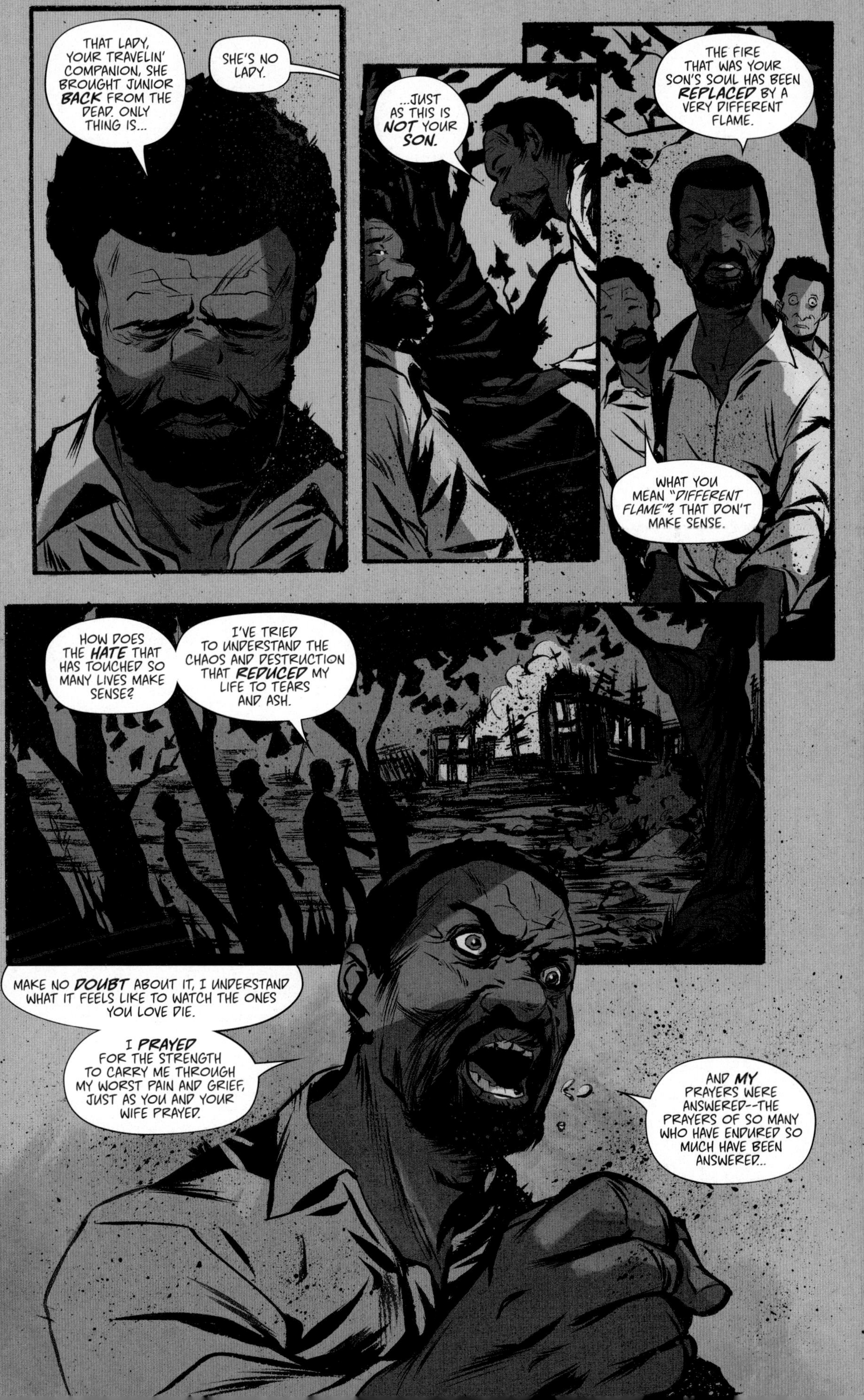
THAT LADY, YOUR TRAVELIN' COMPANION, SHE BROUGHT JUNIOR BACK FROM THE DEAD. ONLY THING IS...
SHE'S NO LADY.
...JUST AS THIS IS NOT YOUR SON.
THE FIRE THAT WAS YOUR SON'S SOUL HAS BEEN REPLACED BY A VERY DIFFERENT FLAME.
WHAT YOU MEAN "DIFFERENT FLAME"? THAT DON'T MAKE SENSE.
HOW DOES THE HATE THAT HAS TOUCHED SO MANY LIVES MAKE SENSE?
I'VE TRIED TO UNDERSTAND THE CHAOS AND DESTRUCTION THAT REDUCED MY LIFE TO TEARS AND ASH.
MAKE NO DOUBT ABOUT IT, I UNDERSTAND WHAT IT FEELS LIKE TO WATCH THE ONES YOU LOVE DIE.
I PRAYED FOR THE STRENGTH TO CARRY ME THROUGH MY WORST PAIN AND GRIEF, JUST AS YOU AND YOUR WIFE PRAYED.
AND MY PRAYERS WERE ANSWERED--THE PRAYERS OF SO MANY WHO HAVE ENDURED SO MUCH HAVE BEEN ANSWERED...

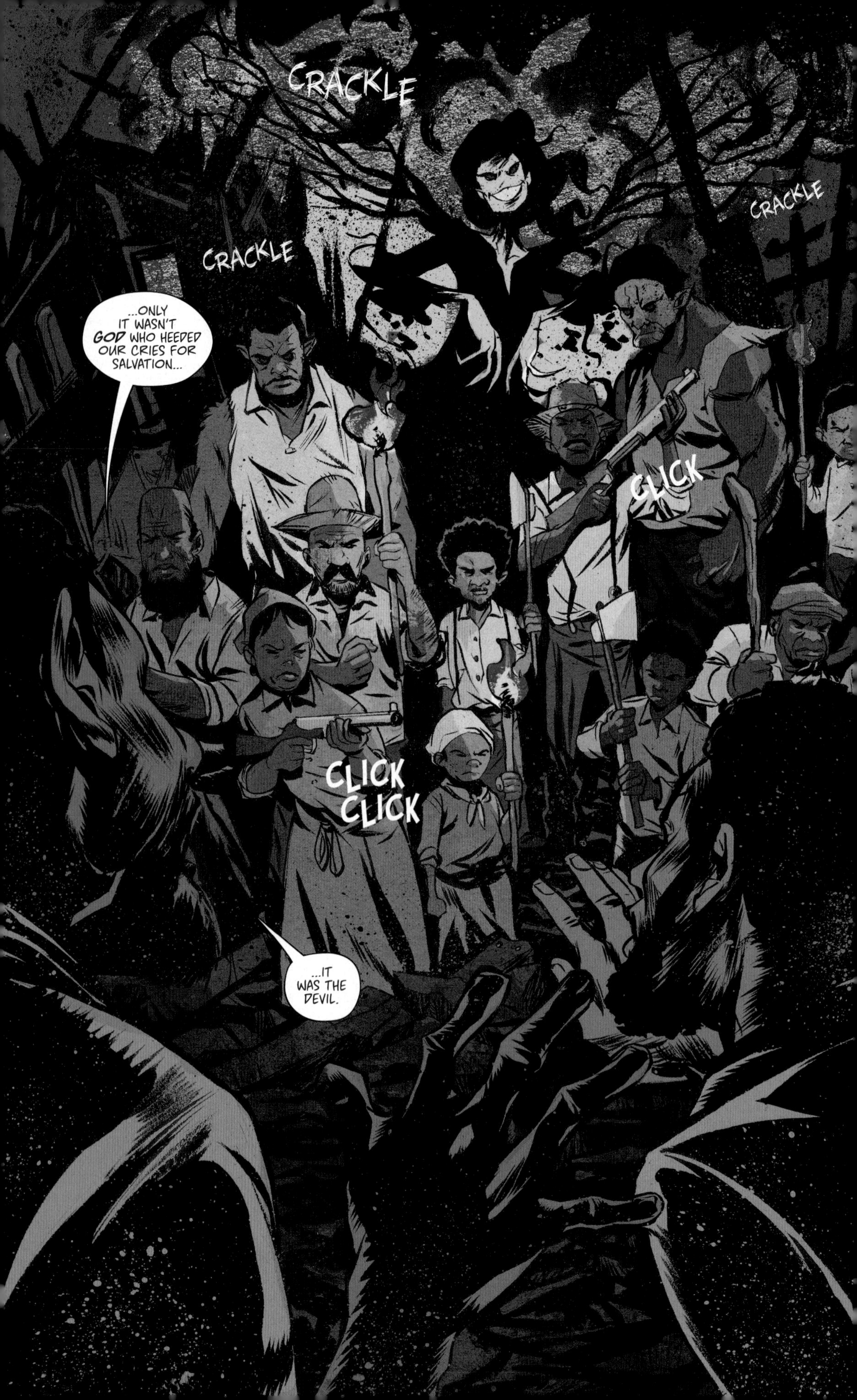
CRACKLE
CRACKLE
CRACKLE
...ONLY IT WASN'T **GOD** WHO HEEDED OUR CRIES FOR SALVATION...
CLICK
CLICK CLICK
...IT WAS THE DEVIL.

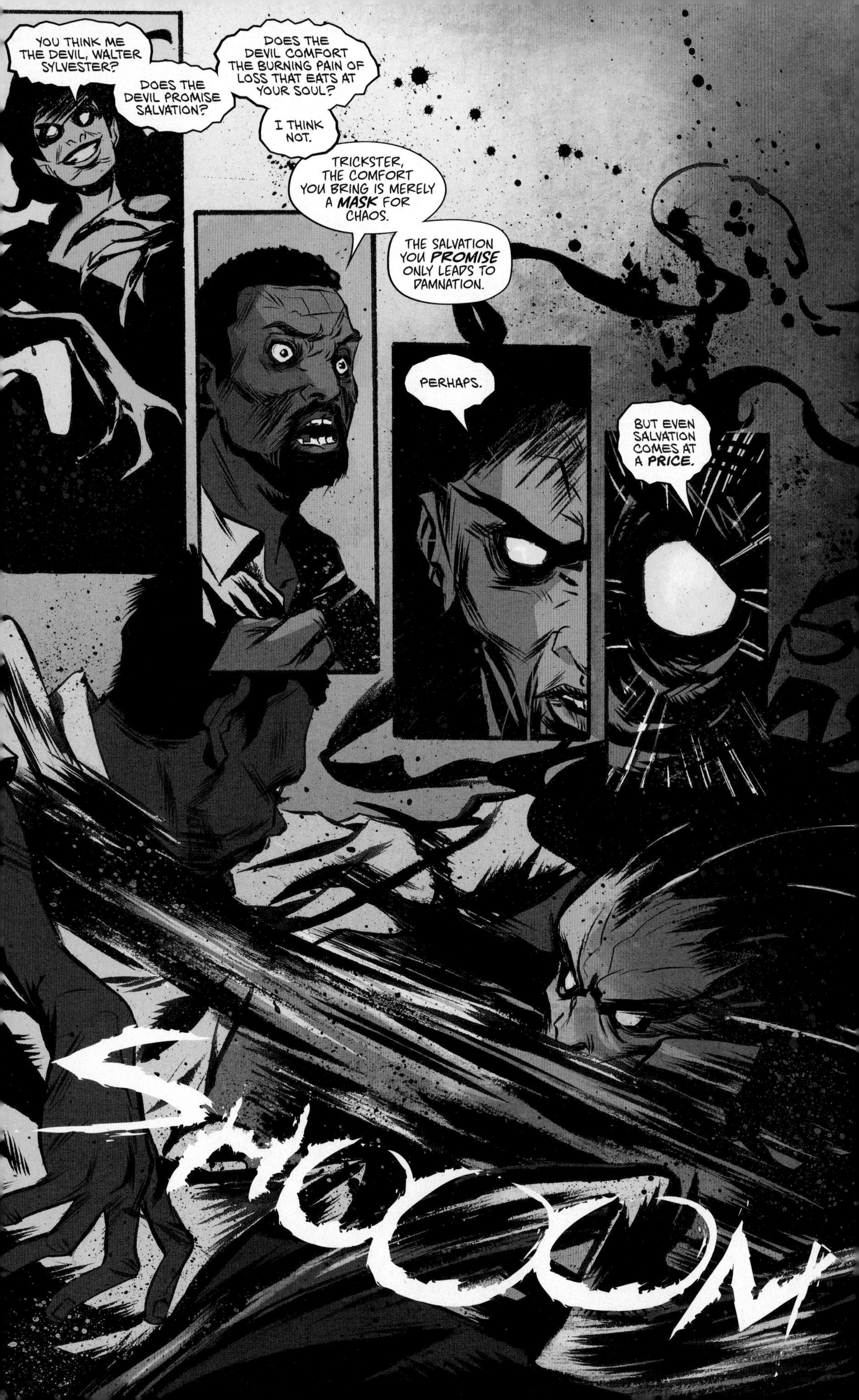
YOU THINK ME THE DEVIL, WALTER SYLVESTER?
DOES THE DEVIL PROMISE SALVATION?
DOES THE DEVIL COMFORT THE BURNING PAIN OF LOSS THAT EATS AT YOUR SOUL?
I THINK NOT.
TRICKSTER, THE COMFORT YOU BRING IS MERELY A MASK FOR CHAOS.
THE SALVATION YOU PROMISE ONLY LEADS TO DAMNATION.
PERHAPS.
BUT EVEN SALVATION COMES AT A PRICE.
SHOOOM

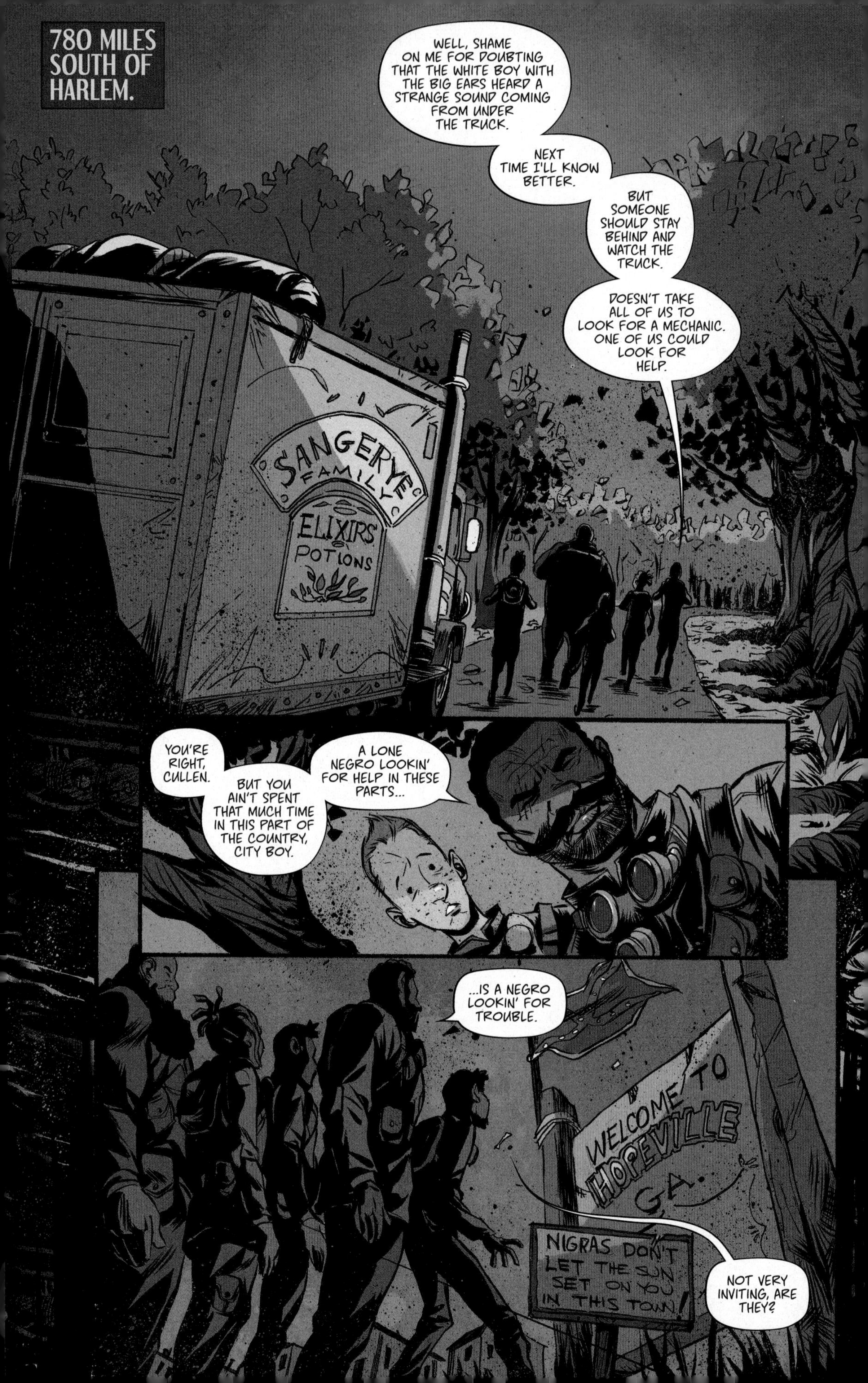
780 MILES SOUTH OF HARLEM.
WELL, SHAME ON ME FOR DOUBTING THAT THE WHITE BOY WITH THE BIG EARS HEARD A STRANGE SOUND COMING FROM UNDER THE TRUCK.
NEXT TIME I'LL KNOW BETTER.
BUT SOMEONE SHOULD STAY BEHIND AND WATCH THE TRUCK.
DOESN'T TAKE ALL OF US TO LOOK FOR A MECHANIC. ONE OF US COULD LOOK FOR HELP.
SANGERYE FAMILY
ELIXIRS' POTIONS
YOU'RE RIGHT, CULLEN.
BUT YOU AIN'T SPENT THAT MUCH TIME IN THIS PART OF THE COUNTRY, CITY BOY.
A LONE NEGRO LOOKIN' FOR HELP IN THESE PARTS...
...IS A NEGRO LOOKIN' FOR TROUBLE.
WELCOME TO HOPEVILLE GA.
NIGRAS DON'T LET THE SUN SET ON YOU IN THIS TOWN!
NOT VERY INVITING, ARE THEY?

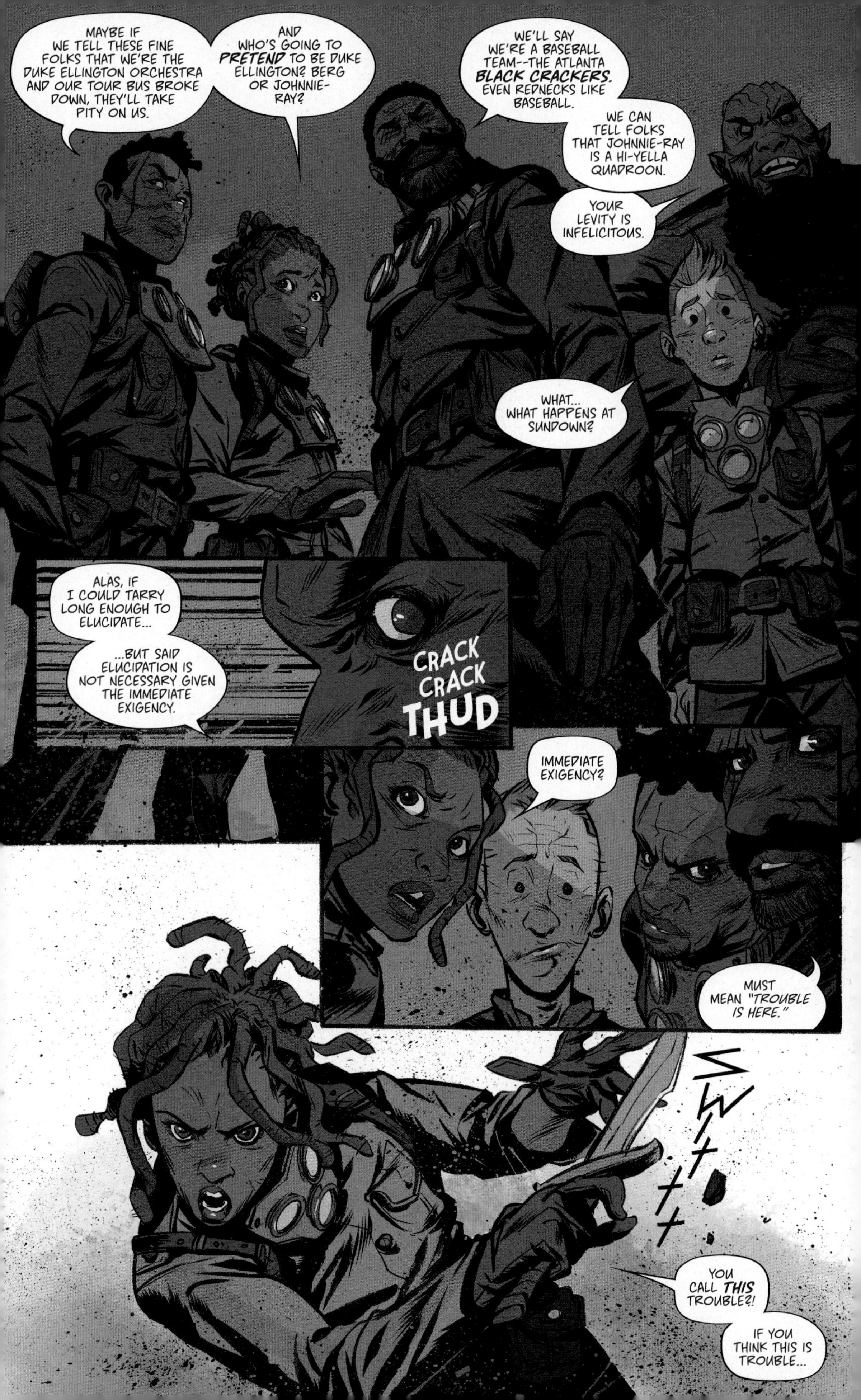
MAYBE IF WE TELL THESE FINE FOLKS THAT WE'RE THE DUKE ELLINGTON ORCHESTRA AND OUR TOUR BUS BROKE DOWN, THEY'LL TAKE PITY ON US.
AND WHO'S GOING TO *PRETEND* TO BE DUKE ELLINGTON? BERG OR JOHNNIE-RAY?
WE'LL SAY WE'RE A BASEBALL TEAM--THE ATLANTA *BLACK CRACKERS.* EVEN REDNECKS LIKE BASEBALL.
WE CAN TELL FOLKS THAT JOHNNIE-RAY IS A HI-YELLA QUADROON.
YOUR LEVITY IS INFELICITOUS.
WHAT... WHAT HAPPENS AT SUNDOWN?
ALAS, IF I COULD TARRY LONG ENOUGH TO ELUCIDATE...
...BUT SAID ELUCIDATION IS NOT NECESSARY GIVEN THE IMMEDIATE EXIGENCY.
CRACK CRACK THUD
IMMEDIATE EXIGENCY?
MUST MEAN "TROUBLE IS HERE."
SWITTT
YOU CALL *THIS* TROUBLE?!
IF YOU THINK THIS IS TROUBLE...

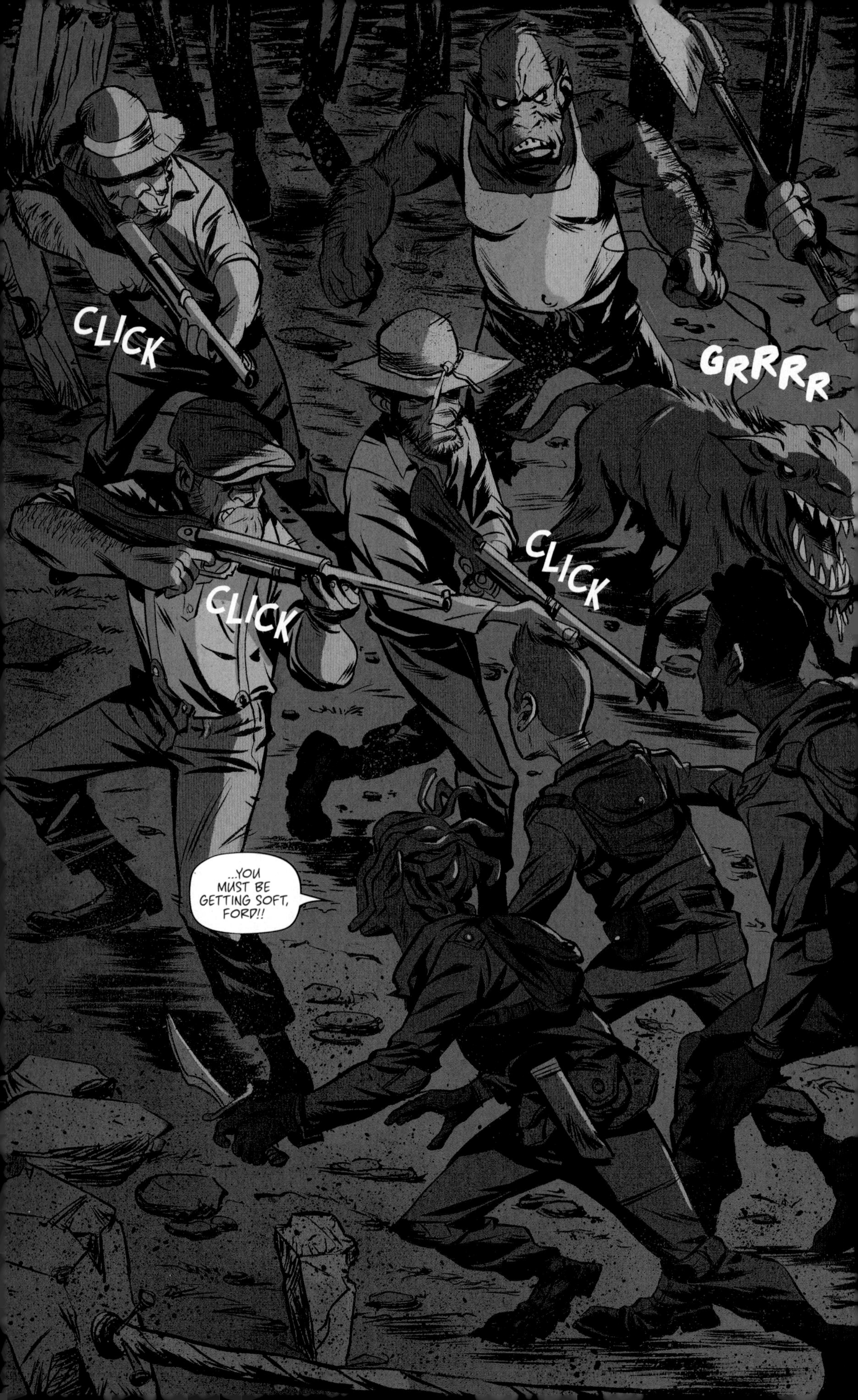
CLICK
GRRRR
CLICK
CLICK
...YOU MUST BE GETTING SOFT, FORD!!

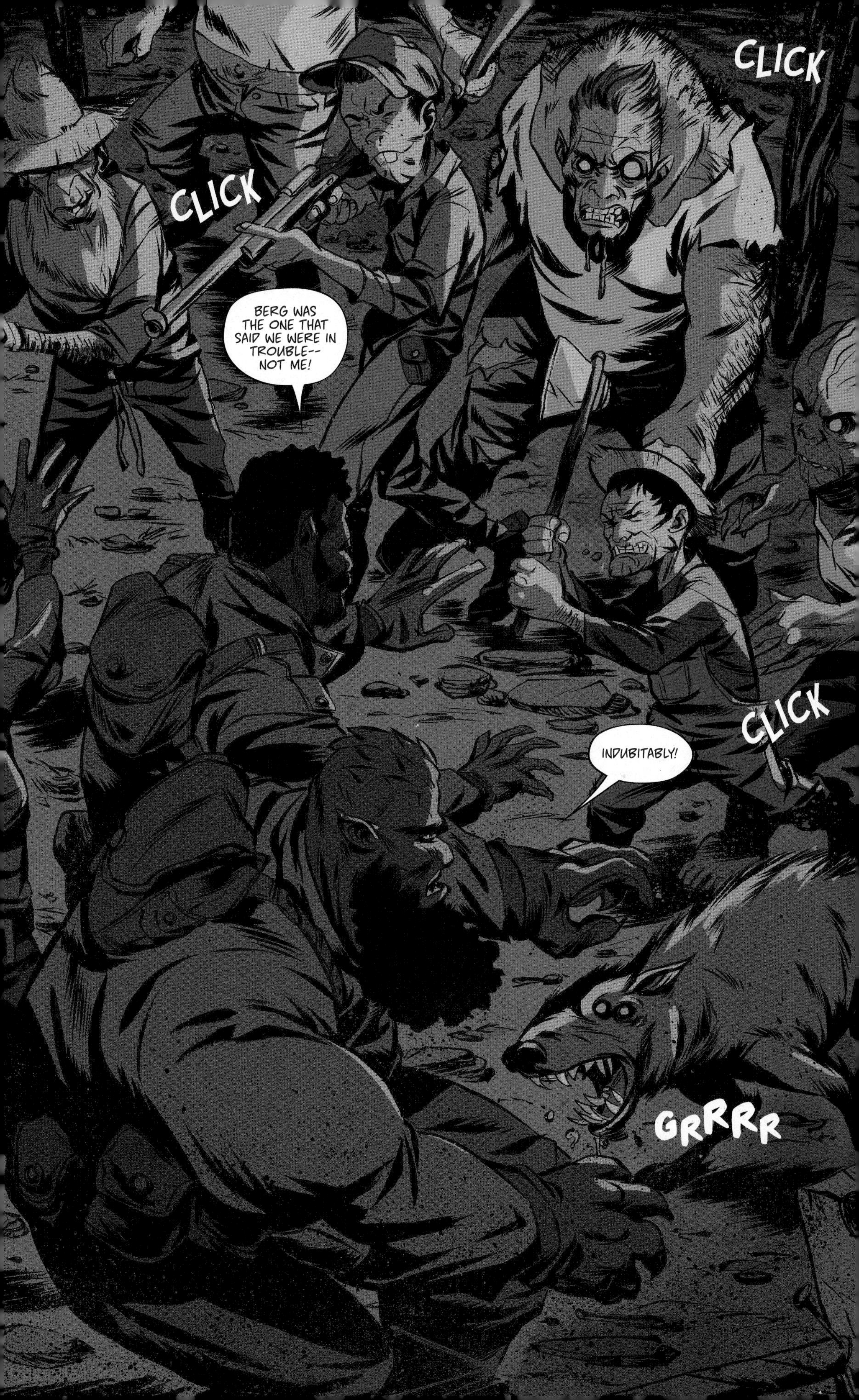
CLICK
CLICK
BERG WAS THE ONE THAT SAID WE WERE IN TROUBLE-- NOT ME!
CLICK
INDUBITABLY!
GRRRR

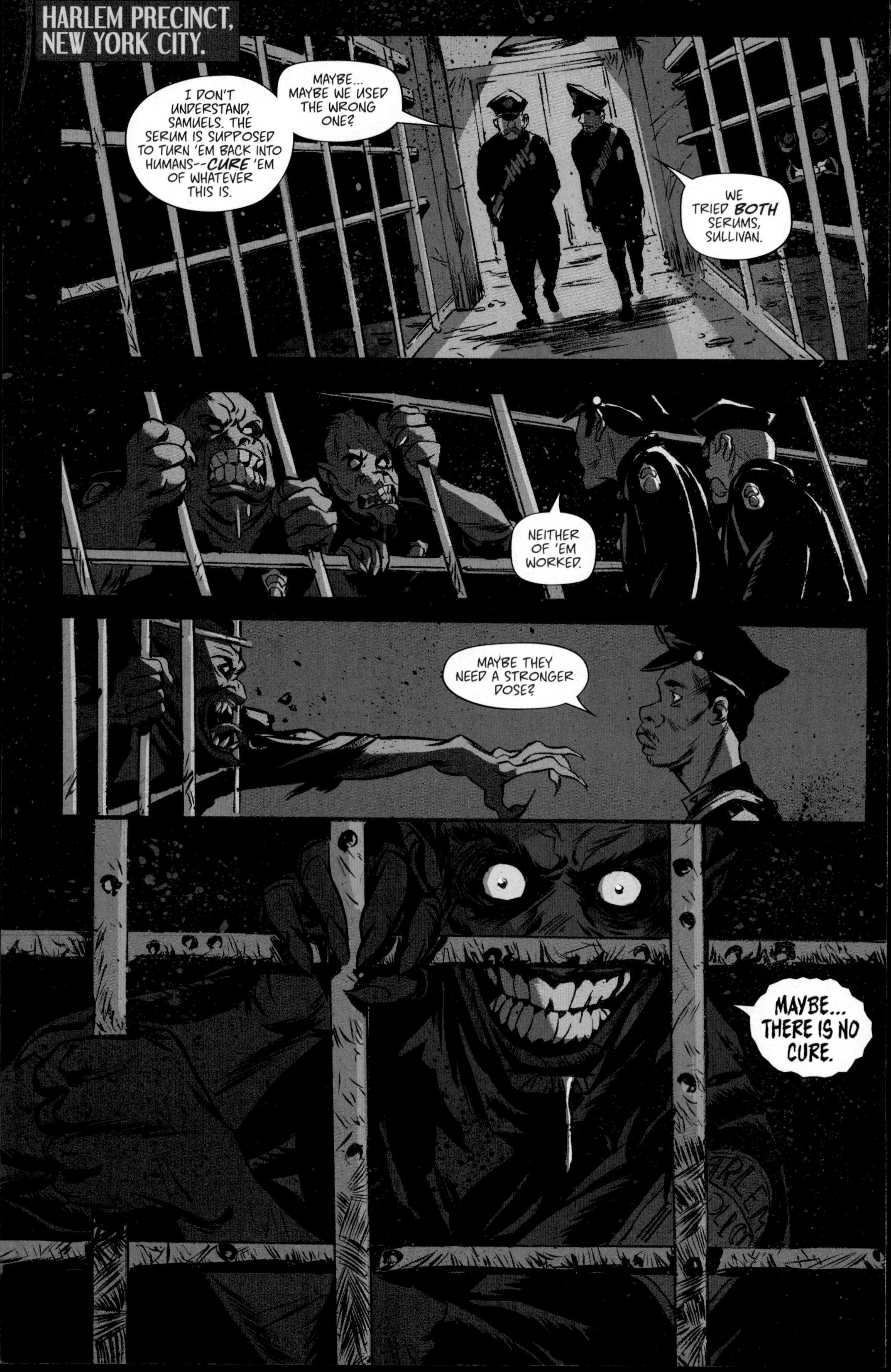
HARLEM PRECINCT, NEW YORK CITY.
I DON'T UNDERSTAND, SAMUELS. THE SERUM IS SUPPOSED TO TURN 'EM BACK INTO HUMANS--CURE 'EM OF WHATEVER THIS IS.
MAYBE... MAYBE WE USED THE WRONG ONE?
WE TRIED BOTH SERUMS, SULLIVAN.
NEITHER OF 'EM WORKED.
MAYBE THEY NEED A STRONGER DOSE?
MAYBE... THERE IS NO CURE.

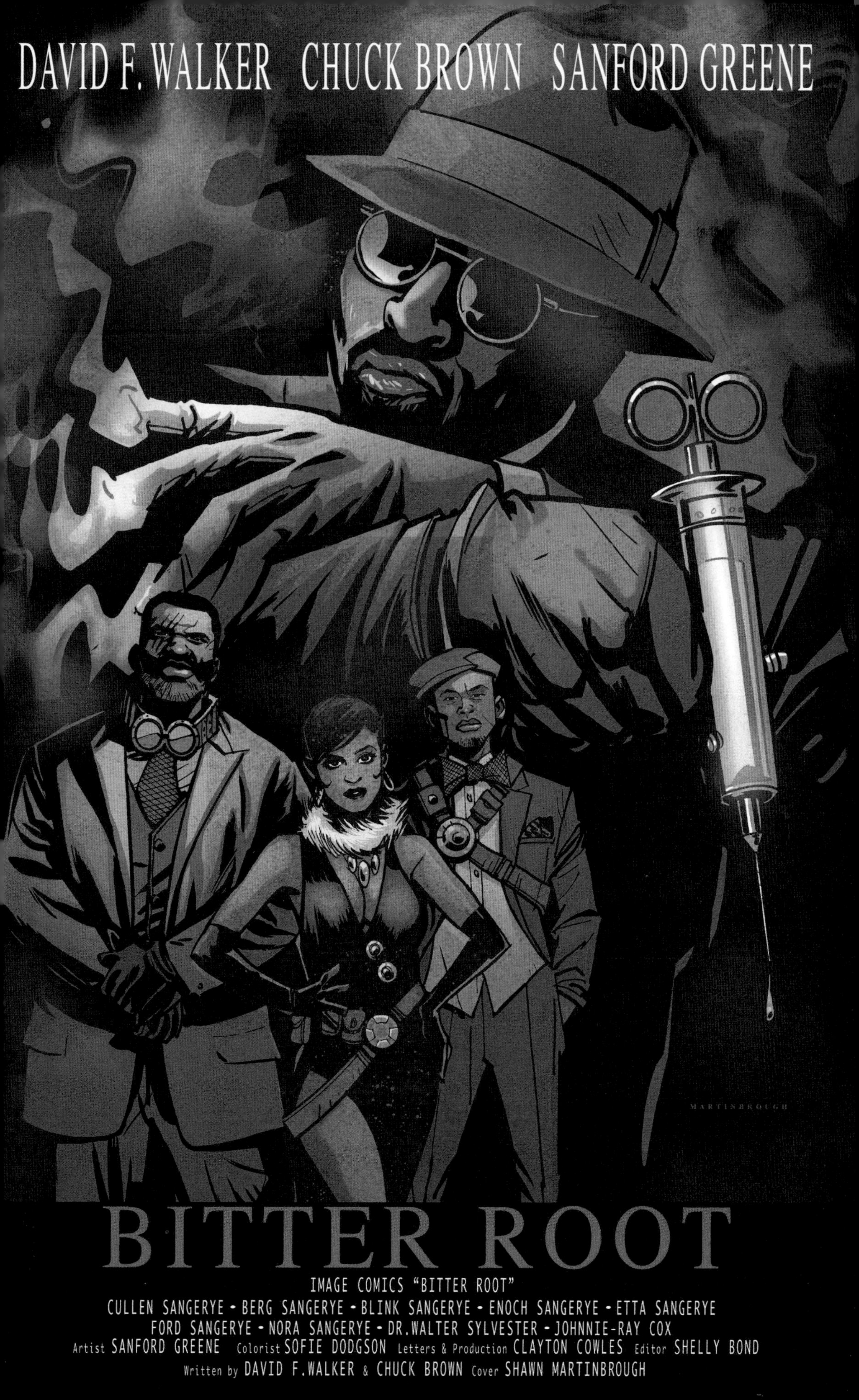
DAVID F. WALKER CHUCK BROWN SANFORD GREENE
MARTINBROUGH
BITTER ROOT
IMAGE COMICS "BITTER ROOT"
CULLEN SANGERYE - BERG SANGERYE - BLINK SANGERYE - ENOCH SANGERYE - ETTA SANGERYE
FORD SANGERYE - NORA SANGERYE - DR.WALTER SYLVESTER - JOHNNIE-RAY COX
Artist SANFORD GREENE Colorist SOFIE DODGSON Letters & Production CLAYTON COWLES Editor SHELLY BOND
Written by DAVID F.WALKER & CHUCK BROWN Cover SHAWN MARTINBROUGH

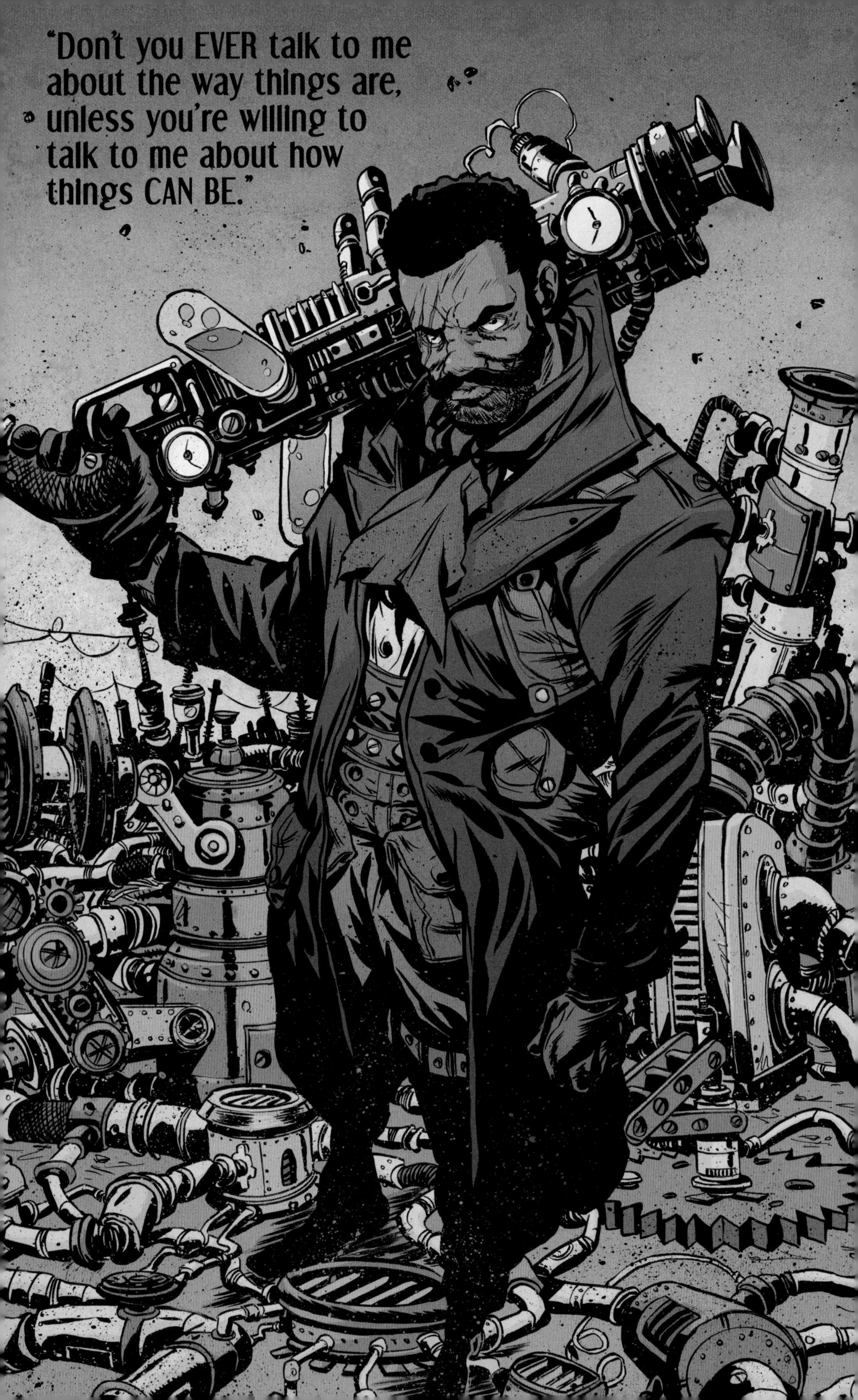
"Don't you EVER talk to me about the way things are, unless you're willing to talk to me about how things CAN BE."

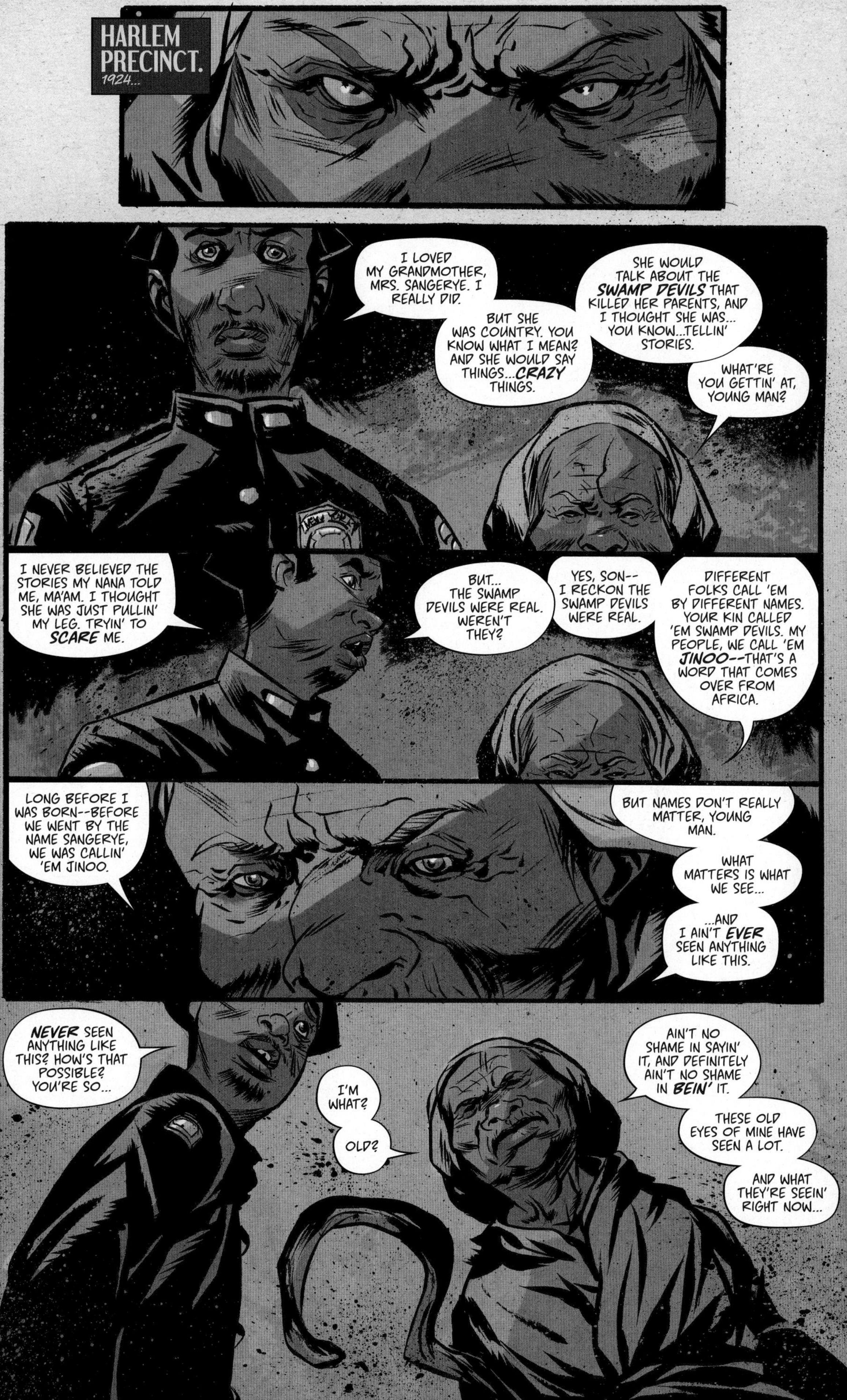
HARLEM PRECINCT. 1924...
I LOVED MY GRANDMOTHER, MRS. SANGERYE. I REALLY DID.
BUT SHE WAS COUNTRY. YOU KNOW WHAT I MEAN? AND SHE WOULD SAY THINGS...CRAZY THINGS.
SHE WOULD TALK ABOUT THE SWAMP DEVILS THAT KILLED HER PARENTS, AND I THOUGHT SHE WAS... YOU KNOW...TELLIN' STORIES.
WHAT'RE YOU GETTIN' AT, YOUNG MAN?
I NEVER BELIEVED THE STORIES MY NANA TOLD ME, MA'AM. I THOUGHT SHE WAS JUST PULLIN' MY LEG. TRYIN' TO SCARE ME.
BUT... THE SWAMP DEVILS WERE REAL. WEREN'T THEY?
YES, SON-- I RECKON THE SWAMP DEVILS WERE REAL.
DIFFERENT FOLKS CALL 'EM BY DIFFERENT NAMES. YOUR KIN CALLED 'EM SWAMP DEVILS. MY PEOPLE, WE CALL 'EM JINOO--THAT'S A WORD THAT COMES OVER FROM AFRICA.
LONG BEFORE I WAS BORN--BEFORE WE WENT BY THE NAME SANGERYE, WE WAS CALLIN' 'EM JINOO.
BUT NAMES DON'T REALLY MATTER, YOUNG MAN.
WHAT MATTERS IS WHAT WE SEE...
...AND I AIN'T EVER SEEN ANYTHING LIKE THIS.
NEVER SEEN ANYTHING LIKE THIS? HOW'S THAT POSSIBLE? YOU'RE SO...
I'M WHAT?
OLD?
AIN'T NO SHAME IN SAYIN' IT, AND DEFINITELY AIN'T NO SHAME IN BEIN' IT.
THESE OLD EYES OF MINE HAVE SEEN A LOT.
AND WHAT THEY'RE SEEIN' RIGHT NOW...

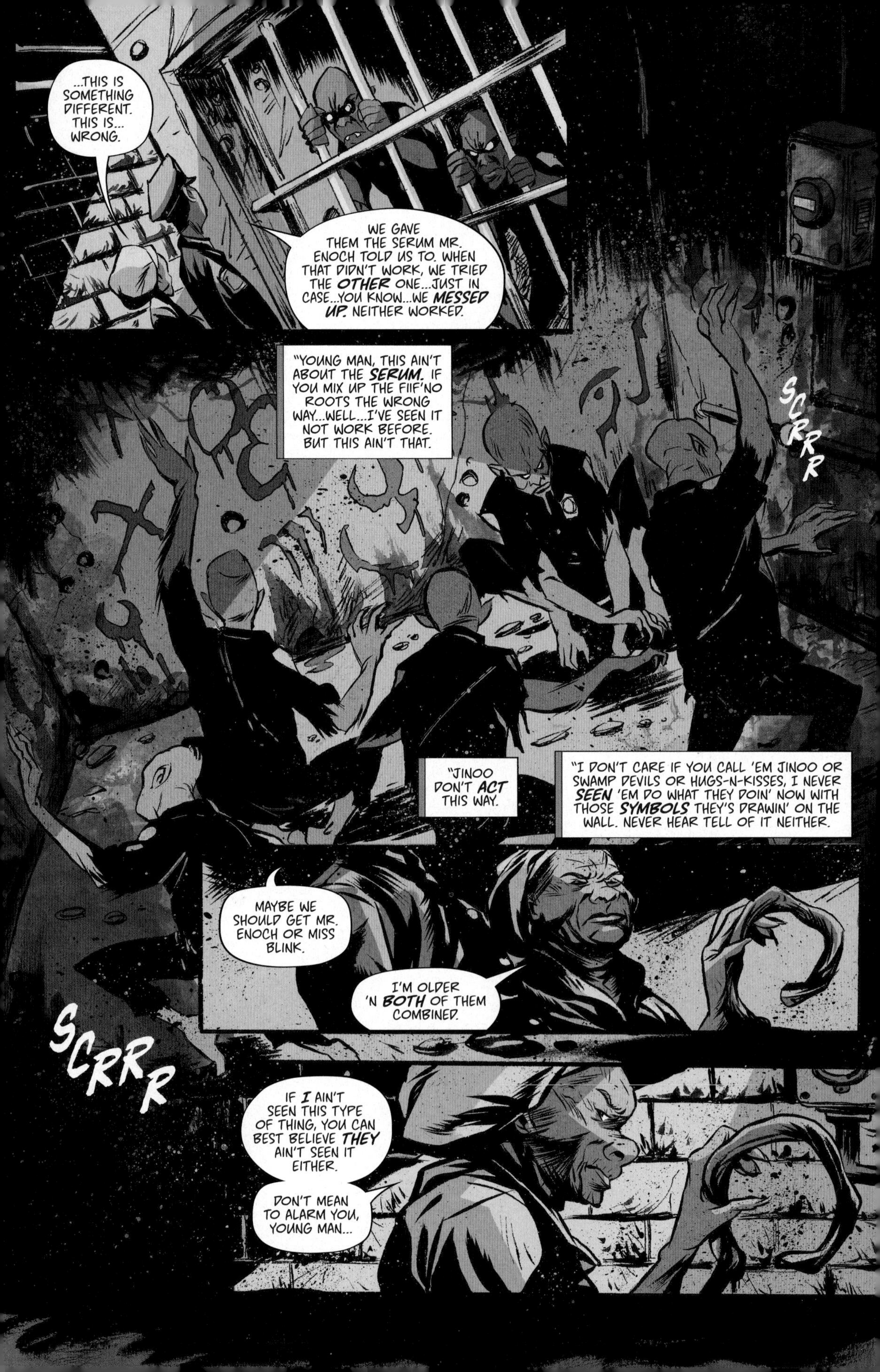
...THIS IS SOMETHING DIFFERENT. THIS IS... WRONG.
WE GAVE THEM THE SERUM MR. ENOCH TOLD US TO. WHEN THAT DIDN'T WORK, WE TRIED THE OTHER ONE...JUST IN CASE...YOU KNOW...WE MESSED UP. NEITHER WORKED.
"YOUNG MAN, THIS AIN'T ABOUT THE SERUM. IF YOU MIX UP THE FIIF'NO ROOTS THE WRONG WAY...WELL...I'VE SEEN IT NOT WORK BEFORE. BUT THIS AIN'T THAT.
SCRRR
"JINOO DON'T ACT THIS WAY.
"I DON'T CARE IF YOU CALL 'EM JINOO OR SWAMP DEVILS OR HUGS-N-KISSES, I NEVER SEEN 'EM DO WHAT THEY DOIN' NOW WITH THOSE SYMBOLS THEY'S DRAWIN' ON THE WALL. NEVER HEAR TELL OF IT NEITHER.
MAYBE WE SHOULD GET MR. ENOCH OR MISS BLINK.
I'M OLDER 'N BOTH OF THEM COMBINED.
SCRRR
IF I AIN'T SEEN THIS TYPE OF THING, YOU CAN BEST BELIEVE THEY AIN'T SEEN IT EITHER.
DON'T MEAN TO ALARM YOU, YOUNG MAN...

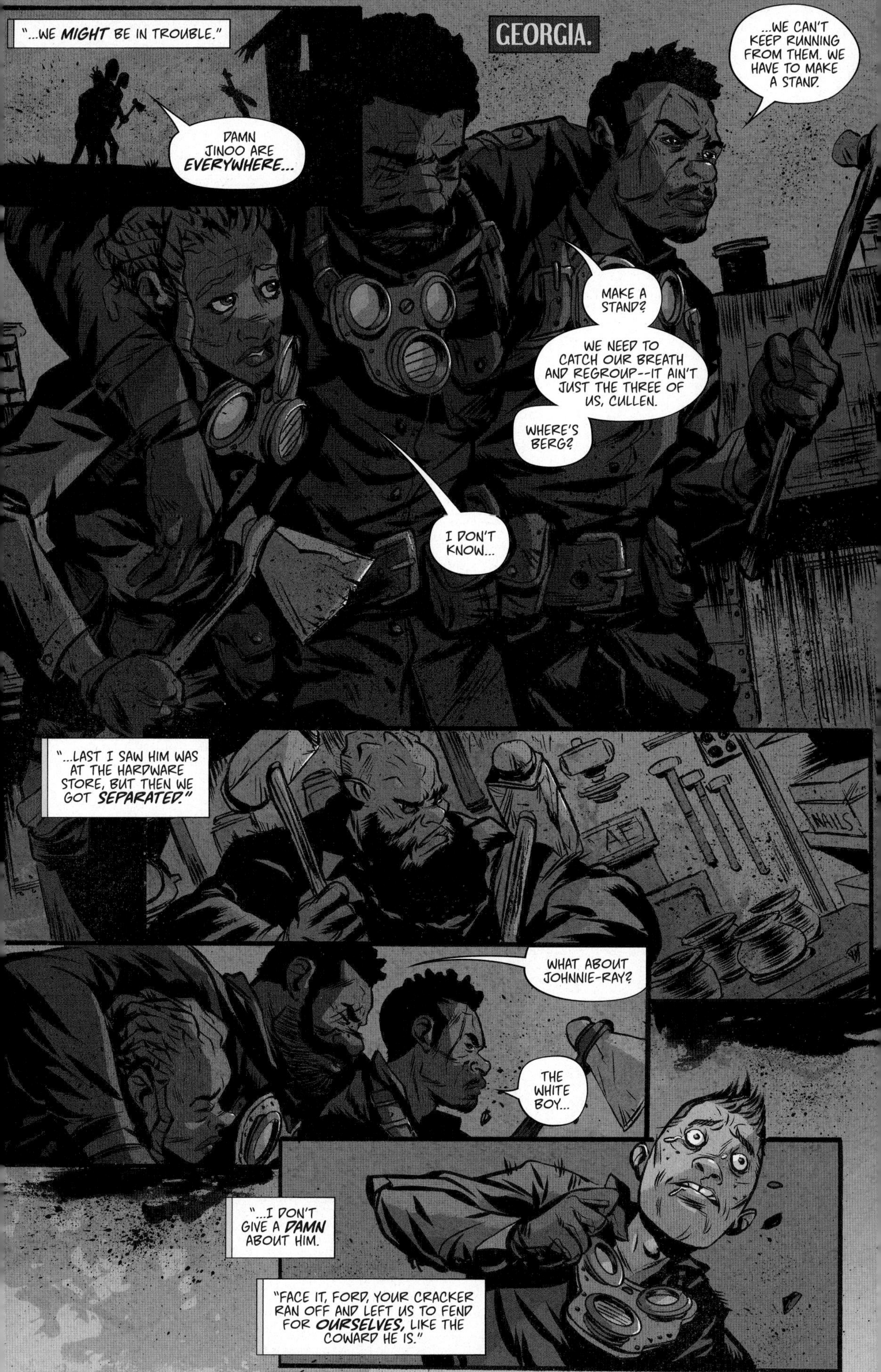
"...WE MIGHT BE IN TROUBLE."
GEORGIA.
DAMN JINOO ARE EVERYWHERE...
...WE CAN'T KEEP RUNNING FROM THEM. WE HAVE TO MAKE A STAND.
MAKE A STAND?
WE NEED TO CATCH OUR BREATH AND REGROUP--IT AIN'T JUST THE THREE OF US, CULLEN.
WHERE'S BERG?
I DON'T KNOW...
"...LAST I SAW HIM WAS AT THE HARDWARE STORE, BUT THEN WE GOT SEPARATED."
NAILS
WHAT ABOUT JOHNNIE-RAY?
THE WHITE BOY...
"...I DON'T GIVE A DAMN ABOUT HIM.
"FACE IT, FORD, YOUR CRACKER RAN OFF AND LEFT US TO FEND FOR OURSELVES, LIKE THE COWARD HE IS."

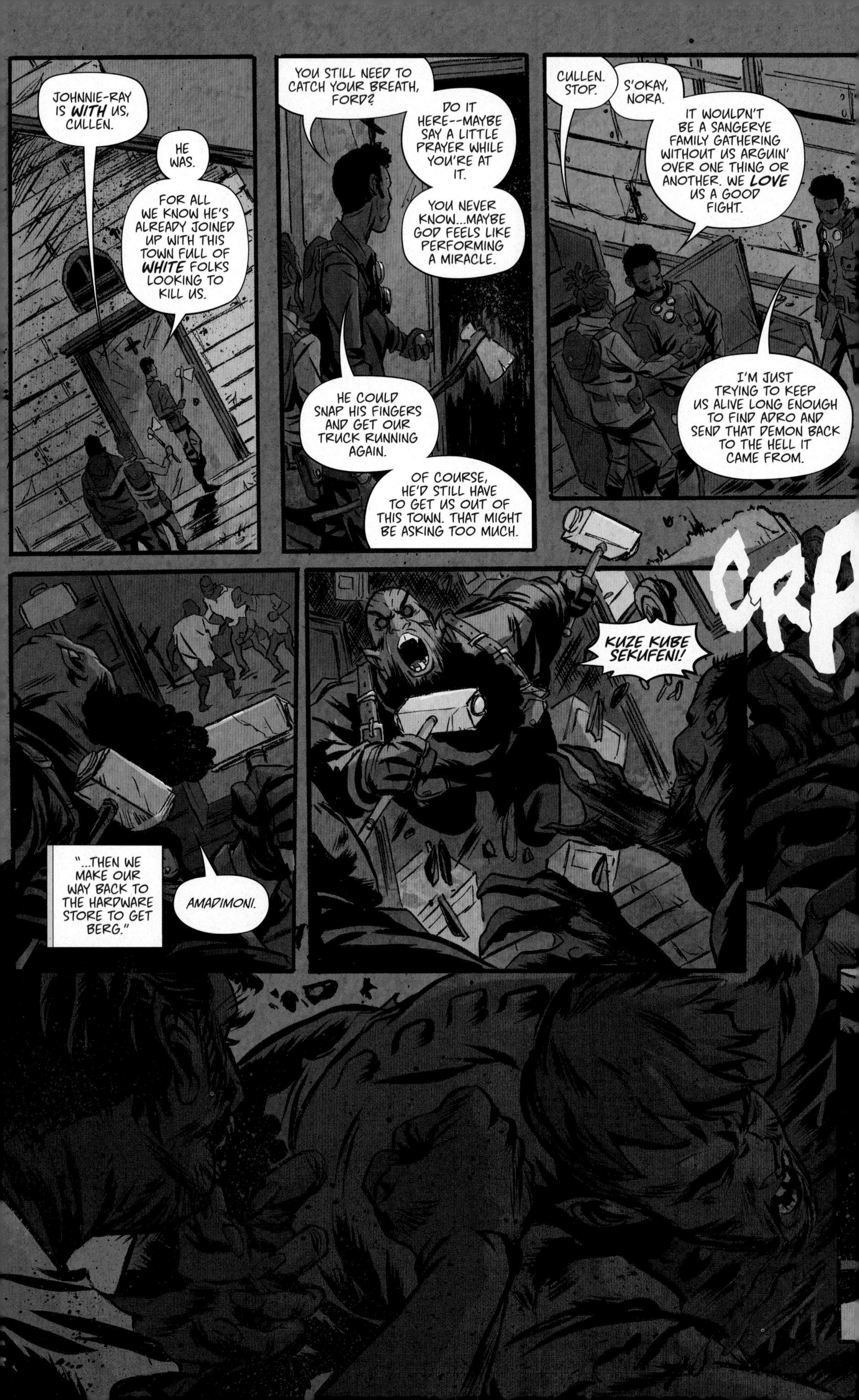
JOHNNIE-RAY IS WITH US, CULLEN.
HE WAS.
FOR ALL WE KNOW HE'S ALREADY JOINED UP WITH THIS TOWN FULL OF WHITE FOLKS LOOKING TO KILL US.
YOU STILL NEED TO CATCH YOUR BREATH, FORD?
DO IT HERE--MAYBE SAY A LITTLE PRAYER WHILE YOU'RE AT IT.
YOU NEVER KNOW...MAYBE GOD FEELS LIKE PERFORMING A MIRACLE.
HE COULD SNAP HIS FINGERS AND GET OUR TRUCK RUNNING AGAIN.
OF COURSE, HE'D STILL HAVE TO GET US OUT OF THIS TOWN. THAT MIGHT BE ASKING TOO MUCH.
CULLEN. STOP.
S'OKAY, NORA.
IT WOULDN'T BE A SANGERYE FAMILY GATHERING WITHOUT US ARGUIN' OVER ONE THING OR ANOTHER. WE LOVE US A GOOD FIGHT.
I'M JUST TRYING TO KEEP US ALIVE LONG ENOUGH TO FIND ADRO AND SEND THAT DEMON BACK TO THE HELL IT CAME FROM.
"...THEN WE MAKE OUR WAY BACK TO THE HARDWARE STORE TO GET BERG."
AMADIMONI.
KUZE KUBE SEKUFENI!
CRA

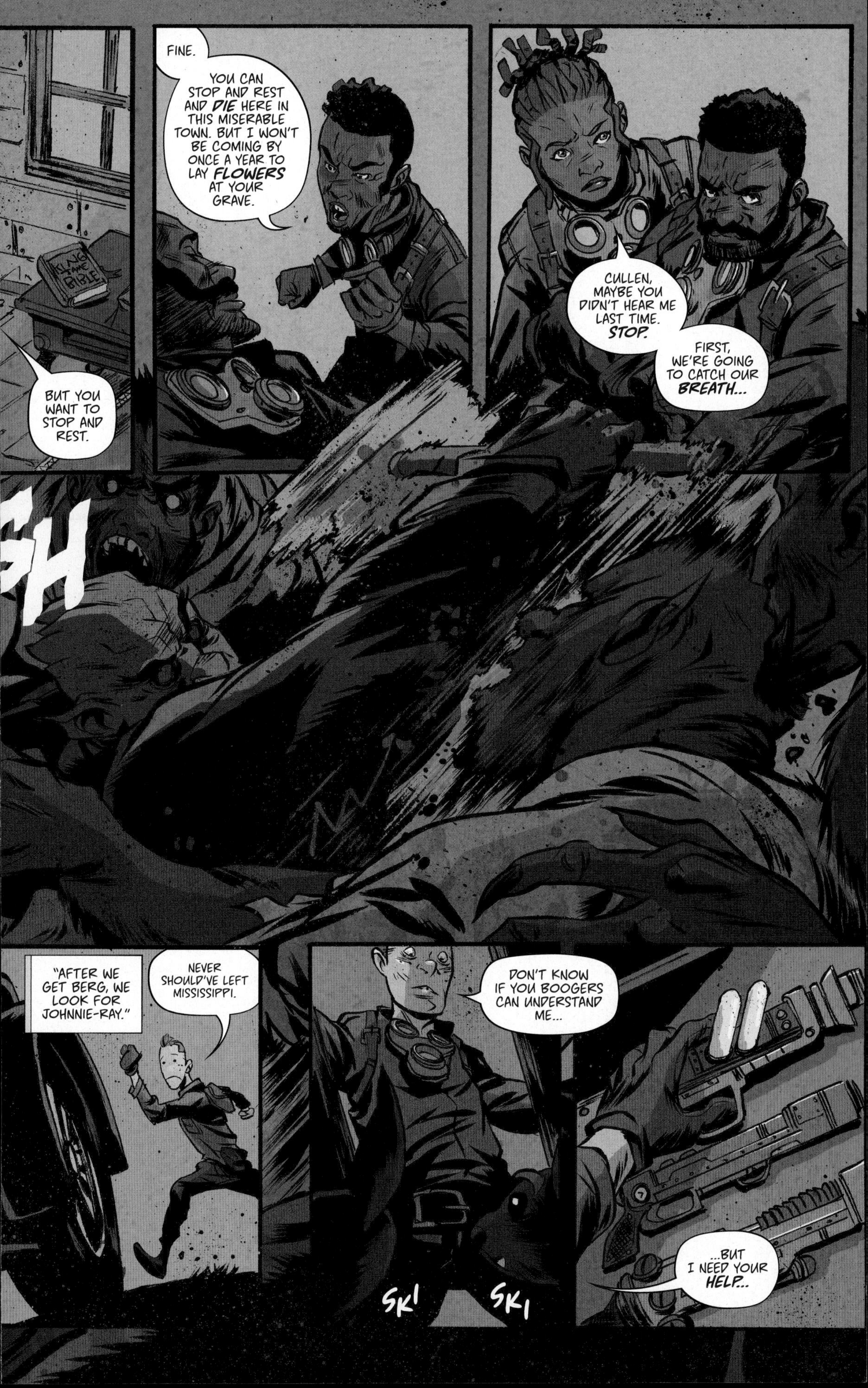

BUT YOU WANT TO STOP AND REST.
FINE.
YOU CAN STOP AND REST AND DIE HERE IN THIS MISERABLE TOWN. BUT I WON'T BE COMING BY ONCE A YEAR TO LAY FLOWERS AT YOUR GRAVE.
CULLEN, MAYBE YOU DIDN'T HEAR ME LAST TIME. STOP.
FIRST, WE'RE GOING TO CATCH OUR BREATH...
KING JAMES BIBLE
GH
"AFTER WE GET BERG, WE LOOK FOR JOHNNIE-RAY."
NEVER SHOULD'VE LEFT MISSISSIPPI.
DON'T KNOW IF YOU BOOGERS CAN UNDERSTAND ME...
...BUT I NEED YOUR HELP...
SKI
SKI

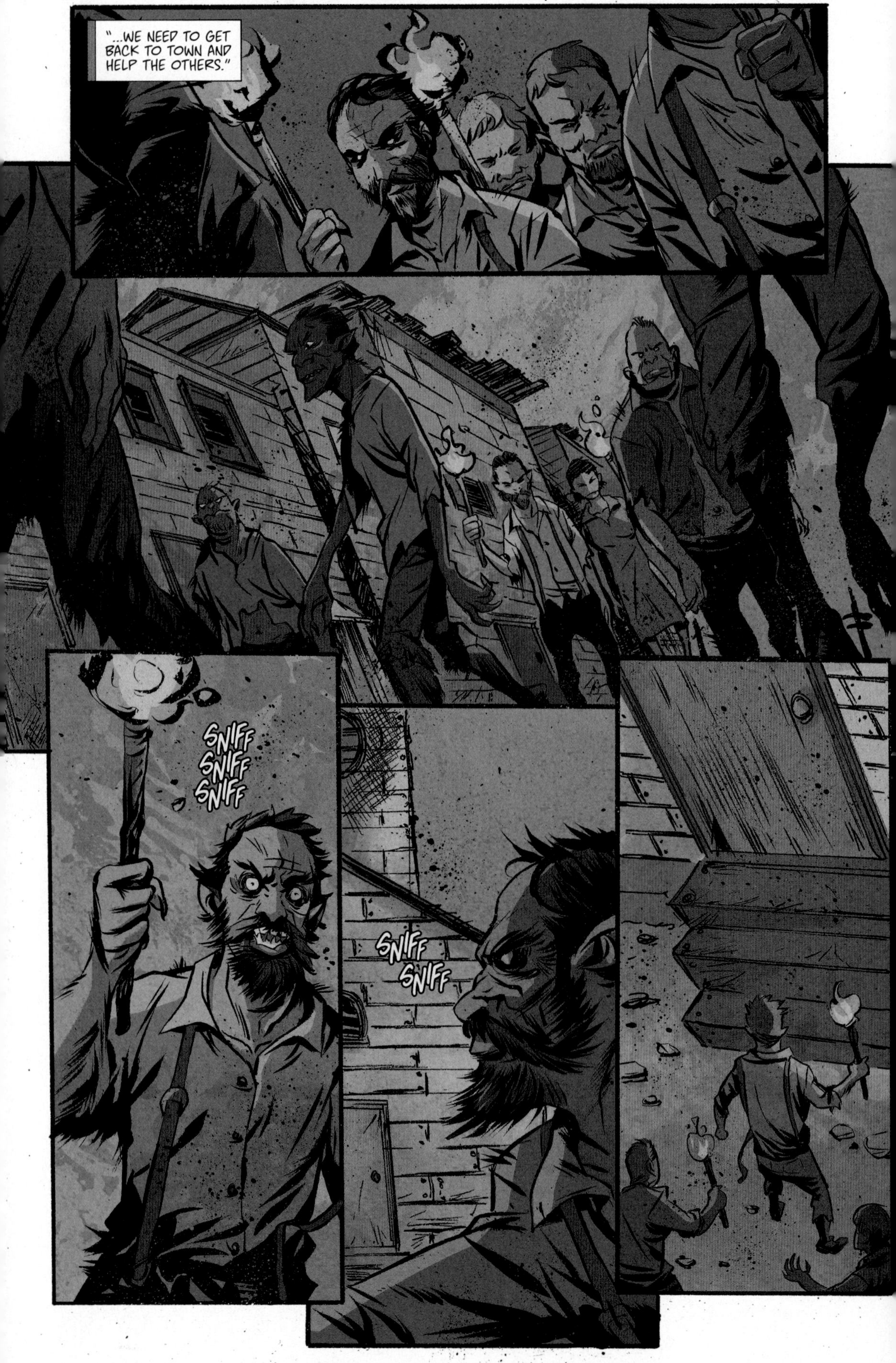
"...WE NEED TO GET BACK TO TOWN AND HELP THE OTHERS."
SNIFF SNIFF SNIFF
SNIFF SNIFF

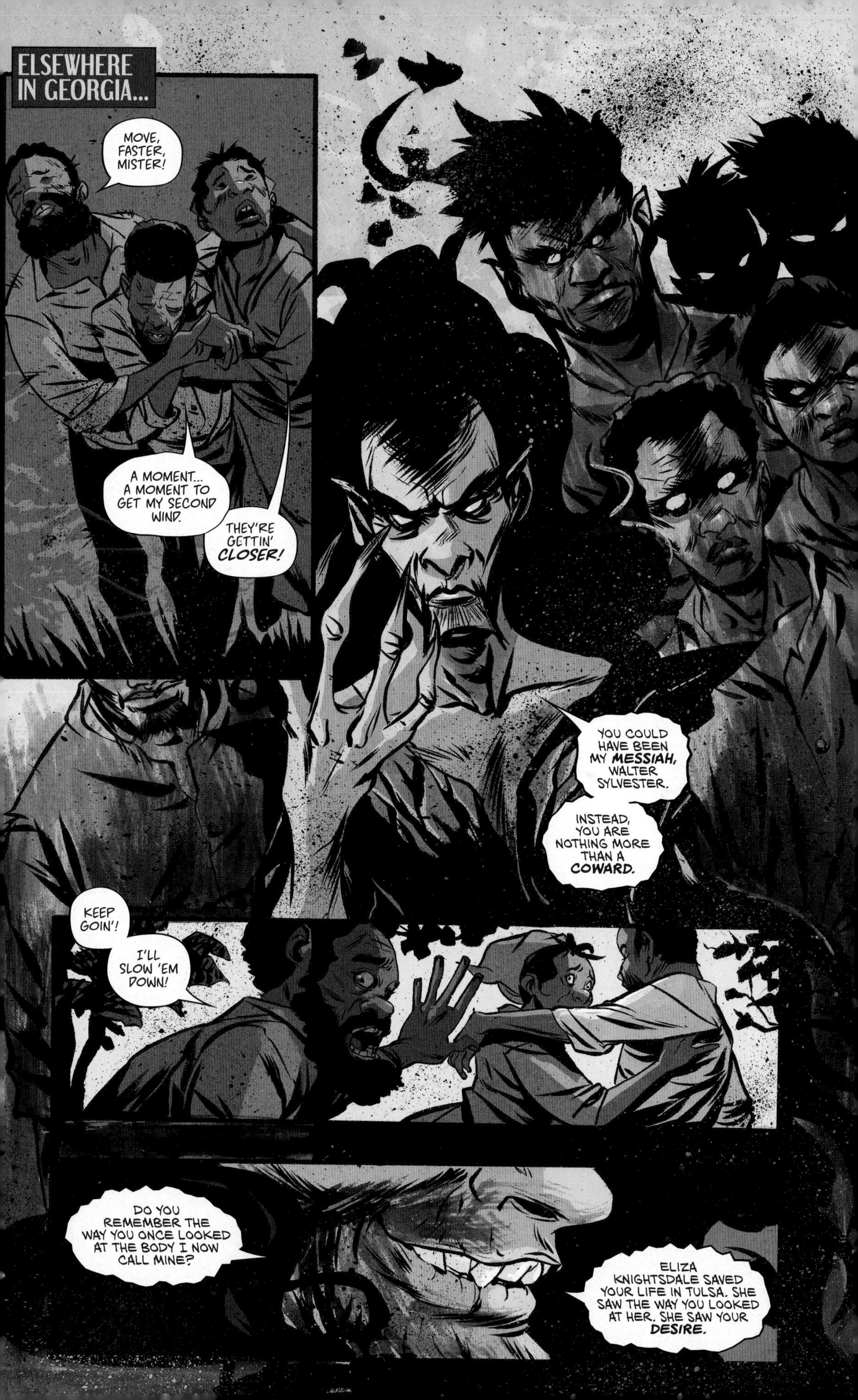
ELSEWHERE IN GEORGIA...
MOVE, FASTER, MISTER!
A MOMENT... A MOMENT TO GET MY SECOND WIND.
THEY'RE GETTIN' CLOSER!
YOU COULD HAVE BEEN MY MESSIAH, WALTER SYLVESTER.
INSTEAD, YOU ARE NOTHING MORE THAN A COWARD.
KEEP GOIN'!
I'LL SLOW 'EM DOWN!
DO YOU REMEMBER THE WAY YOU ONCE LOOKED AT THE BODY I NOW CALL MINE?
ELIZA KNIGHTSDALE SAVED YOUR LIFE IN TULSA. SHE SAW THE WAY YOU LOOKED AT HER. SHE SAW YOUR DESIRE.

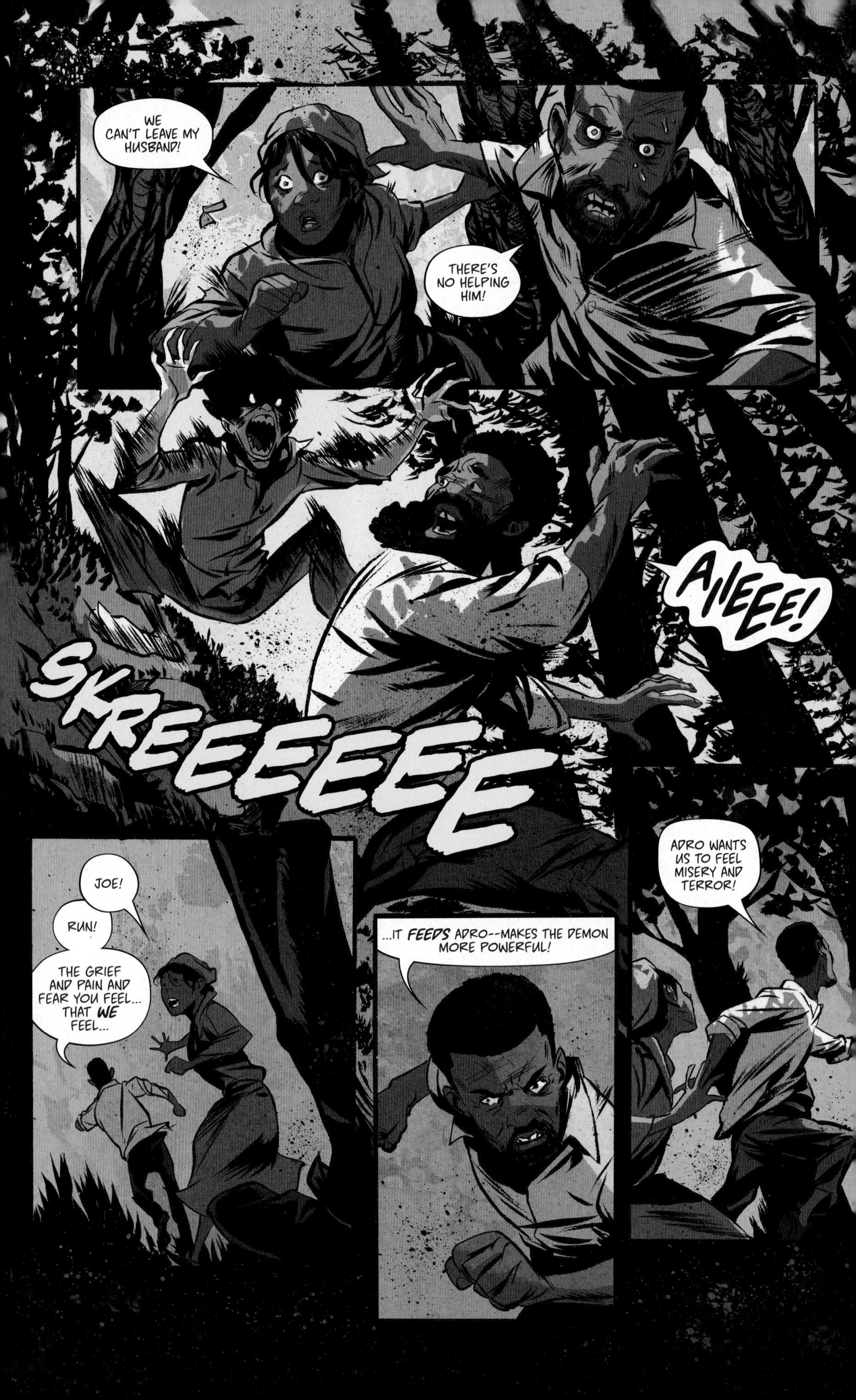
WE CAN'T LEAVE MY HUSBAND!
THERE'S NO HELPING HIM!
AIEEEE!
SKREEEEEEEE
JOE!
RUN!
THE GRIEF AND PAIN AND FEAR YOU FEEL... THAT WE FEEL...
...IT FEEDS ADRO--MAKES THE DEMON MORE POWERFUL!
ADRO WANTS US TO FEEL MISERY AND TERROR!

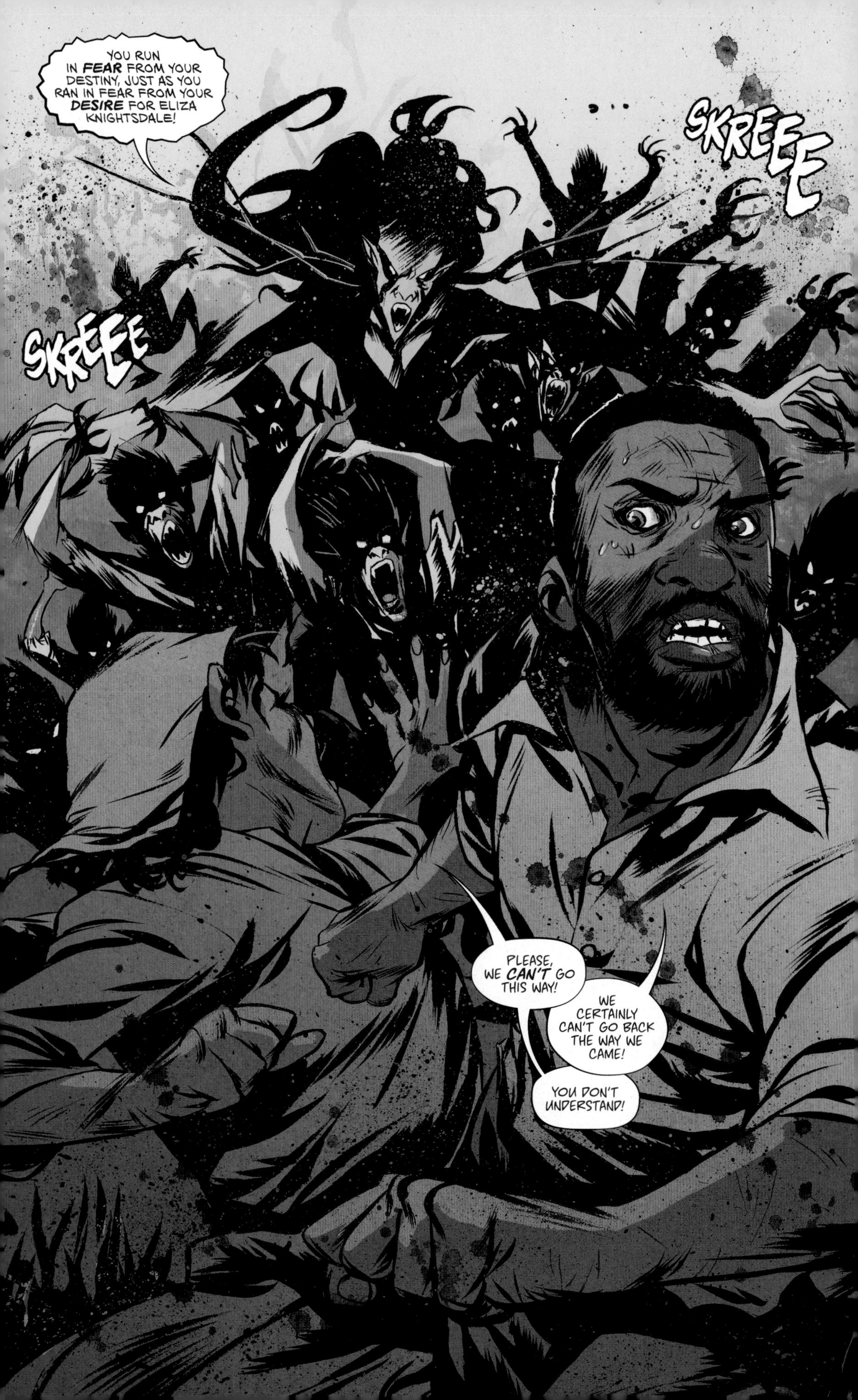
YOU RUN IN **FEAR** FROM YOUR DESTINY, JUST AS YOU RAN IN FEAR FROM YOUR **DESIRE** FOR ELIZA KNIGHTSDALE!
SKREEEE
SKREEE
PLEASE, WE **CAN'T** GO THIS WAY!
WE CERTAINLY CAN'T GO BACK THE WAY WE CAME!
YOU DON'T UNDERSTAND!

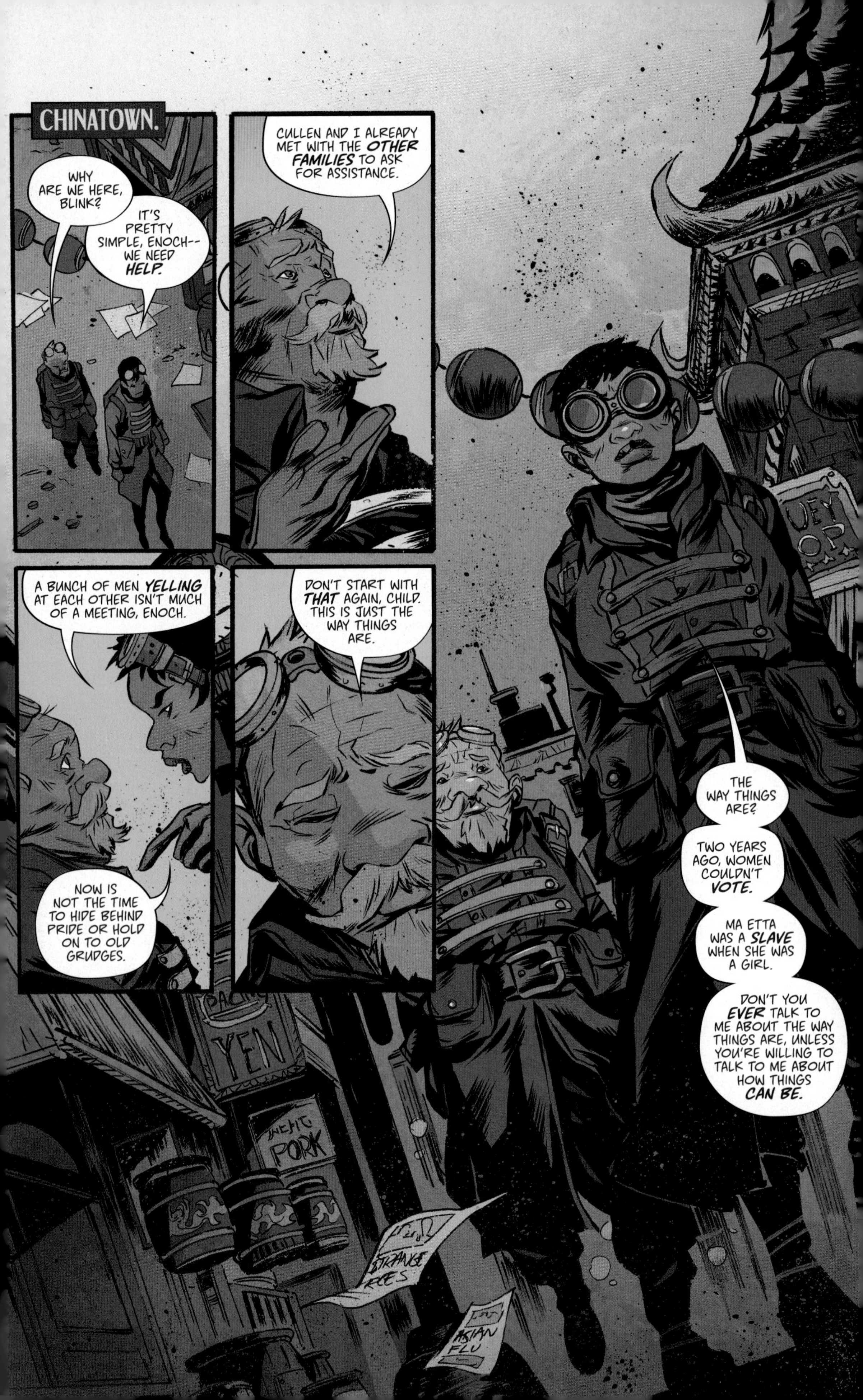
CHINATOWN.
WHY ARE WE HERE, BLINK?
IT'S PRETTY SIMPLE, ENOCH-- WE NEED HELP.
CULLEN AND I ALREADY MET WITH THE OTHER FAMILIES TO ASK FOR ASSISTANCE.
A BUNCH OF MEN YELLING AT EACH OTHER ISN'T MUCH OF A MEETING, ENOCH.
NOW IS NOT THE TIME TO HIDE BEHIND PRIDE OR HOLD ON TO OLD GRUDGES.
DON'T START WITH THAT AGAIN, CHILD. THIS IS JUST THE WAY THINGS ARE.
THE WAY THINGS ARE?
TWO YEARS AGO, WOMEN COULDN'T VOTE.
MA ETTA WAS A SLAVE WHEN SHE WAS A GIRL.
DON'T YOU EVER TALK TO ME ABOUT THE WAY THINGS ARE, UNLESS YOU'RE WILLING TO TALK TO ME ABOUT HOW THINGS CAN BE.
YEN
PORK
ASIAN FLU

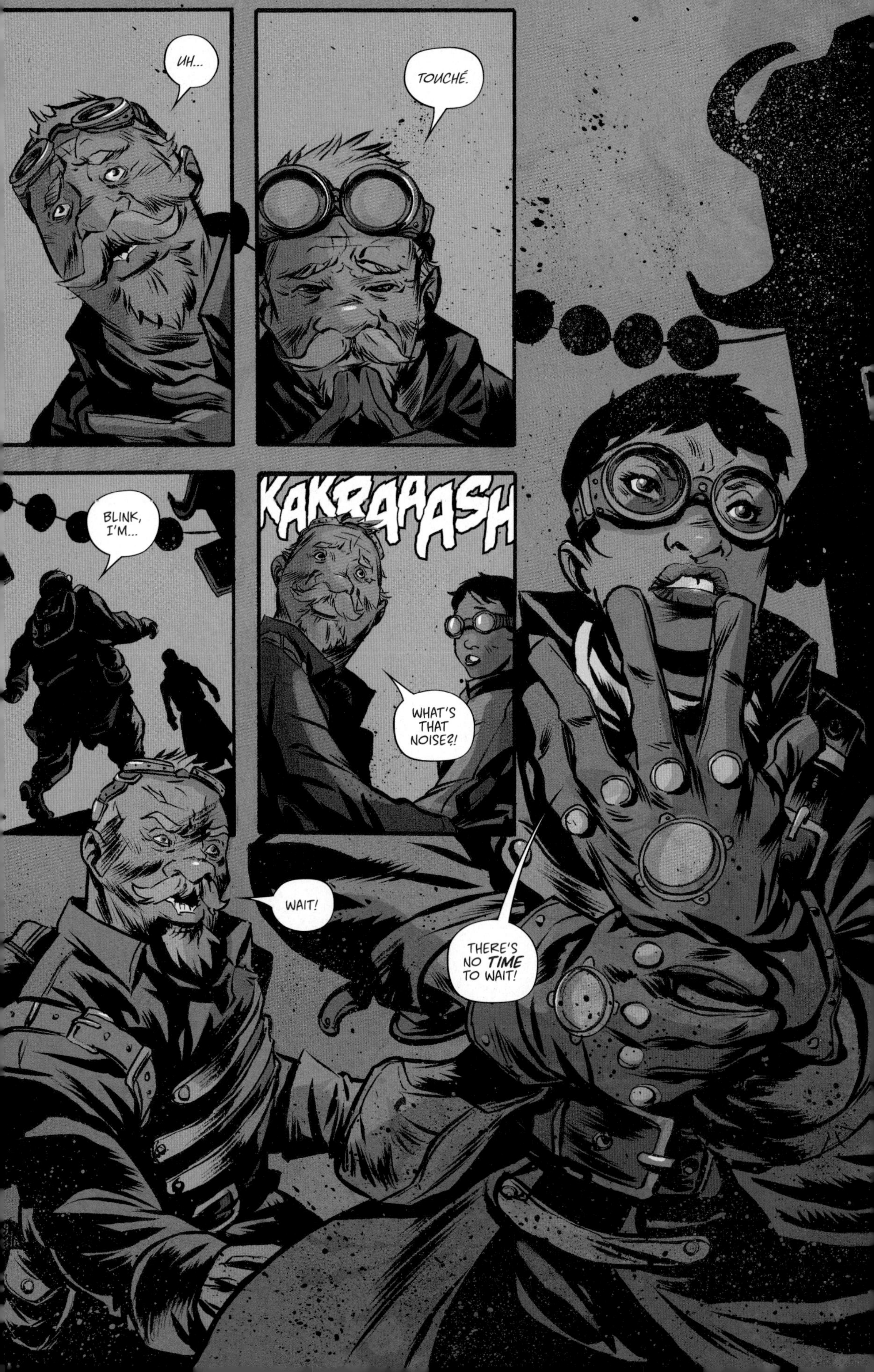
UH...
TOUCHÉ.
BLINK, I'M...
KAKRAAAASH
WHAT'S THAT NOISE?!
WAIT!
THERE'S NO TIME TO WAIT!

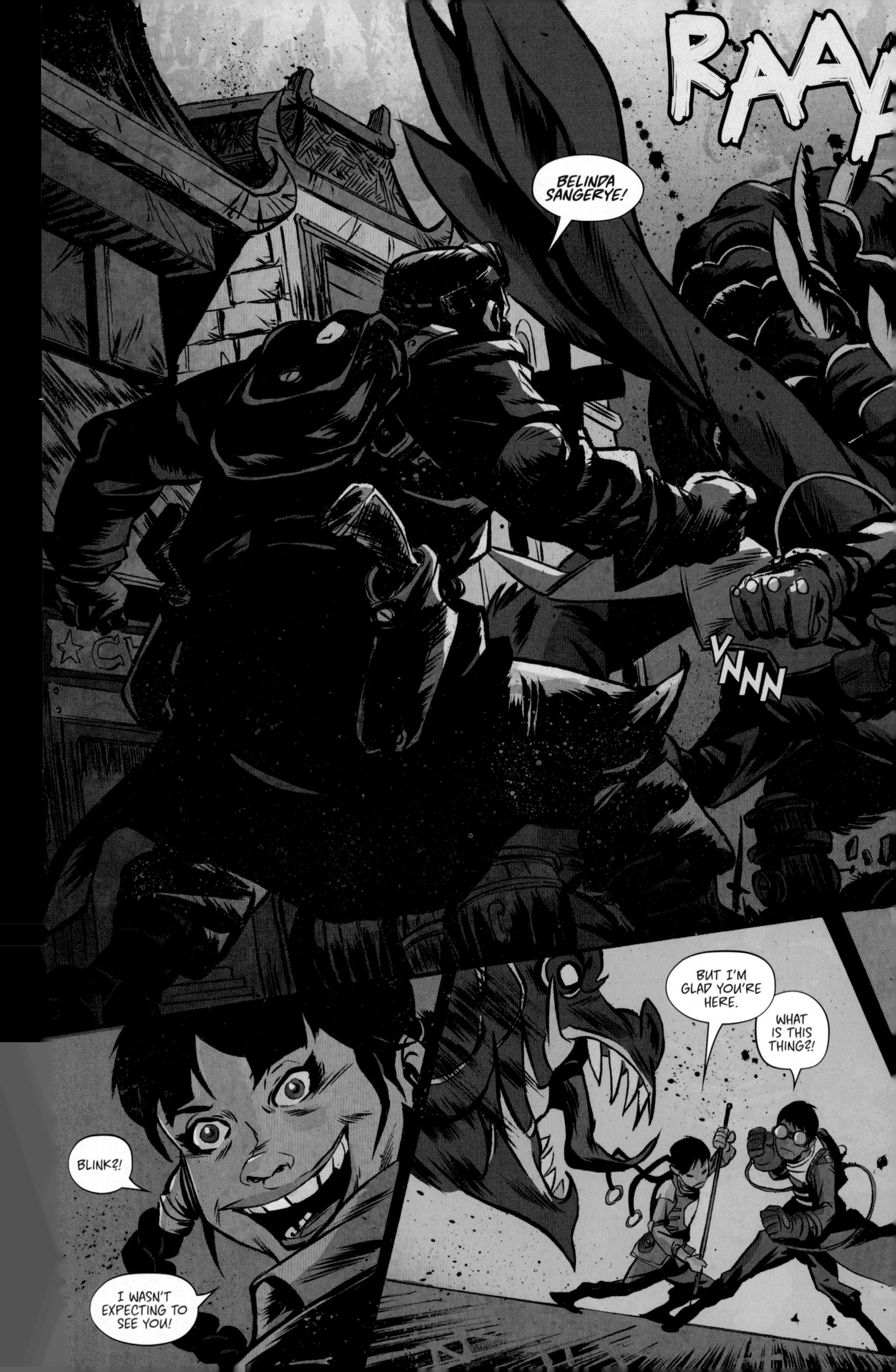
RAAA
BELINDA SANGERYE!
VNNN
BLINK?!
I WASN'T EXPECTING TO SEE YOU!
BUT I'M GLAD YOU'RE HERE.
WHAT IS THIS THING?!

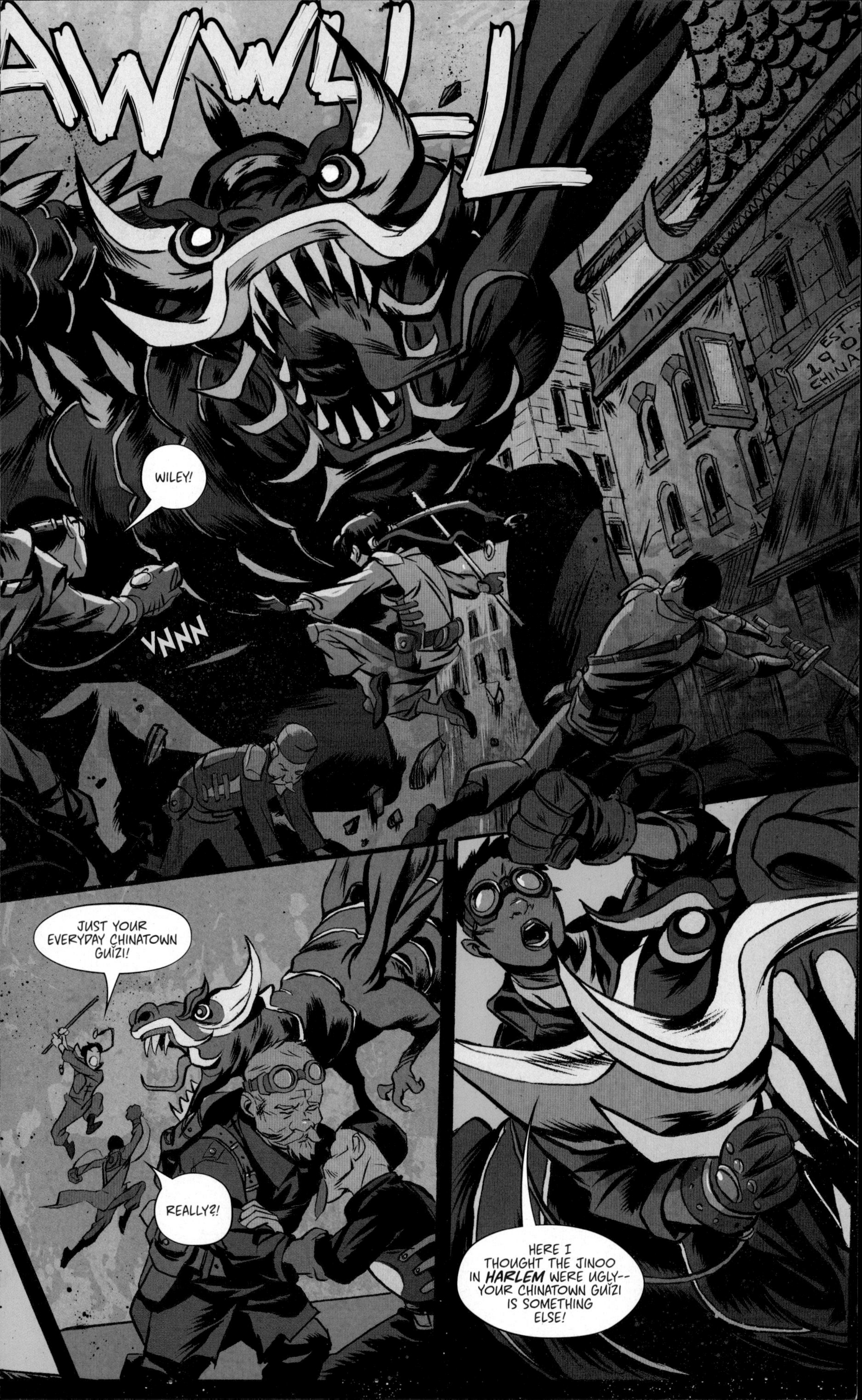
AWWLLL
WILEY!
VNNN
JUST YOUR EVERYDAY CHINATOWN GUÏZI!
REALLY?!
HERE I THOUGHT THE JINOO IN HARLEM WERE UGLY-- YOUR CHINATOWN GUÏZI IS SOMETHING ELSE!

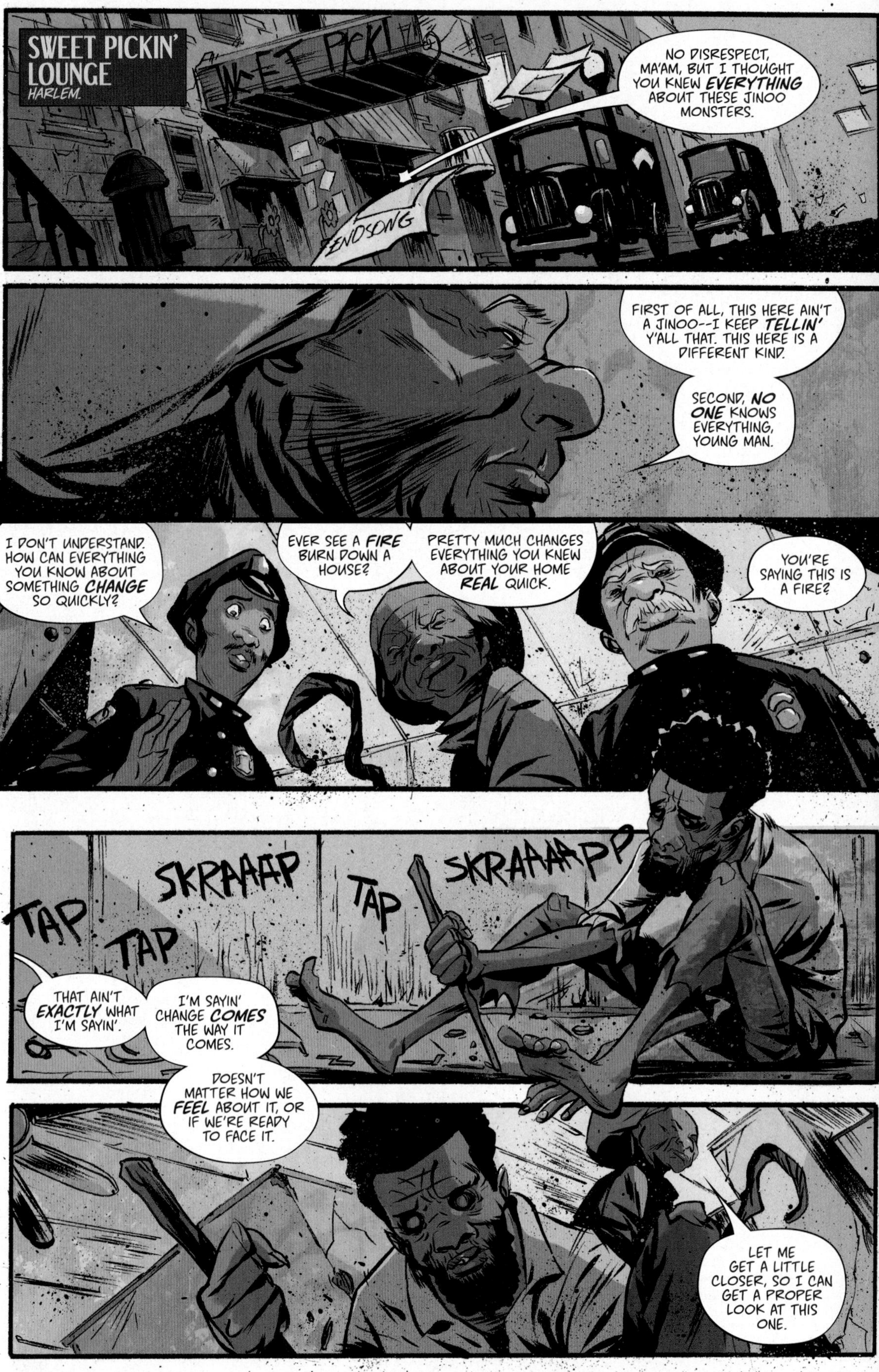
SWEET PICKIN' LOUNGE
HARLEM.
NO DISRESPECT, MA'AM, BUT I THOUGHT YOU KNEW EVERYTHING ABOUT THESE JINOO MONSTERS.
ENDSONG
FIRST OF ALL, THIS HERE AIN'T A JINOO--I KEEP TELLIN' Y'ALL THAT. THIS HERE IS A DIFFERENT KIND.
SECOND, NO ONE KNOWS EVERYTHING, YOUNG MAN.
I DON'T UNDERSTAND. HOW CAN EVERYTHING YOU KNOW ABOUT SOMETHING CHANGE SO QUICKLY?
EVER SEE A FIRE BURN DOWN A HOUSE?
PRETTY MUCH CHANGES EVERYTHING YOU KNEW ABOUT YOUR HOME REAL QUICK.
YOU'RE SAYING THIS IS A FIRE?
TAP
SKRAAAP
TAP
TAP
SKRAAAAPP
THAT AIN'T EXACTLY WHAT I'M SAYIN'.
I'M SAYIN' CHANGE COMES THE WAY IT COMES.
DOESN'T MATTER HOW WE FEEL ABOUT IT, OR IF WE'RE READY TO FACE IT.
LET ME GET A LITTLE CLOSER, SO I CAN GET A PROPER LOOK AT THIS ONE.

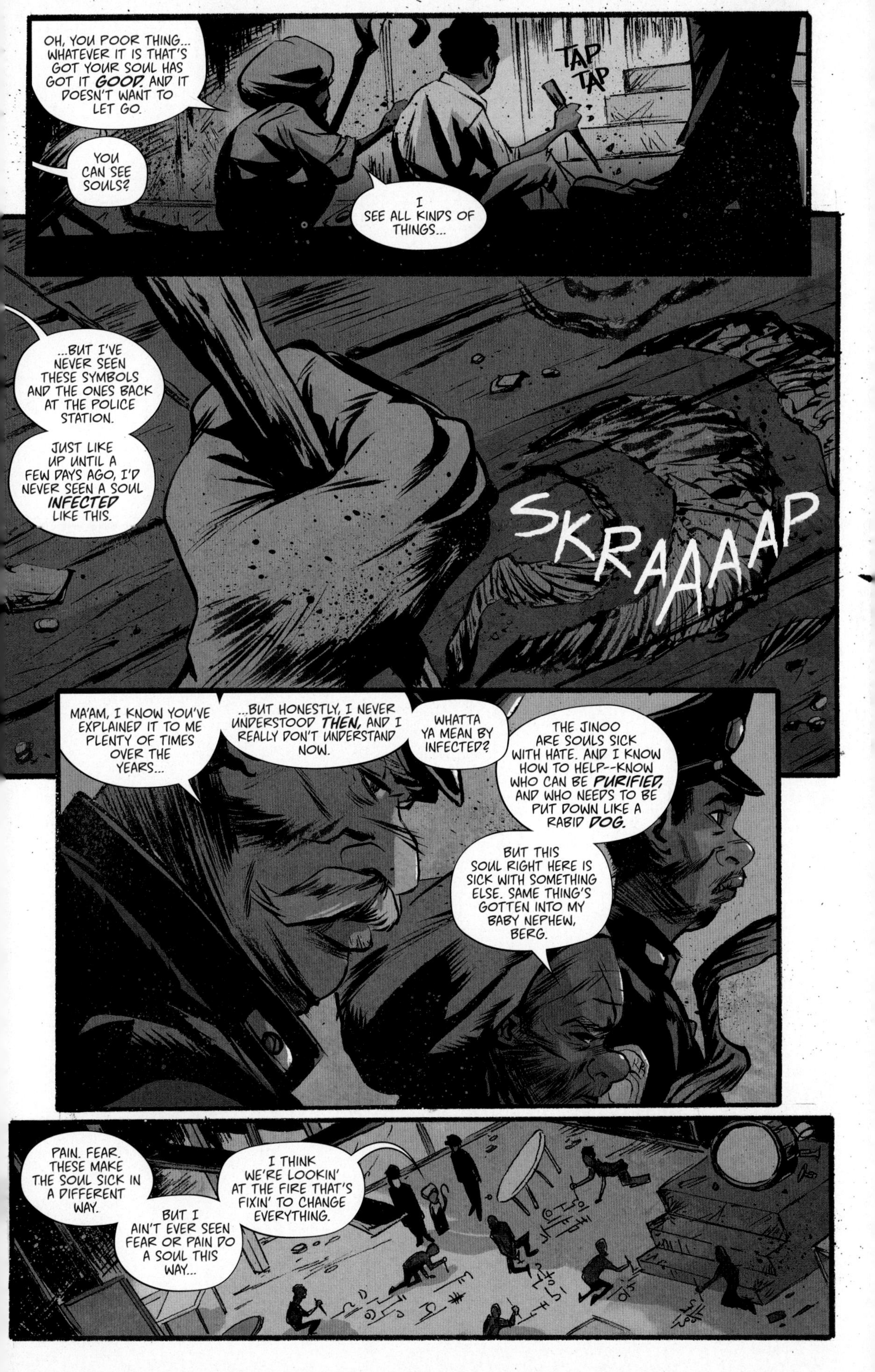
OH, YOU POOR THING... WHATEVER IT IS THAT'S GOT YOUR SOUL HAS GOT IT GOOD. AND IT DOESN'T WANT TO LET GO.
TAP TAP
YOU CAN SEE SOULS?
I SEE ALL KINDS OF THINGS...
...BUT I'VE NEVER SEEN THESE SYMBOLS AND THE ONES BACK AT THE POLICE STATION.
JUST LIKE UP UNTIL A FEW DAYS AGO, I'D NEVER SEEN A SOUL INFECTED LIKE THIS.
SKRAAAAP
MA'AM, I KNOW YOU'VE EXPLAINED IT TO ME PLENTY OF TIMES OVER THE YEARS...
...BUT HONESTLY, I NEVER UNDERSTOOD THEN, AND I REALLY DON'T UNDERSTAND NOW.
WHATTA YA MEAN BY INFECTED?
THE JINOO ARE SOULS SICK WITH HATE. AND I KNOW HOW TO HELP--KNOW WHO CAN BE PURIFIED, AND WHO NEEDS TO BE PUT DOWN LIKE A RABID DOG.
BUT THIS SOUL RIGHT HERE IS SICK WITH SOMETHING ELSE. SAME THING'S GOTTEN INTO MY BABY NEPHEW, BERG.
PAIN. FEAR. THESE MAKE THE SOUL SICK IN A DIFFERENT WAY.
BUT I AIN'T EVER SEEN FEAR OR PAIN DO A SOUL THIS WAY...
I THINK WE'RE LOOKIN' AT THE FIRE THAT'S FIXIN' TO CHANGE EVERYTHING.

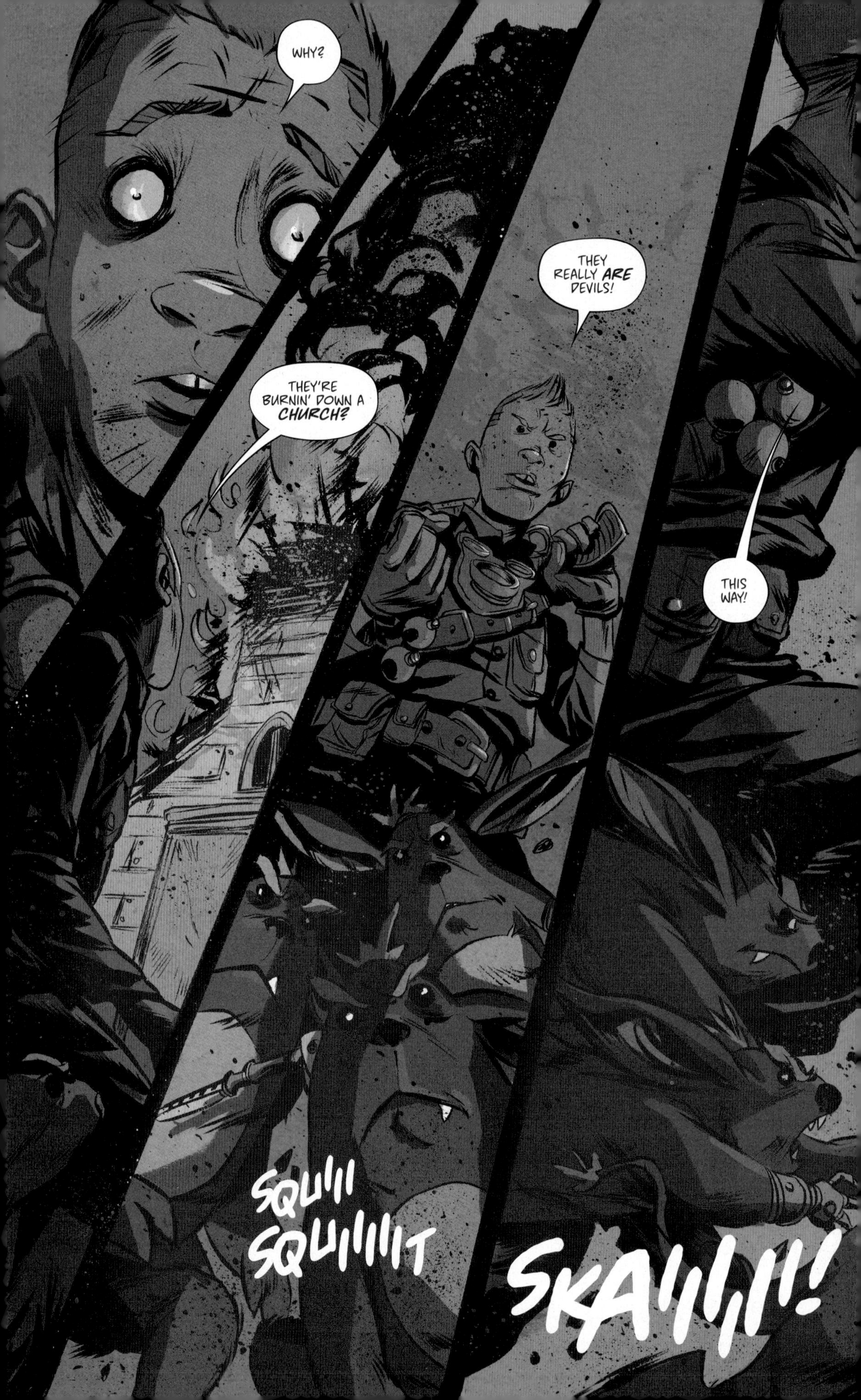
WHY?
THEY'RE BURNIN' DOWN A CHURCH?
THEY REALLY ARE DEVILS!
THIS WAY!
SQUIIII SQUIIIIIT
SKAIIIIII!

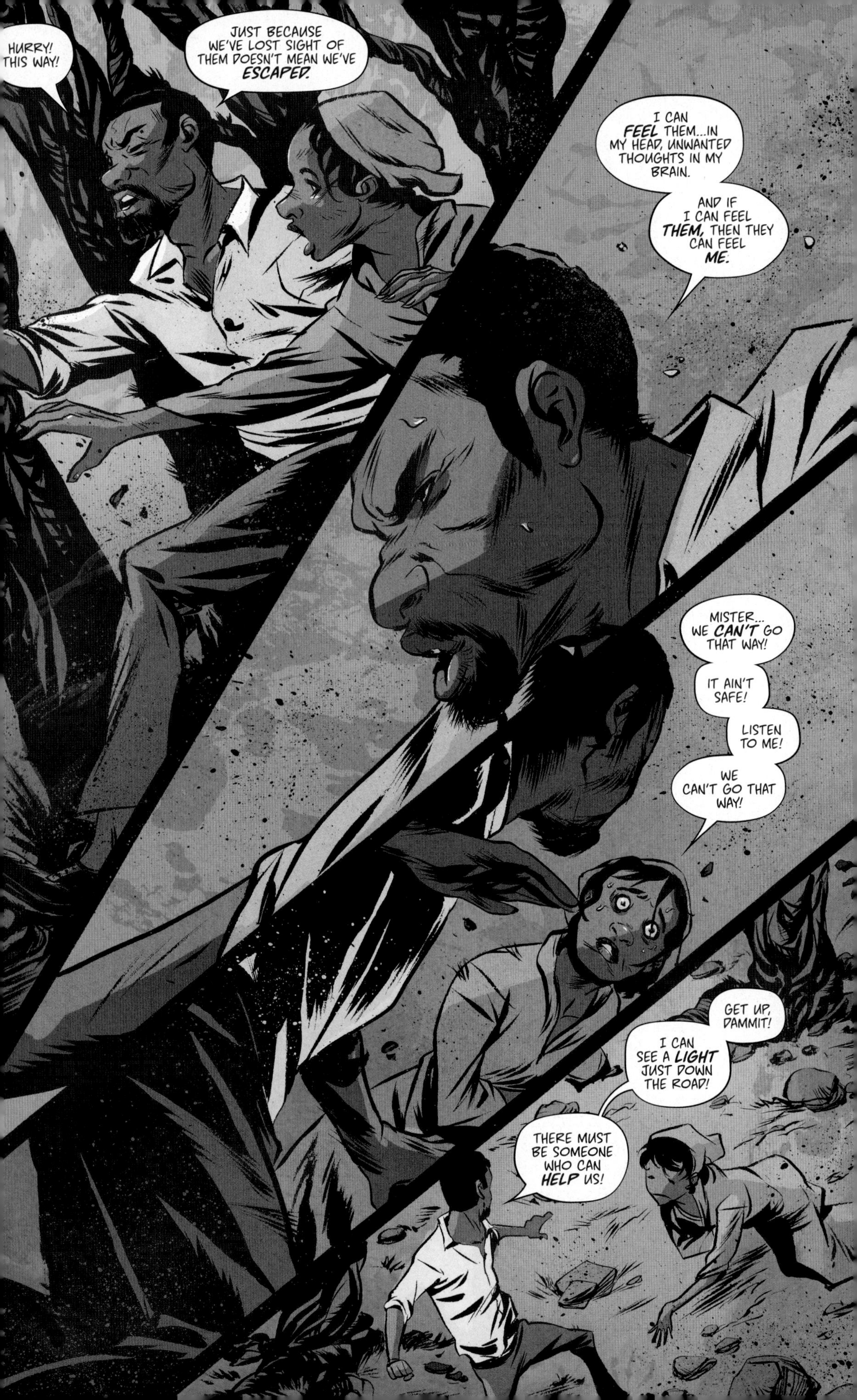
HURRY! THIS WAY!
JUST BECAUSE WE'VE LOST SIGHT OF THEM DOESN'T MEAN WE'VE ESCAPED.
I CAN FEEL THEM...IN MY HEAD, UNWANTED THOUGHTS IN MY BRAIN.
AND IF I CAN FEEL THEM, THEN THEY CAN FEEL ME.
MISTER... WE CAN'T GO THAT WAY!
IT AIN'T SAFE!
LISTEN TO ME!
WE CAN'T GO THAT WAY!
GET UP, DAMMIT!
I CAN SEE A LIGHT JUST DOWN THE ROAD!
THERE MUST BE SOMEONE WHO CAN HELP US!

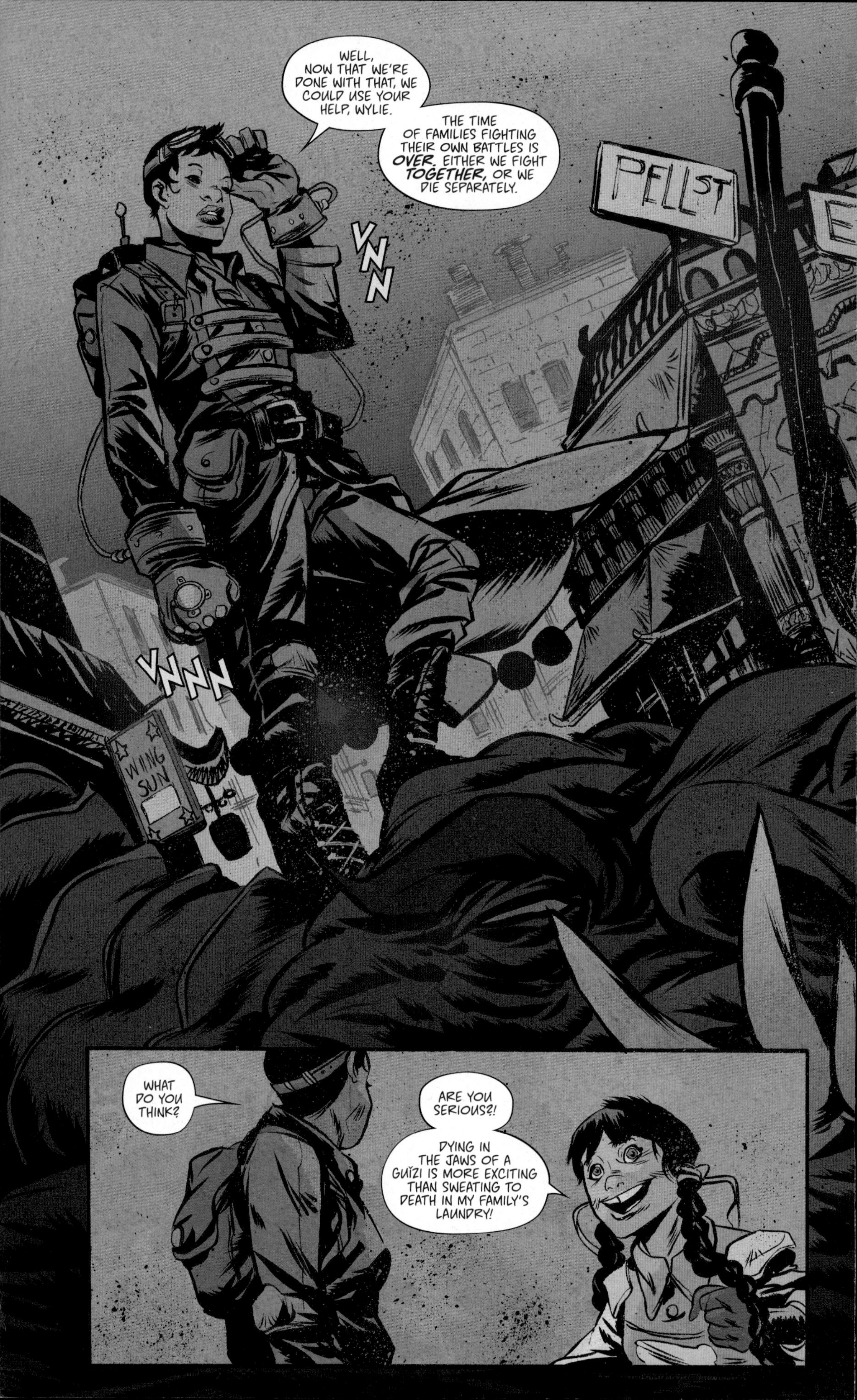
WELL, NOW THAT WE'RE DONE WITH THAT, WE COULD USE YOUR HELP, WYLIE.
THE TIME OF FAMILIES FIGHTING THEIR OWN BATTLES IS OVER. EITHER WE FIGHT TOGETHER, OR WE DIE SEPARATELY.
PELL ST
VNN
VNNN
WING SUN
WHAT DO YOU THINK?
ARE YOU SERIOUS?!
DYING IN THE JAWS OF A GUÏZI IS MORE EXCITING THAN SWEATING TO DEATH IN MY FAMILY'S LAUNDRY!

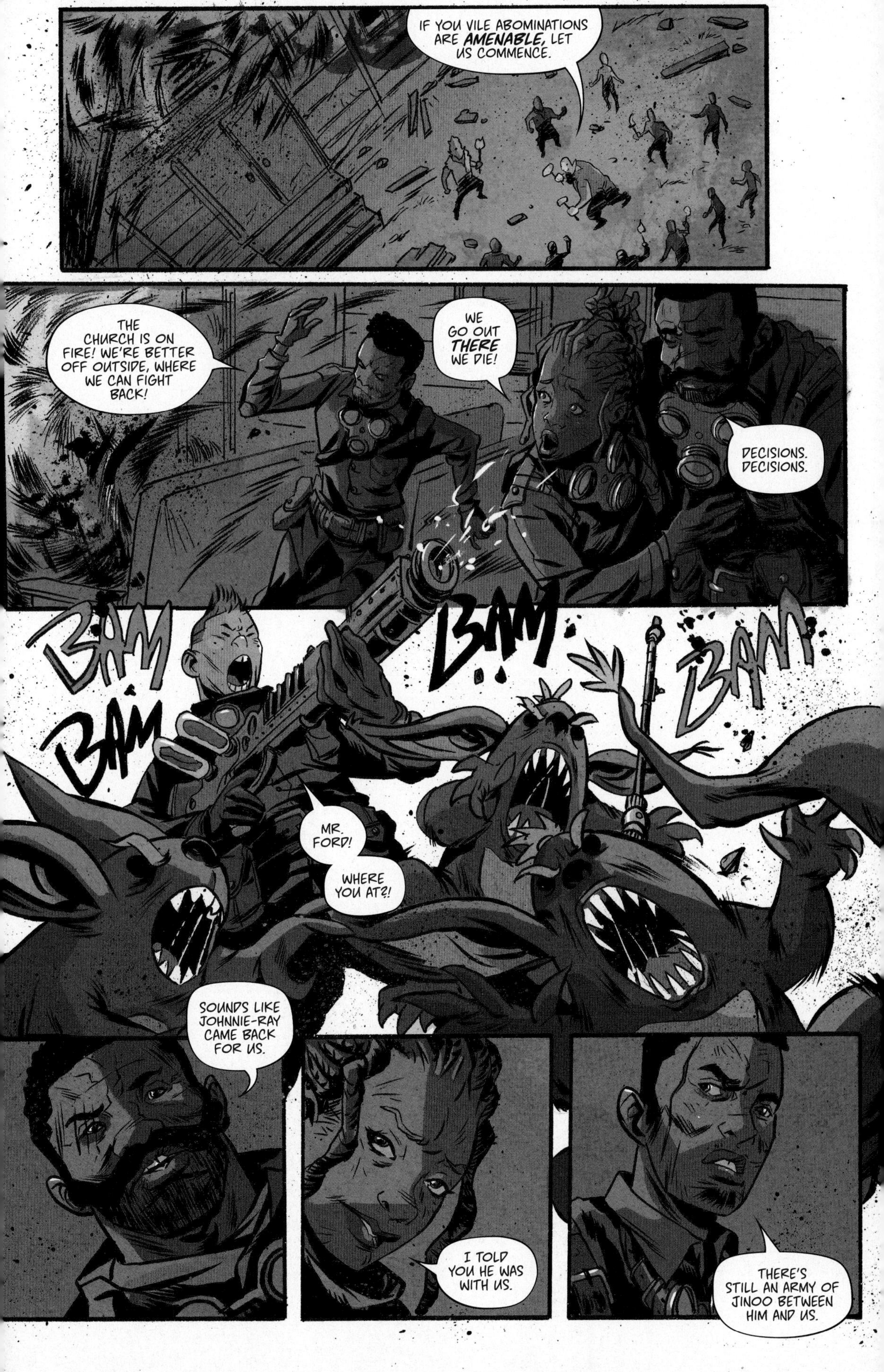
IF YOU VILE ABOMINATIONS ARE AMENABLE, LET US COMMENCE.
THE CHURCH IS ON FIRE! WE'RE BETTER OFF OUTSIDE, WHERE WE CAN FIGHT BACK!
WE GO OUT THERE WE DIE!
DECISIONS. DECISIONS.
BAM
BAM
BAM
BAM
MR. FORD!
WHERE YOU AT?!
SOUNDS LIKE JOHNNIE-RAY CAME BACK FOR US.
I TOLD YOU HE WAS WITH US.
THERE'S STILL AN ARMY OF JINOO BETWEEN HIM AND US.

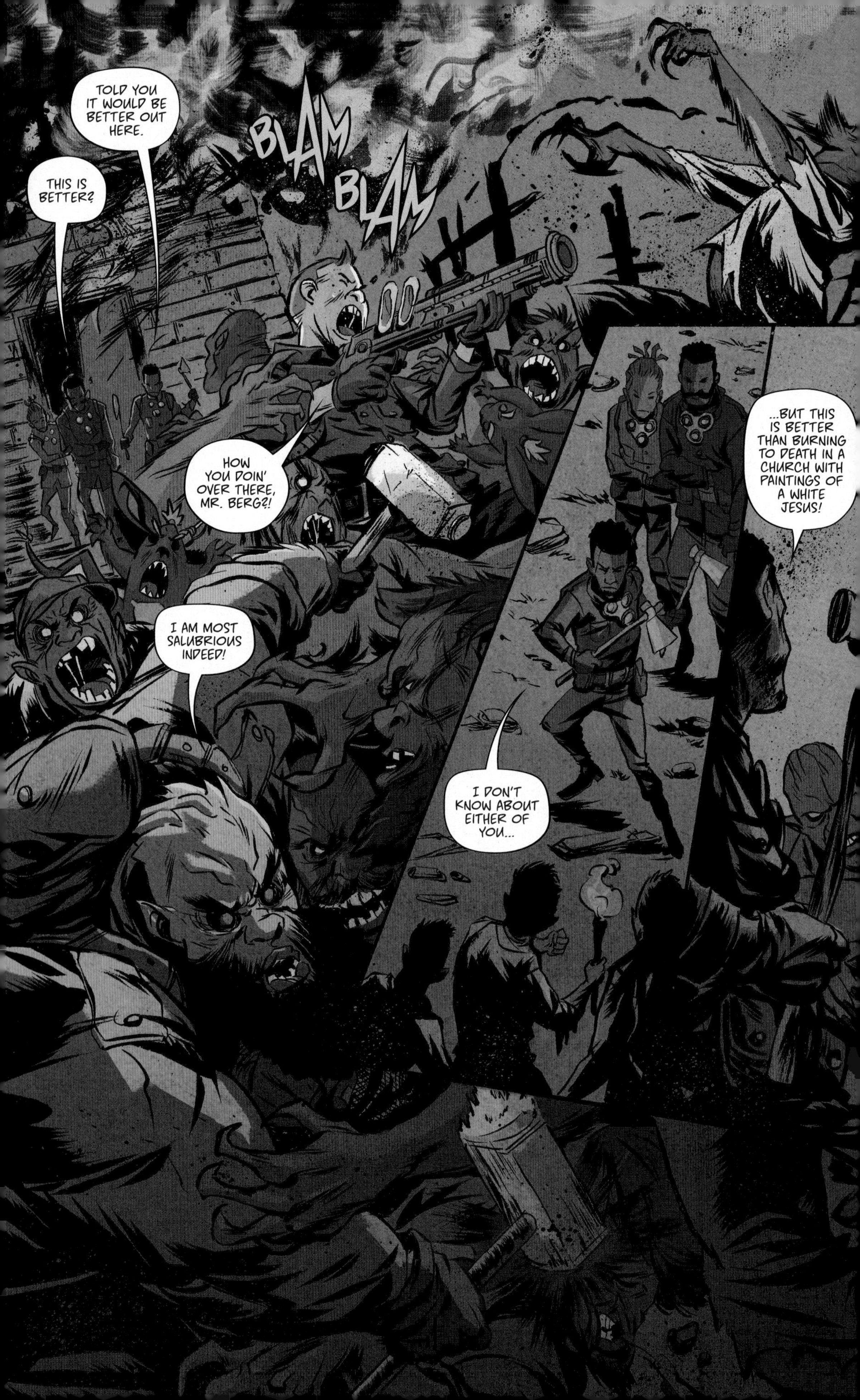
TOLD YOU IT WOULD BE BETTER OUT HERE.
THIS IS BETTER?
BLAM BLAM
HOW YOU DOIN' OVER THERE, MR. BERG?!
I AM MOST SALUBRIOUS INDEED!
I DON'T KNOW ABOUT EITHER OF YOU...
...BUT THIS IS BETTER THAN BURNING TO DEATH IN A CHURCH WITH PAINTINGS OF A WHITE JESUS!

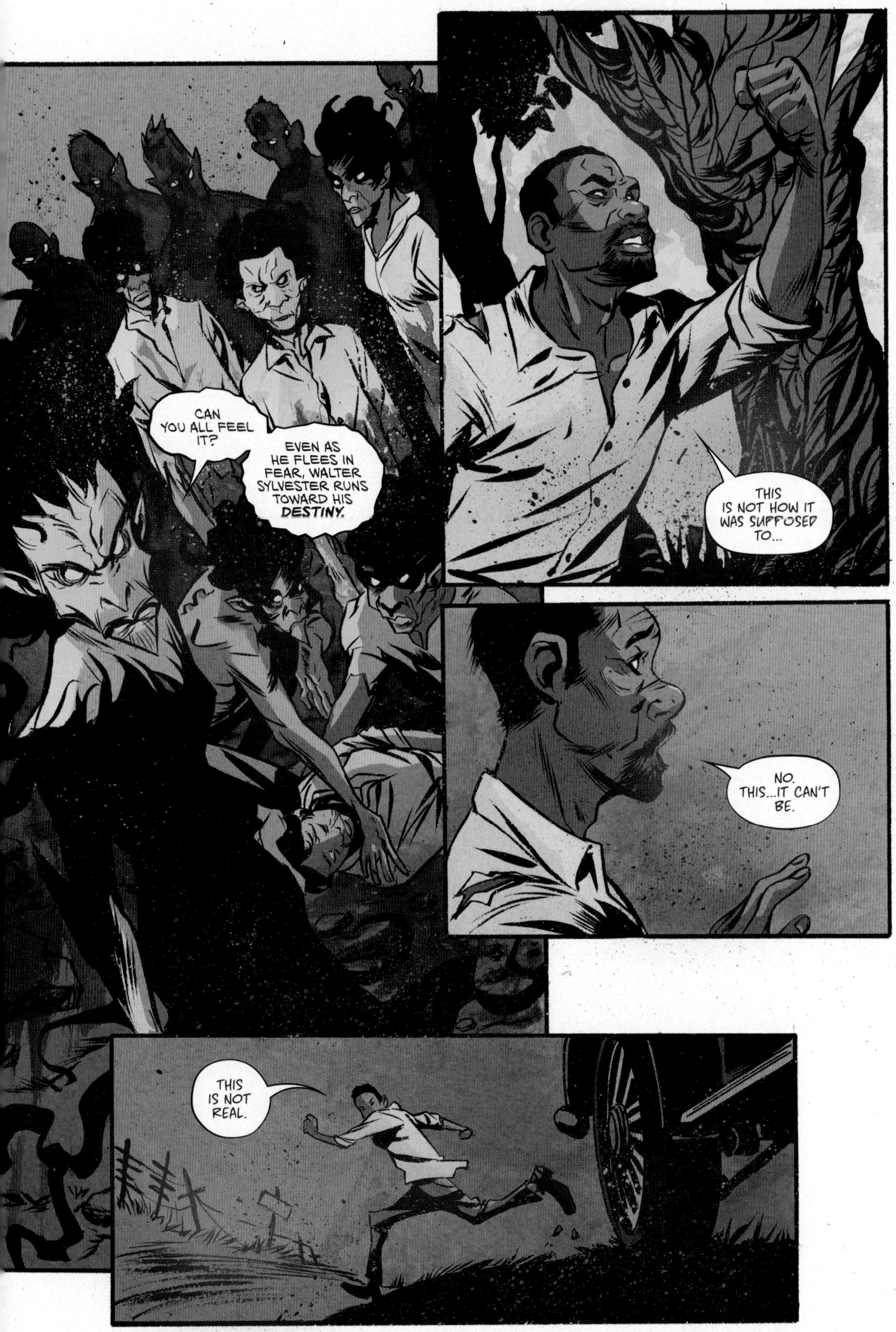
CAN YOU ALL FEEL IT?
EVEN AS HE FLEES IN FEAR, WALTER SYLVESTER RUNS TOWARD HIS **DESTINY.**
THIS IS NOT HOW IT WAS SUPPOSED TO...
NO. THIS...IT CAN'T BE.
THIS IS NOT REAL.

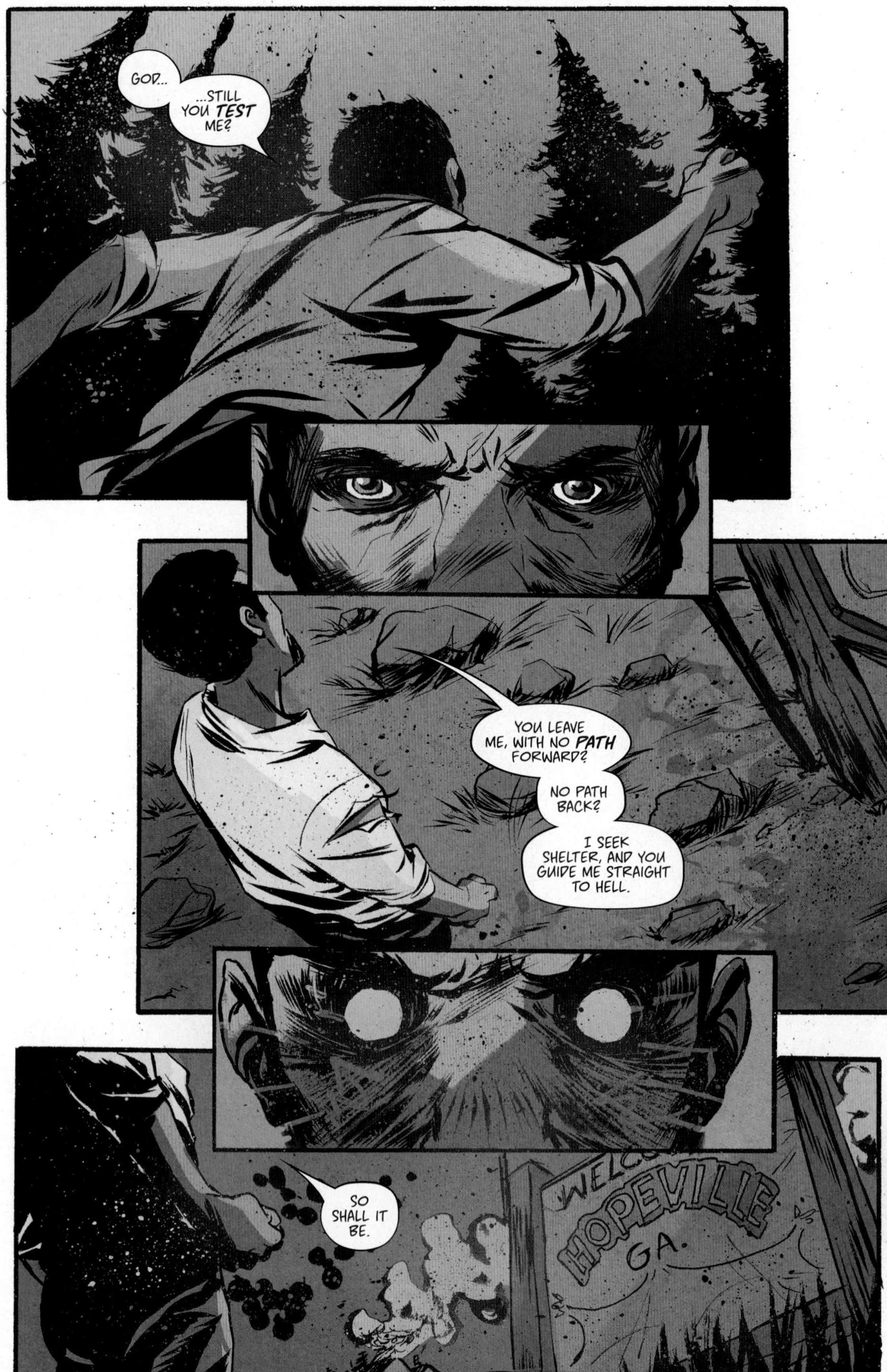
GOD...
...STILL YOU TEST ME?
YOU LEAVE ME, WITH NO PATH FORWARD?
NO PATH BACK?
I SEEK SHELTER, AND YOU GUIDE ME STRAIGHT TO HELL.
SO SHALL IT BE.
HOPEVILLE
GA.
NIGRAS DON'T LET THE SUN

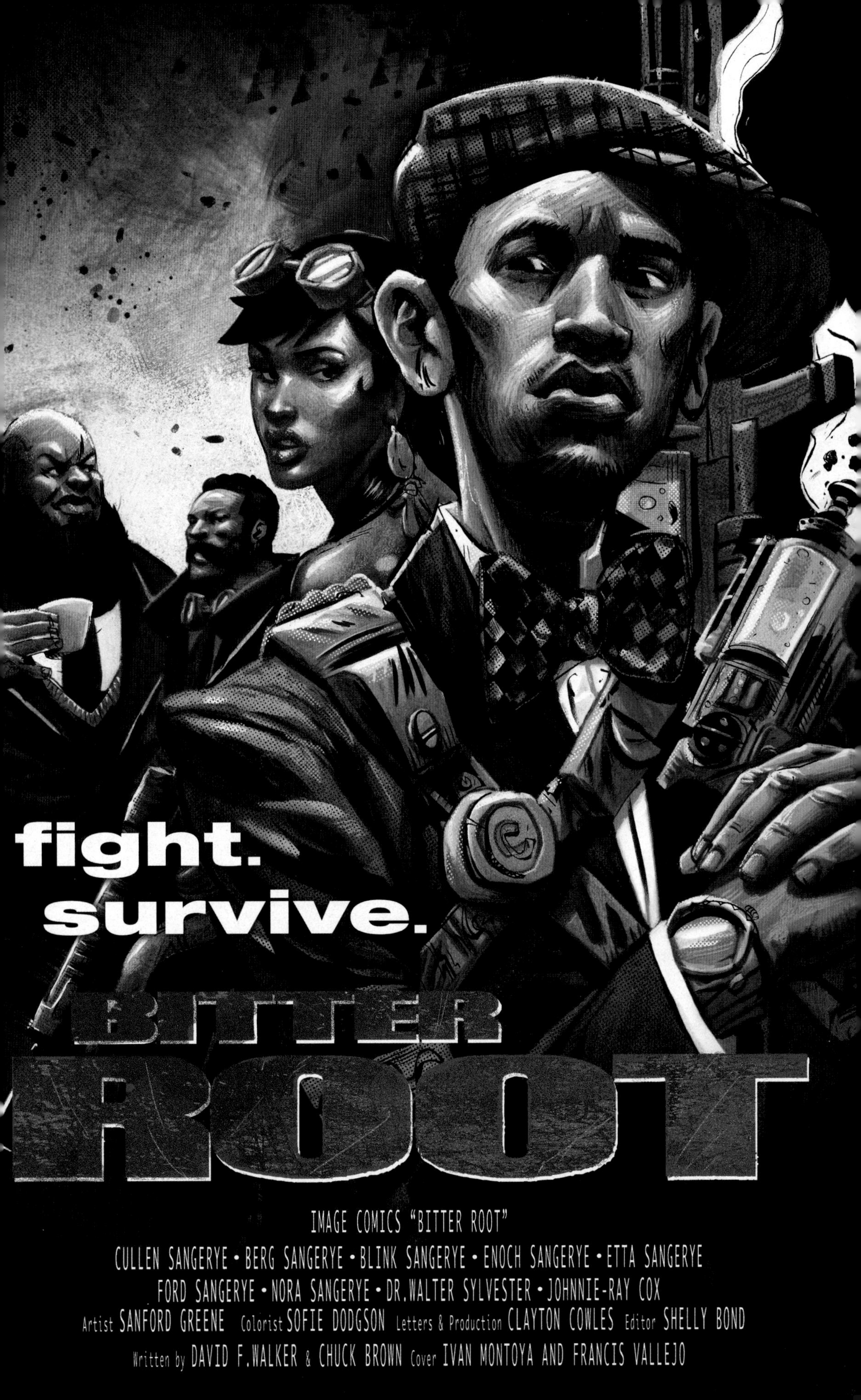
fight.
survive.
BITTER
ROOT
IMAGE COMICS "BITTER ROOT"
CULLEN SANGERYE • BERG SANGERYE • BLINK SANGERYE • ENOCH SANGERYE • ETTA SANGERYE
FORD SANGERYE • NORA SANGERYE • DR.WALTER SYLVESTER • JOHNNIE-RAY COX
Artist SANFORD GREENE Colorist SOFIE DODGSON Letters & Production CLAYTON COWLES Editor SHELLY BOND
Written by DAVID F.WALKER & CHUCK BROWN Cover IVAN MONTOYA AND FRANCIS VALLEJO

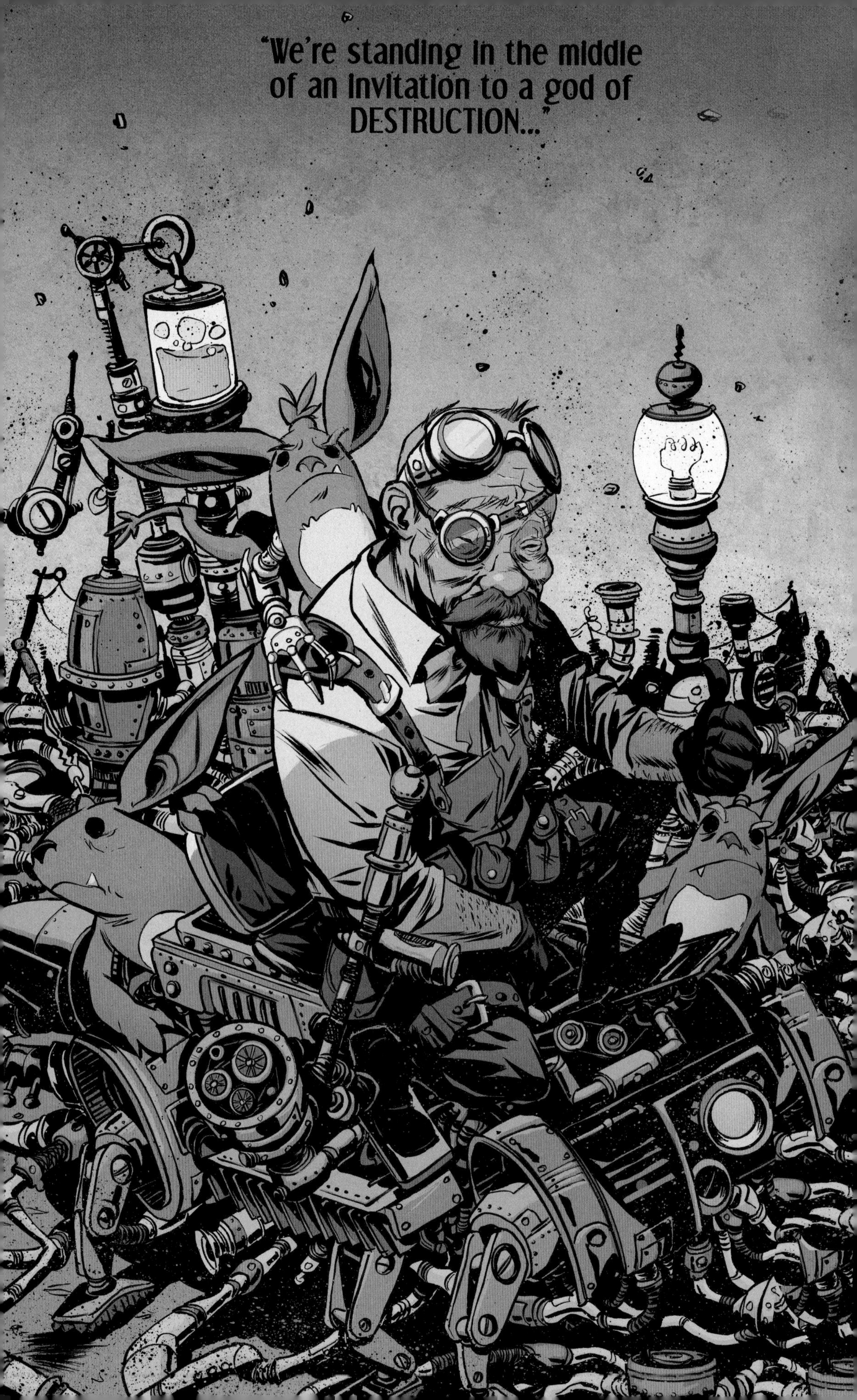
"We're standing in the middle of an invitation to a god of DESTRUCTION..."

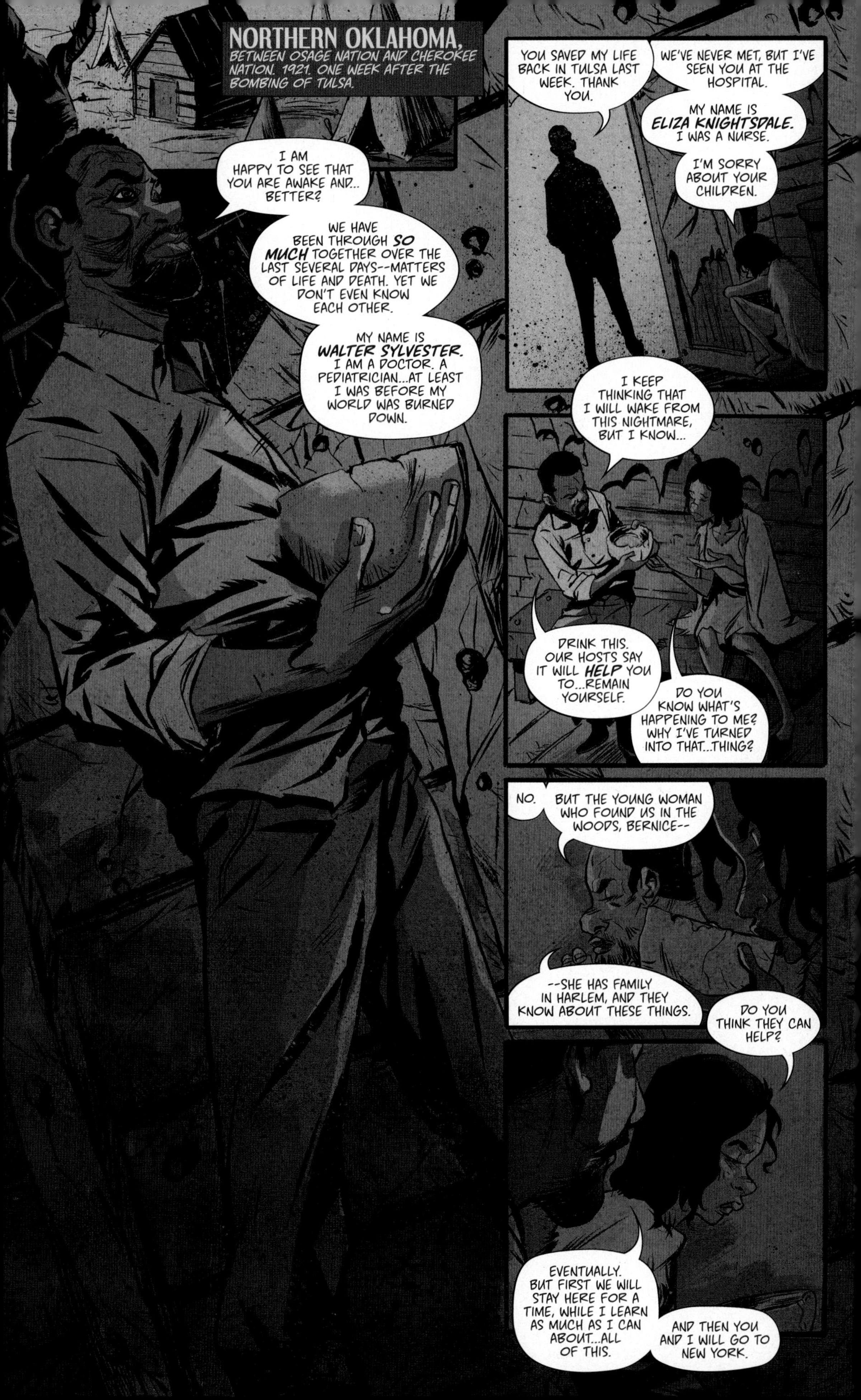
NORTHERN OKLAHOMA,
BETWEEN OSAGE NATION AND CHEROKEE NATION. 1921. ONE WEEK AFTER THE BOMBING OF TULSA.
I AM HAPPY TO SEE THAT YOU ARE AWAKE AND... BETTER?
WE HAVE BEEN THROUGH SO MUCH TOGETHER OVER THE LAST SEVERAL DAYS--MATTERS OF LIFE AND DEATH. YET WE DON'T EVEN KNOW EACH OTHER.
MY NAME IS WALTER SYLVESTER. I AM A DOCTOR. A PEDIATRICIAN...AT LEAST I WAS BEFORE MY WORLD WAS BURNED DOWN.
YOU SAVED MY LIFE BACK IN TULSA LAST WEEK. THANK YOU.
WE'VE NEVER MET, BUT I'VE SEEN YOU AT THE HOSPITAL.
MY NAME IS ELIZA KNIGHTSDALE. I WAS A NURSE.
I'M SORRY ABOUT YOUR CHILDREN.
I KEEP THINKING THAT I WILL WAKE FROM THIS NIGHTMARE, BUT I KNOW...
DRINK THIS. OUR HOSTS SAY IT WILL HELP YOU TO...REMAIN YOURSELF.
DO YOU KNOW WHAT'S HAPPENING TO ME? WHY I'VE TURNED INTO THAT...THING?
NO.
BUT THE YOUNG WOMAN WHO FOUND US IN THE WOODS, BERNICE--
--SHE HAS FAMILY IN HARLEM, AND THEY KNOW ABOUT THESE THINGS.
DO YOU THINK THEY CAN HELP?
EVENTUALLY. BUT FIRST WE WILL STAY HERE FOR A TIME, WHILE I LEARN AS MUCH AS I CAN ABOUT...ALL OF THIS.
AND THEN YOU AND I WILL GO TO NEW YORK.

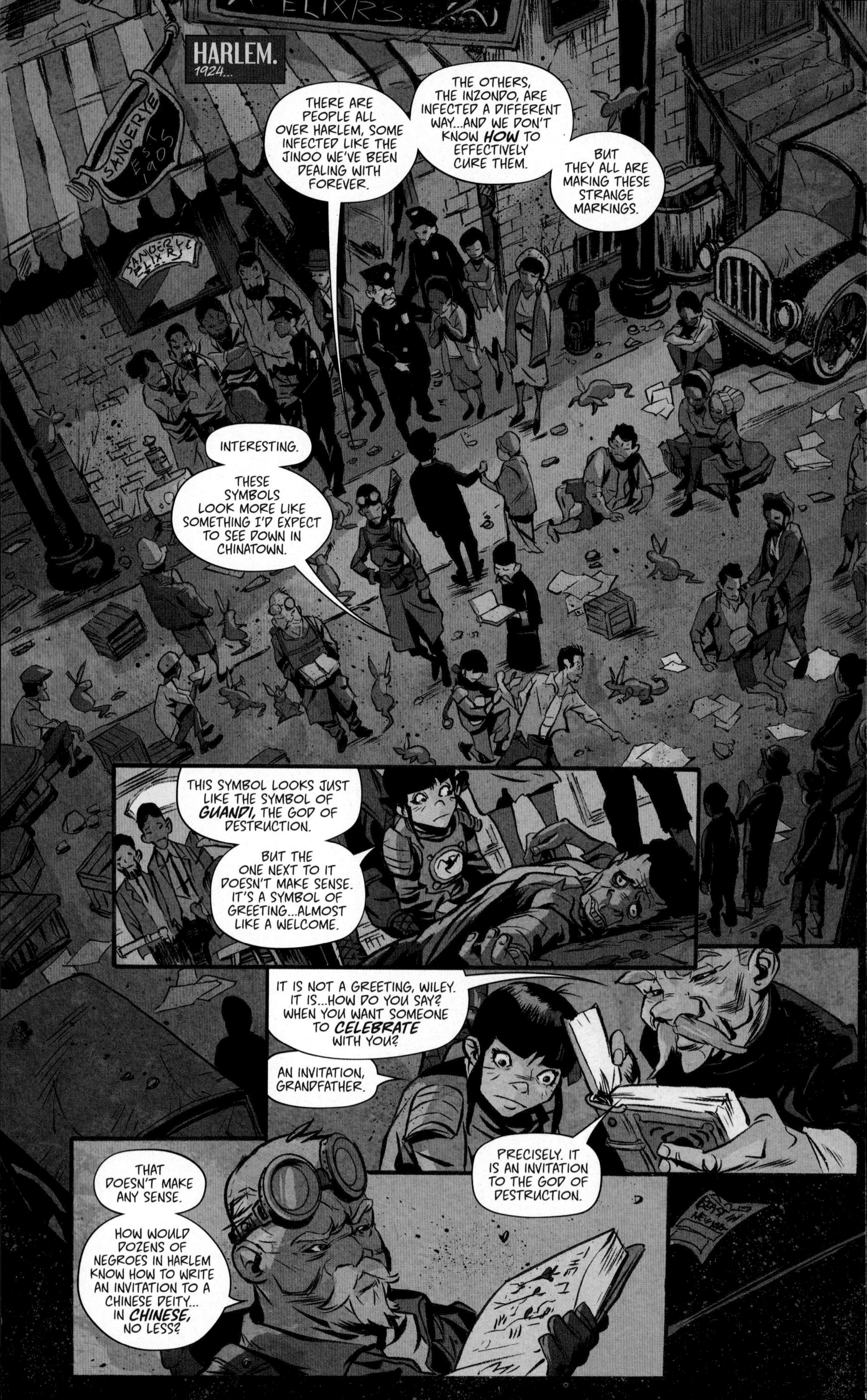

HARLEM. 1924...
SANGERYE EST 1905
THERE ARE PEOPLE ALL OVER HARLEM, SOME INFECTED LIKE THE JINOO WE'VE BEEN DEALING WITH FOREVER.
THE OTHERS, THE INZONDO, ARE INFECTED A DIFFERENT WAY...AND WE DON'T KNOW **HOW** TO EFFECTIVELY CURE THEM.
BUT THEY ALL ARE MAKING THESE STRANGE MARKINGS.
INTERESTING.
THESE SYMBOLS LOOK MORE LIKE SOMETHING I'D EXPECT TO SEE DOWN IN CHINATOWN.
THIS SYMBOL LOOKS JUST LIKE THE SYMBOL OF **GUANDI,** THE GOD OF DESTRUCTION.
BUT THE ONE NEXT TO IT DOESN'T MAKE SENSE. IT'S A SYMBOL OF GREETING...ALMOST LIKE A WELCOME.
IT IS NOT A GREETING, WILEY. IT IS...HOW DO YOU SAY? WHEN YOU WANT SOMEONE TO **CELEBRATE** WITH YOU?
AN INVITATION, GRANDFATHER.
PRECISELY. IT IS AN INVITATION TO THE GOD OF DESTRUCTION.
THAT DOESN'T MAKE ANY SENSE.
HOW WOULD DOZENS OF NEGROES IN HARLEM KNOW HOW TO WRITE AN INVITATION TO A CHINESE DEITY... IN **CHINESE,** NO LESS?

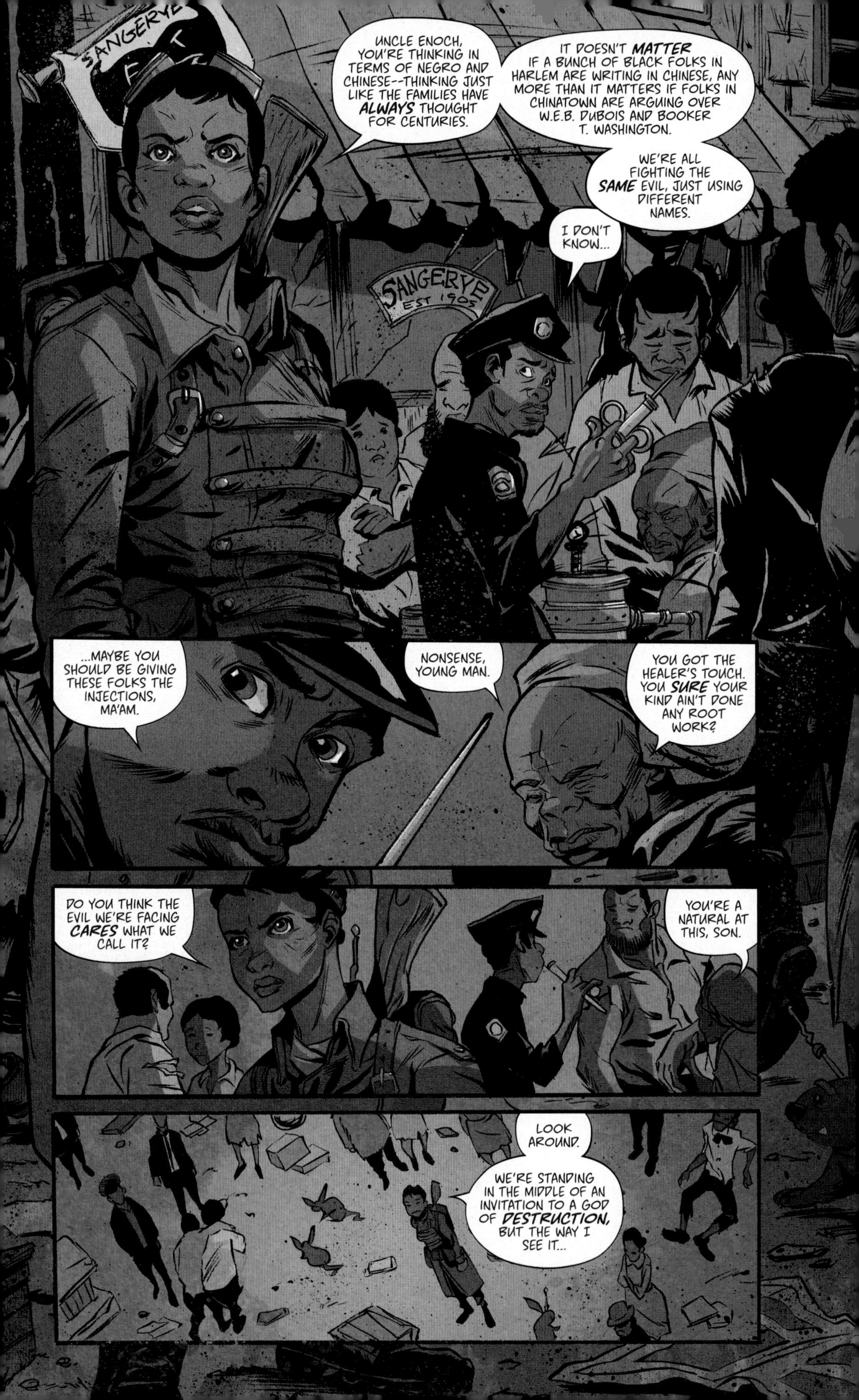
SANGERYE
UNCLE ENOCH, YOU'RE THINKING IN TERMS OF NEGRO AND CHINESE--THINKING JUST LIKE THE FAMILIES HAVE ALWAYS THOUGHT FOR CENTURIES.
IT DOESN'T MATTER IF A BUNCH OF BLACK FOLKS IN HARLEM ARE WRITING IN CHINESE, ANY MORE THAN IT MATTERS IF FOLKS IN CHINATOWN ARE ARGUING OVER W.E.B. DUBOIS AND BOOKER T. WASHINGTON.
WE'RE ALL FIGHTING THE SAME EVIL, JUST USING DIFFERENT NAMES.
I DON'T KNOW...
SANGERYE EST 1905
...MAYBE YOU SHOULD BE GIVING THESE FOLKS THE INJECTIONS, MA'AM.
NONSENSE, YOUNG MAN.
YOU GOT THE HEALER'S TOUCH. YOU SURE YOUR KIND AIN'T DONE ANY ROOT WORK?
DO YOU THINK THE EVIL WE'RE FACING CARES WHAT WE CALL IT?
YOU'RE A NATURAL AT THIS, SON.
LOOK AROUND.
WE'RE STANDING IN THE MIDDLE OF AN INVITATION TO A GOD OF DESTRUCTION, BUT THE WAY I SEE IT...

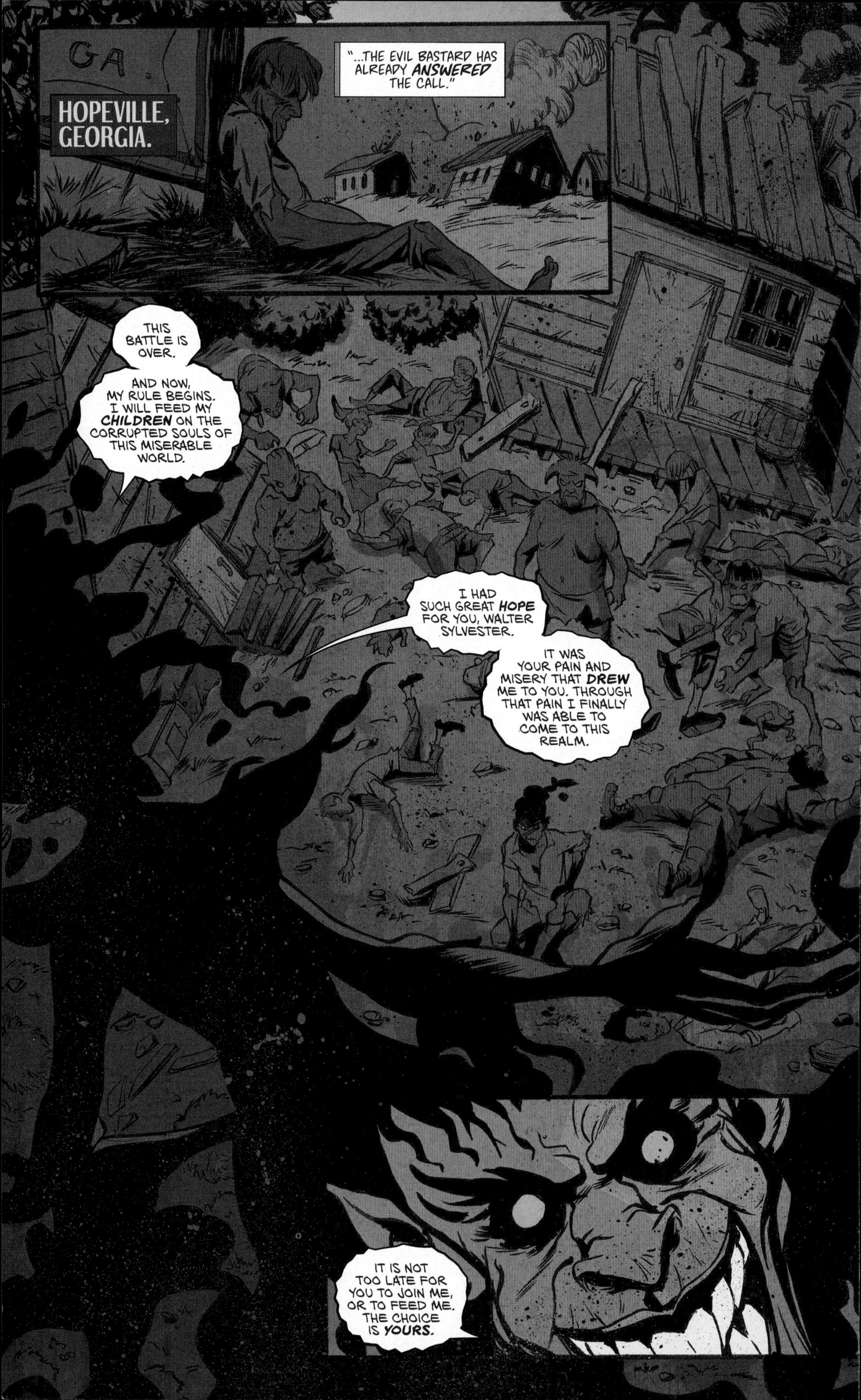
HOPEVILLE, GEORGIA.
"...THE EVIL BASTARD HAS ALREADY ANSWERED THE CALL."
GA
THIS BATTLE IS OVER.
AND NOW, MY RULE BEGINS. I WILL FEED MY CHILDREN ON THE CORRUPTED SOULS OF THIS MISERABLE WORLD.
I HAD SUCH GREAT HOPE FOR YOU, WALTER SYLVESTER.
IT WAS YOUR PAIN AND MISERY THAT DREW ME TO YOU. THROUGH THAT PAIN I FINALLY WAS ABLE TO COME TO THIS REALM.
IT IS NOT TOO LATE FOR YOU TO JOIN ME, OR TO FEED ME. THE CHOICE IS YOURS.

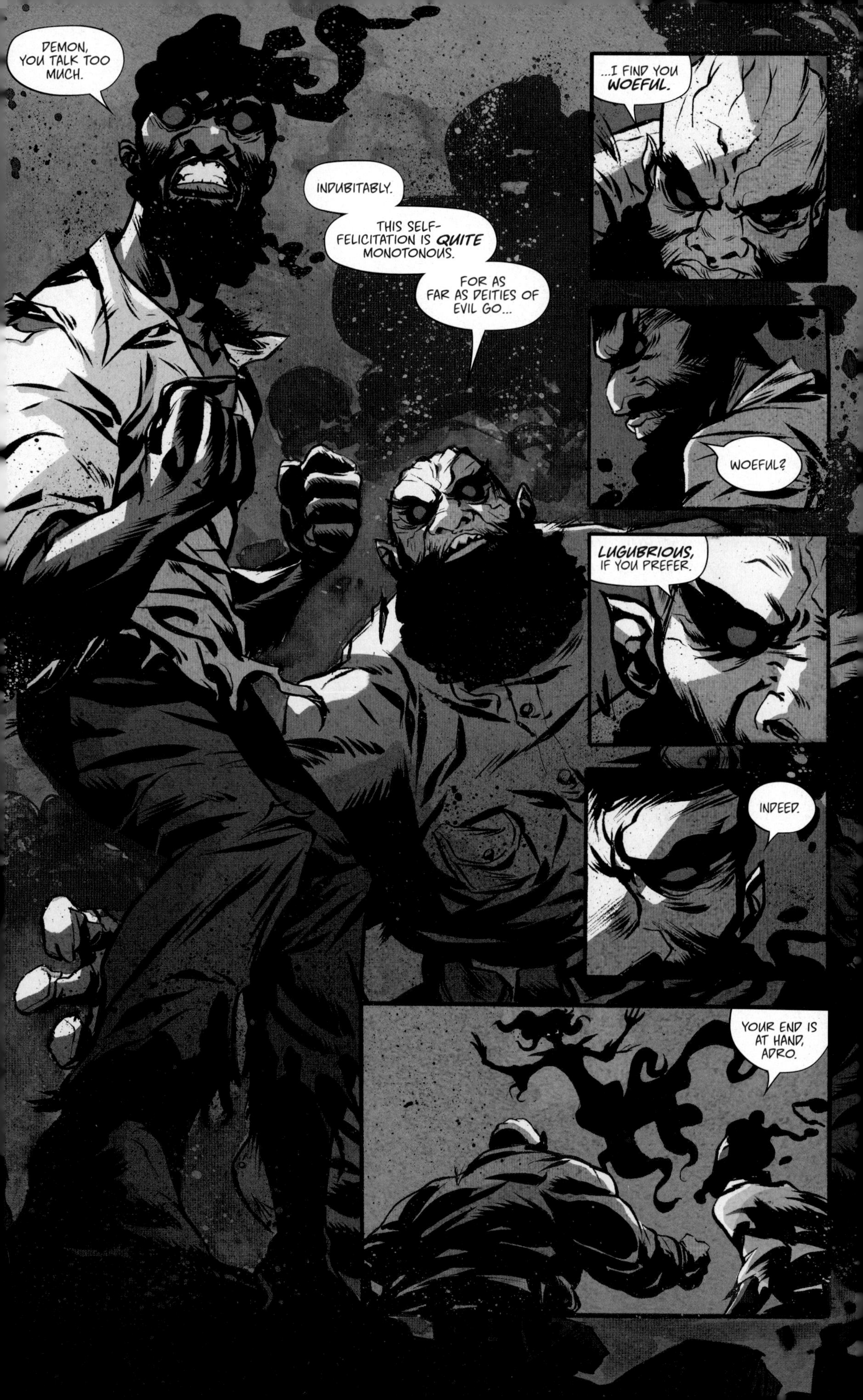
DEMON, YOU TALK TOO MUCH.
INDUBITABLY.
THIS SELF-FELICITATION IS *QUITE* MONOTONOUS.
FOR AS FAR AS DEITIES OF EVIL GO...
...I FIND YOU *WOEFUL.*
WOEFUL?
LUGUBRIOUS, IF YOU PREFER.
INDEED.
YOUR END IS AT HAND, ADRO.

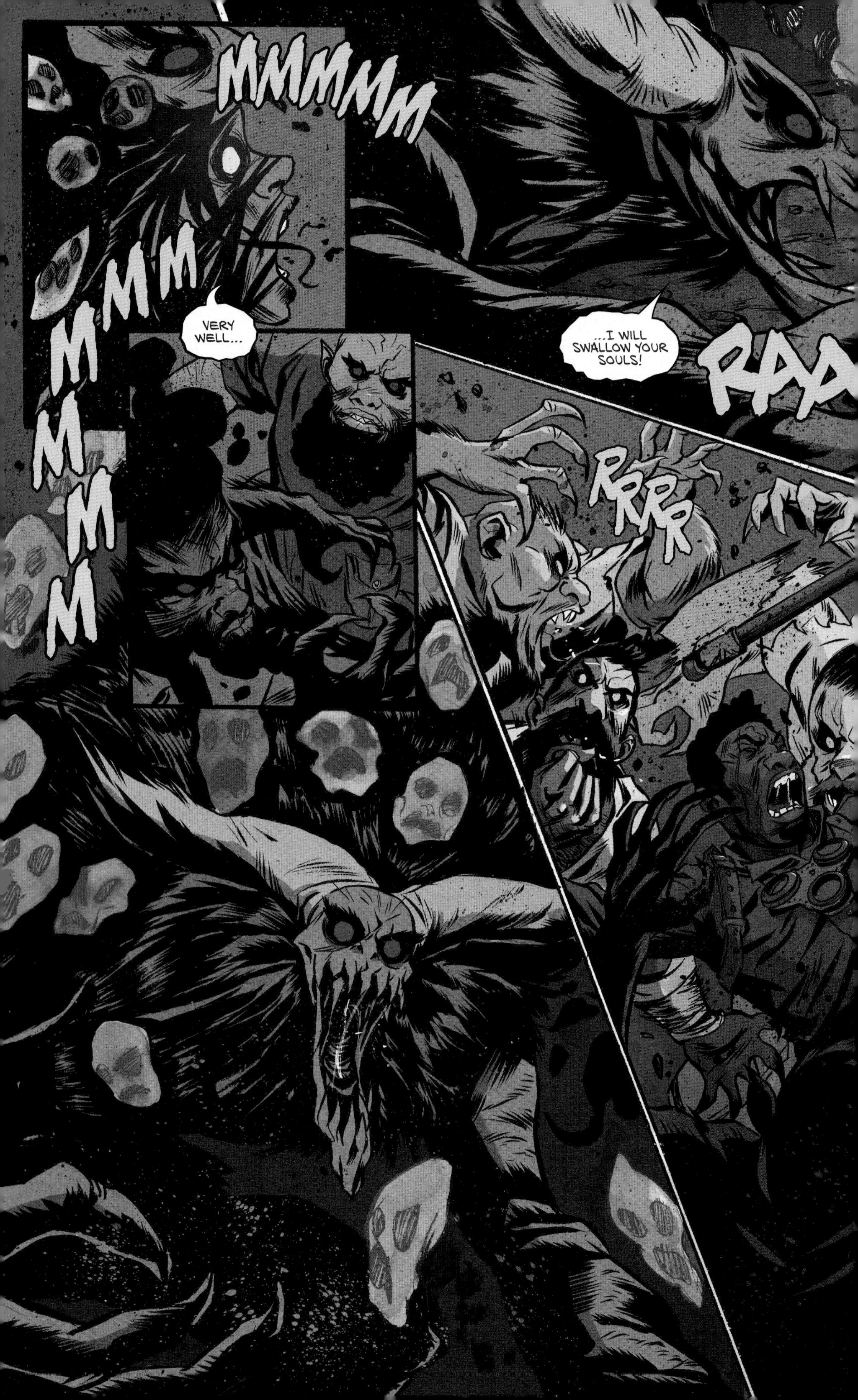
MMMMMM
MMMMMMMMM
VERY WELL...
...I WILL SWALLOW YOUR SOULS!
RAA
RRRR

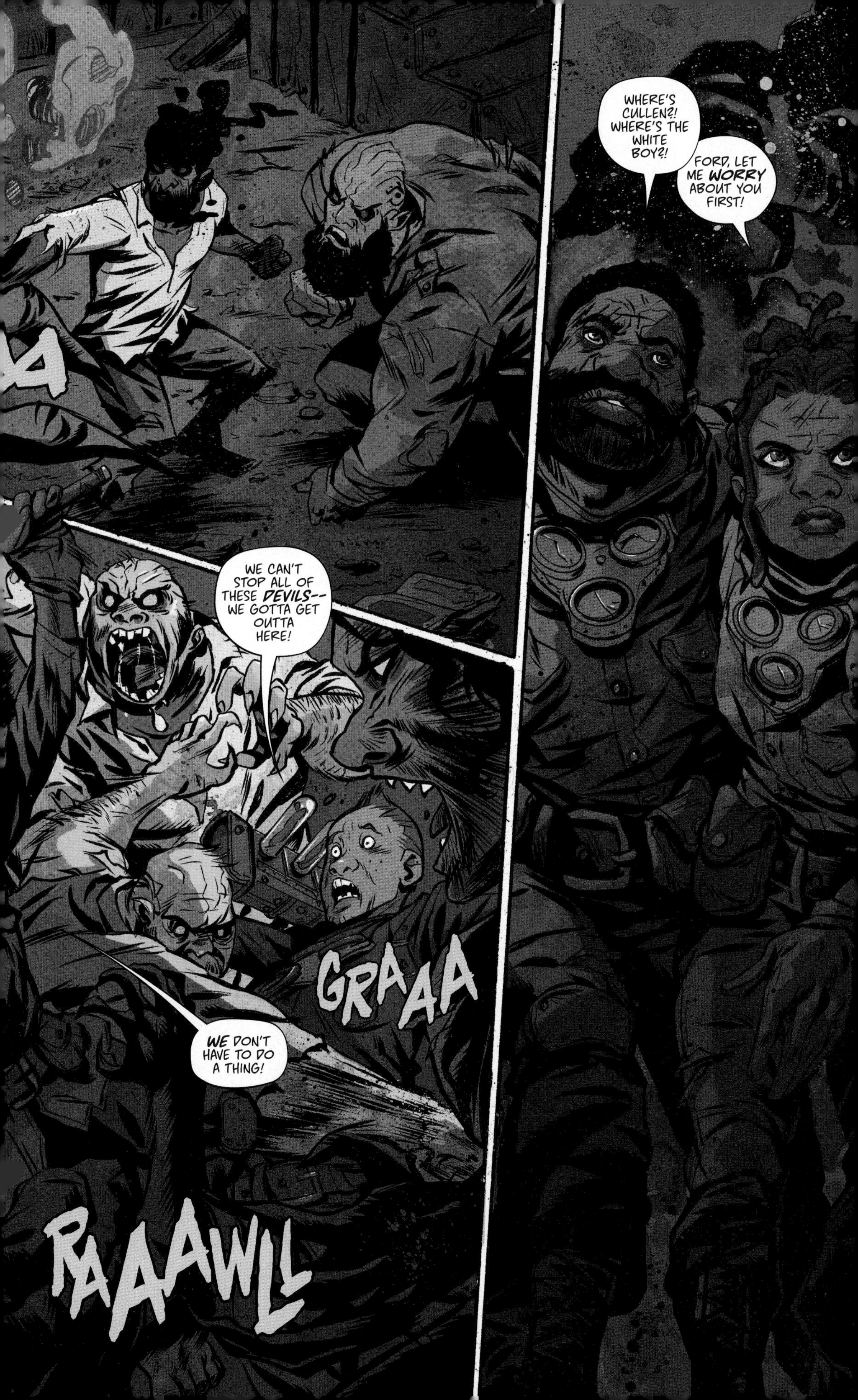
WE CAN'T STOP ALL OF THESE DEVILS-- WE GOTTA GET OUTTA HERE!
GRAAA
WE DON'T HAVE TO DO A THING!
RAAAWLL
WHERE'S CULLEN?! WHERE'S THE WHITE BOY?!
FORD, LET ME WORRY ABOUT YOU FIRST!

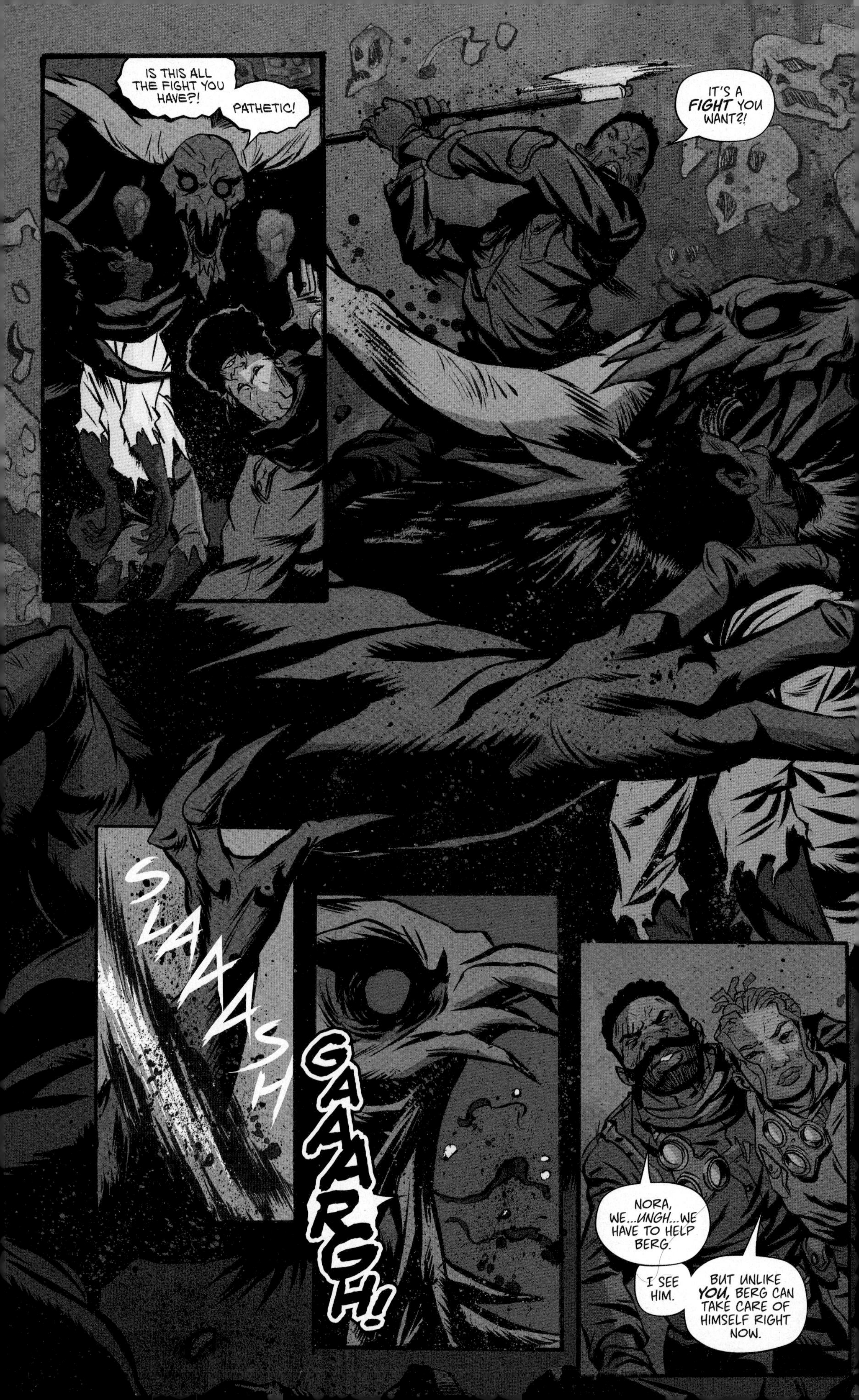
IS THIS ALL THE FIGHT YOU HAVE?!
PATHETIC!
IT'S A **FIGHT** YOU WANT?!
SLAAAASH
GAAARGH!
NORA, WE...*UNGH*...WE HAVE TO HELP BERG.
I SEE HIM.
BUT UNLIKE **YOU,** BERG CAN TAKE CARE OF HIMSELF RIGHT NOW.

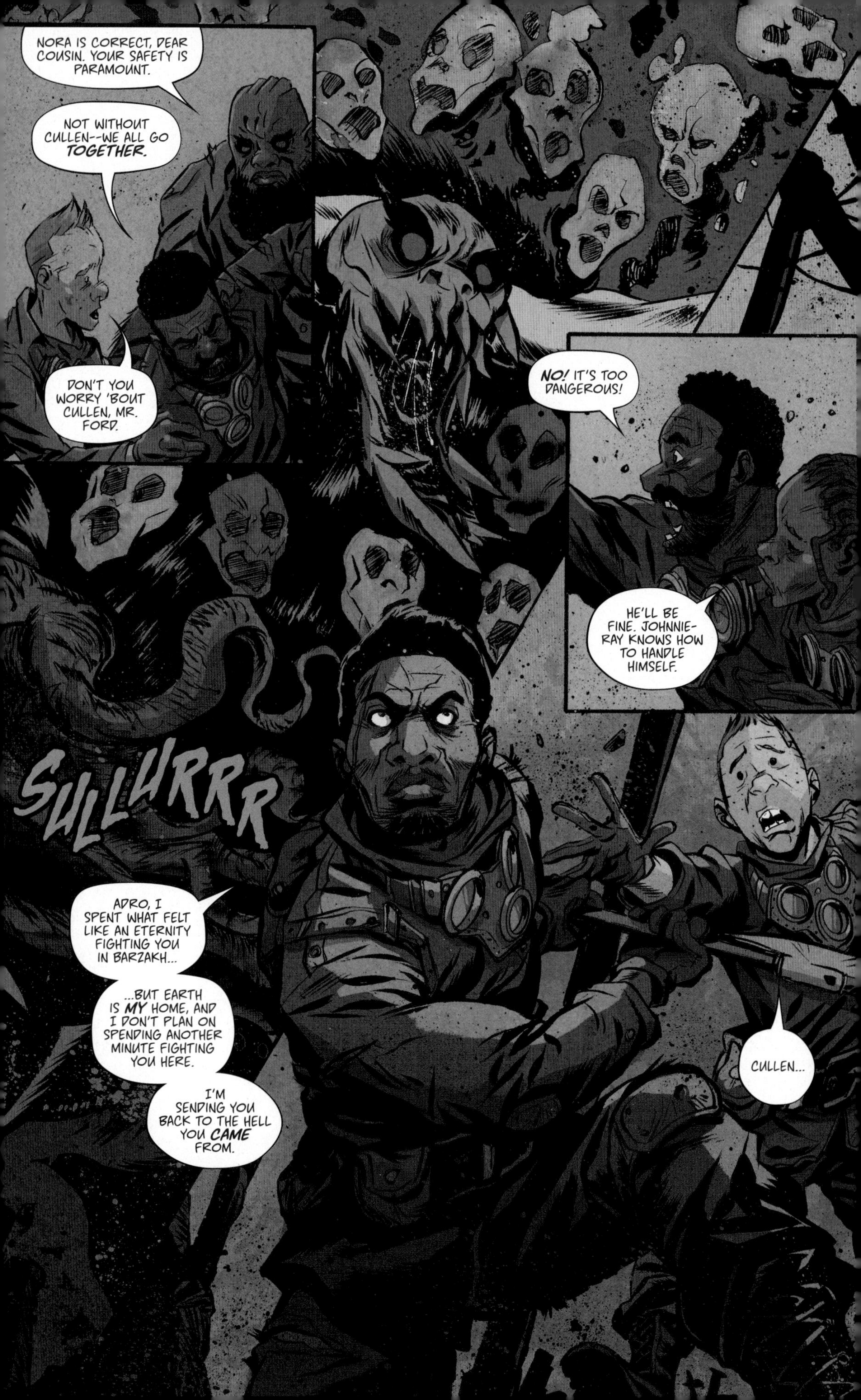
NORA IS CORRECT, DEAR COUSIN. YOUR SAFETY IS PARAMOUNT.
NOT WITHOUT CULLEN--WE ALL GO **TOGETHER.**
DON'T YOU WORRY 'BOUT CULLEN, MR. FORD.
NO! IT'S TOO DANGEROUS!
HE'LL BE FINE. JOHNNIE-RAY KNOWS HOW TO HANDLE HIMSELF.
SULLURRR
ADRO, I SPENT WHAT FELT LIKE AN ETERNITY FIGHTING YOU IN BARZAKH...
...BUT EARTH IS **MY** HOME, AND I DON'T PLAN ON SPENDING ANOTHER MINUTE FIGHTING YOU HERE.
I'M SENDING YOU BACK TO THE HELL YOU ***CAME*** FROM.
CULLEN...

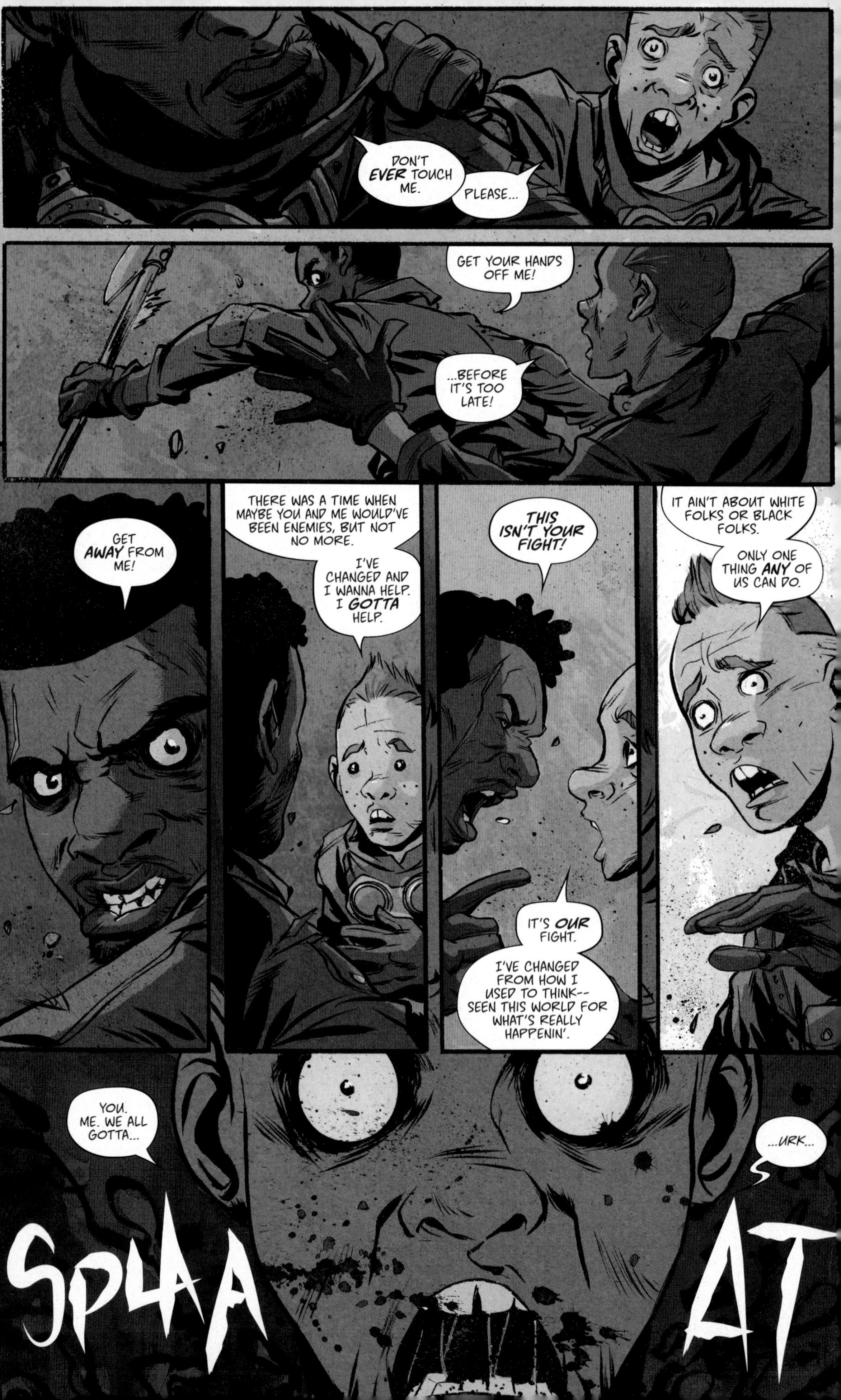
DON'T EVER TOUCH ME.
PLEASE...
GET YOUR HANDS OFF ME!
...BEFORE IT'S TOO LATE!
GET AWAY FROM ME!
THERE WAS A TIME WHEN MAYBE YOU AND ME WOULD'VE BEEN ENEMIES, BUT NOT NO MORE.
I'VE CHANGED AND I WANNA HELP. I GOTTA HELP.
THIS ISN'T YOUR FIGHT!
IT'S OUR FIGHT.
I'VE CHANGED FROM HOW I USED TO THINK-- SEEN THIS WORLD FOR WHAT'S REALLY HAPPENIN'.
IT AIN'T ABOUT WHITE FOLKS OR BLACK FOLKS.
ONLY ONE THING ANY OF US CAN DO.
YOU. ME. WE ALL GOTTA...
...URK...
SPLAAT

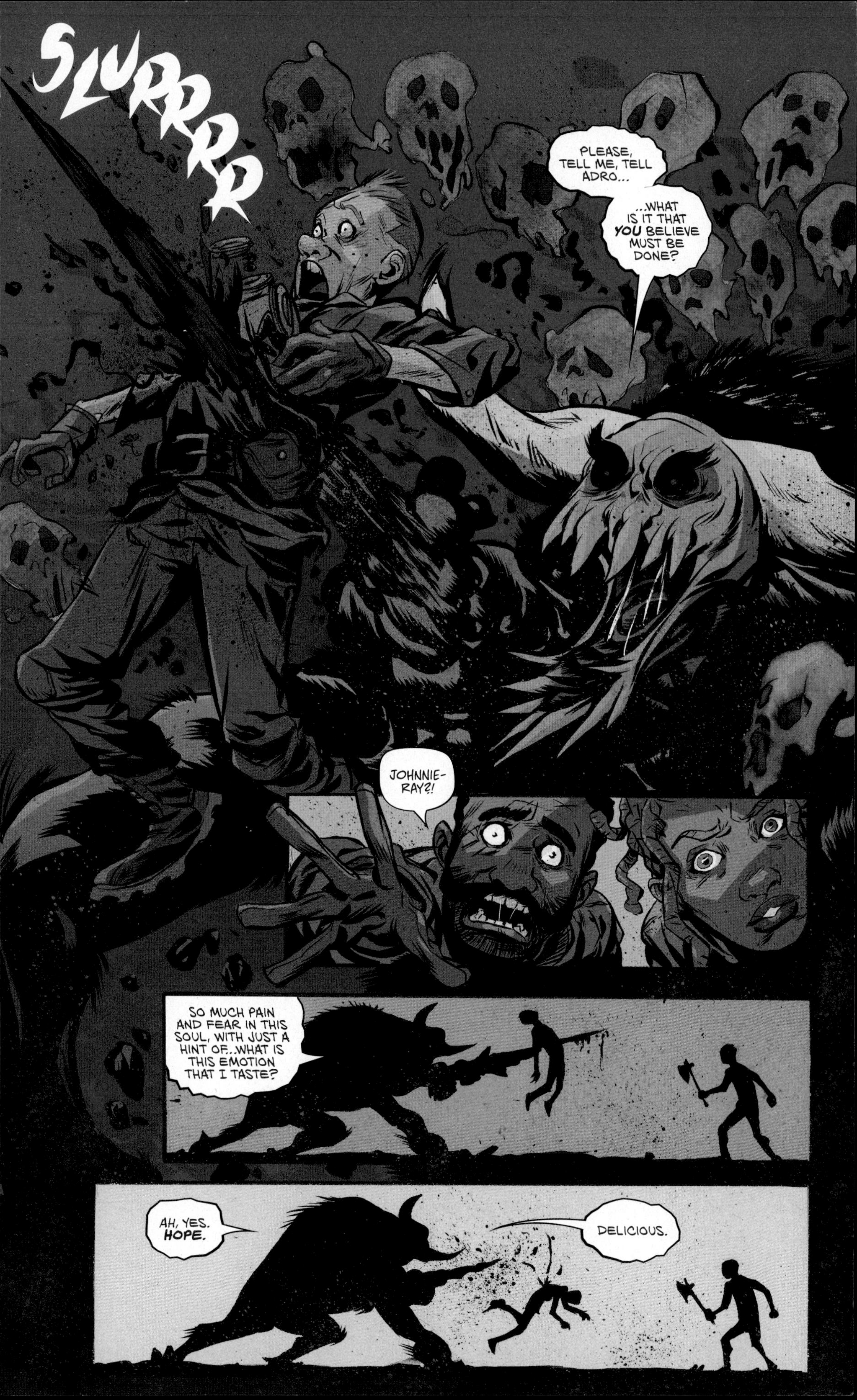
SLURRRR
PLEASE, TELL ME, TELL ADRO...
...WHAT IS IT THAT YOU BELIEVE MUST BE DONE?
JOHNNIE-RAY?!
SO MUCH PAIN AND FEAR IN THIS SOUL, WITH JUST A HINT OF..WHAT IS THIS EMOTION THAT I TASTE?
AH, YES. HOPE.
DELICIOUS.

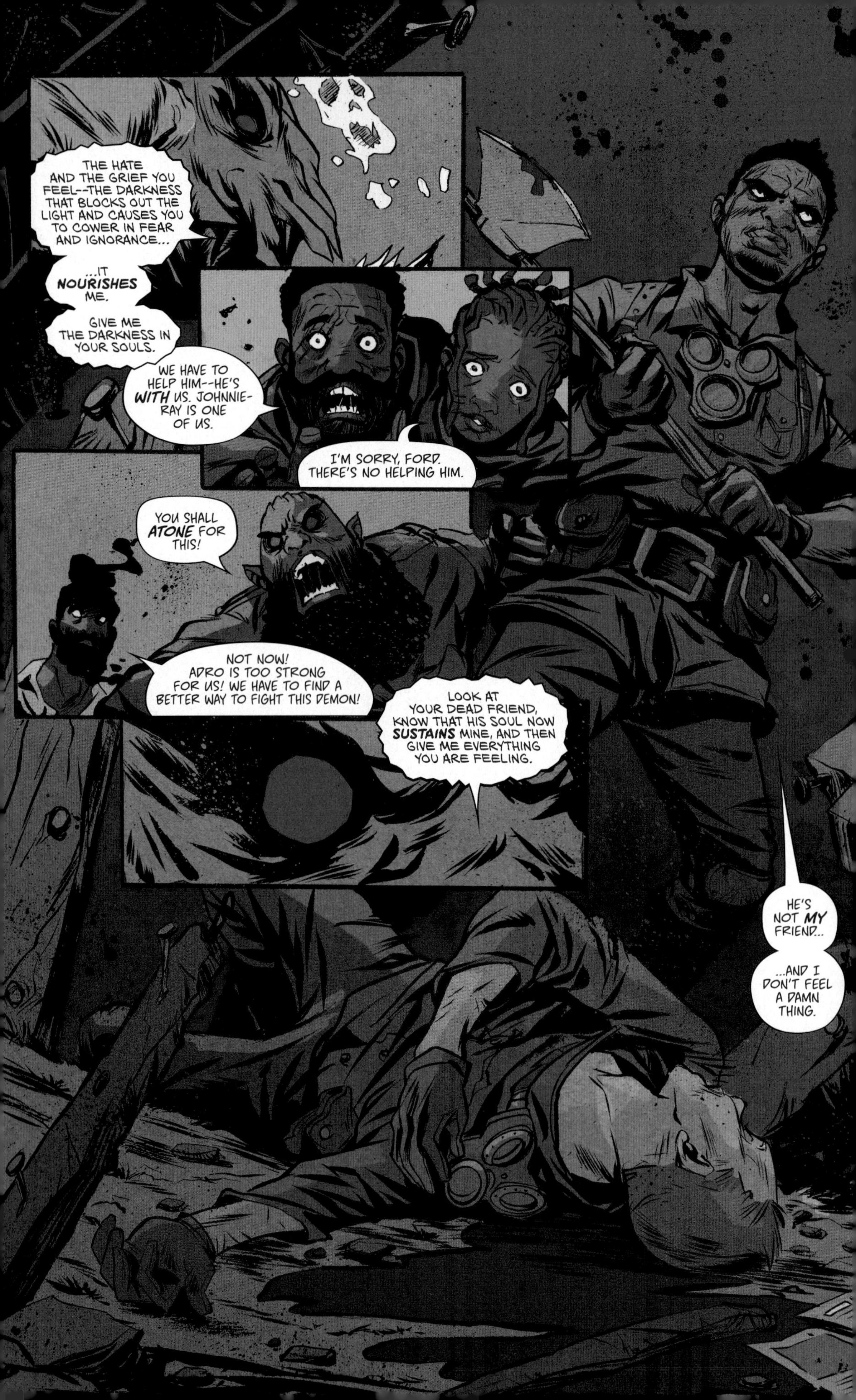
THE HATE AND THE GRIEF YOU FEEL--THE DARKNESS THAT BLOCKS OUT THE LIGHT AND CAUSES YOU TO COWER IN FEAR AND IGNORANCE...
...IT NOURISHES ME.
GIVE ME THE DARKNESS IN YOUR SOULS.
WE HAVE TO HELP HIM--HE'S WITH US. JOHNNIE-RAY IS ONE OF US.
I'M SORRY, FORD. THERE'S NO HELPING HIM.
YOU SHALL ATONE FOR THIS!
NOT NOW! ADRO IS TOO STRONG FOR US! WE HAVE TO FIND A BETTER WAY TO FIGHT THIS DEMON!
LOOK AT YOUR DEAD FRIEND, KNOW THAT HIS SOUL NOW SUSTAINS MINE, AND THEN GIVE ME EVERYTHING YOU ARE FEELING.
HE'S NOT MY FRIEND...
...AND I DON'T FEEL A DAMN THING.

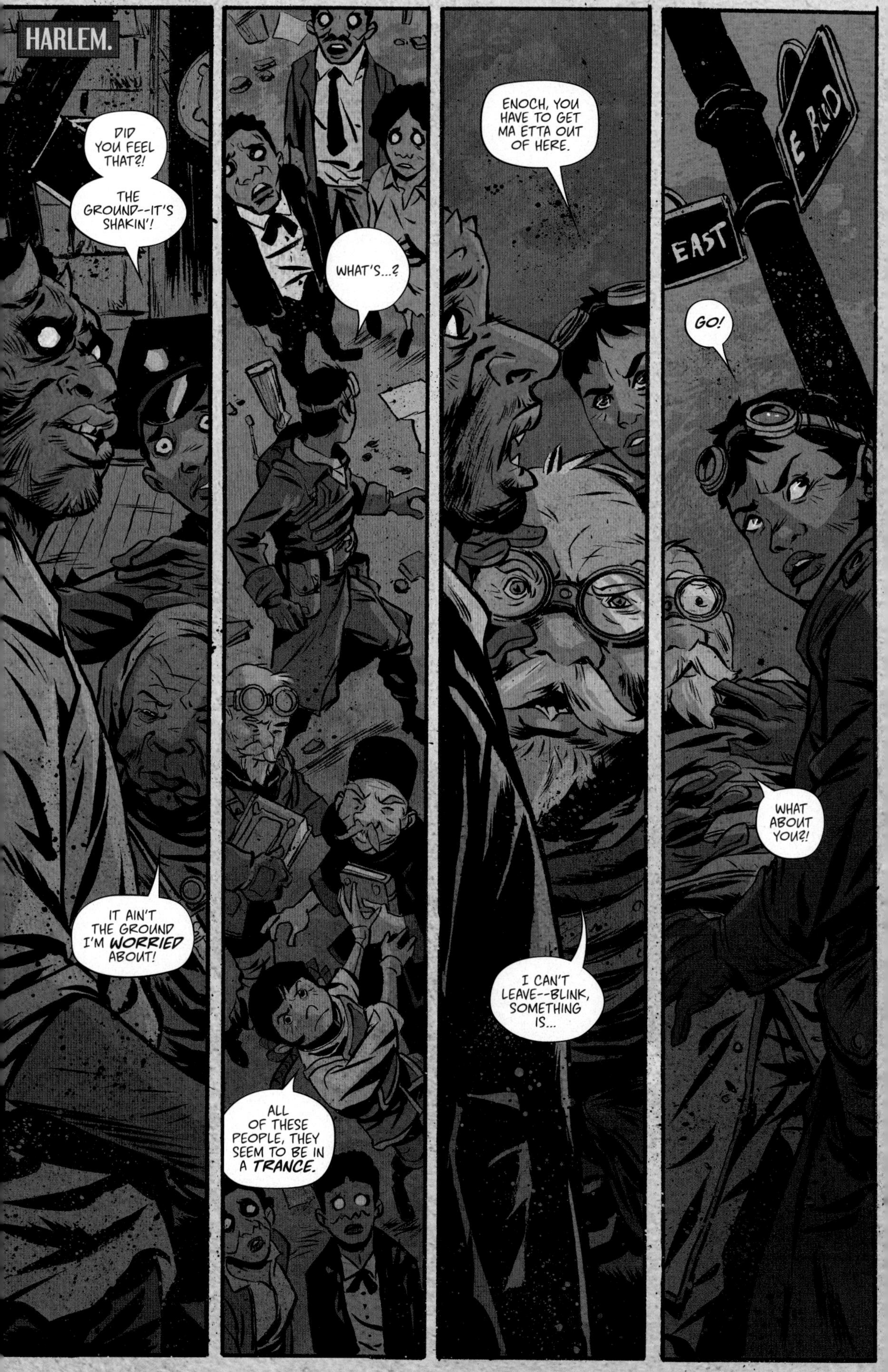
HARLEM.
DID YOU FEEL THAT?!
THE GROUND--IT'S SHAKIN'!
IT AIN'T THE GROUND I'M WORRIED ABOUT!
WHAT'S...?
ALL OF THESE PEOPLE, THEY SEEM TO BE IN A TRANCE.
ENOCH, YOU HAVE TO GET MA ETTA OUT OF HERE.
I CAN'T LEAVE--BLINK, SOMETHING IS...
EAST
GO!
WHAT ABOUT YOU?!

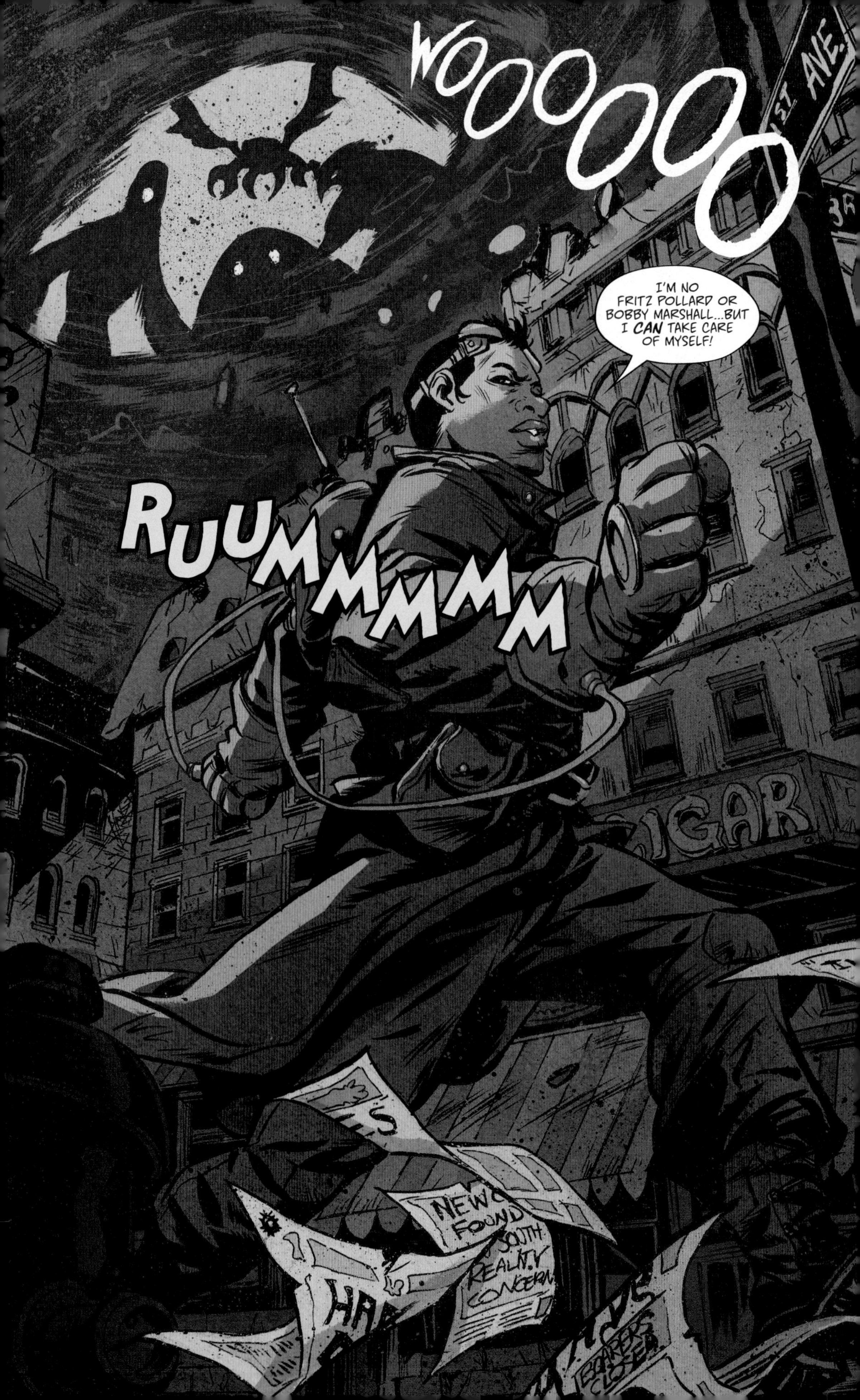
WOOOOOO
1ST AVE.
I'M NO FRITZ POLLARD OR BOBBY MARSHALL...BUT I CAN TAKE CARE OF MYSELF!
RUUMMMMMMM
CIGAR

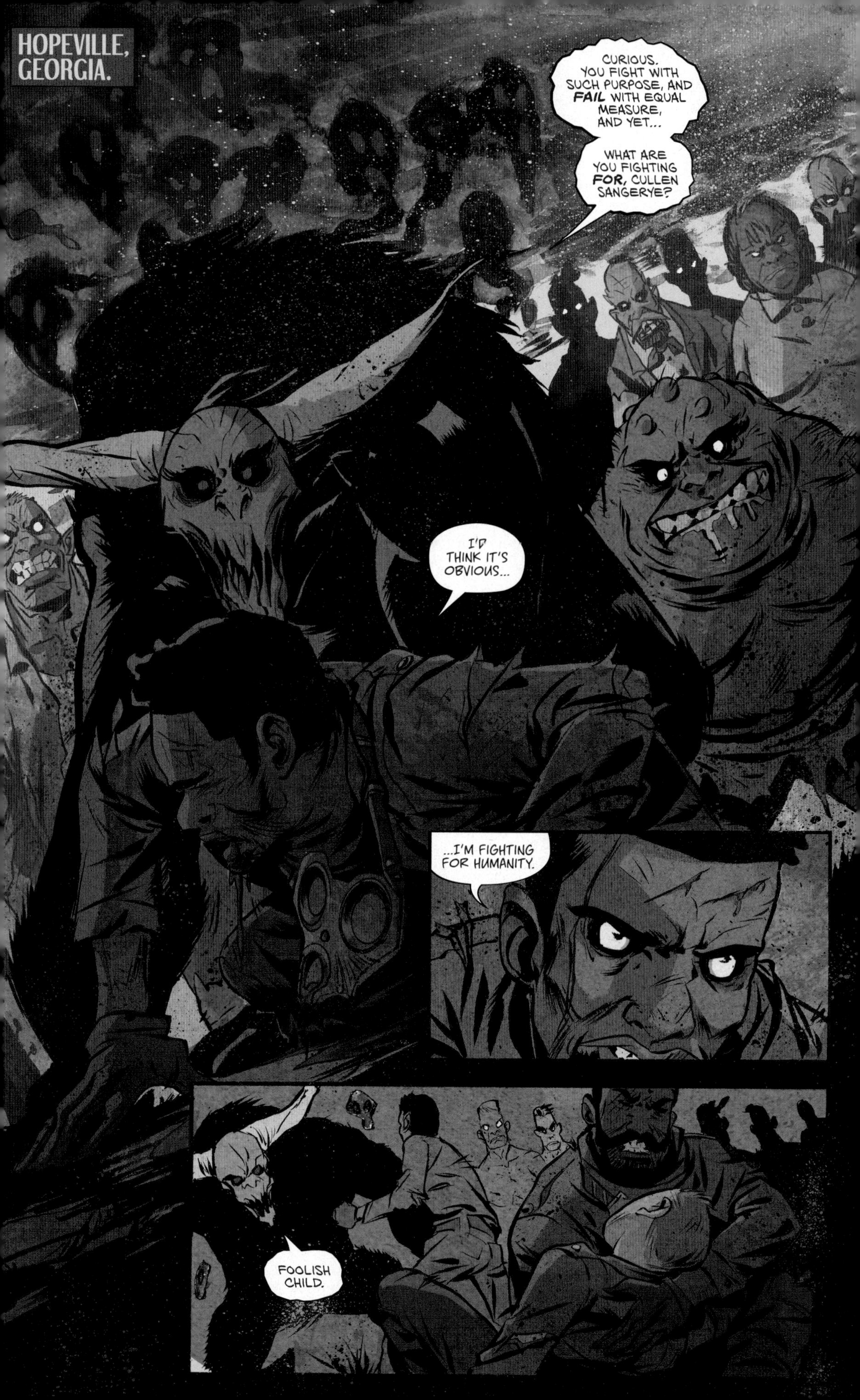
HOPEVILLE, GEORGIA.
CURIOUS. YOU FIGHT WITH SUCH PURPOSE, AND FAIL WITH EQUAL MEASURE, AND YET...
WHAT ARE YOU FIGHTING FOR, CULLEN SANGERYE?
I'D THINK IT'S OBVIOUS...
...I'M FIGHTING FOR HUMANITY.
FOOLISH CHILD.

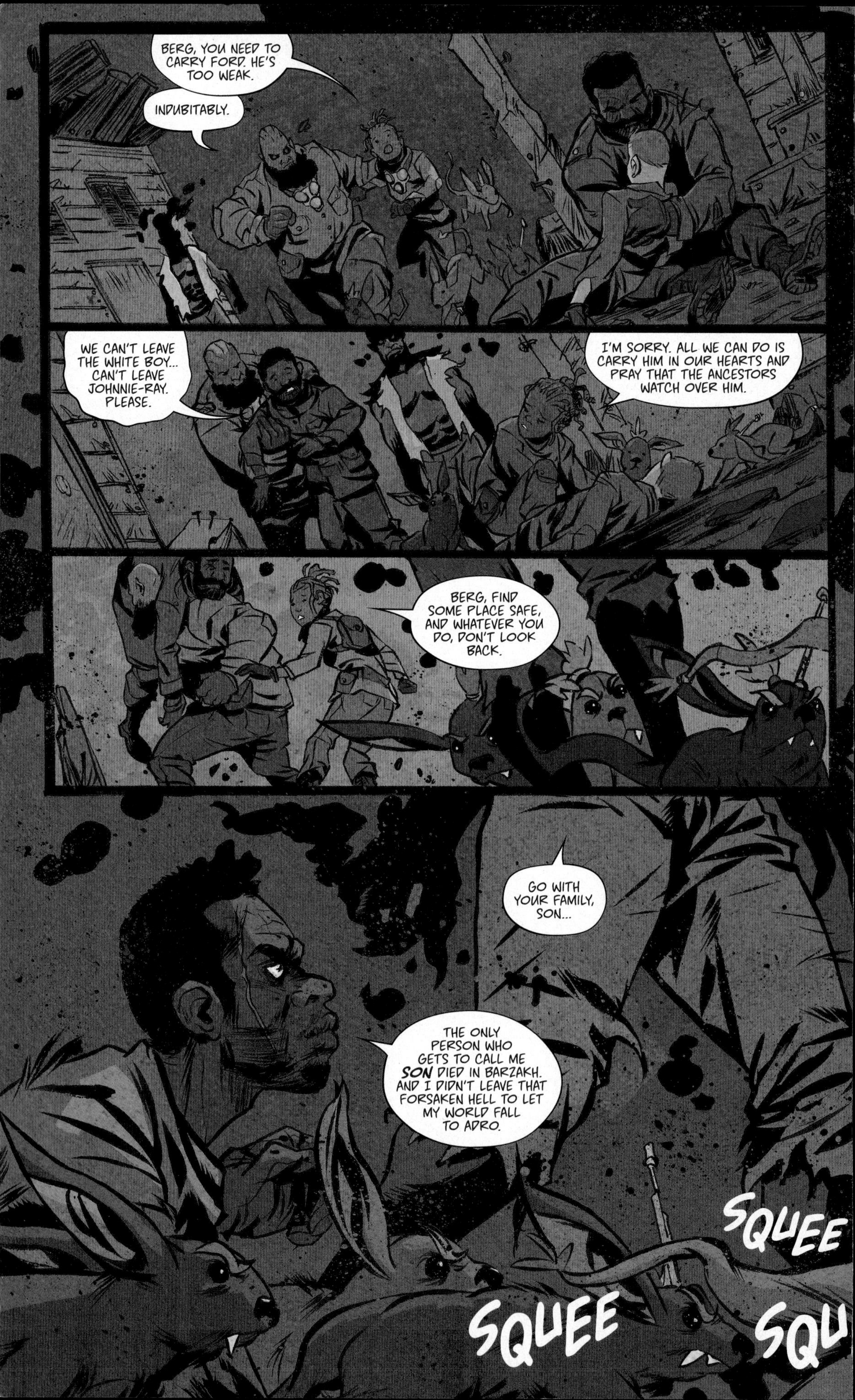
BERG, YOU NEED TO CARRY FORD. HE'S TOO WEAK.
INDUBITABLY.
WE CAN'T LEAVE THE WHITE BOY... CAN'T LEAVE JOHNNIE-RAY. PLEASE.
I'M SORRY. ALL WE CAN DO IS CARRY HIM IN OUR HEARTS AND PRAY THAT THE ANCESTORS WATCH OVER HIM.
BERG, FIND SOME PLACE SAFE, AND WHATEVER YOU DO, DON'T LOOK BACK.
GO WITH YOUR FAMILY, SON...
THE ONLY PERSON WHO GETS TO CALL ME SON DIED IN BARZAKH. AND I DIDN'T LEAVE THAT FORSAKEN HELL TO LET MY WORLD FALL TO ADRO.
SQUEE
SQUEE
SQU

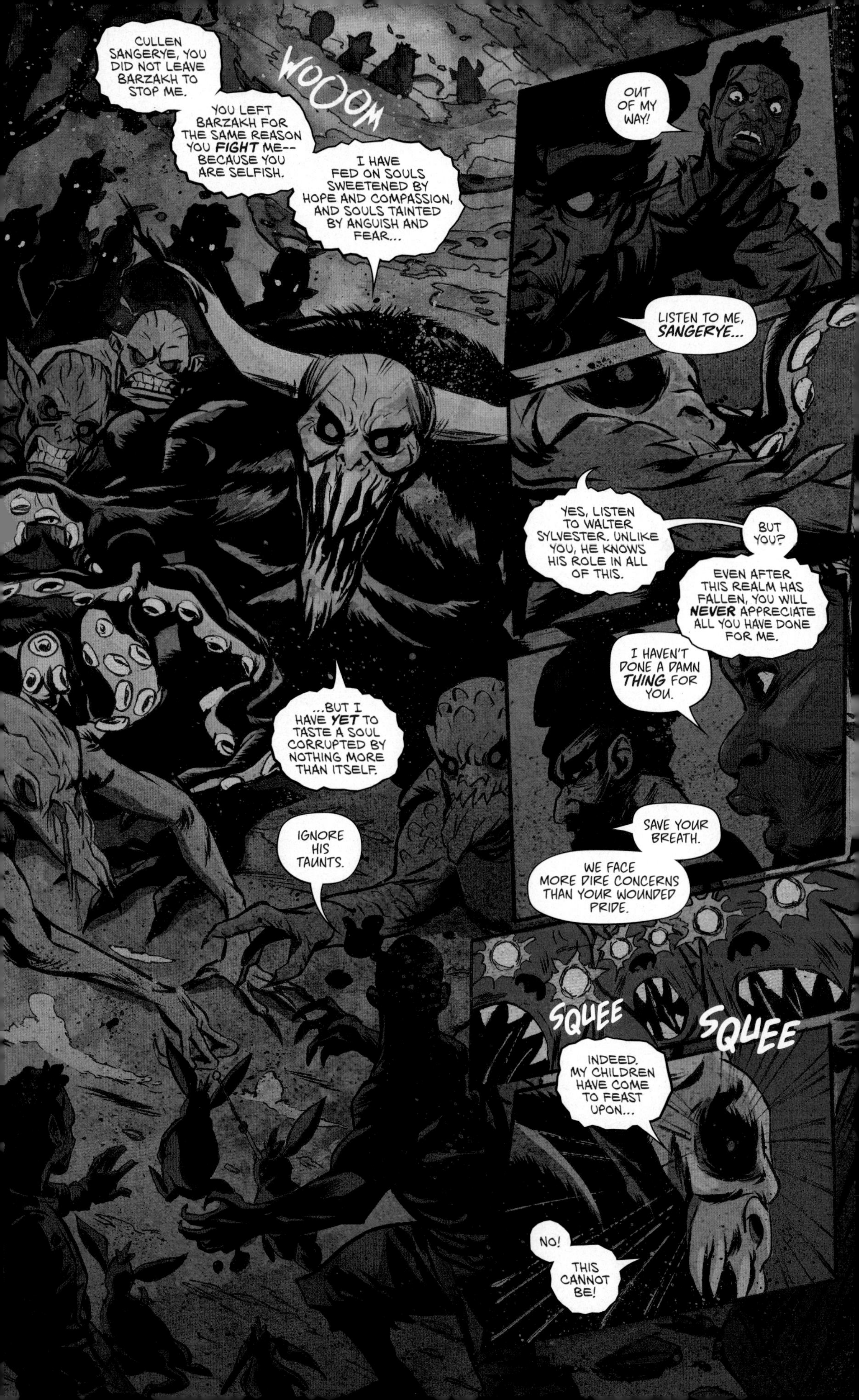
CULLEN SANGERYE, YOU DID NOT LEAVE BARZAKH TO STOP ME.
YOU LEFT BARZAKH FOR THE SAME REASON YOU FIGHT ME--BECAUSE YOU ARE SELFISH.
WOOOM
I HAVE FED ON SOULS SWEETENED BY HOPE AND COMPASSION, AND SOULS TAINTED BY ANGUISH AND FEAR...
OUT OF MY WAY!
LISTEN TO ME, SANGERYE...
YES, LISTEN TO WALTER SYLVESTER. UNLIKE YOU, HE KNOWS HIS ROLE IN ALL OF THIS.
BUT YOU?
EVEN AFTER THIS REALM HAS FALLEN, YOU WILL NEVER APPRECIATE ALL YOU HAVE DONE FOR ME.
I HAVEN'T DONE A DAMN THING FOR YOU.
...BUT I HAVE YET TO TASTE A SOUL CORRUPTED BY NOTHING MORE THAN ITSELF.
IGNORE HIS TAUNTS.
SAVE YOUR BREATH.
WE FACE MORE DIRE CONCERNS THAN YOUR WOUNDED PRIDE.
SQUEE
SQUEE
INDEED. MY CHILDREN HAVE COME TO FEAST UPON...
NO!
THIS CANNOT BE!

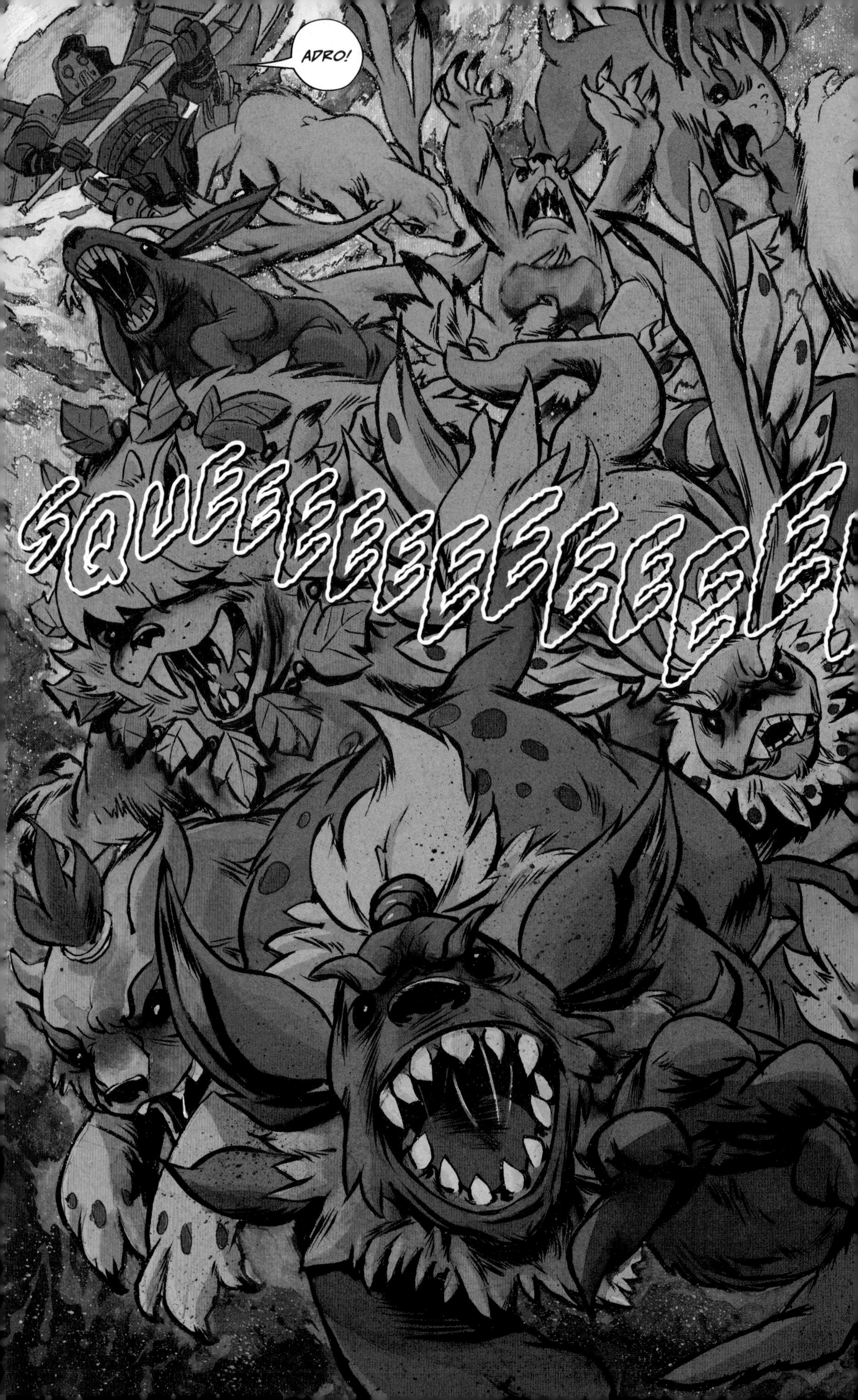
ADRO!
SQUEEEEEEEEEEEEE

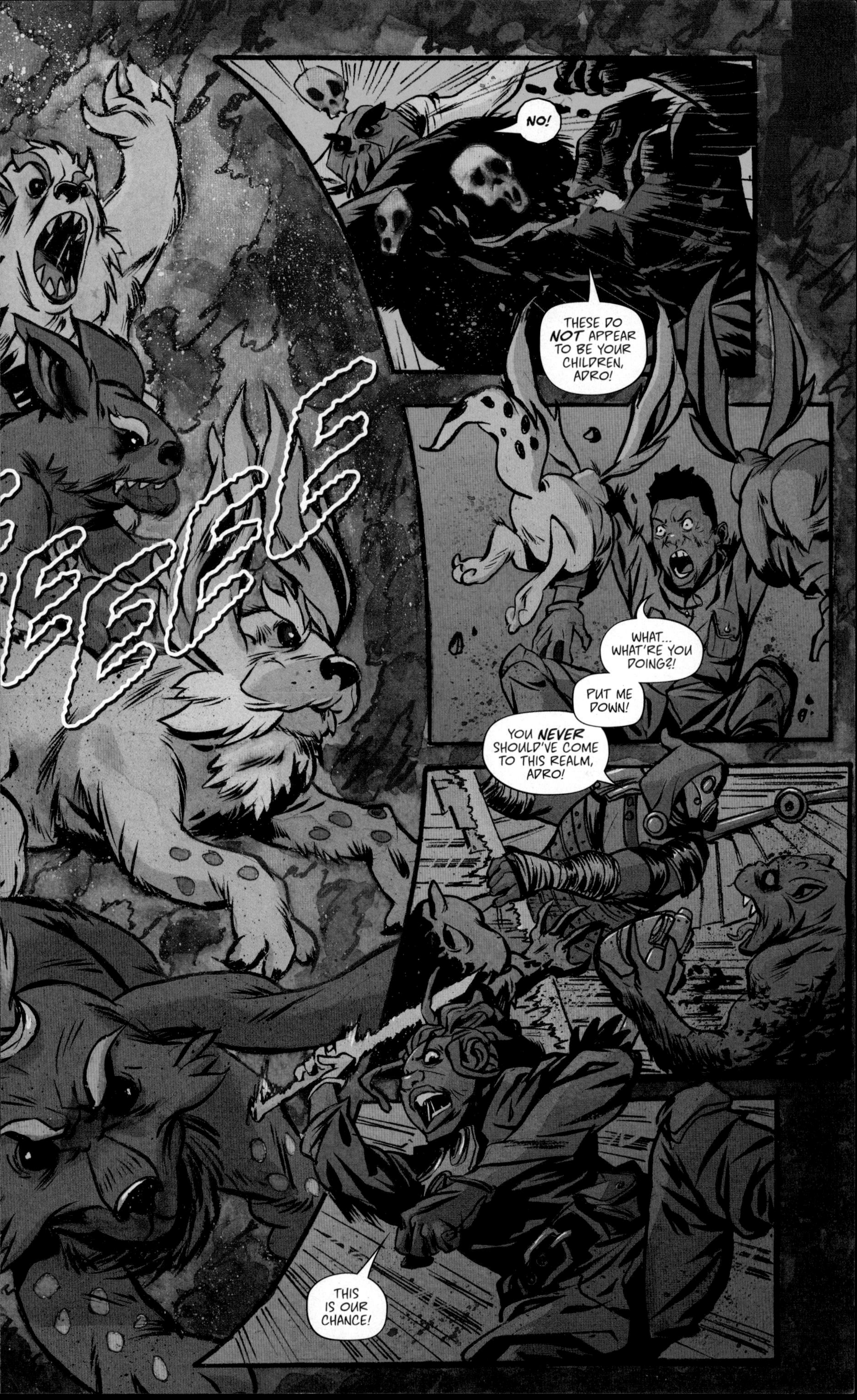
NO!
THESE DO NOT APPEAR TO BE YOUR CHILDREN, ADRO!
WHAT... WHAT'RE YOU DOING?!
PUT ME DOWN!
YOU NEVER SHOULD'VE COME TO THIS REALM, ADRO!
THIS IS OUR CHANCE!

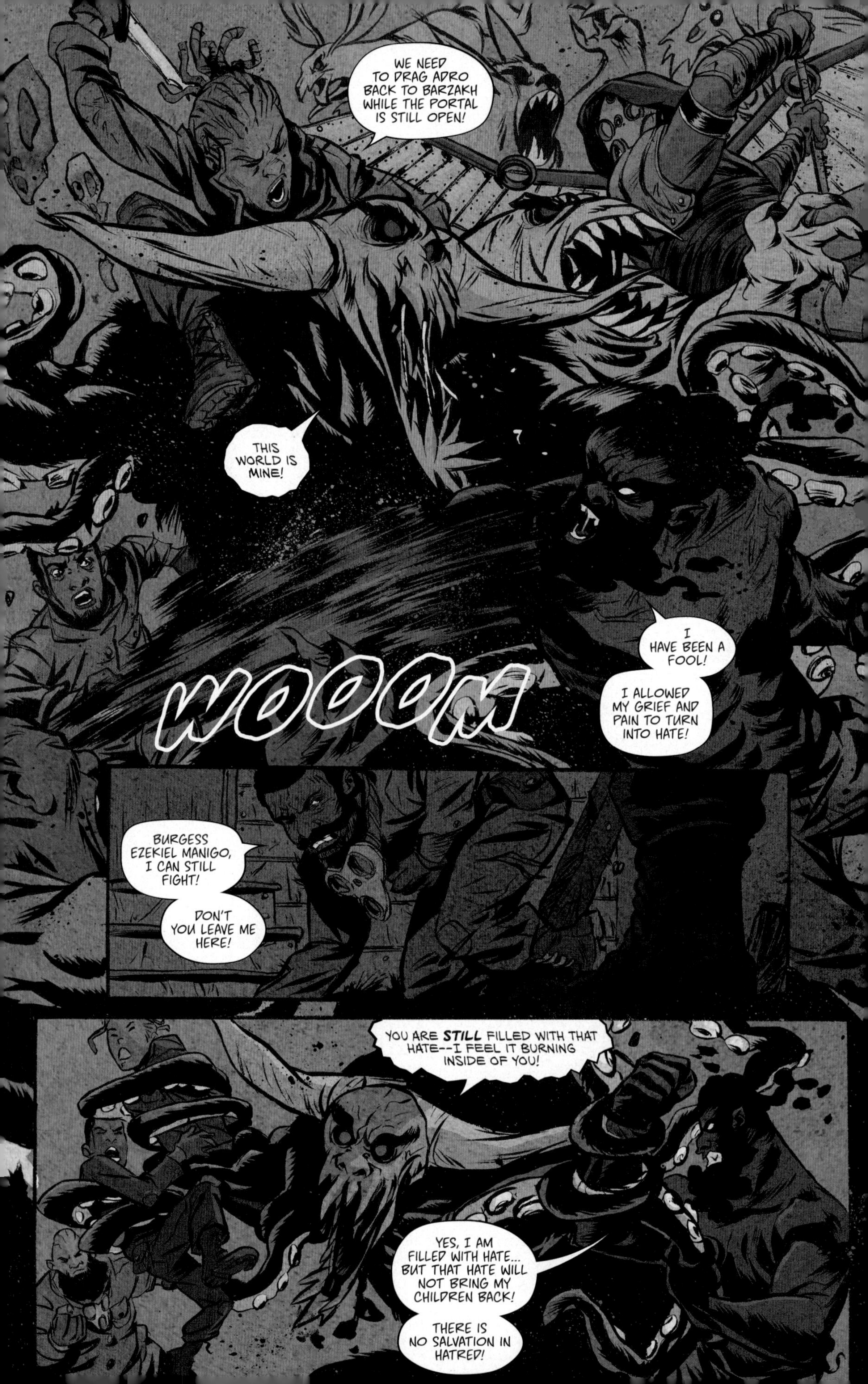
WE NEED TO DRAG ADRO BACK TO BARZAKH WHILE THE PORTAL IS STILL OPEN!
THIS WORLD IS MINE!
WOOOM
I HAVE BEEN A FOOL!
I ALLOWED MY GRIEF AND PAIN TO TURN INTO HATE!
BURGESS EZEKIEL MANIGO, I CAN STILL FIGHT!
DON'T YOU LEAVE ME HERE!
YOU ARE STILL FILLED WITH THAT HATE--I FEEL IT BURNING INSIDE OF YOU!
YES, I AM FILLED WITH HATE... BUT THAT HATE WILL NOT BRING MY CHILDREN BACK!
THERE IS NO SALVATION IN HATRED!

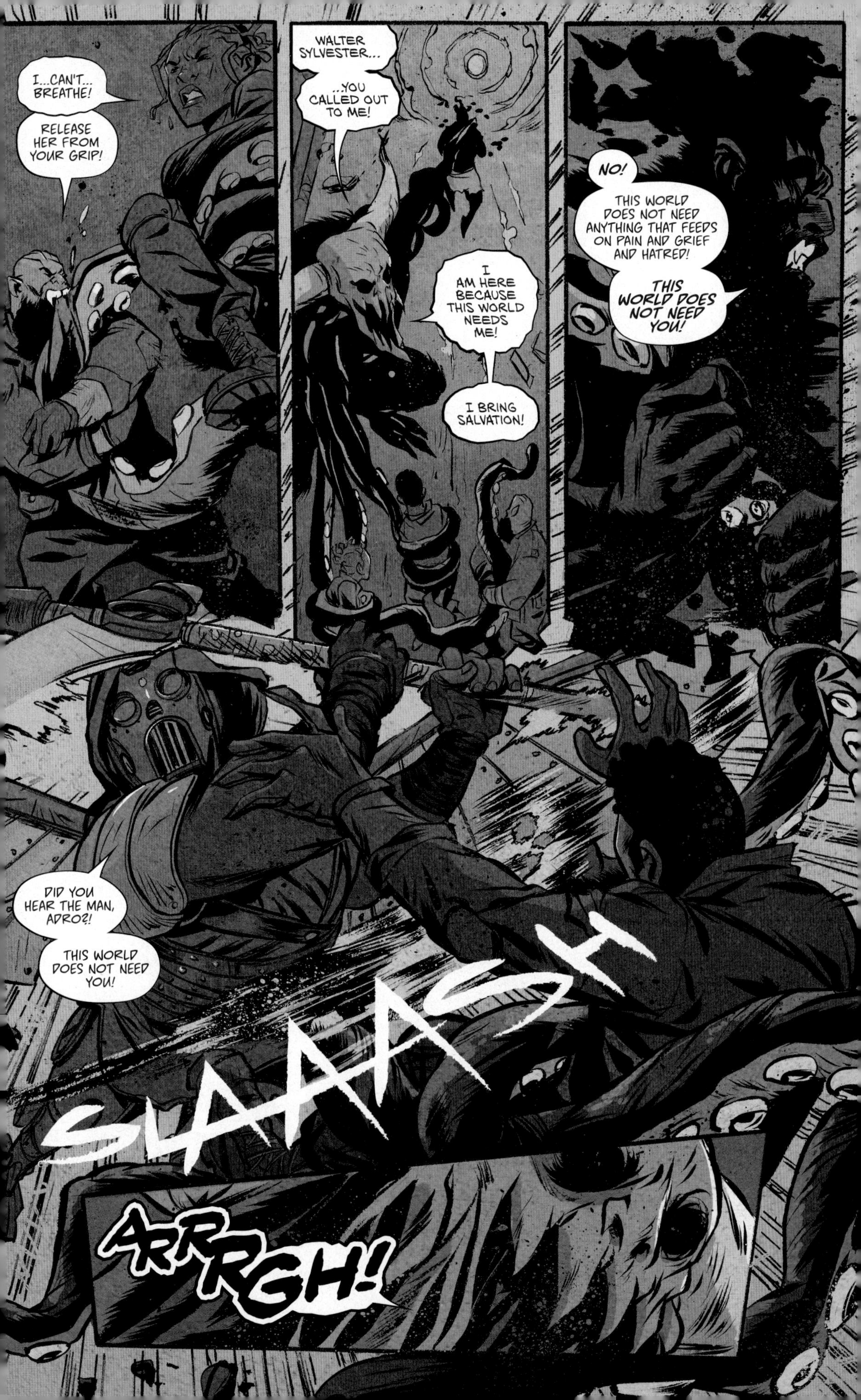
I...CAN'T... BREATHE!
RELEASE HER FROM YOUR GRIP!
WALTER SYLVESTER...
...YOU CALLED OUT TO ME!
I AM HERE BECAUSE THIS WORLD NEEDS ME!
I BRING SALVATION!
NO!
THIS WORLD DOES NOT NEED ANYTHING THAT FEEDS ON PAIN AND GRIEF AND HATRED!
THIS WORLD DOES NOT NEED YOU!
DID YOU HEAR THE MAN, ADRO?!
THIS WORLD DOES NOT NEED YOU!
SLAAASH
ARRRGH!

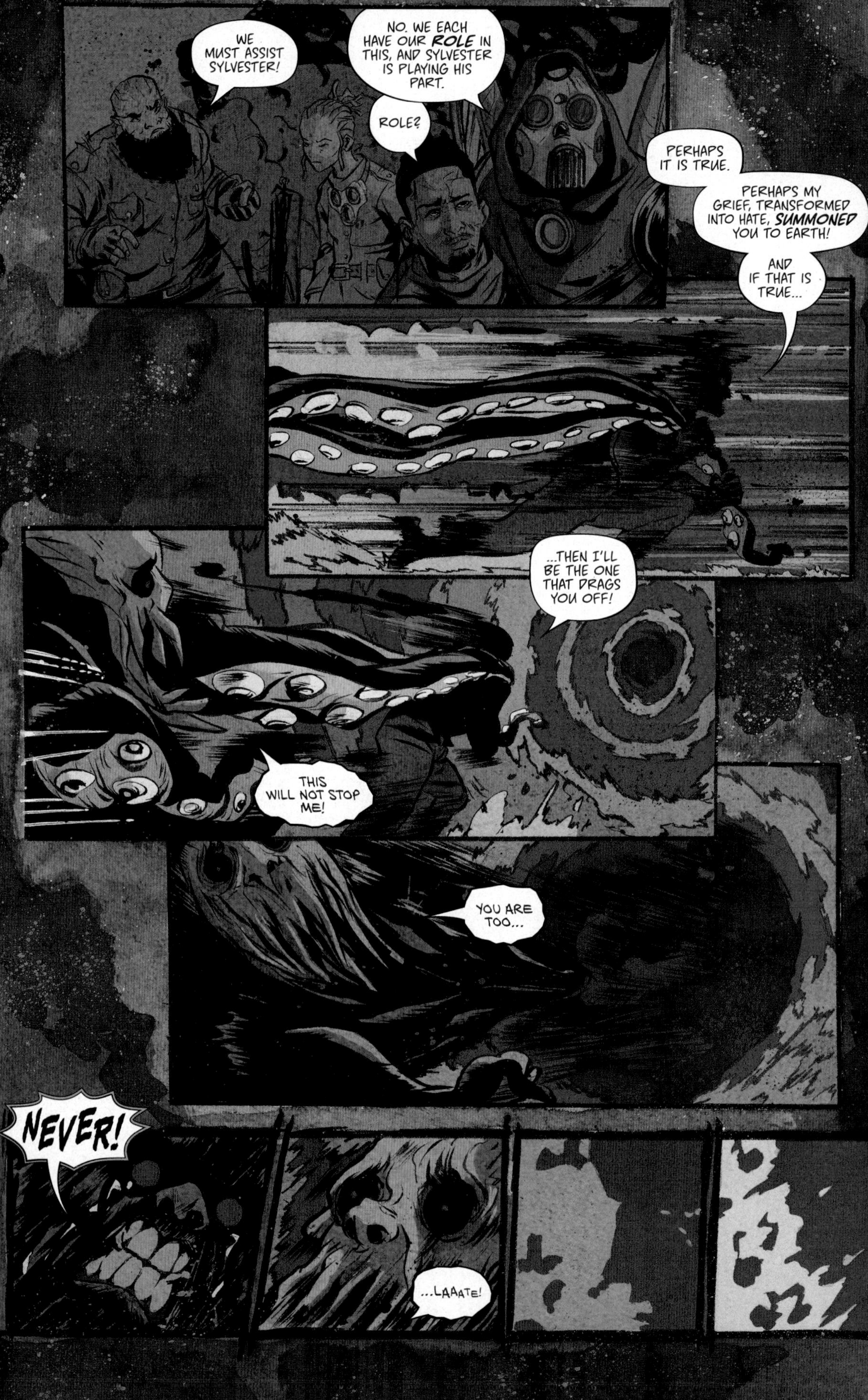
WE MUST ASSIST SYLVESTER!
NO. WE EACH HAVE OUR ROLE IN THIS, AND SYLVESTER IS PLAYING HIS PART.
ROLE?
PERHAPS IT IS TRUE.
PERHAPS MY GRIEF, TRANSFORMED INTO HATE, SUMMONED YOU TO EARTH!
AND IF THAT IS TRUE...
...THEN I'LL BE THE ONE THAT DRAGS YOU OFF!
THIS WILL NOT STOP ME!
YOU ARE TOO...
NEVER!
...LAAATE!

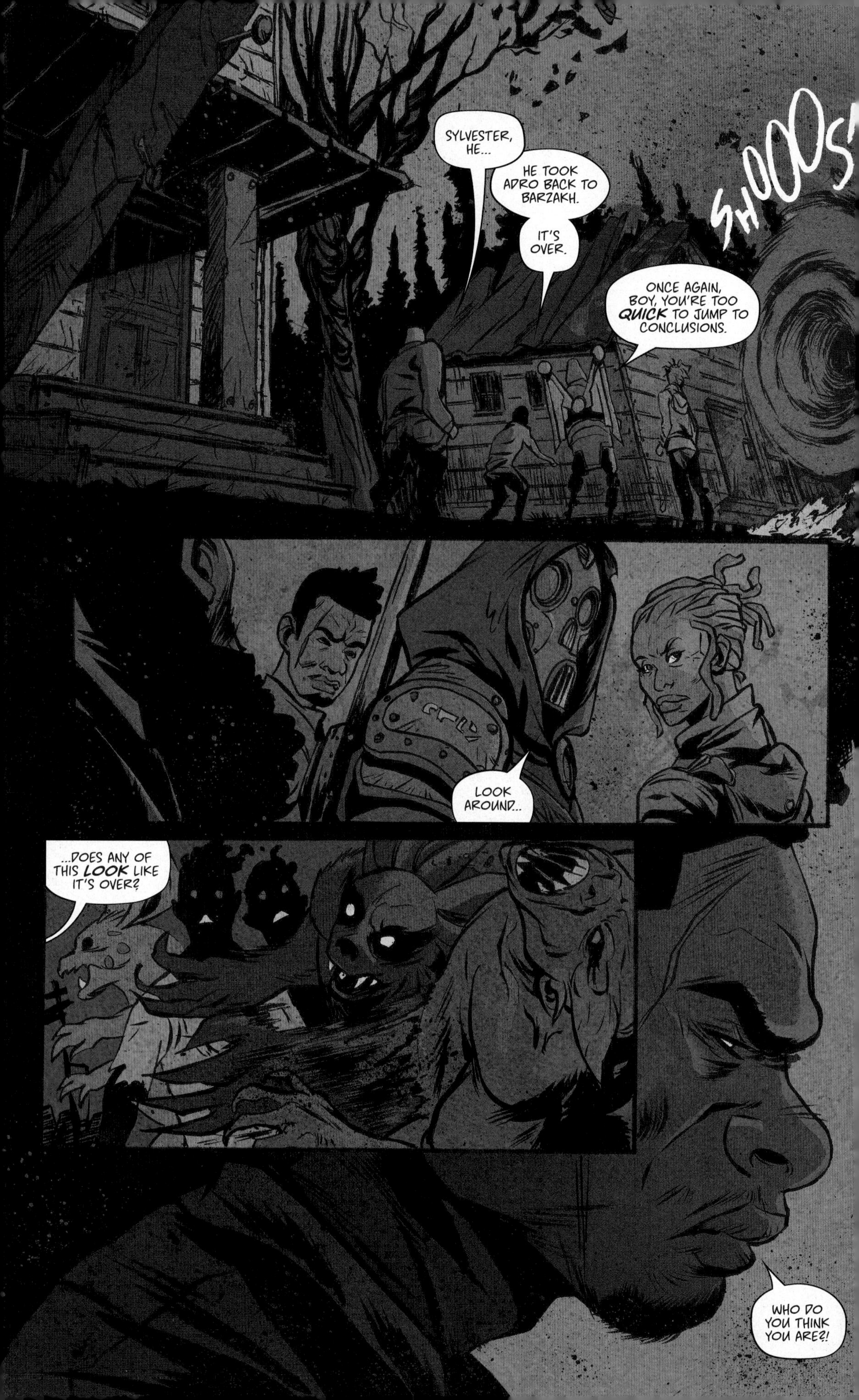
SYLVESTER, HE...
HE TOOK ADRO BACK TO BARZAKH.
IT'S OVER.
SHOOOSH
ONCE AGAIN, BOY, YOU'RE TOO QUICK TO JUMP TO CONCLUSIONS.
LOOK AROUND...
...DOES ANY OF THIS LOOK LIKE IT'S OVER?
WHO DO YOU THINK YOU ARE?!

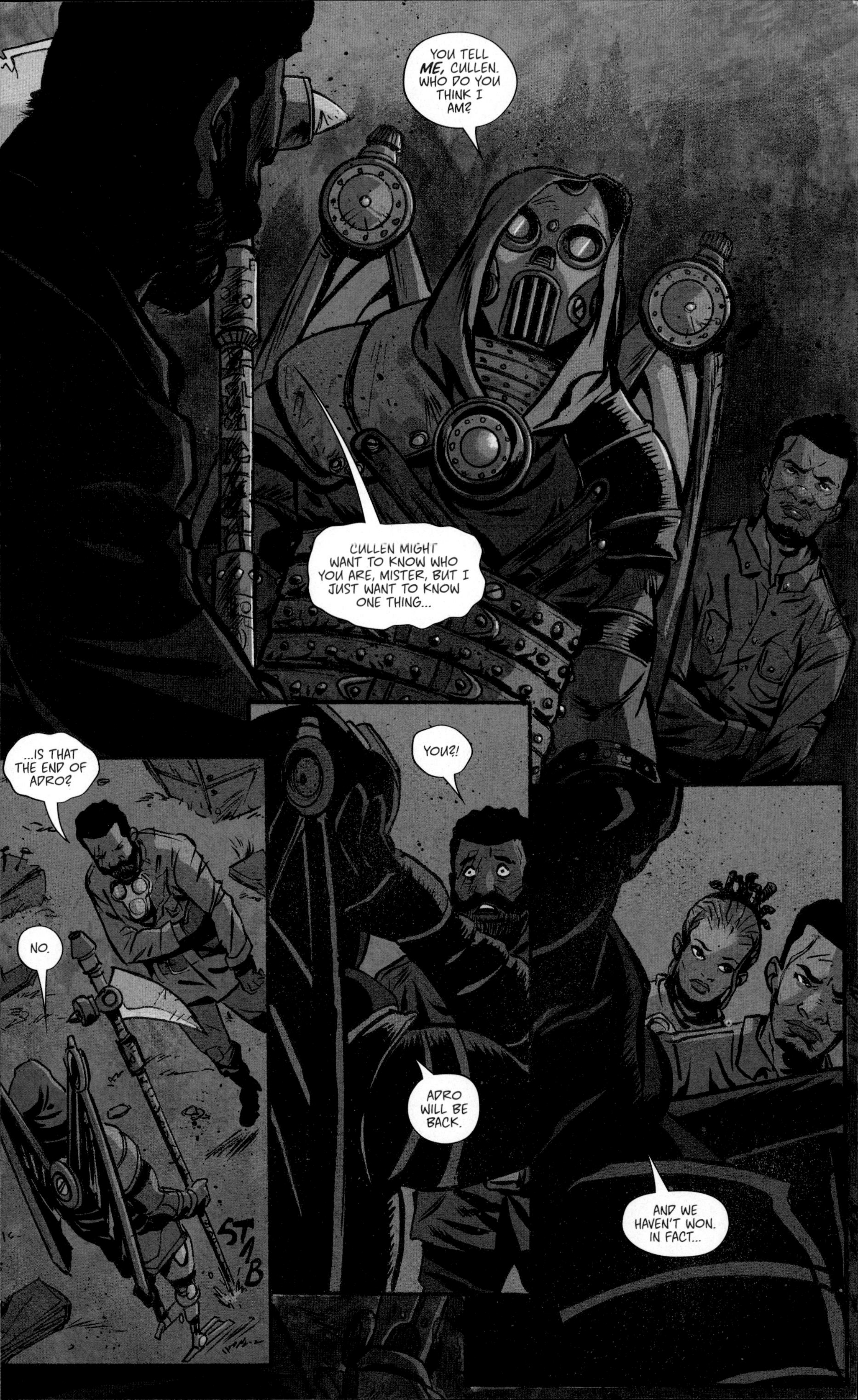
YOU TELL ME, CULLEN. WHO DO YOU THINK I AM?
CULLEN MIGHT WANT TO KNOW WHO YOU ARE, MISTER, BUT I JUST WANT TO KNOW ONE THING...
...IS THAT THE END OF ADRO?
NO.
STAB
YOU?!
ADRO WILL BE BACK.
AND WE HAVEN'T WON. IN FACT...

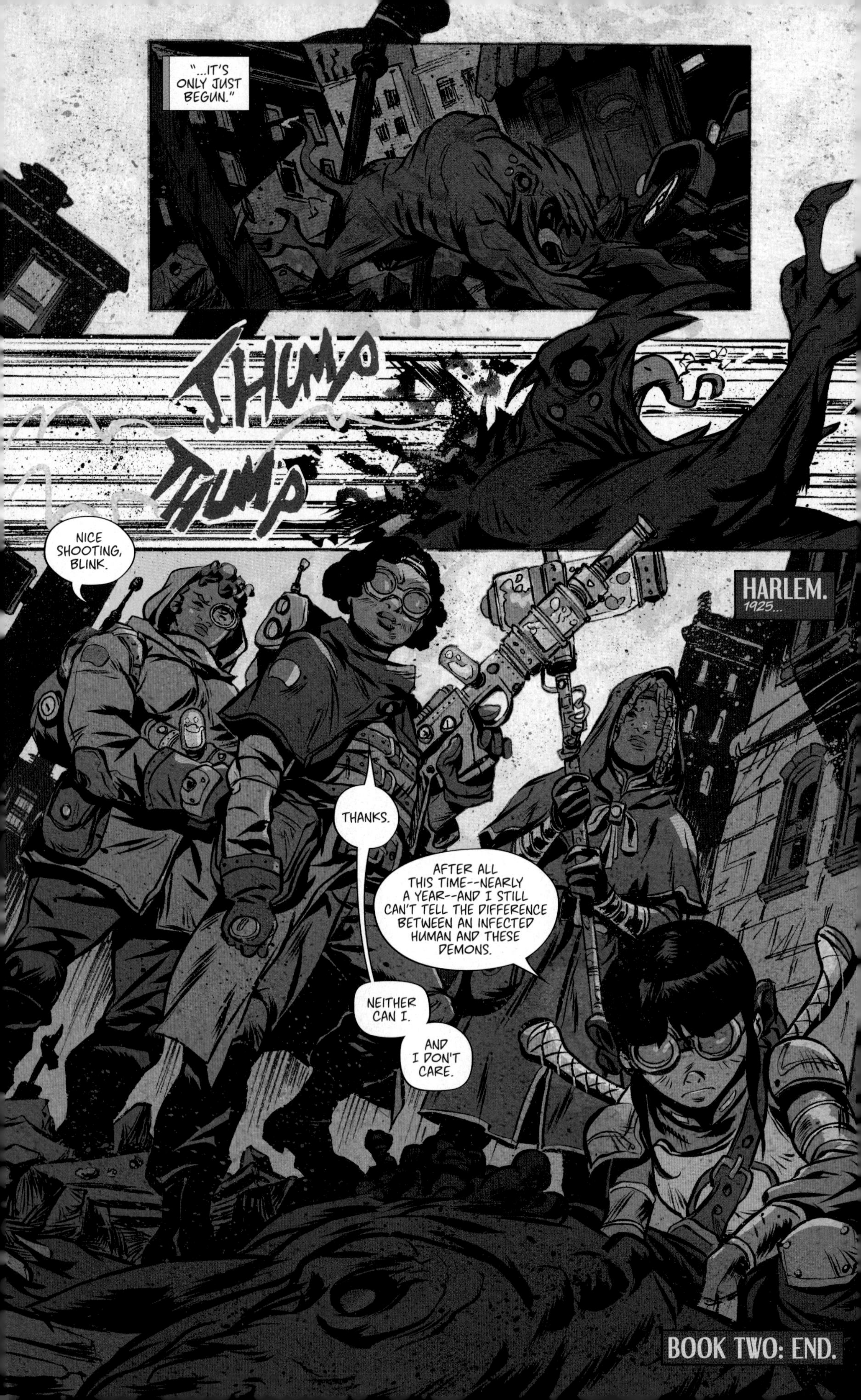
"...IT'S ONLY JUST BEGUN."
THUMP
THUMP
NICE SHOOTING, BLINK.
HARLEM. 1925...
THANKS.
AFTER ALL THIS TIME--NEARLY A YEAR--AND I STILL CAN'T TELL THE DIFFERENCE BETWEEN AN INFECTED HUMAN AND THESE DEMONS.
NEITHER CAN I.
AND I DON'T CARE.
BOOK TWO: END.

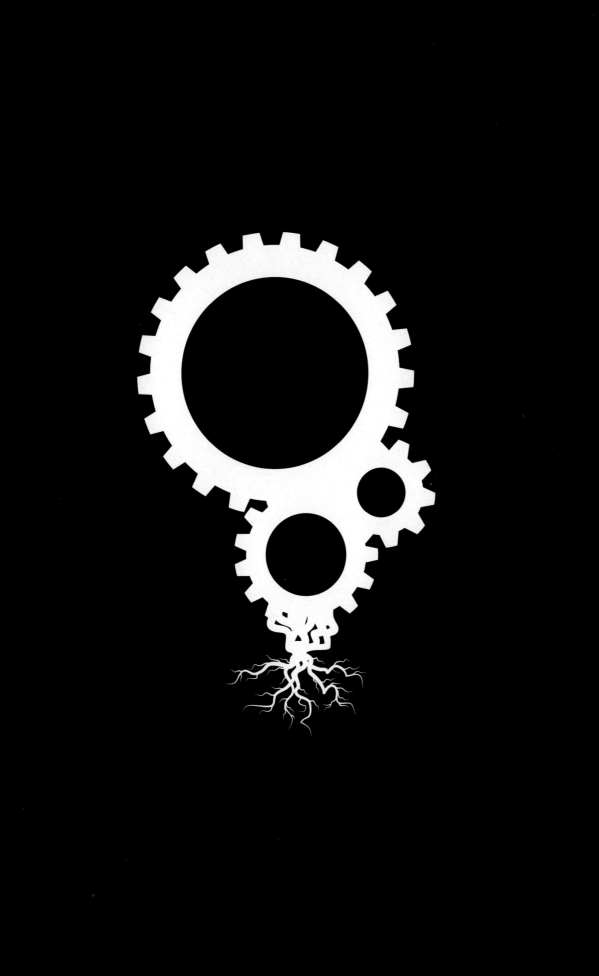

BITTER ROOT:
DRAGGING UP AMERICA'S DARKEST DAYS
Dexter Nelson II

DEXTER NELSON II is the Exhibition Manager and Curator of Comic Books for **OKPOP**, a division of the Oklahoma Historical Society based in Tulsa, Oklahoma. He received his Master's degree in Museum Studies from The University of Central Oklahoma and his Bachelor's degree in History with a minor in Liberal Arts at the University of Science and Arts of Oklahoma.

Dexter has been working in the Museum field for nearly a decade while contributing to comic book letter pages and pursuing a second book, following his published Master's thesis "Pow! The Mythological Enemy of the United States and the Comic Book Super Hero." Dexter's field of emphasis centers on comic books as a lens to view American culture. When he isn't working on exhibitions or conducting research, Dexter can be found reading/collecting comic books or spending time with his lovely family.

Superman was an advocate for Franklin D. Roosevelt's New Deal in his premiere issue in 1938. Captain America's debut comic book featured the hero punching Adolf Hitler in the face. The X-Men depict America's turbulent relations with minorities. The devastating events of both the Oklahoma City Federal Bombing and the terrorist attack on September 11th are illustrated in *Captain America and The Falcon #3* and *The Amazing Spider-Man #36*, respectively. Comic books have always been a medium that mirrors real world events which have seeped into American's zeitgeist; *Bitter Root* carries on this proud tradition in a new way.

Bitter Root takes place during the Harlem Renaissance of the 1920s. It is a series that mixes steam punk, magic and history together for a rich narrative focused on the Sangerye family and their uphill crusade against evil. Within the Sangerye family there are differing approaches on how to deal with their demonic prey. Ma Etta, the matriarch, believes humans possessed by evil can be cured. Other more militant members of the family, like Ford, believe the only way to help the possessed is to purge them from existence. While Etta and Ford are set in their ways, the three younger members, Blink, Berg and Cullen, are trying to find their own posture when dealing in the family business. In following the comic book tradition *Bitter Root* uses American history as a basis for its fantastical world. The nuance in what *Bitter Root* is doing is that the event it is referencing has not yet disseminated fully into popular culture. In fact, the Tulsa Race Massacre has largely been hidden away from the public.

The Tulsa Race Massacre*, formally known as the Tulsa Race Riot, happened in North Tulsa's Greenwood district between May 31st and June 1st in 1921. This event followed the Red Summer of 1919, where violence against African Americans greatly increased. The term Red Summer was the result of post war tensions from World War I, coupled with growing labor shortages for industrial jobs, and white America fearing the rise of Russian Communists. During this violent era, lynching, arson and general violence against African Americans went unpunished. This idea of mob justice would carry on to Tulsa, Oklahoma in 1921. The violence in Tulsa began with white citizens attempting to lynch Dick Rowland, a black man, for what they believed had been an assault on Sarah Page, a white woman, in an elevator. This event marked the first time incendiary devices were dropped on American soil, by Americans in planes, and the destruction of one of America's most prosperous black communities. All thirty-five city blocks of what was known as "Black Wall Street" were destroyed. Since the massacre there have been varying accounts of the total number of fatalities. Conservative estimates are around 30 people whereas local estimates are closer to 300. We may never know the total loss of life.

Despite a majority of the land being destroyed, Greenwood was rebuilt within a few years and was even considered more prosperous, with over one hundred new black-owned businesses operating in the area. Greenwood would continue to thrive until the early 1960s when desegregation, and later urban renewal, caused many to leave the area.

The massacre was possible due to the combination of a rise in vigilantism beginning in 1919 across the Unit-ed States and racial tensions of the time. To this day, none of the white perpetrators have been brought to justice and efforts for reparations for the relatives of survivors has not come.

Bitter Root's connection to this saga in American history is that the sto-ry's primary antagonists are survi-vors of the massacre. The hate and anger they experienced that night transformed them into monster-like creatures. In doing this, Walker and his team have created a villain, Dr. Sylvester, manufactured directly by racism. The origins of Dr. Syl-vester and Miss Knightsdale were previously unknown to readers, but based upon the few glimpses of their story we'd previously seen, we knew the horrific events of 1921 played a major role in them being in Harlem, where they are currently battling the Sangerye family. This portrays an accurate depiction of survivors of the massacre, many left to neigh-boring cities, while some returned to rebuild. The basis of Dr. Sylvester is the trauma he suffered during the massacre and how it affected him. This in a way reflects the real world struggles and anxieties of being Af-rican American today. Only time will tell if he will continue his con-flict with the Sangerye family or if he will realize the culprits of the Tulsa Massacre are his true enemies. Re-gardless of the outcome, *Bitter Root's* fruitfulness is the binary depictions of both sides of a complicated issue: How should African Americans act towards racism? This is evident in the more positive, redeeming ap-proach the Sangerye Family chooses as opposed to the violent approach of Dr. Sylvester. One side seeks to heal where the other prefers to scorch earth.

"Hatred, which could destroy so much, never failed to destroy the man who hated, and this was an immutable law."
- James Baldwin

MIA ARAUJO

There have been a variety of books and documentaries concerning the massacre, but none have gained the popularity of *Bitter Root*. This epic tale from David F. Walker, Chuck Brown and Sanford Greene grapples with a tragedy that America has swept under the rug until recently. Our current divisive and hostile cultural climate has caused many to reevaluate their identity and their place in this country. This idea is vividly expressed within minority commu-nities who struggle with hate, discrimination and unequal power structures. Through this lens *Bitter Root* serves as a cautionary tale of how ugly one can become when our humanity is abandoned and hatred and bigotry are left to fester. Hopefully, this comic book, and potential future film, will spark a much needed conversation about America's difficult history of inequality and of what can be done to rectify it.

It is believed that the powers of the time wanted to label the event as a "riot" in order to block any assistance the area would have received through insurance agencies.

BITTER ROOT AND THE BLACK SPECULATIVE LEGACY OF ZORA NEALE HURSTON

REYNALDO ANDERSON currently serves as an Associate Professor of Communication and Chair of the Humanities department at Harris-Stowe State University in Saint Louis, Missouri. Reynaldo has not only served as an executive board member of the Missouri Arts Council, he has previously served at an international level working for prison reform with C.U.R.E. International in Douala Cameroon, and as a development ambassador recently assisting in the completion of a library project for the Sekyere Afram Plains district in the country of Ghana. Reynaldo publishes extensively in the area of Afrofuturism, communication studies, and the African diaspora experience. Reynaldo is currently the executive director and co-founder of the **Black Speculative Arts Movement (BSAM)** a network of artists, curators, intellectuals and activists. Finally, he is the co-editor of the book *Afrofuturism 2.0: The Rise of Astro-Blackness* published by Lexington books, co-editor of *Cosmic Underground: A Grimoire of Black Speculative Discontent* published by Cedar Grove Publishing, the volume *The Black Speculative Art Movement: Black Futurity, Art+Design* also from Lexington press, and the co-editor of *Black Lives, Black Politics, Black Futures*, special issue of *TOPIA: Canadian Journal of Cultural Studies*.

Black speculative thought, writing and graphic illustration is practiced around the world. The Black speculative tradition emerged in the 19th century as a response to scientific racism, technology of the industrial revolution, Imperialism and slavery in an anti-Black world. Furthermore, it was this Black speculative tradition that insisted on placing the Black/African experience as central to the emergence of the modern era and modernity as an alternative narrative to the hegemonic power of the White western literary imagination and social science tradition. Interestingly enough, an example of this Black speculative tradition is currently embodied in the sequential work by the creators of the comic *Bitter Root* visually representing aspects of the legacy of Zora Neale Hurston, Harlem as a place, and her practice in the Black folklore/conjure tradition. More specifically, this connection between *Bitter Root* and Hurston is a reflection of the Black speculative tradition and modernity, conjure and the current renaissance moment.

Zora Neale Hurston was born in Notasulga, Alabama on January 7, 1891. Her family later relocated to Eatonville, Florida. Hurston's creative practice emerged during an era in the late 19th century and early 20th century when there was an occult revival in the western world. For example, in Germany thinkers like Rudolph Steiner and others were impacted by the Theosophy movement and sought to reconcile aspects of the occult esoteric with modernity. Furthermore, Hurston's work in the esoteric arena paralleled the emergence of the scholarship of Gershom Shalom (1897-1982) on Jewish mysticism and the Kabbalah as a counter history. Other contemporaries of Hurston were Rollo Ahmed, occult advisor of voodoo and esoteric matter to British practitioner Dennis Wheatley, and the Garveyite occultist Black Herman. Hurston also belonged to a collective of Black luminaries of the Harlem Renaissance like Aaron Douglas, and writer George Schuyler, and they were heavily involved in the philosophies and mysticism of George Gurdjieff and Peter D. Ouspensky. Across the Atlantic, during the same era, future generations of Nigerian writers were impacted by D. O. Fagunwa in his 1939 novel *Forest of a Thousand Daemons: A Hunter's saga*. Moreover, aspects of this literary tradition are clearly present in the sequential work of the creators of the *Bitter Root* narrative with their artistry, storytelling, and representation of the conjure tradition of the Sangerye family.

The conjure tradition has deep roots in the African diaspora community. Furthermore, the practice of Africanist Hoodoo (African American influenced) or Vodun (Haitian influenced) in urban enclaves across America was not unusual. These practitioners frequently engaged other esoteric philosophies and a significant number of conjure men and women studied, interpreted and incorporated the work of alchemists like Cornelius Agrippa, John Dee or Paracelsus, in their practice. Hurston's work during this period would be pivotal in its account of Black folklore, modernity, magic and the connection to Africa. Moreover, Hurston brings her training as an anthropologist at Barnard College in New York City under the tutelage of Franz Boas to her work. For example, her most well known novel *Their Eyes Were Watching God* brings out the tension of race, class, folk tradition and modernity championing Black folk culture as a serious art form and foundational to the

"Art must discover and reveal the beauty which predjudice and caricature have overlaid."

—*Alain Locke,* co-founder of the New Negro Movement

Black vernacular tradition. In a similar vein, the work of *Bitter Root* sequentially captures this tension of race, class and tradition in a cosmopolitan space as the Sangerye family must contend with dark forces in a modern urban environment and is part and parcel an artistic legacy of the work of Zora Neale Hurston and the resurgence of Black speculative thought in the early 21st century.

Zora Neale Hurston's work, in attempting to reconcile the esoteric and modern social sciences, precedes the work of Sun Ra's Myth-Science, the hyperstition theory of writer Nick Land, and foreshadows the development of Critical Race Design Studies by John Jennings. For example, her book *Mules and Men* (1935) clearly reflects the influence of modern anthropology and ethnographic research techniques introduced by Franz Boas. This rigorous use of design technique is present in the *Bitter Root* series as its creators bring to life in its pages the Black speculative tradition. Accordingly, the current Black Speculative Renaissance that has emerged and is embodied in Black futuristic/aesthetic collectives around the world, is in pursuit of what Zora Neale Hurston was doing generations ago: they are trying to make the *unseen* seen, and the *invisible* visible, and at the end of days, all will be revealed.

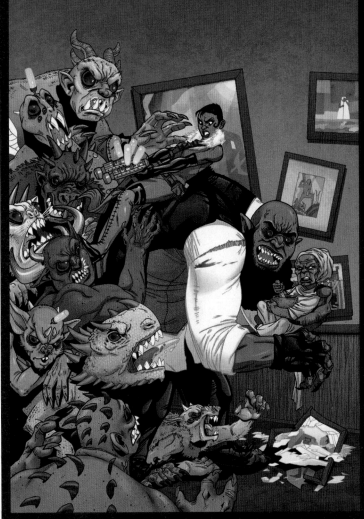

art by **BRIDGET CONNEL**

BITTER TWITTER:

@BITTERROOT18 | @Cbrown803 | @sanfordgreene | @DavidWalker1201

BITTER TRUTHS curated and designed by **John Jennings** / tw @JIJennings
Research Assistant: **Edgardo Delgadillo-Aguilera**

Repeater
Leila Taylor
Darkly
Black History and America's Gothic Soul

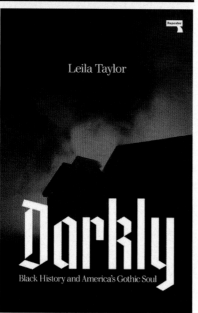

To quote Harlem Renaissance poet and legend Langston Hughes: **"Black is...Black ain't".** Leila Taylor's extraordinary new book from Repeater Press does a compelling, personal and intellectually stimulating pass at unpacking that statement. In her book ***Darkly: Black History and America's Gothic Soul***, Taylor weaves together an investigation into Blackness and the Gothic that comes across as personal memoir, art criticism, and insightful historic analysis. The graphic designer and media scholar slips effortlessly from music criticism, to intersectional identity politics, to semiotic analysis of the construction of Blackness itself. In the book she states: ***"Blackness in America is still in the middle, residing in the place between opposites: living in the present while carrying the past, being human but perceived as other, considered both a person and a product, both American and foreign, neither here nor there."*** Much like the creature from ***Frankenstein*** or the letters that connect the narrative of Bram Stoker's ***Dracula***, Taylor is putting forth that we, as Black people, are very much an epistolary; woven together like the quilts that covered our ancestors' broken backs. Through using her own experiences as a Black woman in America and a lover of the Goth culture, she maps out the overlaps between that cultural space and the uncanny and surreal exprience of what it feels like to be a liminal creature covered in the shroud of thing we did not create: Blackness itself. *–John Jennings*

HORROR NOIRE
ORIGINAL

Horror Noire: A History of Black Horror is a film birthed from the popularity of Jordan Peele's film ***Get Out*** and based on the book of the same name by Professor Robin Means Coleman published in 2011. ***Get Out*** is a horror movie directed, written, and starring a Black man, that went on to win the Best Original Screenplay Oscar. Something that even five years ago would have been deemed far-fetched. "Black people don't watch horror!" was a common phrase that is steeped in the erasure of our past within the genre and ***Horror Noire*** works hard to set the record straight.

A Shudder exclusive, ***Horror Noire*** seeks to track the evolution of Blackness and Black people in the horror film genre. Shot with interviews from prominent Black scholars and actors within the genre seated in a dark movie theater. We get this one-on-one intimate setting that is reminiscent of gathering around a fire for scary storytime. Keith David, Ashley Blackwell, Richard Lawson, and Tony Todd, to name a few, go back and forth, piecing together our journey through this medium. From ***Birth of A Nation***, (which is rightfully included in this documentary) to ***Get Out, Horror Noire*** makes sure to not sugarcoat Black people's roots in horror. Tananarive Due, acclaimed author, professor at UCLA, and co-producer of this documentary, lends the historical elements to the film by giving context to the political climates surrounding the making of many of these films. Something that viewers decades later tend to lose in the cult popularity surrounding some of these movies.

Watching this film, I was taken aback by the depth this documentary delves in to at the beginning. Where I would personally think to start in the 60s with the seminal George Romero film ***Night of The Living Dead,*** they go to the literal beginning of filmmaking with ***Birth of A Nation***. ***Birth of A Nation*** is a movie made in 1915 and its heroes are members of the Ku Klux Klan. A film I had to sit through many times in my film classes. That even in 2012 was being taught as "one of the best films ever made." However, ***Horror Noire*** says the one thing I always thought, if you are Black, ***Birth of A Nation*** is a blood-curdling movie. The KKK saving a white woman from being accosted by the obsessed Black male slave ends with a lynching. The conclusion deemed a happy ending at the time is a nightmarish reality for the Black folks.

The documentary walks us through the evolution of that myopic trope in ***Birth of A Nation*** from monster, to sacrificial lamb, to hero. As someone who likes to think of themself as well-versed in scary movies, this documentary opened my eyes. There were so many things I had never known and films I had never heard of before. For example, ***Ganja & Hess,*** and how Jada Pinkett was the first Black final girl in the movie ***Tales From The Crypt: Demon Knight***.

Horror is the mirror that reflects society at itself, and it is no wonder that Black horror films have had a Renaissance. Starting with ***Get Out***, ***The Girl With All The Gifts***, ***Us***, ***Sweetheart***, and the upcoming reboot of ***Candyman***. ***Horror Noire: A History of Black Horror*** shows us our past within horror and builds a foundation where Black horror can thrive. *—Jazmine Joyner* (**@jazmine_joyner**). Note: also check out ***Horror Noire*** screenwriter Ashley Blackwell **@GraveyardSister**!

BITTER ROOT'S MA ETTA AS INDEX FOR HEALING FROM EPIGENETIC TRAUMAS

DONNA-LYNN WASHINGTON is an Adjunct Lecturer in English at Kingsborough Community College in Brooklyn, NY. She is the editor for the book *Conversations: John Jennings* to be published from University Press of Mississippi 2020. Miss Washington is the senior editor and a senior writer at *ReviewFix* and has contributed to *Critical Insights: Frank Yerby* an academic anthology. Her essay is called 'Frank Yerby and His Readers'. This book is to be published by University Press of Mississippi in 2020. She has also contributed entries to the *Encyclopedia of Black Comics*, published in 2017. Miss Washington has a M.A in English from Brooklyn College.

HBO's *Watchmen* shook me to my core when it aired. And no other episode resonated with me more than "The Extraordinary Being" in which the protagonist Angela Abar (Regina King) relives the life of her grandfather by ingesting a drug called Nostalgia. She experiences all of his memories, which include becoming a police officer, his lynching, sexual experiences with his wife and a white costumed hero and becoming the hero Hooded Justice. A Black man having to makeup in semi-whiteface, carrying a rope, wearing a hooded robe did not escape my love of irony. I tweeted about it saying that Angela has given meaning to ancestral PTSD. Essentially, this is our pain, this is why we're angry; it resonated deeply as Angela experienced the pain of her ancestor as if it were her own. Shannon Sullivan discusses how "people of color can biologically inherit the deleterious effect of white racism." It's based on the theory of *epigenetics*, which posits the possibility that "biomarkers shape an individual's vulnerability to PTSD development, thereby contributing to a heterogeneous response to trauma" (Heinzelmann and Gill). This led me back to *Bitter Root: Volume One*. If we are able to inherit our ancestral PTSD where our triggers are various forms of racism, then what would happen if we could inherit the coping skills to deal with them?

Ma Etta is a character I've been drawn to from her first appearance. Her short frame at times shows her gently resting on her gnarled cane, as if ready to use it as a weapon if necessary. Sanford Greene's art portrays the many faces of Ma Etta in various emotional states, though always lined with piercing, intelligent, knowing eyes. She gives her family strength and knowledge through her root-working, but I believe more so through her ability to understand the monsters her family traditionally fights. The deniability of Black folks who refuse to associate with the Sangeryes, the racism of whites in both the North and South all contribute to the manifestation of the monsters that need to be brought down.

In the first issue Ma Etta explains how the women in the family utilize their minds, while physical battle is left to the men. When she says this, there is a portrait of smiling, young Black people who are blissfully ignorant of their faiths. For me that's where the horror lies, where people may die or become demon-like creatures through hatred or ignorance. That portrait demonstrates the loss of family through the horrors of racism. And even though Ma Etta changes her stance and thanks Blink for not listening to her, she keeps that trauma with her. This helps her to be able to carry on for her family and for herself.

It's clear how the narrative being set during the Harlem Renaissance reinforces the necessity of Ma Etta's beliefs. I am reminded of Jesse Redmon Fauset and her moniker as the midwife of the Harlem Re-naissance. As an editor of W.E.B. Du Bois' magazine *The Crisis*, Fauset helped give birth and cared for the literary voice of Black America by emphasizing the average, middle-class Black people. Her novel *Plum Bun* exemplifies this as the protagonist Angela Murray passes for white only to out herself when another Black art student is racially discriminated against. What Angela does in this 1929 narrative actively supports a Black woman's fight against the horrors of racism. She does this after having to first subvert the social construct of race and hide who she really is to survive.

These related acts are illustrations of the effect of racial oppression that is inherited in the very DNA that Black people share. We continually fight on all fronts; even the most microscopic ones.

Like the Yoruba African deity Aya who is both warrior and caretaker of the earth, Ma Etta is a direct descendent of psychological resilience. Her capacity to "recover quickly…from, or resist being affected by a misfortune, shock, illness" (OED.com) alongside her age goes to her ability to adapt. She is "within the context of family, community and religious beliefs" (Jackson Z et al 1) along with her ability to have withstood "intergenerational exposures to 250 years of chattel slavery followed by 150 years of systemic discrimination" (1) makes her the answer to ancestral trauma. This has led me to believe that if we can inherit this pain, then *Bitter Root's* Ma Etta may have a salve for that if not a cure to reclaim our strength or power in giving us the resources to fight against the monster that is racism.

My Grenadian maternal grandmother and Trinidadian paternal great-grandmother were my Ma Etta, and when they died much of the family history died with them. But their ability to endure and thrive under oppressive circumstances, like epigenetics, or ancestral PTSD, have been passed down. Yes, we may carry the trauma of our ancestors, but we also inherit the tools that defeat those traumas.

Sources:

Gill, Jessica and Morgan Heinzelmann. "Epigenetic Mechanisms Shape the Biological Response to Trauma and Risk for PTSD: A Critical Review." *Nursing Research and Practice*, Volume 2013. Hindawi Publishing Corporation

Jackson et al. "Intergenerational Resilience in Response to the Stress and Trauma of Enslavement and Chronic Exposure to Institutionalized Racism." *Journal of Clinical Epigenetics,* Vol. 4 No 3:15 pp 1-7

"Jessie Faucet: Midwife to The Harlem Renaissance." *New Crisis.* Vol. 107 Issue 4 July/August 2000

"Resilience" Oxford English Dictionary.com

Sullivan, Shannon. "Inheriting Racist Disparities in Health: Epigenetics and the Transgenerational Effects of White Racism." *Critical Philosophy of Race,* Vol 1 No. 2, Penn State University Press, 2013

"Anybody depending on somebody else's gods is depending on a fox not to eat chickens."

— *Zora Neale Hurston*

Ma Etta by Sanford Greene

CONJURE + COLLAGE AS CREATIVE RESISTANCE

STACEY ROBINSON is an Assistant Professor of Graphic Design at the University of Illinois and an Arturo Schomburg fellow who completed his Masters of Fine Art at the University at Buffalo. His multimedia work discusses ideas of "Black Utopias" as decolonized spaces of peace by considering Black affluent, self-sustaining communities, Black protest movements and the art that document(ed) them.

His recent exhibition *'Binary Con-Science'* explores ideas of W.E.B. Du Bois's "double consciousness" as a Black cultural adaptation, and a means of colonial survival. His exhibition *'Branding the AfroFuture'* looks at designing and construct-ing Black futures through various cultural, collage aesthetics.

His latest graphic novel, *'I Am Alfonso Jones'* with writer Tony Medina and John Jennings, is available from Lee & Low books. He is currently a Nasir Jones Hip Hop Reserch Fellow at Harvard University.

I first started appreciating the word conjure in 2014 at an Afrofuturism-themed conference called AstroBlackness. Previously, I'd only thought about conjure culture as it was depicted in stereotypical bugged-eyed African or Caribbean peoples drinking blood, dancing with snakes, killing chickens, etc. These visuals didn't at all appeal to a burgeoning artist/scholar in the second year of graduate school grappling with the complexity of Du Boisian double-consciousness in the way I was depicting it, as being Black and other. Especially being Black with a complex religious past. Most of which was influenced by Christian colonialism and all of which contradicted and outright rejected the depictions of Black conjure culture. During this conference I learned to appreciate the idea of conjure ushering in Black liberated futures, something I'd never thought possible outside the rejections of African-centered thoughts and practices in Christianity. Webster defines conjure in part as "to summon by or as if by invocation or incantation," "to affect or effect by or as if by magic." As I dove deeper into Black ancestral studies, I accepted Christianity's African-based influences of the Holy Ghost as a trance state, the breaking and eating of Christ's body through the symbol of bread, and the refilling of a new spirit within us through the drinking of wine symbolized as Christ's blood.

Culture always advances through the collaging together of new ideas housed on the foundations of thought, respect, preservation of the past, and the dream of a further advancing narrative. It's the conjuring of ancient culture, the evocation, incantation, summoning, the pleads, demands, all with payments required. Writer Kinitra Brooks often leans into the ideas of conjure through the examination her matriarchal lineage. It's with her work that I began to understand the intricacies of conjure women are hearers, healers, and harmers. They can hear you plead, heal incurable sicknesses, and/or harm oppressive slave masters, and if you've ever watched a Stephen King, or Joe Hill series, conjure women are often the ancillary matriarchal figures that undergird everyone else's survival, most times at the expense of themselves.

The visual representation of collage through conjuring exists in Romare Bearden's 1960s-70s series of *Conjur Woman*. These images transcend a fixed narrative, while retaining the secrets within a supernatural Black woman. These are precursors to 'Black Girl Magic' as a movement. I imagine his early upbringing in North Carolina and his migration to Harlem furthered his understanding of a unified and complicated Black narrative of cultural resistance. Yet, how would Bearden's collages have evolved without Picasso's influence? Furthermore, what would Picasso's legacy be without the influence of unnamed African sculptors? Not so bitter-rooted in the culture is the conjuring of African aesthetics and practices throughout the world. The weightier influences of conjure as Black resistance are also thematic in the work of African American author, essayist, political activist and lawyer Charles Waddell Chesnutt's seminal 1899 book *The Conjure Woman*. Conjure and collage seem synonymous in cultures wherever Black people are colonized. Influences exist through the matriarchs of Bearden, Picasso, and *Bitter Root's* matriarch Ma Etta.

Among the many cultural lessons residing in the action-packed pages of *Bitter Root*, one that reoccurs in the underground conjure world of the Harlem Renaissance, is the multifacity of cultures expressed within Black collective resistance in daily life. These influences to our collective world culture traveled across the Atlantic, through the Middle Passage and many times conveyed in the plain sight of Colonial Christianity as escape plans sung through Negro Spirituals, Pig Latin, and braided hair patterns that illustrated freedom maps, to name a few. It's the examination of oral, written, hair woven, and drummed communication operating as Saul Williams' manifesto of "Coded Language," where he states "Whereas, break-beats have been the missing link connecting the diasporic community to its drum-woven past…"

Our "drum-woven past" became something new in the Americas via a resistance culture of darker-hued citizens. Just as the culture of Hip-Hop born initially in the South Bronx drew influences from the neighboring New York boroughs, even in its early days the collaboration of culture was evident through the sonic resonance of German electronic, Southern Blues, Soul, Rock, and Afro-Cuban music. What would "Rap" be without the precursors of The Last Poets, Gil Scott-Heron, or James Brown's "Excuse me cat, while I rap" in his 1971 song "Escape-ism"? How would "Graffiti" look without the influences of Abstract Expressionism and comic books? When would DJing have evolved without the ingenuity of Grandmaster Flash piecing together discarded technology and a dream of looping together music without a break in sound? How would Break-dancing exist without Capoeira? What would Knowledge be without Marcus Garvey, or Nobel Drew Ali? These Five Elements are foundational to a culture that birthed the communities of the South Bronx that resembled the aesthetic of a post-apocalypse in many of the documented images. How would the British music scene of the 80s have evolved without the residence of Black working-class Caribbeans who brought Roots, Dub, and Reggae with them? Without this, would there have been a punk movement in the same place "Heavy Metal" music was birthed through the appropriation Blues records before sampling restrictions were regulated? Or even at the risk of being meta, what's Sanford Greene's brilliantly dynamic story-telling without the influence of graffiti, and I guarantee a dope Hip-Hop playlist? Even his precursory style is more evident of the Hip-Hop cultural influence.

Black music and cultural production have always been resistant, activist and the galvanization of people seeking change. We are conjurers by tradition. Tapping into the past, resurrecting and collaging together forgotten sounds, aesthetics, and thought as social change movements that call forth a new narrative. It's this resistance to normalized culture that regulates oppressed people to the sidelines that keeps Black people pushing the boulder back up hill. Far too often we are pushed even further beyond the sidelines and erased from our own narratives, so often that ironically it in itself becomes cultural normality. Remember the Black Lives Matter-themed Pepsi commercial. We **wish** social justice would be actualized by simply giving a White police officer an icy-cold, thirst-quenching beverage as people dance to the beat of justice in the background.

BERG'S BOOKSHELF:

*the literature of **Bitter Root***

THE NEW NEGRO
VOICES OF THE HARLEM RENAISSANCE
EDITED BY ALAIN LOCKE

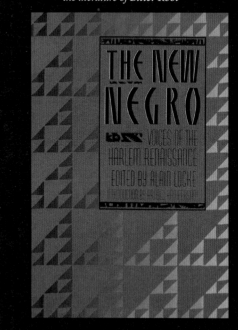

The New Negro is an anthology edited by Alain LeRoy Locke that showcases various works of poetry, fiction, and essays not only from him, but other central figures from the Harlem Renaissance like Zora Neale Hurston, W.E.B. Du Bois, Langston Hughes, Claude McKay, Jean Toomer, Eric Walrond, Richard Bruce Nugent, and many more. This book highlights the philosophy of the "New Negro" through the essay Locke wrote and is reinforced by the other literary works that figures of the Harlem Renaissance implemented. Besides reinforcing the "New Negro" through their works, they complement the philosophy with other themes like "Self Expression", "Renewal and Rebirth", and "Jazz and Blues", by the poetical, artistic, and fictitious works showcased in it. By showing the life and the struggles of the "Negro" in America through these literary works, with the philosophy and the art, the themes conjured and concepts given to the reader and the Black man shows what is needed to do for them to have political, social, and artistic change in their lives.

— Edgardo Delgadillo-Aguilera

BITTER TWITTER:

@BITTERROOT18 | @Cbrown803 | @sanfordgreene | @DavidWalker1201

BITTER TRUTHS curated and designed and edited by **John Jennings / tw @JIJennings**
Research Assistant: **Edgardo Delgadillo-Aguilera**

Africa has a strong, deep, rich oral tradition. In many countries across West Africa, this tradition is preserved by the griots, who function as historians, storytellers, poets, or musicians. Often, the griot is the preserver of the history of a family, a clan, and sometimes of the nation. This is done by narrating how the nation was founded along with their outstanding achievements, victories, or exploits. In addition to their function as a storyteller or historian, a griot was also the keeper and custodian of the culture and traditions of generations past, particularly through an oral memory. As such they are often positioned as societal leaders due to their position as educator, cultural critic, and advisor to rulers and kings.

TO THE GRIOT IN TIMES OF TERROR

MICHAEL NORTON DANDO earned his PhD in Curriculum and Instruction with a focus on multicultural education from the University of Wisconsin-Madison and is currently an Assistant Professor of Communication Arts and Literature at St. Cloud State University in Minnesota. An award-winning author, artist, educator, and scholar with two decades of classroom experience, his research and writing explore ways teachers and schools collaborate with communities to build collective, civically engaged, democratic opportunities and systems for social justice education. Particularly, his research examines ways youth employ various cultural forms, including hip-hop and comics, to create social, cultural, and political identities that generate educational opportunities for sustained, critical, democratic engagement for social justice.

The griot embodies an explicitly socio-cultural and particularly political role in African diasporic tradition as an individual who is deeply connected to the soul and spirit of a people. So close is this link that in the language of the Mandinka, "griot" translates to "blood." They are literally seen as the culture's life blood, as a griot's role is not simply rehashing a rehearsed past, but doing so for a particular purpose or to impart a particular wisdom, knowledge, or social critique. In this way, a griot's role pushed how a culture thought, how they dialogued, and how they envisioned themselves in the future. Contemporary examples include anti-apartheid activist Steve Biko, the works of novelist Octavia Butler, and Africanjujuist Nnedi Okorafor.

Over time, the role of the griot took up varied forms including musician, town crier, or entertainer, eventually becoming what we might understand to be modern media practitioners such as the hip-hop emcee, film director, and indeed comic book creative. These modern day griots, which include the *Bitter Root* team, tell stories that desperately need telling to provide hope, solidarity, and the ability to envision differently; reminding us of what makes us human, and why it is something worth fighting for. So why do we need *Bitter Root* now?

In responding to this question, it is necessary to return to the roles and responsibilities of the griot as artist, author, and activist in contemporary democratic society--namely radical truth tellers. American novelist, playwright, essayist, poet, and activist James Baldwin noted that it is the artist's duty to "disturb the peace," that is to shake up the entrenched notions and seemingly natural understandings of the status quo that can often breed complacency and a sense of resignation to the so-called way of things. Pointedly, it is incumbent on the artist to render the invisible, visible. And this is precisely what *Bitter Root* does. Walker, Greene, and Brown have used their considerable talents to disrupt the status quo as they invite readers into a complex conversation regarding the persistent presence and functions of race and belonging, as well as the dehumanizing nature of racialized hatred and trauma. This struggle for humanization is, as Brazilian educational theorist Paulo Freire notes, a "central concern" in the fight for freedom and liberation, one further complicated by considering W.E.B. DuBois' concept of the color line. The Sangerye family inhabits this space of (un)belonging in that they have for generations been saving a world that denies their basic humanity from actual monsters born of its own hatred. The Sangeryes exist in a state of tension with regard to humanity from Blink pushing back against patriarchal notions of gender roles, to their varied perspectives on dealing with Jinoo who are both monsters and humans. *Bitter Root* asks its audience to thoroughly consider who counts as a human being and the implications of that answer.

In his writing, DuBois refers to "second-sight," the ability of African Americans to see themselves not only as they truly are, but also as the Other that (White) America imagines them to be. The griot's ability to communicate the liminal nature of the second-sight DuBois describes illuminates a perspective that can serve to shift the fundamental arrangement of knowledge that produces these liminal positions by introducing new objects of knowledge. So, in many ways the griot's mandate is to be a teller of truths, especially those that often operate unseen or unrecognized by those in power or by the status quo. Like the Sangerye family, generation after generation the griot defends humanity against forces that many cannot see because they have become absorbed or infected by that which would destroy them. Like the Ethnopunk blasters Berg, Ford, Blink, and Cullen wield, a griot provides healing and protection to a community by way of ancestral memory, knowledge and lifeways.

Human history is written in blood. A culture is sustained through the stories it tells. The Sangereys' story carries with it in its blood, in its DNA, or sangre in French Creole culture, the stories of real-life monster hunters of generations past such as Bayard Rustin, Mamie Till, Fannie Lou Hamer, and scores of others fighting every day for the survival of their families and for democracy itself. Moreover this story honors the legacy of those who have taken up the fight today such as Tarana Burke or Bree Newsome. And in so doing these stories afford people the opportunity to imagine better. To hope. Because as author, lawyer, and activist Bryan Stevenson notes,

"...hopelessness is the enemy of justice. Hope allows us to push forward, even when the truth is distorted by the people in power. It allows us to stand up when they tell us to sit down, and to speak when they say be quiet."

And so, it is the responsibility of the griot to tell of what the world might be, could be, and should be. One that Langston Hughes foresaw when he swore that America "would be" for him someday. In order to begin to realize a more just, caring, and humanizing world, it is necessary for us to keep alive ways to imagine a better world that fosters the belief in a world in which right matters and where a loving, reconciling justice is sought in the face of mighty odds. Part of an artist's responsibility is to provide hope and solidarity in troubled times, to illuminate the parts of the human spirit that will not and must not be extinguished. It is a griot's responsibility to keep the flames of democracy alive and a legacy that *Bitter Root* continues to uphold for future generations

BERG'S BOOKSHELF:
*the literature of **Bitter Root***

Quicksand is a novel published in 1928 and a winner of the Harmon Foundation Prize. It is based on the life of Nella Larsen, a novelist and short story writer of the Harlem Renaissance. Larsen was a nurse and a teacher, born from a Danish Mother and Black West Indian Father. The semi-autobiographical book's main character, Helga Crane, is of the same interracial parentage. The book's narrative states that her father left Helga and her mother while she was an infant and her mother remarries. This time, she marries a white man. As the story progresses, she faces a lot of issues with her identity and discrimination throughout her entire life. *Quicksand* follows Helga from childhood to adulthood, as she faces oppression, struggles with identity and, and looks for acceptance both in Harlem and Denmark. The themes that the book presents reflect on the struggles of the Black American and what they have to overcome in their daily lives. *Quicksand* does a good job of showcasing the many struggles, challenges, and problems needed to be addressed and fought against through the perspective of a biracial woman wrestling with her internal conflicts and spiritual duality. W.E.B. DuBois stated that *Quicksand* was the "best piece of fiction that Negro America has produced since the heyday of Chesnutt [.]" Just like Berg in *Bitter Root*, DuBois is painfully aware of what is being faced by the main character. The themes of the book actually echo DuBois' most famous work *The Souls of Black Folk*. *Bitter Root* picks up this tension around who is perceived or worthy to be American and turns it on its ear. A clear example is seen in *Bitter Root #1* when Berg and Cullen are stopped and accused by the policemen of "harming" the white man whom they helped. Another example of the way *Bitter Root* deals with tensions around identity can be seen in Blink, who is chastised for fighting on the frontlines like her male cousins. The tensions around gender roles in *Bitter Root* parallel Helga's struggles with the male gaze. One can imagine that Berg, by reading *Quicksand*, not only sees the gravity of the struggles of the character Helga Crane, but now has more insight on how to further combat the social issues that surround him. He can more readily parse out those intersectional issues in order to create a way of seeing that leads to finding a better path for the Black American in society.

—Edgardo Delgadillo-Aguilera

BLACK MAGIC WOMAN:

an interview with
DR. EBONY
ELIZABETH
THOMAS

EBONY E. THOMAS is Associate Professor in the Literacy, Culture, and International Educational Division at the University of Pennsylvania's Graduate School of Education. A former Detroit Public Schools teacher and National Academy of Education/Spencer Foundation Postdoctoral Fellow, she was a member of the NCTE Cultivating New Voices Among Scholars of Color's 2008-2010 cohort, served on the NCTE Conference on English Education's Executive Committee from 2013 until 2017, and is the immediate past chair of the NCTE Standing Committee on Research. Currently, she serves as co-editor of Research of the Teaching of English, and her most recent book is *The Dark Fantastic: Race and the Imagination from Harry Potter to the Hunger Games* (NYU Press, 2019).

BT: What made you want to become a professor?

EET: My FAMU, Wayne State, and Michigan professors all encouraged me to become a professor someday! But becoming a children's literature professor happened when I met Phil Nel and Karin Westman at the first international Harry Potter fan conference, Nimbus-2003. I was co-chair of programming, and presented a paper titled "Imperial Harry: The Potter Books in the Postcolonial Context," inspired by Roderick McGillis' edited volume with a similar subtitle, *Voices of the Other: Children's Literature in the Postcolonial Context.* Karin and Phil came up to me after the session and suggested that I consider a career as a children's literature scholar. 17 years later, that's exactly what I am!

BT: What is the "Dark Fantastic" and what brought you to it?

EET: In *The Dark Fantastic*, I explored the way that race operates in the popular fantastic traditions of the West, primarily within mainstream speculative transmedia that is produced in the United States and England, and marketed to youth and young adults all over the world. Proposing that Black characters in such stories were trapped in a cycle that I named the dark fantastic, my analysis of popular young adult media revealed pernicious movement through four stages: spectacle, hesitation, violence, and haunting. Specifically, I argued that Black girl characters show up in imagined storyworlds as monstrous, invisible, and always dying. Their frightening fates mirror the realities of imperiled Black girlhoods in the real world. Only through emancipation—either through Black feminist storytelling or agentive youth restorying—could such characters escape the cycle.

Breaking this cycle requires rethinking our assumptions about magical child and teen characters. It requires reimagining who deserves magic in stories. Rethinking the cartographies of the imagination requires more than a paint-by-numbers approach to endarkening speculative fiction for youth and young adults. Such rethinking requires that we comprehensively redraw the maps of our minds, investigating the shape of our thoughts that have been formed and reformed through reading children's literature, young adult fiction, and speculative storytelling.

BT: What are some of your favorite speculative narratives and why?

EET: There are so many favorites that I've encountered over the course of my lifetime. As a child, I loved Virginia Hamilton's *The People Could Fly* and *The Dark Way*, as well as Madeleine L'Engle's *A Wrinkle in Time* quartet. As a teen, it was all Octavia Butler, all the time, capped by her *Parables* duology the summer after my senior year of high school.

As a young adult, I was into *Harry Potter, His Dark Materials*, and through that fandom, read a lot of mainstream science fiction and fantasy written by White canonical authors: Isaac Asimov, Marion Zimmer Bradley, Orson Scott Card, Richard C. Clarke, Philip K. Dick, George R.R. Martin, J.R.R. Tolkien, and many, many more. I wish someone had clued me in on the various controversies associated with some of them, but 20 years ago, it's as if you weren't a real nerd if you weren't reading those authors.

I will say I've heard nothing but great things about George R.R. Martin. He's definitely someone I'd love to meet, because his novels and *Star Trek* helped me get through the tenure track. Also, I wish I'd discovered Ursula K. LeGuin earlier in life. I didn't get to meet her through her words until I had a PhD.

Lately, I've been loving the Black girl magic fantasy novels of Nnedi Okorafor, Tomi Adeyemi, Dhonielle Clayton, Zetta Elliott, and L.L. McKinney. I fell in love with N.K. Jemisin's Broken Earth trilogy and can't wait for it to be adapted. I think P. Djeli Clark is a genius. Season 4 of *The Expanse* was the best genre show on TV, second only to HBO's *Watchmen* adaptation. I am so proud of the work that K. Tempest Bradford is doing with *Writing the Other*, and am inspired by adrienne maree brown and Walidah Imarisha's vision that "all organizing is speculative fiction."

I wish I'd read more short stories along the way. Shout out to Sheree Renee Thomas' groundbreaking anthology *Dark Matter* and its sequel; they were lights for us SFF Blerds when the landscape was bleak.

BT: What do you want people to take away from your book and how you think it can affect their everyday lives?

EET: I'd love for folks to walk away from *The Dark Fantastic* with new lenses for their reading, viewing, and participation in fan communities. My hope is for the reader to begin to see the selected stories, and by extension, all speculative storytelling, from the perspective of a Black girl reader, sitting at home, trying to find herself in magic, in the future, in the imagination. I want the reader to see what we see (to quote Social Justice Books' SWWS group) when they look at these stories. I want them to never look at these stories the same way again.

BT: Does your pedagogy affect your own fiction writing? If so, how?

EET: Long ago, I used to read chapters from my novel-that-I-hope-will-someday-be-published to my high school students. But I think I didn't really think of novel writing as pedagogical until I revisited the manuscript after more than a decade away from it. When I was in my late teens and 20s, and created the characters, I related to them as peers. Today, they feel more like students I once taught, my nieces and nephews, and their friends. That distancing has helped me as I revise.

After I sell this book, I'd like to put on my scholar hat and reflect on the long, strange trip that was the 20 years (25+ since I got the characters) between conception and publication. I don't know that such a long incubation period is ideal, but then again, *The Dark Fantastic* also was slow cooked. I came up with the idea for the book in the mid-2000s, and began to write it in early 2014. So maybe that's my process: slow cooked books. These days, I'm content with that.

"When I conjure these memories, they are of the present to me, because after all, the artist is a kind of enchanter in time."
–Romare Bearden

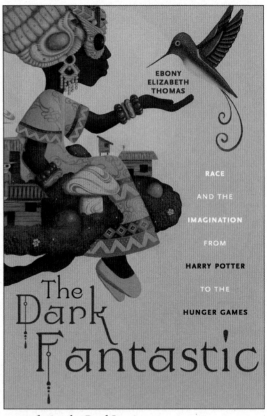

EBONY ELIZABETH THOMAS

RACE AND THE IMAGINATION FROM HARRY POTTER TO THE HUNGER GAMES

The Dark Fantastic

cover design by Paul Lewin
@paullewinart

BITTER TWITTER:

@BITTERROOT18 | @Cbrown803 | @sanfordgreene | @DavidWalker1201

BITTER TRUTHS curated and designed and edited by **John Jennings** / tw **@JIJennings**
Research Assistant: **Edgardo Delgadillo-Aguilera**

BITTER TRUTHS

DEEP STRUCTURES:
TECHNOSOCIAL
MEANINGS OF THE
BITTER ROOT LOGO

DAMIAN DUFFY is a cartoonist, scholar, writer, curator, lecturer, teacher, and a Glyph Comics, Eisner Comics, and Bram Stoker Award-winning, #1 New York Times bestselling graphic novelist. He holds an MS and Ph.D. in Library and Information Sciences from the University of Illinois at Urbana-Champaign, where he is on faculty, teaching courses on computers & culture, and social media & global change. Duffy's work includes the ground-breaking artshows *Other Heroes: African American Comics Creators, Characters, and Archetypes, Out of Sequence: Underrepresnted Voices in American Comics,* and is the co-author of underground cult classic graphic novel *The Hole: Consumer Culture vol. 1.* Duffy is also the co-editor of *Black Comix: African American Independent Comix Art and Culture* and the sequel *Black Comix Returns.* He is also an adaptor of two of Octavia E. Butler's novels into graphic novels; *Kindred* and *Parable of the Sower.* Duffy lives in Champaign, Illinois with his wife and two children.

"Truth must be dug up from the past and presented to the circle of scholastics in scientific form and then through stories and dramatizations that will permeate our educational system."
— Carter G. Woodson

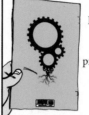

Let's dig into that logo on the back cover—in the properly Langston Hughes sense of "dig and be dug in return."

It's a cyborg image . . .

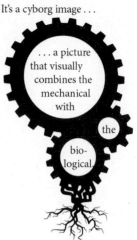

. . . a picture that visually combines the mechanical with the bio-logical.

The conjurepunk crest thus symbolizes the combinations of technology and conjurework used by the Sangereye family. But beyond that, the logo also provides visual metaphor for the overall technological, social, and historical contexts of *Bitter Root.*

For instance, considered cartographic-ally, the logo functions as an abstract mapping of the demographic shifts that preceded the race riots of the Red Summer of 1919, true events that haunt the Sangereye's opening story arc: The Great Migration . . .

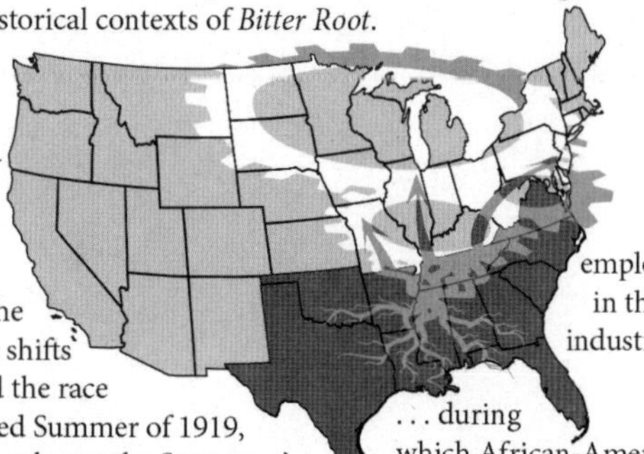

. . . for employment in the more industrialized North.

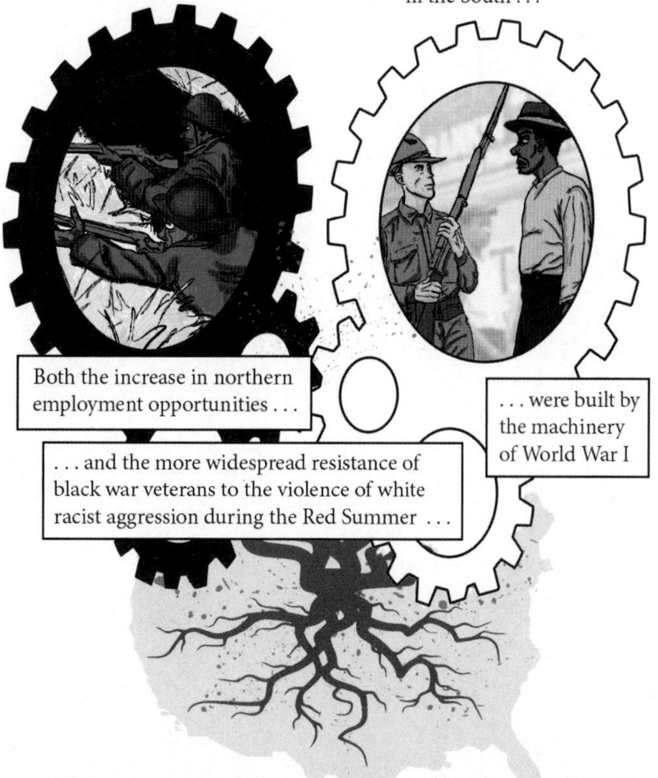

. . . during which African-Americans left agricultural work in the South . . .

Both the increase in northern employment opportunities . . .

. . . were built by the machinery of World War I

. . . and the more widespread resistance of black war veterans to the violence of white racist aggression during the Red Summer . . .

White supremacist violence is of course much older, soaked into the roots of the U.S.—along with Indigenous and African Diasporic blood.

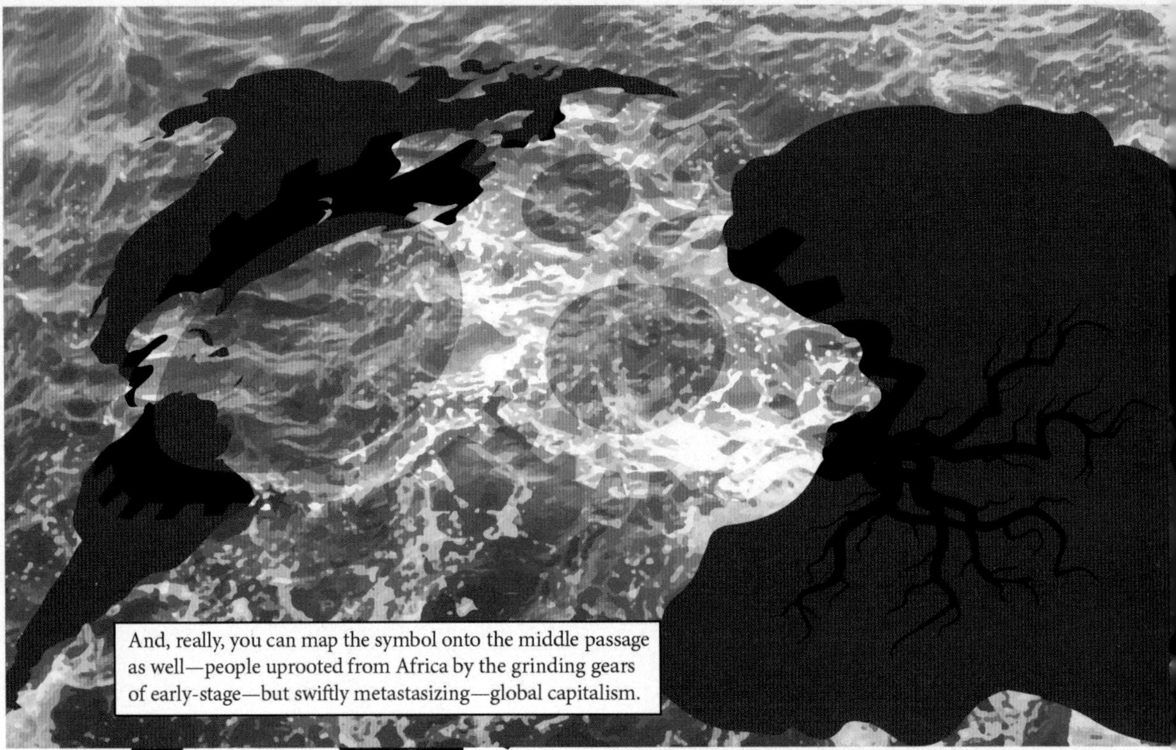
And, really, you can map the symbol onto the middle passage as well—people uprooted from Africa by the grinding gears of early-stage—but swiftly metastasizing—global capitalism.

But, *Bitter Root* isn't a story about division, but about connections.

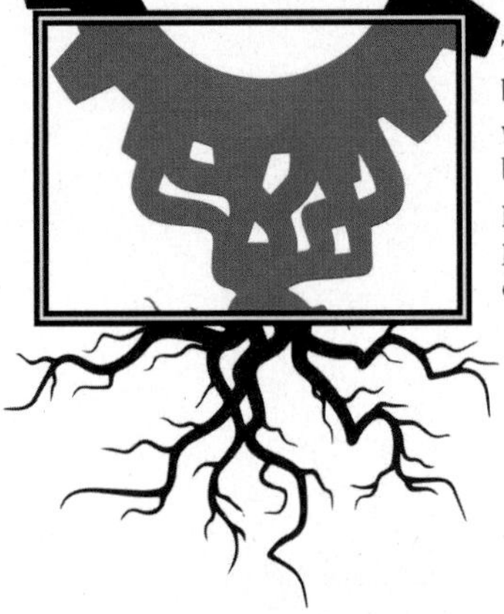

The Sangereye's build armor, weapons, and beliefs from the places where past and present entangle.

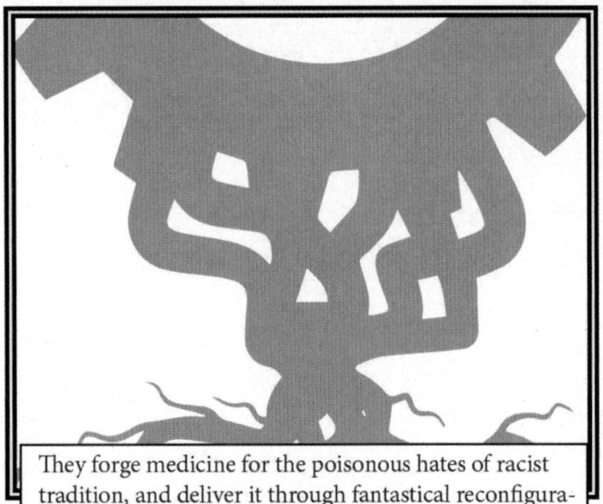

They forge medicine for the poisonous hates of racist tradition, and deliver it through fantastical reconfigurations of the real world weapons field tested in what was once naively considered the war to end all wars.

It is in this syncretic space, in the place where the gears and roots overlap and intertwine, that we find the logos most insightful visual representation of Harlem Renaissance history that the fiction of *Bitter Root* represents.

Bitter Root is a story of supernatural battles and family demons, that resonates not just because of the storytelling skills of Brown, Walker, Greene, Dodgson, and Cowles, but because those skills have been turned to a nuanced dramatization of the historically heavy horror of being black in the United States.

It is a logographic invocation of what Houston A. Baker, Jr. calls the "counter-modernism" of African-American cultural production, both during the Harlem Renaissance, and beyond it—a combination of modernist aesthetic experimentation with "an ever-present, folk or vernacular drive that moves always up, beyond, and away from whatever forms of oppression a surrounding culture next devises" (96).[1]

[1] Baker Jr, Houston A. *Modernism and the Harlem Renaissance*. University of Chicago Press, 2013.

PLAYING IN THE DARK:

an interview with
Horror Pioneer
BRANDON MASSEY

BRANDON MASSEY sold his first short story in 1996 to a speculative fiction magazine. Three years later, he self-published *Thunderland*, his first novel. After managing to sell a few thousand copies on his own, Kensington Publishing Corp signed him to a deal and republished the novel in 2002. Since then, Massey has published up to three books a year, ranging from thriller novels such as *The Other Brother* and *Don't Ever Tell*, vampire fiction such as *Dark Corner*, and short story collections such as *Twisted Tales*; he's also edited multiple anthologies in his *Dark Dreams* series, featuring the short works of acclaimed authors from Eric Jerome Dickey to Tananarive Due. Massey currently lives with his family near Atlanta, GA, and continues to write every day. To stay posted on his latest book news, be sure to visit his website at *www.brandonmassey.com* and sign up for his free newsletter.

It's not hyperbolic to state that black cultural production around the speculative is not only in vogue, but has reached an international level of impact and visibility. Black speculative culture and Afrofuturism have been mainstream, and this has been the case in multiple genres and media. Jordan Peele's groundbreaking horror film *Get Out* has now helped to catapult smart, political, Afrocentric horror to the forefront. However, long before Jordan Peele's work, there has been the work of a number of black horror writers working in the shadows.

One such pioneer is Brandon Massey. Massey's first novel *The Dark Corner* and his co-edited *Dark Dreams* series, which collected short stories by black authors, helped set the bar and the tone for the black experience in the genre of horror. Now almost two decades later and almost just as many books, Brandon Massey has released his new novel *The Quiet Ones*. Bitter Truths reached out to this master of the macabre to see what terrifying tales he is working on now.

What was your gateway into horror narratives and what were some of your favorites?

One of my earliest experiences with the genre was when my mom took me to see *Alien* in the theater. Yes, I was only six at the time--and probably shouldn't have been there. But it made a powerful impression on me, as you can imagine. It was terrifying. It was also exhilarating, like riding the world's most exciting roller coaster. After that, I was hooked.

When did you decide to become a writer and editor of horror?

The genre chose me, really. I started seriously pursuing writing as a teenager and originally wanted to write fantasy and sci-fi, two genres I also loved. But whenever I sat down to write, my stories always took these unexpected turns into frightening places.

I didn't see anyone like me writing these kind of stories. I've always been a bit of a contrarian by nature so I said, "Well, why not me?"

Why do you think horror is useful for black people to engage in politically?

Horror helps you deal with fear--with the possibility of the "worst that can happen." When I look around our current political landscape I find a lot to be afraid of--extremist views, the enormous gap between the wealthy and the lower classes, the tribalism, our country's overall level of apathy and cynicism in regard to the political process. I think at times like the present, people actually want and appreciate horror because usually in a horror tale, someone survives at the end. I think we can all use some survival tactics and coping mechanisms these days.

What inspired you to become an editor?

I'm more of an "occasional" editor, honestly. It's not something I've done for many years, but at the time it was an opportunity to provide exposure to fresh voices, to give back. All anyone needs is a chance to shine. It's been gratifying to find that some of the talented writers who were published for the first time in one of my anthologies have gone on to long-term pro careers.

What, if any, negative issues have occurred from you being involved in creating horror stories and editing them?

When I started publishing in 1999, 2000 or so, there was a bit of pushback from the audience that typically is most invested in works by African American authors. One reader I met at a signing accused me of writing books about "demons" and shoved my book back in my face as if it might burn her. It was a bizarre response but back then I was getting a fair number of questions about why I was writing this material, and whether something was wrong with me. Or they just flat out refused to read it. That resistance has started to erode over time but in the beginning it was discouraging.

What scares you?

Losing my family. Losing my health--psychological and physical. Being trapped in a situation entirely out of my control.

What is your new book about and what inspired it?

The Quiet Ones is a story about a woman who is trying to make her life whole by finding the sister from whom she has been separated for twenty-five years. It's inspired by my ongoing obsession with family ties and secrets, which I've written about in multiple books.

If you were editing a book on black horror now, who would you include?

I'd love to include Walter Mosley, NK Jemisin, and Victor LaValle.

What horror film still scares you today?

'*The Exorcist*' still disturbs me and probably always will. It effectively exploits that primal fear of the unknown, of being at the mercy of something beyond your control and even comprehension.

What advice would you give POC who want to do horror stories?

Be authentic. Learn the craft.

"One thing I know that's true about horror fans of any color is they like to be scared. And the easiest place to be scared is in a new thing."

—*Tananarive Due*

THE QUIET ONES
BRANDON MASSEY
AUTHOR OF FRENZIED AND NANA

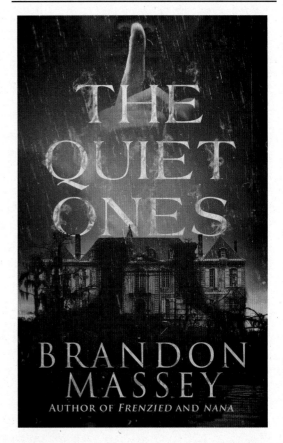

BITTER TWITTER:

@BITTERROOT18 | @Cbrown803 | @sanfordgreene | @DavidWalker1201

BITTER TRUTHS curated and designed and edited by **John Jennings / tw @JIJennings**
Research Assistant: **Edgardo Delgadillo-Aguilera**

AMPUTATING WHITENESS

MATTHEW TEUTSCH is the Director of the Lillian E. Smith Center at Piedmont College. He maintains Interminable Rambling, a blog about literature, composition, culture, and pedagogy. He has published articles and book reviews in various venues including *LEAR, MELUS, Mississippi Quarterly, African American Review, Callaloo, Black Perspectives,* and *Bitter Southerner.* His research focus is African American, Southern, and Nineteenth Century American literature. He is the editor of *Rediscovering Frank Yerby: Critical Essays* (UPM 2020), and his current project examines Christopher Priest's run on *Black Panther.* Follow him on Twitter @ SilasLapham.

When we first meet Johnnie-Ray Knox in Mississippi, we see him dressed in Klan robes taking part in a attempted lynching of a Black man who supposedly messed with the purity of a white Southern woman. Ford Sangerye intervenes and kills the infected Jinoo. Johnnie-Ray, though, does not turn into a Jinoo, and Ford warns Johnnie-Ray, "Keep your soul clean, Johnnie-Ray Knox. Otherwise, next time I won't leave you standing." Johnnie-Ray's initial appearance reminds me of two images. The first is a photograph taken by Todd Robertson during a Klan rally in Gainesville, GA, in 1992. The image shows a young white boy, probably about two years old, dressed in Klan robes touching his reflection in a riot shield that a Black Georgia State Trooper holds in his hands. The boy is enraptured with himself, his own visage, and he completely ignores his surroundings, including the trooper holding the shield. In his self-absorption, he reaches his finger out to touch his own facsimile.

Robertson's photograph reminds me of Lillian Smith's words regarding the narcissism and self-absorption of whiteness. In "Are We Not All Confused?" from the Spring 1942 issue of *South Today*, Smith writes about Southern liberals who argued for change and an end to segregation before America's involvement in World War II, but who fell silent during the war. She writes, "Under stress men tend to revert to early patterns of behavior. . . . White southerners are rigorously trained in childhood to believe in their whiteness. They are trained in distinctions, segregations, special privileges, as they are trained in their toilet habits."

One's education in racism, hate, and oppression begins in childhood, and one could argue from the moment one enters into the world and the pen leaves a mark in the box labeled "Race." It takes a lifetime to disentangle one's self from its grip. That is why Ford, as he talks with the grandparents of the young man whom Johnnie-Ray and the others were about to lynch, says, "I don't purify. I amputate." The roots of racism run deep. They're in our education system. On our television. On our movie screens. In our video games. In our music. In our comics. In our grocery stores. To rid oneself of the roots, one must burn them out, scorching them into oblivion, before they seep so deep into the soul that eradicating them becomes nearly impossible.

The other image I thought about with Johnnie-Ray's introduction was Reginald Marsh's *This is Her First Lynching*, a piece he did for the NAACP's 1935 "An Art Commentary on Lynching". In Marsh's piece, a crowd of white townspeople move to the left of the image, towards a lynching victim off of the canvas. The glow from the fire that burns the victim dances on their faces. Two townspeople hold a little girl aloft so she can see. She sits in the air, finger to her chin, as she takes in the grotesque violence. The visages of the townspeople are distorted, illuminating the Jinoo within each of them. The girl's face looks innocent, as if her soul, like Johnnie-Ray's, is still clean. How long will this last? How long till the Jinoo infects her? If it does, will she be able to rid herself of the infection? Will she have to amputate a part of herself?

Will the young girl be like the Jinoo that Ford kills? Or, will she be like Johnny-Ray Knox? Over the course of *Bitter Root*, Johnnie-Ray becomes an ally to the Sangerye family. We see him lead Ford to a gatekeeper in Northern Mississippi. We see him cleaning the Sangerye's shop and serving soup to people in Harlem after the battle with Dr. Sylvester. We see him in the tunnels underneath New York City with Cullen, Blink, and Nora as they come across Adro's handiwork. We see him heading down to Georgia with some of the Sangeryes to confront Adro.

In spite of all of this, Berg points out to Johnny-Ray that even though he sees Johnny-Ray as an ally "this equanimity is tenuous at best." The roots still exist in Johnny-Ray, and this fact reminds me of an anecdote Smith provides in *Killers of the Dream* (1949).

Smith writes about hosting interracial dinners at her home in Northeast Georgia in the 1940s, and she points out that one white woman, even "though her conscience was serene" and she believed in integration, could not shake the deeply rooted thought that breaking bread with a Black woman was a taboo against civil society. The woman became "seized by an acute nausea which disappeared only when the meal was finished." The woman knew that the nausea arose from, as she termed it, the "bottom of her personality" which she traced back to "her childhood training."

Philosopher George Yancy sums up the white woman's reaction in this way: "This is an incredible example because it demonstrates that having a serene conscience or having an epistemologically correct belief does not ipso facto militate against the impact of one's white racism." The white woman knew, in her head, what she was doing was right. Yet, her childhood training told her otherwise, revealing the part of herself that had not yet been amputated.

We do not know how Johnny-Ray's story will play out. Has he amputated his past? Has he scorched the roots of his racism? Or, do they lie dormant, waiting to surface?

BERG'S BOOKSHELF:
*the literature of **Bitter Root***

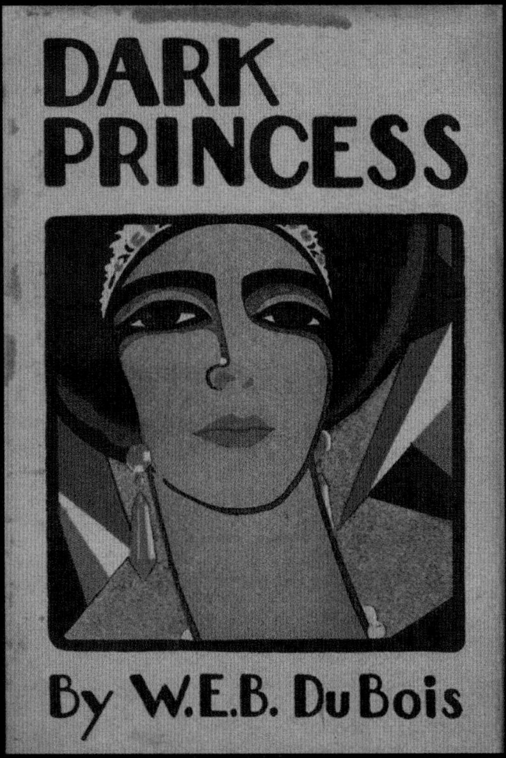
DARK
PRINCESS
By W.E.B. Du Bois

The sociologist, activist, and one of the central figures of the Harlem Renaissance, William Edward Burghardt (W.E.B.) Du Bois, serialized a novel of great importance entitled *Dark Princess* in 1928. The story focuses on Matthew Townes, a college student from the University of Manhattan studying obstetrics. Unfortunately, due to his status as a Black American, he was not qualified to finish his studies. In disbelief that he did not qualify, and feeling betrayed by the country he loved, he decided to leave for Germany. Hoping to find a different purpose, he meets Princess Kautilya of Bwodpur who opens his eyes to a world of culture beyond America. Matthews' gradual radicalization happens over five chapters. His adventures expose him to a myriad of experiences from being wrongfully arrested to having a son born of royal blood. Themes that are reflected in the narrative are anti-imperialism, internationalism, international racial solidarity, and exposing racial inequality. Through his journey of transformation is embodied through the romantic interest of Princess Kautilya. The princess seems to read as an avatar of the romanticization of protest, abolishment of racist institutions, unionization, and solidarity of people of color throughout the African Diaspora. One can speculate that *Bitter Root's* Berg would be inspired by DuBois' heroine and learn more about the importance of resistance, unification of people of color throughout the Diaspora, and deploying protest in order to fight against imperialism in America. *Dark Princess* imagines a better future for Black people. It shows that people of color are people of stature and of purpose. Not only is this another story that highlights the experiences of a Black Americans, but idealizes and speculates a world of all colors, equality, and unity. It is a story that attempts to visualize and relate a schema for a better future. I think there's no question that the *Dark Princess* would be on Berg's bookshelf.

WEB Dubois characterizes African-Americans as living in state of double consciousness, "looking at one's self through the eyes of others, measuring one's soul by the tape of a world that looks on in amused contempt and pity." But what if we were to flip the script? What if we were to measure a White man's soul by the tape of a world of men and women whom he has looked on in amused contempt and pity?

Bitter Root does just that.

Bitter Root is among the Blackest of power fantasies, weaving together elements from the horror and superhero genres to tell tales that center Blackness while reconceptualizing the history of race in America. It is the story of the Sangeryes ... a family of Black monster hunters who wield axes, shotguns, swords, and a vast array of root work powered steampunk inspired weaponry. They are engaged in an intergenerational mission to hunt down and eradicate White people who have been transformed into monsters by hate and racism.

Comic books offer a surreal fantastical mix of adventure, crime, horror, humor, and romance targeting white mostly male audiences. Since the creation of *Superman* in 1938, arguably the first costumed superhero, the superhero genre has been so popular in the US that it became synonymous with comic books. The superhero genre is a power fantasy built around people grappling with power. Flight. Speed. Strength. Magic. Technology. Wealth. Whether theses powers were embodied, mediated through objects, the product of knowledge, or skills honed to a preternatural level ... these powers were located in individuals that do not work for the crown or state. They are not beholden. Rather, they choose to put their powers in service of their causes and constituencies.

"Truth, justice, and the American way."

"With great power comes great responsibility."

"Fighting for a world that hates and fears them."

These are more than mere catch phrases. They are statements about the appropriate use of power. And they are very much gendered and racialized in accordance with the identities of the characters, the narrative world they inhabit, and the identities of the target audiences.

These super heroic white power fantasies can and do engage the plights of ethnic and racial minorities. But to what affect and in service whom? When Superman fights for "truth, justice, and the American way" he does so as a white man in the context of a country divided along racial lines, redeeming the system along the way. Spiderman's belief that "with great power comes great responsibility" inspires selfless acts but it renders him feckless when faced with systemic concerns. And the X-Men, no matter how diverse their lineup, inevitably end up fighting for a world that so hates and fears them that their members often die by the hands of the people they are protecting.

What Superman, Spiderman, and the X-Men's power fantasies have in common is their service to a multicultural society (a system) founded on democratic principles that is dominated by white people who want to be better out of a sense of civility, fairness, and inclusivity. Racism undercuts these ideals. Fighting racism redeems the system but fully realizing the humanity of racial and ethnic others. After all, you can have civility, fairness, and inclusivity in a world that still diminishes

AMONG THE BLACKEST OF POWER FANTASIES

STANFORD CARPENTER,PhD is a Cultural Anthropologist, Comic Scholar, Comic Creator, and former Archaeologist. Dr. Carpenter is co-creator of the forthcoming NPR Affiliate podcast *Brother-Story and the Correspondent*, an ethnographic and journalistic take on comics, culture, and the lives of the people who create and consume them. He is on the advisory boards of Abrams ComicArts' Megascope imprint advisory board, the Black & Brown Comix Arts Festival, and Pocket Con Team.

the souls of marginalized people by looking upon them with "amused contempt and pity."

In his articulation of double consciousness, WEB DuBois describes what it is to be on the ass end of a power fantasy, to exist in a framework determined by someone … else. And therein lies the value of a Black power fantasy, of flipping the script, of crafting a world that looks at white people who flirt with racism with "amused contempt and pity."

In *Bitter Root* we have Black creators crafting a power fantasy that centers racism and trauma without centering White people. We see Black men and women shepherd the enslaved to freedom on the underground railroad. We get glimpses of Red Summer and the Greenwood Massacre. We see the struggle and the trauma of survivors as they grapple with what they have experienced. These events and experiences that tap into some of the most horrific Black collective memories are points of entry in an epic battle against hate and racism. An epic battle against hate and racism? Sound a little corny? Maybe so. But that is what the superhero genre does well. It grounds the fantastical, it embodies concepts into (imaginary) physical forms and puts them at odds with one another.

Bitter Root focuses on the Sangeryes, an extended family of monster hunters. When the readers first encounter them, they are battling the jinoo in Harlem. For the most part, they do their best to cure the jinoo through root work. But they do not hesitate to kill the jinoo in self-defense. In *Bitter Root* racism and trauma have an otherworldly transformative quality. When White people commit horrifically violent hatefully racist acts their souls are "tainted by hate," they are transformed into monsters (jinno) that prey on the innocent. The Red Summer and Greenwood were infestations, where the racially motivated hate got so out of control that the jinoo rose up and committed mass murder. While the Black survivors of these are left to a different fate. Their souls "ravaged by great sorrow and pain" render them transformed into inzondo. The inzondo occupy a liminal space. Humans see them as monsters. But the inzondo see themselves as "liberated," setting up one of the most interesting conflicts in the story.

"I am not trouble, young Sangerye," argues Dr. Sylvester, an inzondo transformed by the Tulsa massacre, "I am salvation. Moses led his people to freedom from the oppression of the pharaoh. And I am here to lead our people to freedom."

"By attacking innocent folk?" asks Cullen Sangerye.

"Cullen, there's no reasoning with this devil." Interjects Cullen's uncle, Enoch Sangerye.

"I am not the devil," continues Dr. Sylvester, "It was the devil that made me what I have become, and the devil I am here to destroy. Look around you, Enoch Sangerye. You've seen this before – cities and towns burned to the ground. It always starts with their hate and fear. And it always ends with our deaths. You saw the hell unleashed in the summer of 1919."

What do we make of these wounded survivors filled with righteous rage and empowered with the ability to destroy the source of the traumas that made them? Therein lies the most interesting complication in what could otherwise be a battle between good Black people and evil White racists. The inzondo's origins, their stories, are intimately tied to the Sangeryes. The Sangeryes are descended from conductors of the underground railroad. They and their kin were also there for the Red Summer and Greenwood … and not all of them survived. The same events that created the inzondo also forged the Sangereys into heroes.

In the world of *Bitter Root* racism is bad. Not because it represents a threat to civility, fairness, or inclusivity but because it destroys people, orphans children, and lays waste to communities leaving no one left to bury the dead. This is a world where white people are viewed with "amused contempt and pity" because they live a tragic existence. Racism consumes and transforms them into monsters that need to be eliminated. Yet they are not victims. Rather, they are responsible for racism, the original sin that sets all of this into motion.

" Either America will destroy ignorance or ignorance will destroy the United States."

- *W.E.B. DuBois*

BITTER TWITTER:

@BITTERROOT18 | @Cbrown803 | @sanfordgreene | @DavidWalker1201

BITTER TRUTHS curated and designed and edited by **John Jennings** / tw **@JIJennings**
Research Assistant: **Edgardo Delgadillo-Aguilera**

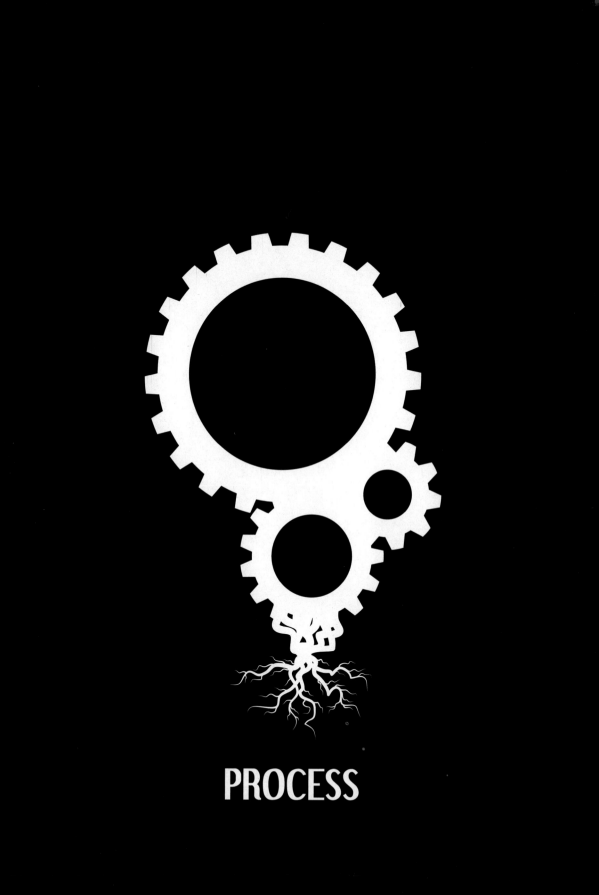

PROCESS

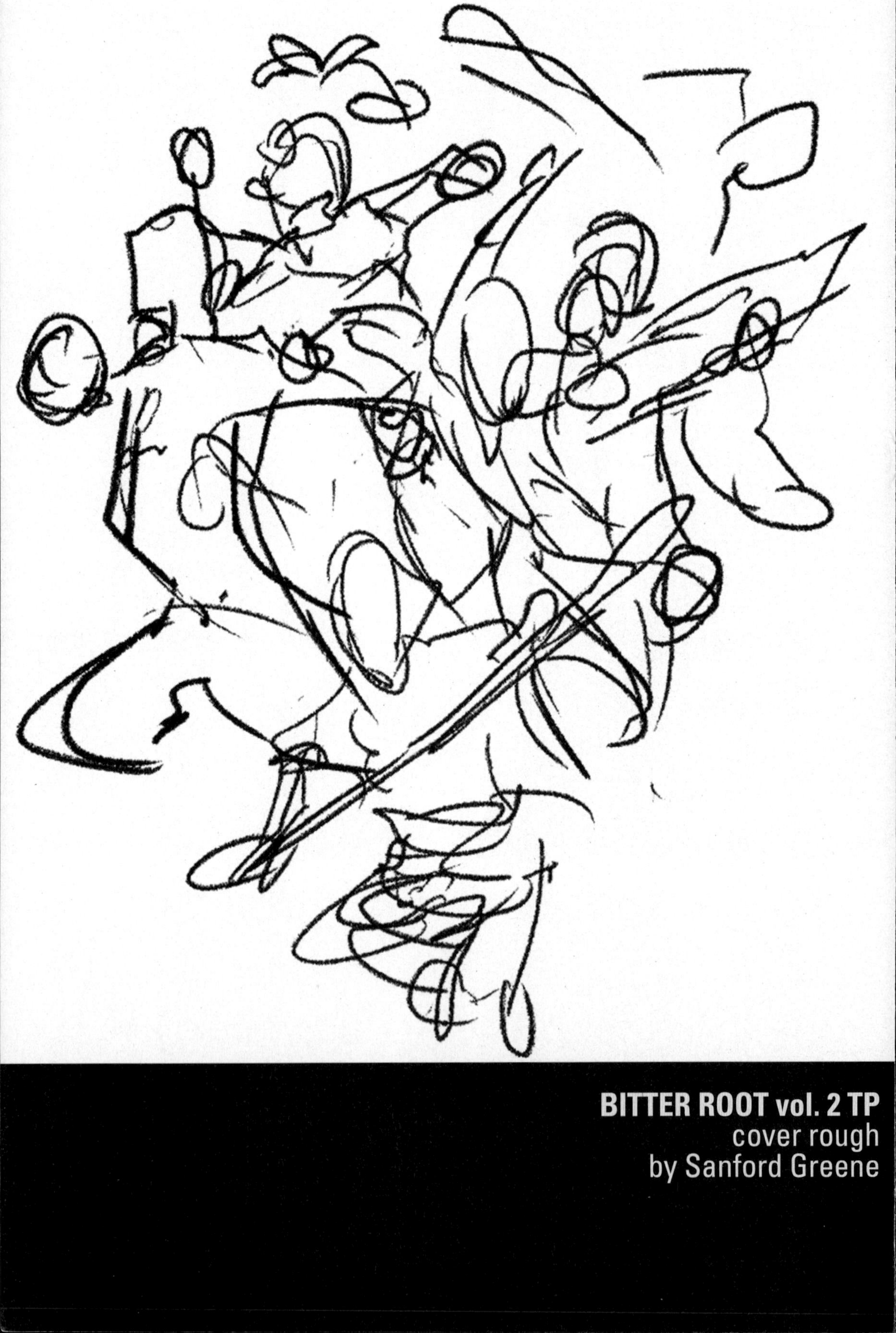

BITTER ROOT vol. 2 TP
cover rough
by Sanford Greene

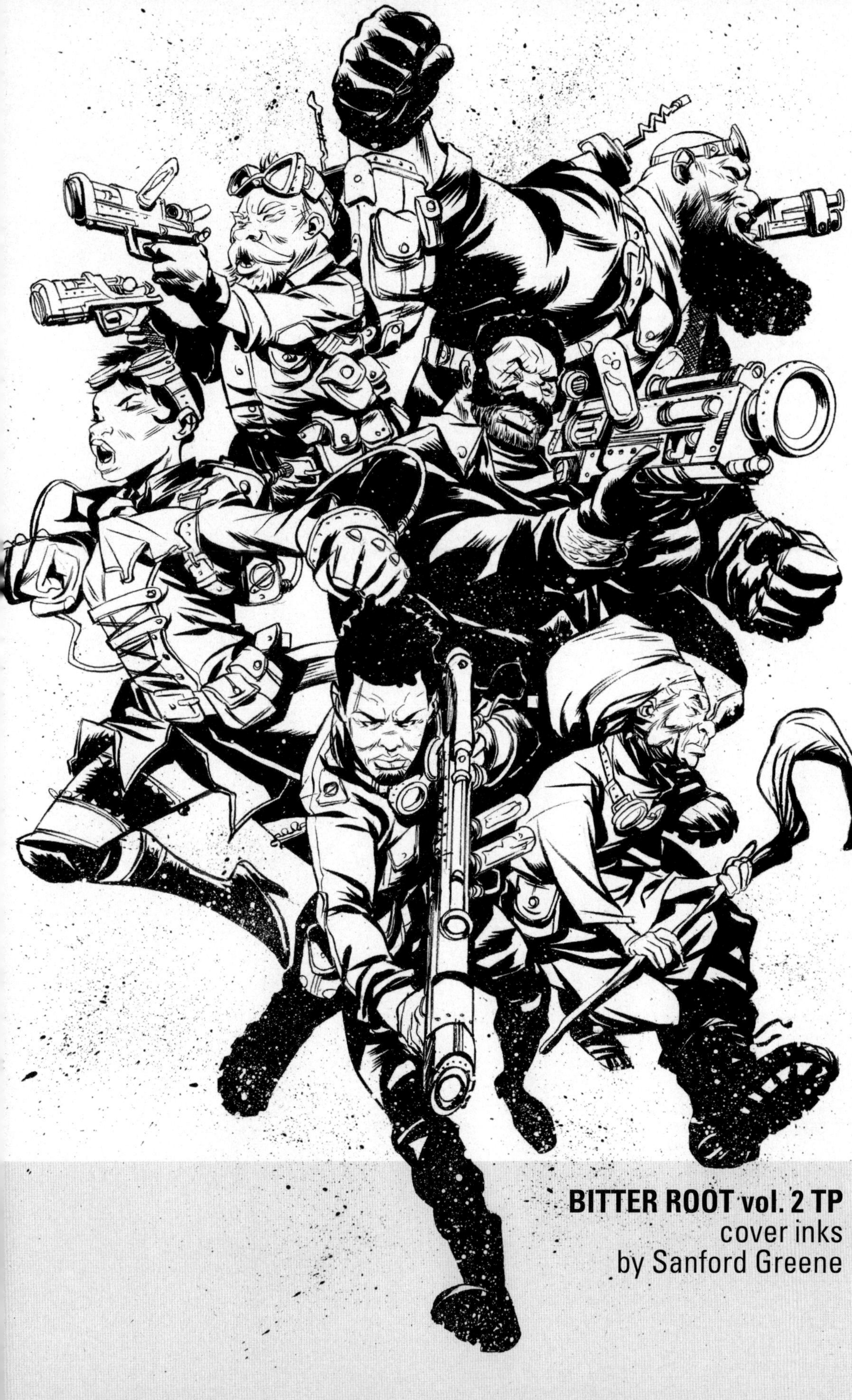

BITTER ROOT vol. 2 TP
cover inks
by Sanford Greene

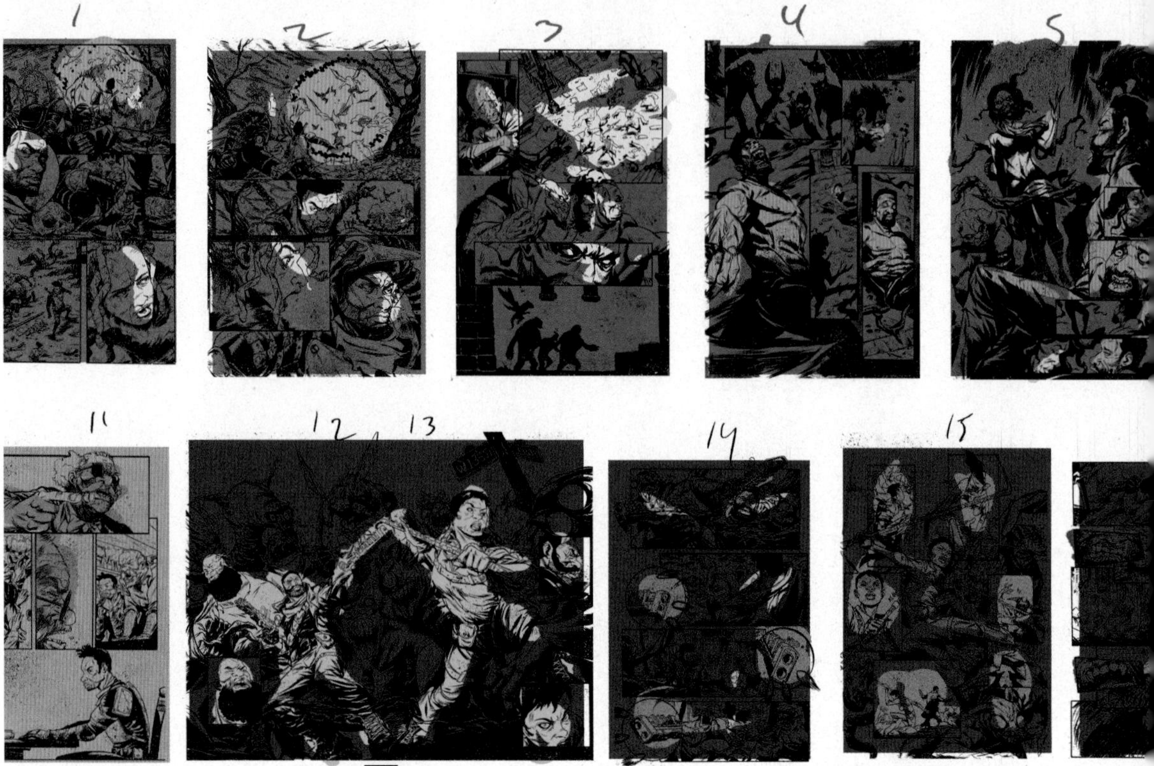
1
2
3
4
5
11
12 13
14
15

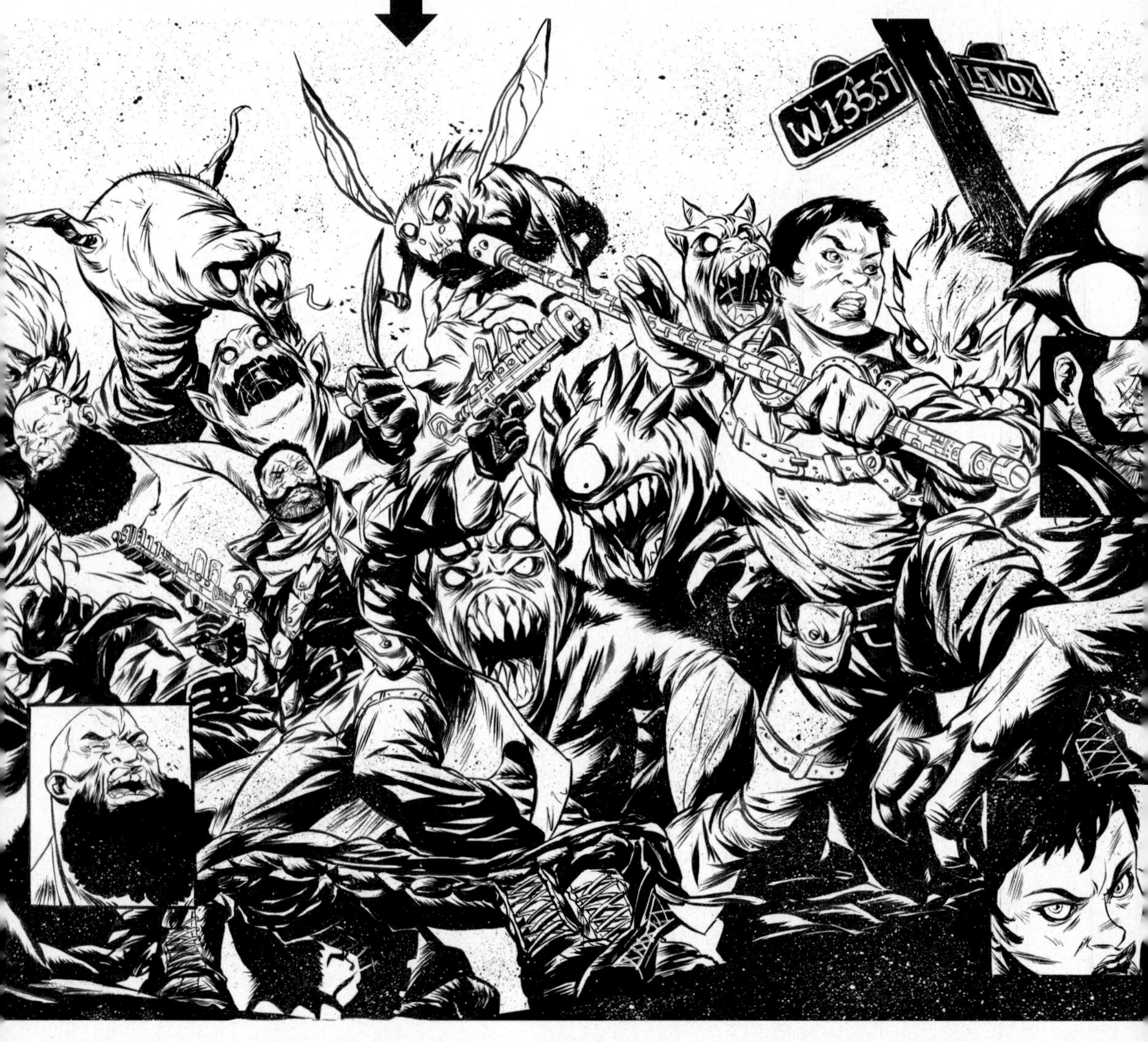
W 135 ST
LENOX

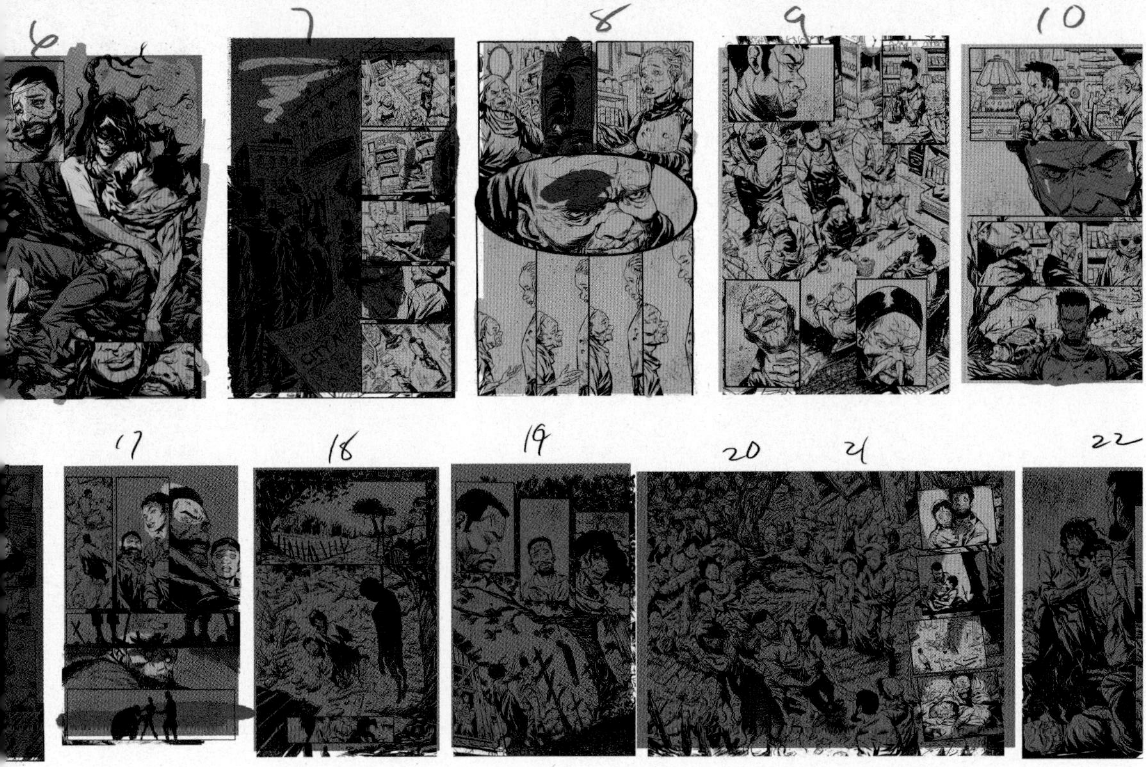

6
7
8
9
10
17
18
19
20
21
22

"Sanford's art is so expressive and lyrical that the colours needed to be vibrant but simple to honour that energy without detracting from his brushstrokes."

—Sofie Dodgson, colorist

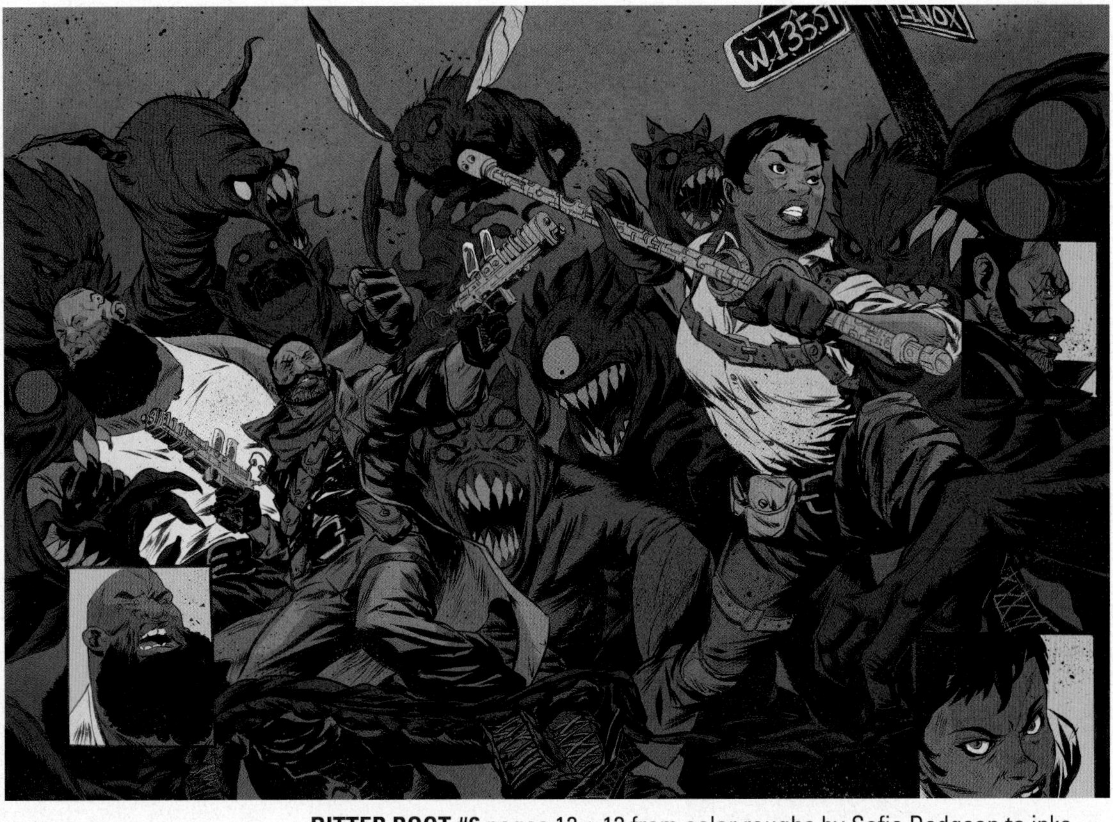

W135ST

BITTER ROOT #6 pages 12 + 13 from color roughs by Sofie Dodgson to inks by Sanford Greene to final color.

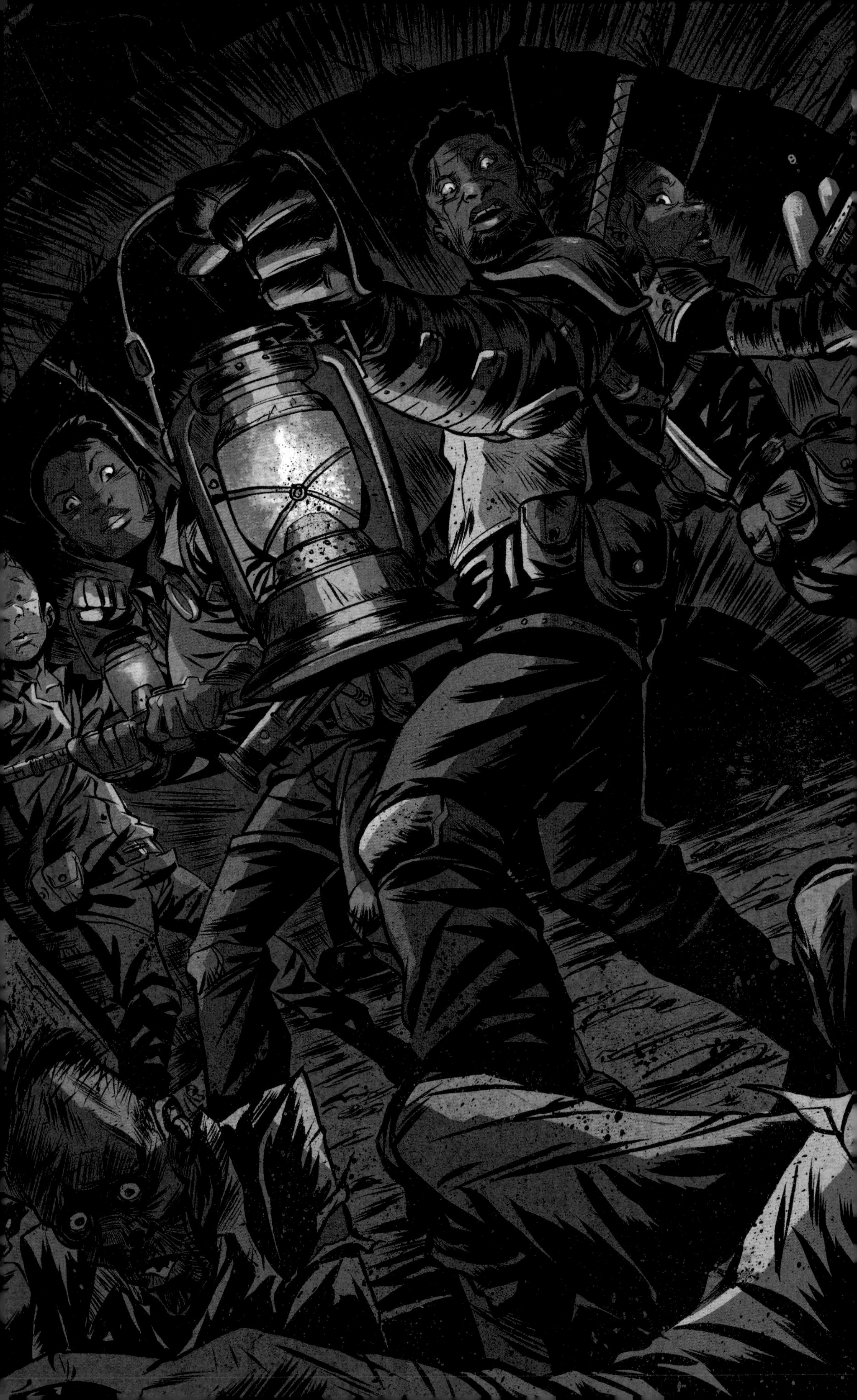

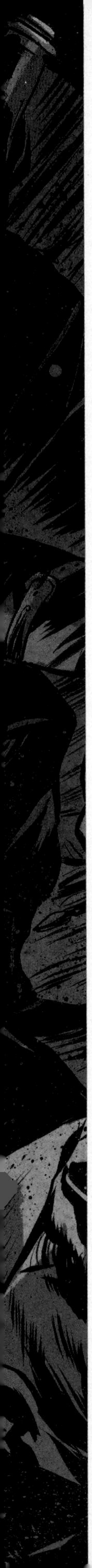

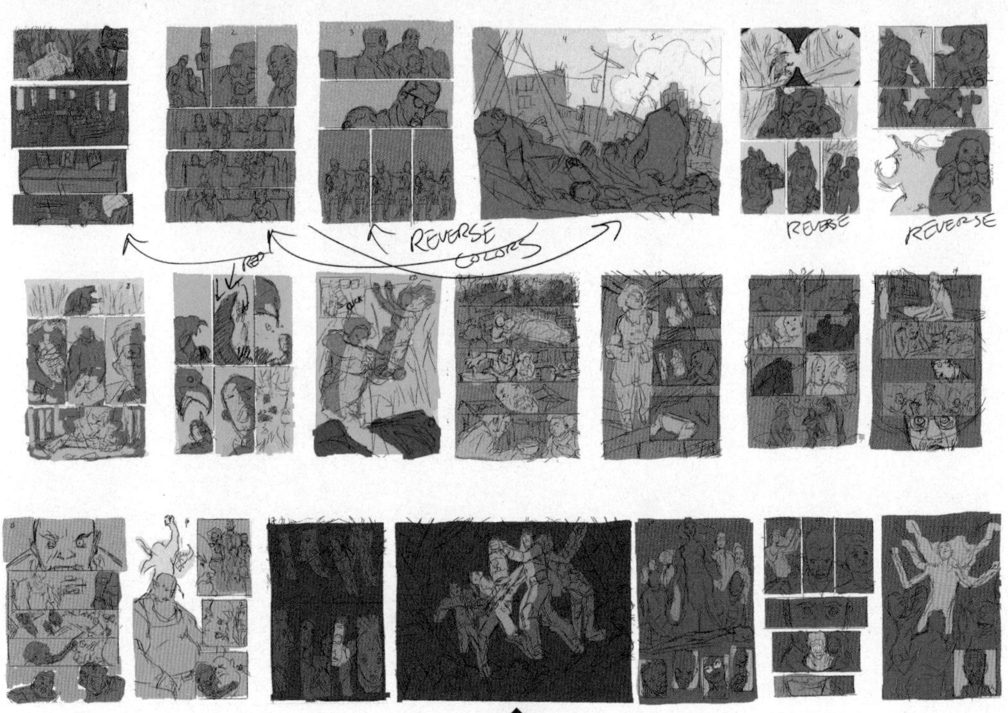
RED
REVERSE COLORS
REVERSE
REVERSE

"Certain colour choices were definitely responses to the artwork — like fills of dark, visceral pink around a character's agonized expression, or a melancholy, muted colour for the background when the characters looked downtrodden."

—*Sofie Dodgson*

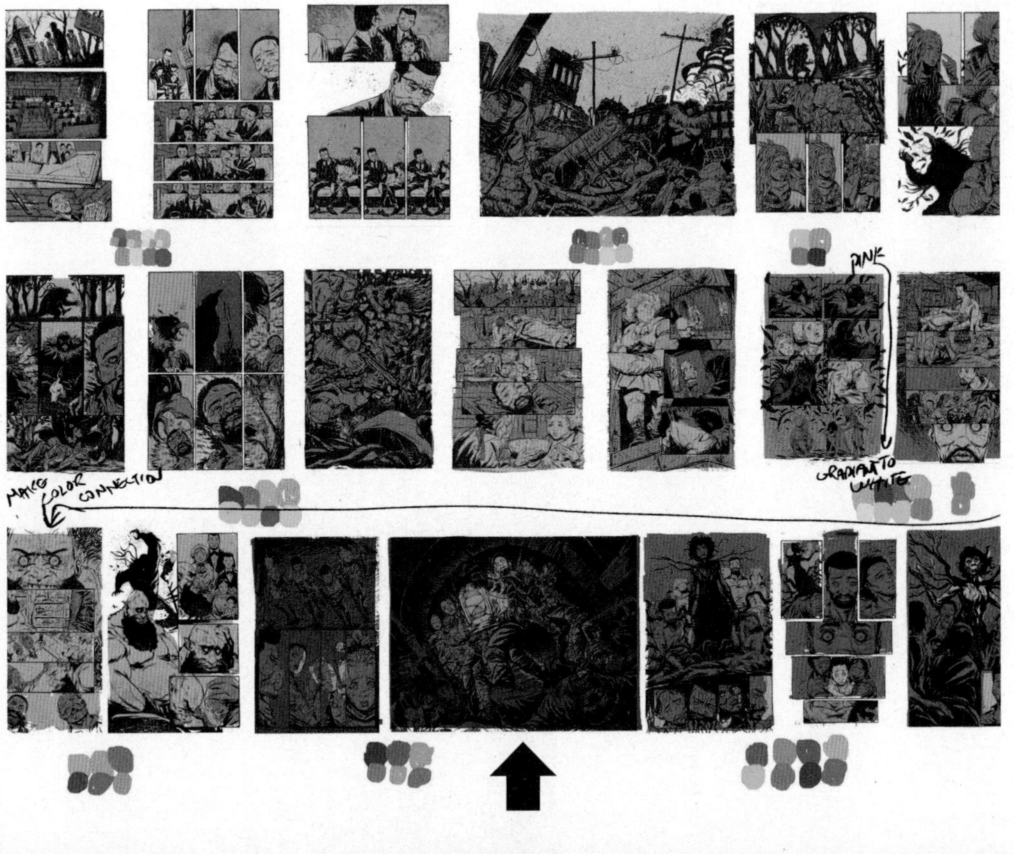
PINK
GRADIANT TO WHITE
MAKE COLOR CONNECTION

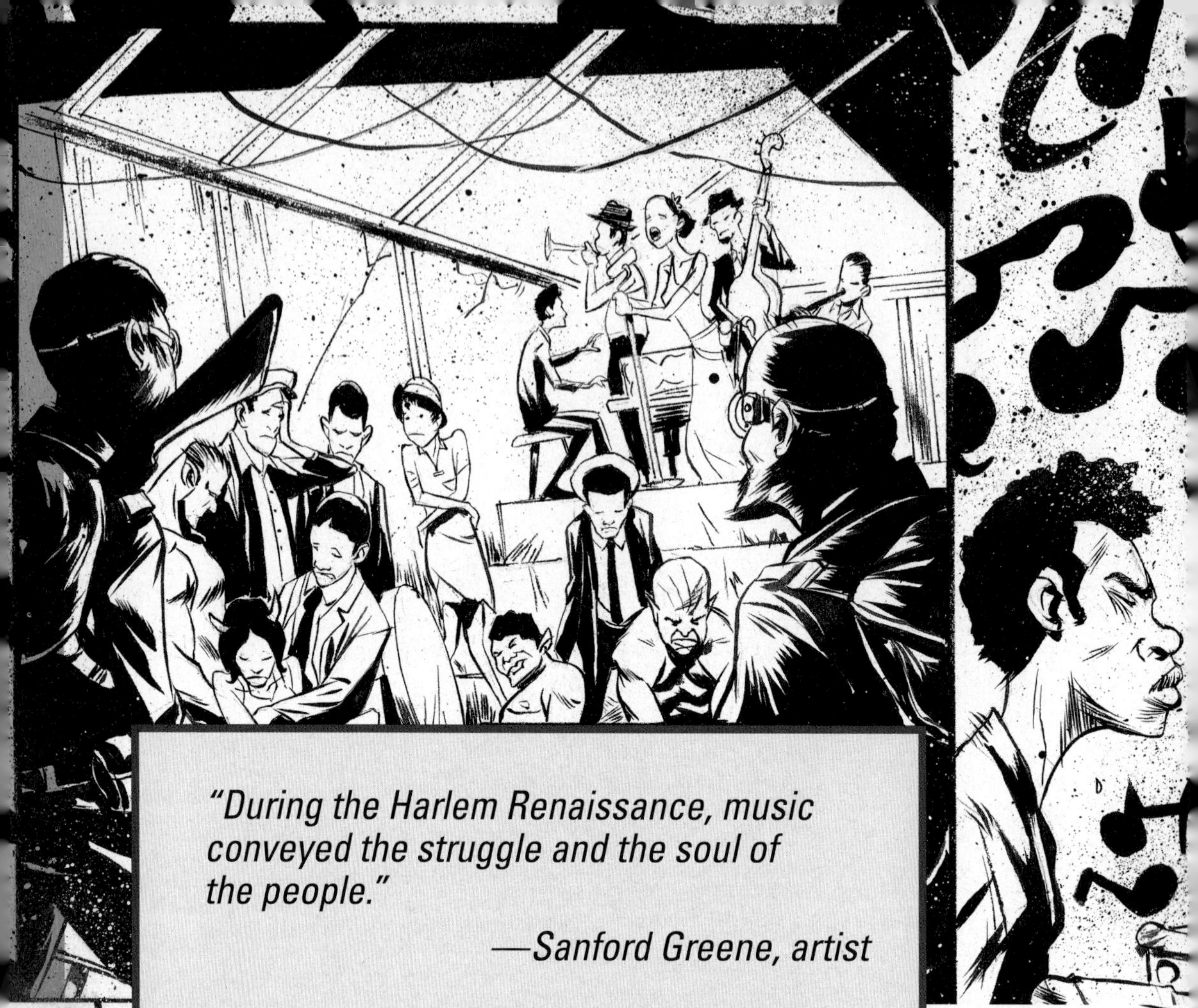

"During the Harlem Renaissance, music conveyed the struggle and the soul of the people."

—Sanford Greene, artist

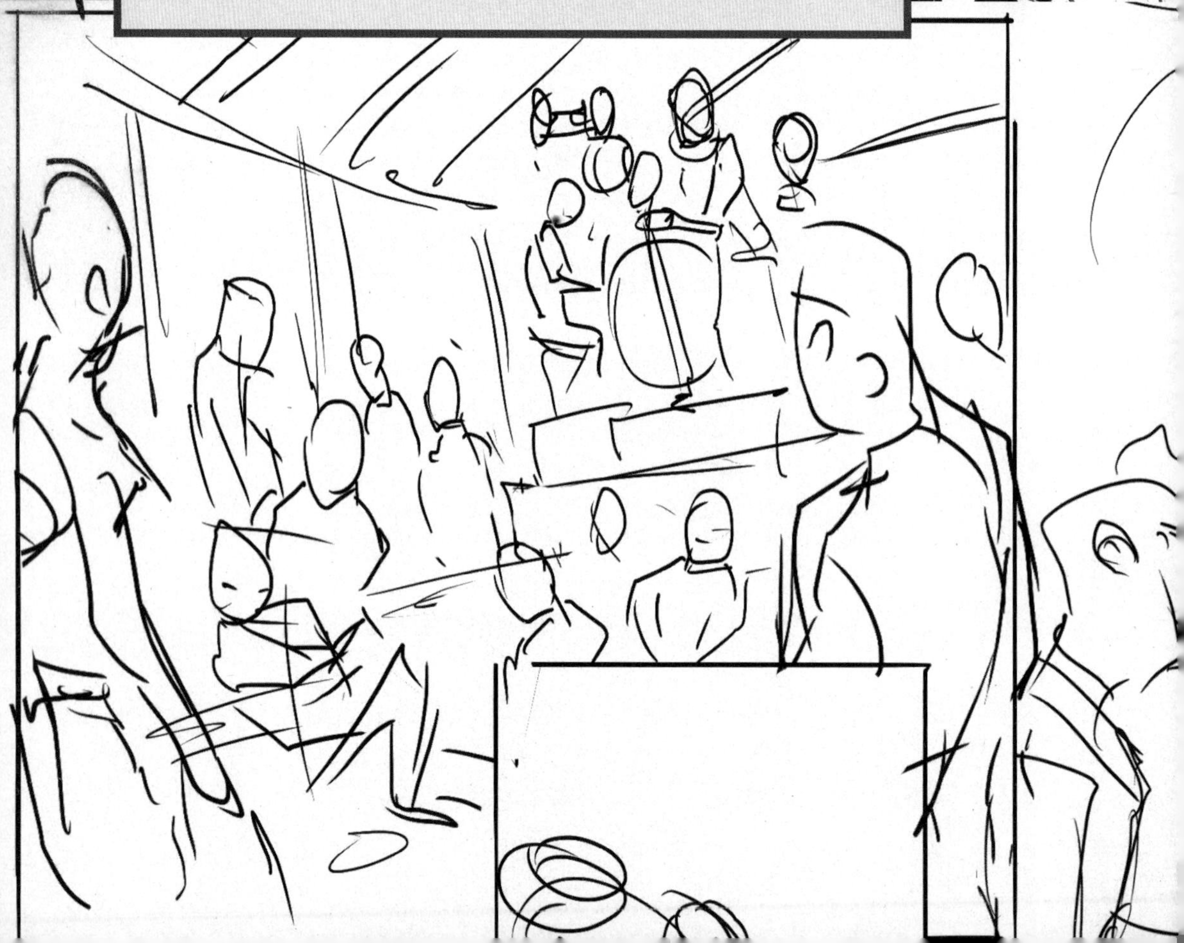

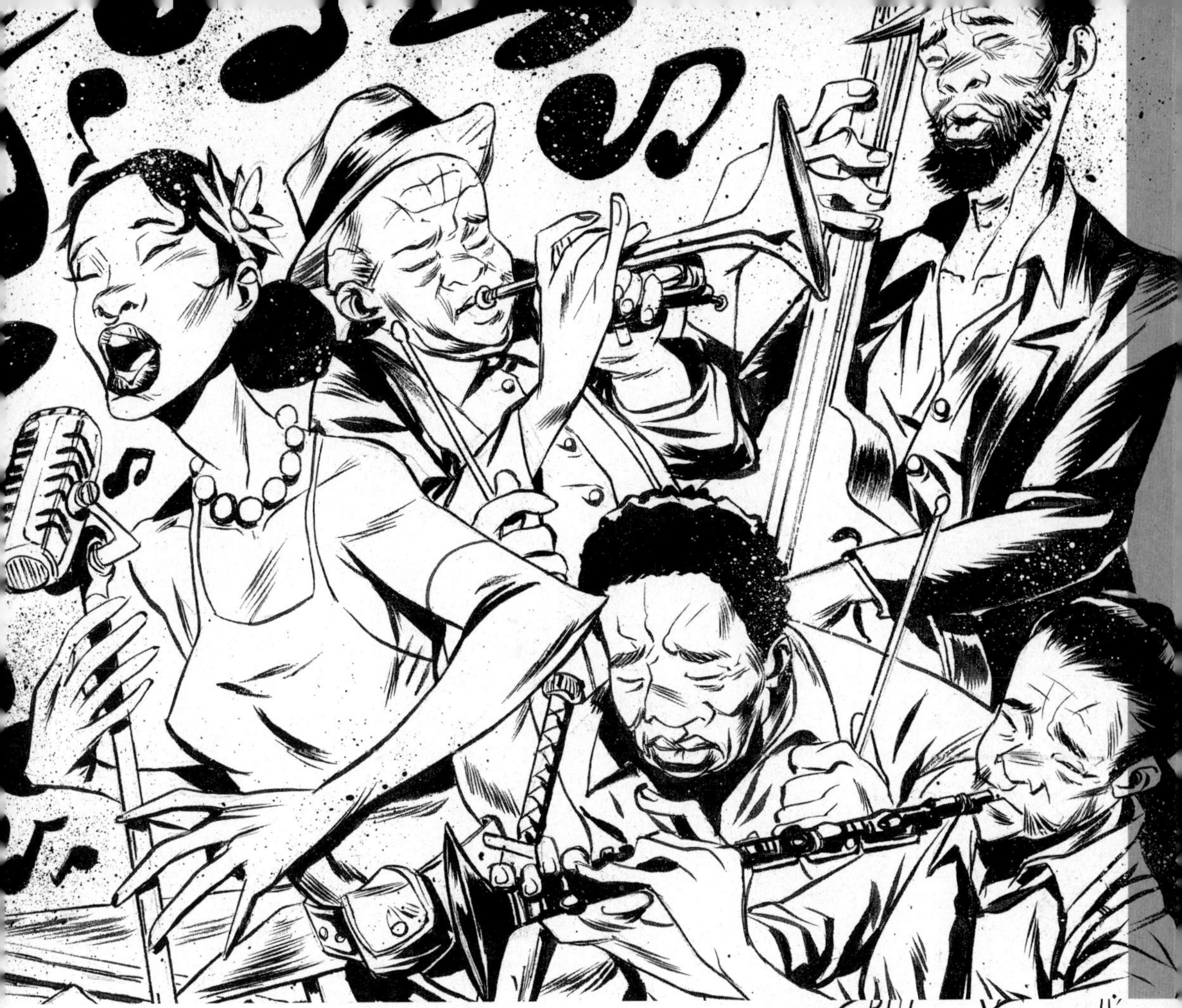

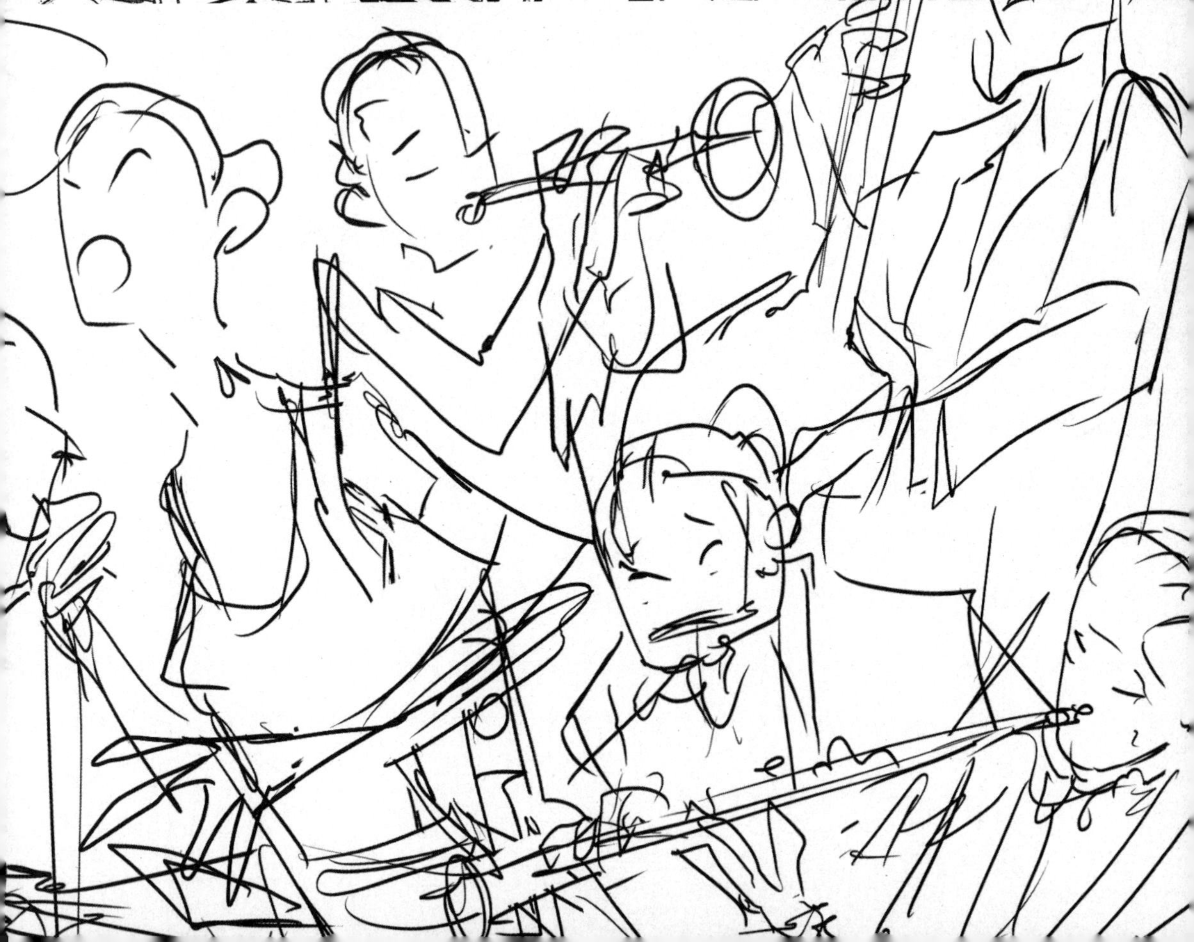

DAVID F. WALKER is an award-winning comic book writer, filmmaker, journalist, and educator. Walker is best known for his work in graphic novels and comics, which includes *The Life of Frederick Douglass* and *The Black Panther Party* (Ten Speed Press), and the Eisner Award-nominated series *Naomi* (DC Comics). He has written for Marvel Comics (*Luke Cage, Occupy Avengers, Power Man and Iron Fist, Nighthawk, Fury, Deadpool*), DC Comics (*Cyborg, Young Justice*), BOOM! Studios (*Planet of the Apes*), and Dark Horse (*Number 13*).

CHUCK BROWN is the Ringo and Eisner Award-winning writer of ON THE STUMP, *1000* and *The Quiet Kind*. He has written comic books for Marvel, Image, Dark Horse, and IDW.

SANFORD GREENE has been a successful cartoonist for over 18 years and is a sequential art instructor at his alma mater, Benedict College. He was recently nominated for a 2020 Ringo Award for Best Artist.

SOFIE DODGSON is a costume designer that lives by the sea and sometimes colours comic books.

CLAYTON COWLES is a 2009 graduate of the Joe Kubert School. He has lettered numerous books for Marvel, DC, Valiant, and Image Comics. He has twice been nominated for the Eisner and Ringo Awards for "Best Lettering." He lives in upstate New York in a house with two cats.

SHELLY BOND has been driven to edit comics and aggravate her favorite freelancers since 1988. She lives in Los Angeles.